Developing Self-Discipline and Preventing and Correcting Misbehavior

George G. Bear

University of Delaware

with

Albert R. Cavalier
University of Delaware

and

Maureen A. Manning
University of Delaware

Boston ■ New York ■ San Francisco
Mexico City ■ Montreal ■ Toronto ■ London ■ Madrid ■ Munich ■ Paris
Hong Kong ■ Singapore ■ Tokyo ■ Cape Town ■ Sydney

To my wife, Patti, who so consistently demonstrates the qualities and skills of effective discipline in her classroom and at home and who was the inspiration for this book. To our sons, Brian and Adam, who have often reminded us that all kids, and adults, misbehave at times.

Senior Editor: *Arnis E. Burvikovs*
Series Editorial Assistant: *Megan Smallidge*
Marketing Manager: *Tara Whorf*
Editorial-Production Service: *Omegatype Typography, Inc.*
Composition and Prepress Buyer: *Linda Cox*
Manufacturing Buyer: *Andrew Turso*
Cover Administrator: *Linda Knowles*
Electronic Composition: *Omegatype Typography, Inc.*

For related titles and support materials, visit our online catalog at www.ablongman.com.

Copyright © 2005 Pearson Education, Inc.

Library of Congress Cataloging-in-Publication-Data

Bear, George G.
    Developing self-discipline and preventing and correcting misbehavior / George G. Bear.
        p. cm.
    Includes bibliographical references and index.
    ISBN 0-205-29353-0 (alk. paper)
    1. School discipline.   2. Problem children—Behavior modification.   3. Self-control.   I. Title.

LB3012.B317 2005
371.5—dc22

                                                                                    2004052674

Printed in the United States of America

10   9   8   7   6   5   4   3   2   1   09   08   07   06   05   04

Photo Credits: pp. 1, 97, 113, 128, 141, 173, 198, 251, 281 George G. Bear; p. 23 Dennis MacDonald/PHOTOEDIT; p. 50 Culver Pictures; p. 73 Leif Skoogfors/CORBIS; p. 225 Jose Luis Pelaez, Inc./CORBIS

CONTENTS

9 Developing Emotional Competencies and Self-Discipline   173

10 Preventing Misbehavior with Effective Classroom Management   198

PREFACE

Perhaps no other phase of human society is causing greater concern in the present generation than the moral trend of young people. There is universal recognition among the civilized nations of the urgent need for the salvaging of civilization. The adult generation is convinced that the moral situation is bad and frantically insists that matters be set right. (Troth, 1930, p. 3)

It is common for books on classroom discipline to begin by presenting evidence that disciplinary problems in today's schools are at a historical high, that crime is rampant in communities and increasing, and that unless schools alter their current practices, the situation will certainly worsen. As seen in the opening quotation, such dire warnings certainly are not new. They can be found in the writings of every generation of American educators, which certainly includes today's.

From the 1700s to the late 1800s *moral education* was the highest priority in the schools and, during the early to mid-1900s, it was *character education*. Both movements shared the same aim—to develop self-discipline. As used throughout this book, self-discipline refers to social and moral responsibility, self-regulation, self-control, and autonomy. Each of these concepts conveys the general idea that students should understand and appreciate differences between right and wrong; recognize the importance of cooperative relationships; make decisions that concern issues of justice, rights, and the welfare of others and act according to their decisions; assume responsibility for their actions; and inhibit socially inappropriate behavior and exhibit prosocial behavior. Teachers who emphasize student self-discipline not only help develop responsible citizens but also prevent many acts of misbehavior while fostering the learning and safety of all students. Thus, they also make the job of teaching easier.

Over the years different strategies for teaching self-discipline have waxed and waned. Change has not always been positive. For example, in recent decades educators have jumped from one bandwagon to another in search of a panacea for the discipline problems of the "modern" era. Popular bandwagons related to school discipline have prospered under many different flags, including moral education, character education, values clarification, moral development, behavior modification, self-esteem building, and various "models" of school discipline. More recent bandwagons include zero tolerance, social skills training, social problem solving, conflict resolution, antibullying programs, positive behavioral supports, emotional intelligence, and once again—character education. Too often these bandwagons are boarded hastily by educators who possess little knowledge of what has *worked* or *failed* in the past, of the issues involved, and of evidence demonstrating in what direction the bandwagon is heading. Unfortunately, the direction often is a dead-end street. Moreover, as is true today, often the wrong bandwagons are boarded when theory and research do exist showing that there are better routes to travel to achieve the aim of developing self-discipline while also creating and maintaining environments that are safe, orderly, and conducive to learning.

How Does This Book Differ from Most Other Books on Classroom Discipline?

Books on classroom discipline and classroom management tend to be one of two types: model focused or techniques focused. The first type espouses one particular model of classroom discipline, which typically is that of the author(s), or presents multiple models of classroom discipline and encourages readers to pick and choose the one model that best fits their personal philosophy. Unfortunately, theory and research in child development and educational psychology are rarely presented in support of these models. Readers are to trust the "theories" of the authors and their claims that the strategies and techniques they present are effective.

The second type of book focuses on techniques for behavior management. Although often grounded in theory and research, such theory and research tend to be narrow and simplistic in perspective. Typically, the basic premise is that behavior is determined by the environment and, by manipulating the classroom or school environment, educators can change or control the behavior of students. Other factors, particularly thought processes and emotions, receive little, if any, attention. To these authors, the aim of classroom discipline is to manage behavior and to teach students how to behave. Typically, "effective" techniques are those that bring about compliance to hard-and-fast rules. Whether or not students learn *why* responsible behavior is important, that they come to value such behavior (other than to receive rewards and avoid punishment), and that they act in accordance with their values (especially when not in the presence of adults) are seldom addressed. What seems to matter the most is simply that students no longer bother their teachers. Much too often the techniques of behavior management, while certainly important especially in correcting misbehavior, are not used in combination with other necessary strategies and techniques for developing self-discipline.

Unlike the two types of books just described, this book offers a more balanced and comprehensive perspective. Drawing from best practices of discipline used throughout the history of American education and from current theory and research in education and psychology, it is argued that whereas the primary aim of discipline should be the development of self-discipline, classroom teachers must adopt a comprehensive approach to classroom discipline that includes three critical components: (1) developing self-discipline, (2) preventing misbehavior with effective classroom management, and (3) correcting misbehavior. A fourth component, remediating and preventing or responding to chronic and serious misbehavior also is important but is more specific to schoolwide discipline, not classroom discipline per se, and is more critical in some schools than others. Thus, the fourth component receives relatively less attention in this book.

The book is designed to serve as a primary text for courses in school discipline and classroom management and as a secondary text for courses in educational psychology, instructional methods, or child and adolescent development. It also should be useful to practicing teachers, administrators, school psychologists, school counselors, and other edu-

Hall, G. S. (1911). *Educational problems* (Vol. 1). New York: D. Appleton.
Troth, P. C. (1930). *Selected readings in character education*. Boston, MA: Beacon Press.

Acknowledgments

I am grateful to the many reviewers of the manuscript, particularly to the many teachers in the courses my wife and I have taught on classroom discipline. Special thanks go to Bob Hampel, educational historian, University of Delaware, who reviewed chapters on history, convincing me that the past *is* relevant to education today; to elementary principals Chuck Hughes and Susan Goglia and assistant high school principal Sharon Denny for reviewing various chapters; to Cal Izard, distinguished professor of psychology, University of Delaware, for reviewing the chapter on emotions; to Karole Kurtz, a graduate assistant, for her invaluable help with references and support materials; to Jeanne Geddes-Keye, principal of the College School, and the teachers and students of the school for giving me plenty of examples to use in the book; to Arnie Burvikovs, editor of Allyn and Bacon, for his patience, guidance, and support; and to the following reviewers of the manuscript, for their invaluable suggestions: Randy L. Brown, University of Central Oklahoma; Karen Engelsen, Pima Community College; Monica A. Lambert, Appalachian State University; Gerald D. McGregor Jr., University of Texas at Tyler; Judie Rhoads, Western Oregon University; Charlene W. Sox, Appalachian State University; and Sue Ann Thorson, University of Maine at Farmington.

cators and mental health specialists interested in issues, strategies, and techniques of classroom and school discipline.

Overview of the Book

The first four chapters focus on critical issues in classroom discipline, beginning with Chapters 1 and 2 examining two traditional aims of American educators: (1) to *teach* or develop student self-control, character, or *self-discipline,* and (2) to *correct* misbehavior for the purpose of creating and maintaining a safe, orderly, and positive learning environment. No other issue in school discipline has been the focus of more controversy than that of *using* discipline to correct misbehavior. Such controversy is examined in Chapter 2, including reasons why punishment *is* necessary in most schools despite its many limitations.

Chapters 3 and 4 explore a wide range of additional issues of classroom discipline, presented in a historical context. In studying the history of school discipline, it might come as a surprise to learn that nearly all strategies and techniques of classroom discipline (both good and bad) that are popular today have been used for decades, if not centuries. The primary purpose of these two chapters is to introduce various approaches, strategies, and techniques for developing self-discipline and correcting misbehavior that have been popular over the centuries, while challenging readers to reflect on their usefulness. Among the critical issues of school discipline that are highlighted are the aim of classroom discipline, the use of harsh forms of punishment, the causes of misbehavior, religious education, moral education, character education, values education, and the legal rights of students (and teachers).

In response to the void caused by the near demise of character education by the end of the 1970s and the rapid increase in discipline problems and school violence new models for teaching self-discipline and managing student behavior rose in popularity during the 1960s, 1970s, and into the 1980s. Three classic models are reviewed. Chapter 5 examines Rudolph Dreikurs's (Dreikurs, 1968; Dreikurs & Cassel, 1972; Dreikurs, Grunwald, & Pepper, 1982) model of logical consequences, or *discipline without tears,* which emphasizes the motives for misbehavior, democratic teaching, and the use of logical consequences and encouragement.

Chapter 6 reviews William Glasser's (1965) *Reality Therapy* and more recent versions of his approach to school discipline, with its emphasis on student responsibility, confronting misbehavior, and classroom meetings. Chapter 7 focuses on perhaps the most popular model of school discipline in history, assertive discipline (Canter & Canter, 1976, 1992, 2001).

These three models were selected for several reasons. First, these three models, or at least their basic concepts, have remained popular for over thirty years. Second, there are few, if any, fundamental issues, concepts, or techniques of school discipline that either Dreikurs, Glasser, or Canter and Canter have failed to address. Among the issues, concepts, and techniques are the psychological needs of students, causes of misbehavior, student choice and responsibility in behavior, the goals of misbehavior, teacher–student relations, classroom meetings, social problem solving, encouragement, logical and natural consequences, modeling, and the systematic use of rewards and punishment. Third, the models present an excellent contrast in philosophy. Whereas the models of Glasser and Dreikurs are student centered and emphasize that the development of self-discipline should be the primary aim of education, assertive discipline is teacher centered and places much greater emphasis on the control and management of student behavior. Finally, because nearly all modern models of school discipline share the same basic concepts and techniques presented by Dreikurs, Glasser, and Canter and Canter (see Table 4.1, pp. 92–93), by reviewing these three classic models there is little need to review the dozens of other "new" models of school discipline.

The second half of the book focuses on practical strategies and techniques that are grounded in recent theory and research. Chapters 8 and 9 focus on developing self-discipline, with Chapter 8 addressing the development of social and moral problem solving and Chapter 9 addressing the development of emotional competencies. These chapters present theory and research supporting the critical roles of social and moral problem solving and emotions in developing self-discipline. They also present multiple practical strategies and techniques for developing social and moral problem-solving skills and emotions linked to self-discipline.

The following chapter, Chapter 10, focuses on evidence-based and practical strategies and techniques of classroom management for preventing behavior problems. It is argued that whereas developing self-discipline and preventing misbehavior with effective classroom management are certainly related, they should be viewed as two distinct components of comprehensive school discipline. That is, effective teachers do not necessarily prevent misbehavior by developing self-discipline, nor do they develop self-discipline by using good classroom management. Because these are separate components of comprehensive school discipline, they often require different strategies and techniques, as presented in this chapter.

Chapters 11 and 12 present a wide range of evidence-based and practical strategies and techniques for correcting misbehavior. Chapter 11 focuses on techniques designed to replace misbehavior with more appropriate behavior. Often these techniques are sufficient for correction. However, in many cases it is necessary that replacement techniques be used in combination with reductive techniques, as presented in Chapter 12, which are more punitive in nature.

The last chapter, Chapter 13, focuses on two separate groups of students: those with disabilities and those with chronic and serious behavior problems. What they have in common is that they benefit from individualized education programs designed to meet their needs. For sure, the same strategies and techniques presented earlier in the book for developing self-discipline and for preventing and correcting misbehavior are effective with these students, most of whom remain in regular classrooms. However, often they require more intensive, sustained, and comprehensive services—or *remediation*—which cannot always be provided in the regular classroom. Such remedial services typically are required following chronic or serious misbehavior, which often results in suspension, expulsion, or placement into another setting. This chapter focuses on the needs for remedial services, the provisions of the Individuals with Disabilities Education Act pertaining to school discipline, and the need for schools to develop and implement necessary plans for preventing and responding to crises that involve school violence.

Supplements to the Text

For instructors choosing to use this as a text, instructional materials are available as pa the Instructor's Manual. These resources are available electronically and access ca arranged by contacting your local representative.

- PowerPoint slides for each chapter
- Chapter summaries and questions for class discussion
- Suggested small group activities, including activity worksheets
- Test bank of over 300 multiple choice and short answer questions
- Proposed syllabus
- Needs Assessment and Implementation Guide for Comprehensive School Disci (as a recommended small group activity)
- Vignettes of Misbehavior (in PowerPoint and Word formats) in which student presented with multiple scenarios and asked to respond

Final Personal Note

In writing this book I have strived to present differing and often contrasting theoretica spectives and a wide range of evidence-based and practical strategies and techniques professor and researcher, I tried to integrate research, strategies, and techniques guid cognitive developmental theory, social cognitive learning theory, emotional theory applied behavior analysis. As a past school administrator and school psychologist continues to work as a school psychologist one day a week in a private school), I reminded myself that basing strategies and techniques on theory and research is not cient: Strategies and techniques also must be realistic and practical. When I forge important point, I was quickly reminded of it by my wife, a fifth-grade teacher, a numerous other classroom teachers enrolled in courses I have taught on classroom pline and classroom management. Finally, as a researcher, school psychologist, paren soccer coach who has met and observed thousands of children and adolescents, I also reminded myself that while nearly all children and adolescents misbehave at one ti another, relatively few fail to become morally and socially responsible citizens. Fo teachers and schools of the past and present deserve much of the credit.

Canter, L. (1976). *Assertive discipline: A take charge approach for today's educator.* Santa Monic Lee Canter and Associates.

Canter, L., & Canter, M. (1992, 2001). *Assertive discipline: Positive behavior management for classroom.* Santa Monica, CA: Canter and Associates.

Dreikurs, R. (1968). *Psychology in the classroom: A manual for teachers.* New York: Harper & Row

Dreikurs, R., & Cassel, P. (1972). *Discipline without tears: What to do with children who misbehav* York: Hawthorn Books.

Dreikurs, R., Grunwald, B. B., & Pepper, F. C. (1982). *Maintaining sanity in the classroom: Cla management techniques.* New York: Harper Collins.

Glasser, W. (1965). *Reality therapy.* New York: Harper & Row.

cators and mental health specialists interested in issues, strategies, and techniques of class-room and school discipline.

Overview of the Book

The first four chapters focus on critical issues in classroom discipline, beginning with Chapters 1 and 2 examining two traditional aims of American educators: (1) to *teach* or develop student self-control, character, or *self-discipline,* and (2) to *correct* misbehavior for the purpose of creating and maintaining a safe, orderly, and positive learning environment. No other issue in school discipline has been the focus of more controversy than that of *using* discipline to correct misbehavior. Such controversy is examined in Chapter 2, including reasons why punishment *is* necessary in most schools despite its many limitations.

Chapters 3 and 4 explore a wide range of additional issues of classroom discipline, presented in a historical context. In studying the history of school discipline, it might come as a surprise to learn that nearly all strategies and techniques of classroom discipline (both good and bad) that are popular today have been used for decades, if not centuries. The primary purpose of these two chapters is to introduce various approaches, strategies, and techniques for developing self-discipline and correcting misbehavior that have been popular over the centuries, while challenging readers to reflect on their usefulness. Among the critical issues of school discipline that are highlighted are the aim of classroom discipline, the use of harsh forms of punishment, the causes of misbehavior, religious education, moral education, character education, values education, and the legal rights of students (and teachers).

In response to the void caused by the near demise of character education by the end of the 1970s and the rapid increase in discipline problems and school violence new models for teaching self-discipline and managing student behavior rose in popularity during the 1960s, 1970s, and into the 1980s. Three classic models are reviewed. Chapter 5 examines Rudolph Dreikurs's (Dreikurs, 1968; Dreikurs & Cassel, 1972; Dreikurs, Grunwald, & Pepper, 1982) model of logical consequences, or *discipline without tears,* which emphasizes the motives for misbehavior, democratic teaching, and the use of logical consequences and encouragement.

Chapter 6 reviews William Glasser's (1965) *Reality Therapy* and more recent versions of his approach to school discipline, with its emphasis on student responsibility, confronting misbehavior, and classroom meetings. Chapter 7 focuses on perhaps the most popular model of school discipline in history, assertive discipline (Canter & Canter, 1976, 1992, 2001).

These three models were selected for several reasons. First, these three models, or at least their basic concepts, have remained popular for over thirty years. Second, there are few, if any, fundamental issues, concepts, or techniques of school discipline that either Dreikurs, Glasser, or Canter and Canter have failed to address. Among the issues, concepts, and techniques are the psychological needs of students, causes of misbehavior, student choice and responsibility in behavior, the goals of misbehavior, teacher–student relations, classroom meetings, social problem solving, encouragement, logical and natural consequences, modeling, and the systematic use of rewards and punishment. Third, the models present an excellent contrast in philosophy. Whereas the models of Glasser and Dreikurs are student centered and emphasize that the development of self-discipline should be the primary aim of education, assertive discipline is teacher centered and places much greater emphasis on the control and management of student behavior. Finally, because nearly all modern models of school discipline share the same basic concepts and techniques presented by Dreikurs, Glasser, and Canter and Canter (see Table 4.1, pp. 92–93), by reviewing these three classic models there is little need to review the dozens of other "new" models of school discipline.

The second half of the book focuses on practical strategies and techniques that are grounded in recent theory and research. Chapters 8 and 9 focus on developing self-discipline, with Chapter 8 addressing the development of social and moral problem solving and Chapter 9 addressing the development of emotional competencies. These chapters present theory and research supporting the critical roles of social and moral problem solving and emotions in developing self-discipline. They also present multiple practical strategies and techniques for developing social and moral problem-solving skills and emotions linked to self-discipline.

The following chapter, Chapter 10, focuses on evidence-based and practical strategies and techniques of classroom management for preventing behavior problems. It is argued that whereas developing self-discipline and preventing misbehavior with effective classroom management are certainly related, they should be viewed as two distinct components of comprehensive school discipline. That is, effective teachers do not necessarily prevent misbehavior by developing self-discipline, nor do they develop self-discipline by using good classroom management. Because these are separate components of comprehensive school discipline, they often require different strategies and techniques, as presented in this chapter.

Chapters 11 and 12 present a wide range of evidence-based and practical strategies and techniques for correcting misbehavior. Chapter 11 focuses on techniques designed to replace misbehavior with more appropriate behavior. Often these techniques are sufficient for correction. However, in many cases it is necessary that replacement techniques be used in combination with reductive techniques, as presented in Chapter 12, which are more punitive in nature.

The last chapter, Chapter 13, focuses on two separate groups of students: those with disabilities and those with chronic and serious behavior problems. What they have in common is that they benefit from individualized education programs designed to meet their needs. For sure, the same strategies and techniques presented earlier in the book for developing self-discipline and for preventing and correcting misbehavior are effective with these students, most of whom remain in regular classrooms. However, often they require more intensive, sustained, and comprehensive services—or *remediation*—which cannot always be provided in the regular classroom. Such remedial services typically are required following chronic or serious misbehavior, which often results in suspension, expulsion, or placement into another setting. This chapter focuses on the needs for remedial services, the provisions of the Individuals with Disabilities Education Act pertaining to school discipline, and the need for schools to develop and implement necessary plans for preventing and responding to crises that involve school violence.

Supplements to the Text

For instructors choosing to use this as a text, instructional materials are available as part of the Instructor's Manual. These resources are available electronically and access can be arranged by contacting your local representative.

- PowerPoint slides for each chapter
- Chapter summaries and questions for class discussion
- Suggested small group activities, including activity worksheets
- Test bank of over 300 multiple choice and short answer questions
- Proposed syllabus
- Needs Assessment and Implementation Guide for Comprehensive School Discipline (as a recommended small group activity)
- Vignettes of Misbehavior (in PowerPoint and Word formats) in which students are presented with multiple scenarios and asked to respond

Final Personal Note

In writing this book I have strived to present differing and often contrasting theoretical perspectives and a wide range of evidence-based and practical strategies and techniques. As a professor and researcher, I tried to integrate research, strategies, and techniques guided by cognitive developmental theory, social cognitive learning theory, emotional theory, and applied behavior analysis. As a past school administrator and school psychologist (who continues to work as a school psychologist one day a week in a private school), I often reminded myself that basing strategies and techniques on theory and research is not sufficient: Strategies and techniques also must be realistic and practical. When I forgot this important point, I was quickly reminded of it by my wife, a fifth-grade teacher, and by numerous other classroom teachers enrolled in courses I have taught on classroom discipline and classroom management. Finally, as a researcher, school psychologist, parent, and soccer coach who has met and observed thousands of children and adolescents, I also often reminded myself that while nearly all children and adolescents misbehave at one time or another, relatively few fail to become morally and socially responsible citizens. For this, teachers and schools of the past and present deserve much of the credit.

Canter, L. (1976). *Assertive discipline: A take charge approach for today's educator.* Santa Monica, CA: Lee Canter and Associates.

Canter, L., & Canter, M. (1992, 2001). *Assertive discipline: Positive behavior management for today's classroom.* Santa Monica, CA: Canter and Associates.

Dreikurs, R. (1968). *Psychology in the classroom: A manual for teachers.* New York: Harper & Row.

Dreikurs, R., & Cassel, P. (1972). *Discipline without tears: What to do with children who misbehave.* New York: Hawthorn Books.

Dreikurs, R., Grunwald, B. B., & Pepper, F. C. (1982). *Maintaining sanity in the classroom: Classroom management techniques.* New York: Harper Collins.

Glasser, W. (1965). *Reality therapy.* New York: Harper & Row.

Hall, G. S. (1911). *Educational problems* (Vol. 1). New York: D. Appleton.
Troth, P. C. (1930). *Selected readings in character education.* Boston, MA: Beacon Press.

Acknowledgments

I am grateful to the many reviewers of the manuscript, particularly to the many teachers in the courses my wife and I have taught on classroom discipline. Special thanks go to Bob Hampel, educational historian, University of Delaware, who reviewed chapters on history, convincing me that the past *is* relevant to education today; to elementary principals Chuck Hughes and Susan Goglia and assistant high school principal Sharon Denny for reviewing various chapters; to Cal Izard, distinguished professor of psychology, University of Delaware, for reviewing the chapter on emotions; to Karole Kurtz, a graduate assistant, for her invaluable help with references and support materials; to Jeanne Geddes-Keye, principal of the College School, and the teachers and students of the school for giving me plenty of examples to use in the book; to Arnie Burvikovs, editor of Allyn and Bacon, for his patience, guidance, and support; and to the following reviewers of the manuscript, for their invaluable suggestions: Randy L. Brown, University of Central Oklahoma; Karen Engelsen, Pima Community College; Monica A. Lambert, Appalachian State University; Gerald D. McGregor Jr., University of Texas at Tyler; Judie Rhoads, Western Oregon University; Charlene W. Sox, Appalachian State University; and Sue Ann Thorson, University of Maine at Farmington.

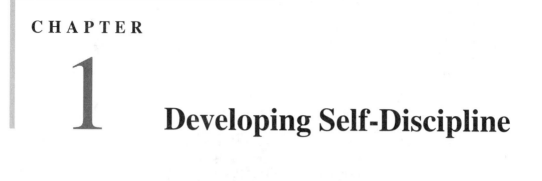

CHAPTER

1 Developing Self-Discipline

GUIDING QUESTIONS

- What is discipline? What is *self-discipline*?
- Should the development of responsible citizenship, or self-discipline, be a primary aim of education? Is it a primary aim in most schools?
- Is it idealistic to expect students to be self-governing or self-disciplined?
- Should schools be held accountable for school discipline, as they are for academic achievement?
- How is self-discipline related to character education, emotional intelligence, and social and emotional learning?

- How might educators balance a student's need for autonomy with the school's need to exert its authority?
- What should be the basic components of a comprehensive program of classroom discipline?

> When public education was established in America, our founding fathers argued that responsible citizenship was to be a primary goal. This was perhaps best reflected in Thomas Jefferson's philosophy that democracy could be protected only by establishing a nation of independently minded, self-governing learners—learners who truly understood that virtuous behavior is critical for democracy's survival. Schools were to imbue students with a moral sense by developing reasoning linked to just and caring behavior. Radically different from the practices of other nations at that time, religion was to play no direct role in this mission and the role of the federal government, if any, would be minimal. For sure, "habits of virtue" were directly taught in the home, church, and community, as well as in school. This was done primarily by means of modeling and reinforcing adherence to rigorous routines of habitual behavior, especially behavior associated with the Puritan ethic of hard work. Punishment also was used—often too much so (Finkelstein, 1989; Hyman, 1990). But the recognized ideal in respect to teaching discipline was not to teach a fear of God, fear of punishment, nor a blind respect for authority. Instead, Jefferson and other leaders of democracy envisioned that public schools would help children overcome their self-interest, or "egoism," by promoting what was perceived at that time to be a moral instinct of care for and duty to others. (Mayo, 1942/1988, p. 300)

> As often experienced by today's educators, Jefferson quickly discovered that when applied to classroom practice, idealism must give way to realism. As noted by historian Fawn Brodie (1974), when Jefferson began his model school of learning (the University of Virginia) "Jefferson at first was in favor of self-government for the students and a minimum of discipline, but a student riot, which he himself at eighty-two helped to quell, and which resulted in three expulsions (one his own nephew) and eleven severe reprimands, convinced him that severer regulations were essential" (p. 604). So began the challenge of democratic educators to develop self-governing, socially responsible individuals while using a "minimum" of externally imposed discipline. (Bear, 1998, p. 14)

For centuries educators have wrestled with issues of classroom discipline. Primary among them has been the relation between *developing* self-discipline, or responsible citizenship, and *using* discipline to manage, correct, or punish misbehavior. There certainly have been periods in American history (perhaps even now) when educators have been more concerned about managing, correcting, and punishing misbehavior than about developing responsible citizenship. However, over the years the primary aim of most educators, including Jefferson, has been to develop self-governing, socially responsible citizens while using a minimum of external control.

These two sides to discipline—developing self-discipline and using discipline to correct misbehavior—are seen in most definitions of discipline. For example, *Webster's New World College Dictionary* (1996, p. 391) gives two definitions that are most applicable to discipline in the context of schooling:

1. "teaching" that "develops self-control" and "character" and
2. "treatment" that "corrects" or "punishes."

These definitions reflect two traditional aims of education in the United States: (1) to *teach* or *develop* student self-control, character, or *self-discipline,* and (2) to help create and maintain a safe, orderly, and positive learning environment using techniques to *correct* misbehavior. Most educators understand that these two aims of classroom discipline are not diametrically opposed, nor are they necessarily antagonistic to one another—*developing* self-discipline and *correcting* misbehavior are equally important. Both are critical to classroom discipline.

The present chapter focuses on what is generally perceived as the more positive side to discipline—the teaching of self-discipline. Terms commonly used interchangeably with self-discipline are reviewed: *responsibility, self-control, autonomy, character, emotional intelligence,* and *social and emotional learning.* Perhaps more importantly, this chapter looks at *why* the development of self-discipline should be a priority. It is clear that when educators teach students skills and abilities associated with self-discipline, they can devote more time to academic instruction and less to the correction of misbehavior. In the following chapter the second aspect of classroom discipline, what is often viewed by many authors of models of classroom discipline as the negative side, receives focus: the *use* of discipline, particularly the use of punishment to correct misbehavior. No other issue in classroom discipline has been the subject of more enduring debate than the role of punishment in correcting misbehavior. Why punishment has remained the most popular strategy for correcting misbehavior is examined, and both advantages and limitations of punishment are discussed. Together, Chapters 1 and 2 challenge readers to reflect on the dual aims of discipline—to develop self-discipline and use discipline to correct misbehavior. More importantly, they challenge readers to consider how these two aims fit into their own philosophies of classroom discipline.

Developing Self-Discipline and Using Discipline: Two National Priorities

The importance of both developing self-discipline and using discipline is seen in recent government initiatives and national polls. With respect to developing self-discipline, the values of responsibility, respect, trustworthiness, justice and fairness, caring, and civic virtue and citizenship have been identified as "core values" by parents, teachers, and youth leaders ("Six Pillars of Character," 1992). National surveys show that a large majority of teachers and parents support these six values (Public Agenda, 1996). Consistent with such public support, values have been specified by the federal government as character values for schools to target in order to receive federal grants for character education (*Federal Register,* 2002). The goal of developing self-discipline also can be seen in the rapidly growing number of federal, state, and locally funded projects designed to teach students various social and emotional skills to prevent and cope with a variety of social problems, including school violence, peer conflict, bullying, and drugs and alcohol (Collaborative for Academic, Social, and Emotional Learning [CASEL], 2003; Elias et al., 1997).

With respect to the second aim of classroom discipline, a focus on correcting (and to a lesser extent preventing) discipline problems is evident in other government initiatives, such as the Gun-Free Schools Act (1994), Goals 2000: Educate America Act (National Education Goals Panel, 1994), and the No Child Left Behind Act (The White House, 2001).

The Gun-Free Schools Act mandates that schools expel any student for at least one year who possesses a gun on school property. Among the goals of Goals 2000 was that every school would provide a disciplined environment conducive to learning by the year 2000. Likewise, with respect to classroom discipline, the more recent No Child Left Behind Act stipulated the following:

- "Laws on the books" are to be aggressively enforced. Schools are encouraged to suspend, expel, and report students to the police for violations of the law, as well as for other disruptive behaviors in the school's code of conduct.
- Schools must allow a student to transfer to another school if the student attends "a persistently dangerous public elementary or secondary school or becomes a victim of a violent crime while in or on the grounds of a public school the student attends."
- School districts "must use federal school-safety funding to establish a plan for keeping schools safe and drug free." These plans must include "appropriate and effective discipline policies; security procedures; prevention activities; student codes of conduct; and a crisis management plan for responding to violent or traumatic incidents on school grounds."
- Schools are encouraged to implement programs that research has shown to "prevent violence in and around schools; prevent the illegal use of alcohol, drugs, and tobacco by young people; and foster a safe and drug-free learning environment that supports academic achievement." Note that an emphasis on *research-supported* practices is seen throughout the No Child Left Behind Act (as well as throughout this book).
- States are required to "report school safety statistics to the public on a school-by-school basis."
- Teachers and other school professionals are protected from lawsuits "when they take reasonable actions to maintain order and discipline in the classroom." This is to help ensure that teachers "maintain discipline and enforce the rules."

The message in these acts is clear: Schools are to *use* discipline to ensure safety and to correct misbehavior. An emphasis on the use of discipline also is seen in the recent increase in *zero tolerance* policies and programs, many of which follow from federal and state legislation. As discussed in Chapter 2, zero tolerance policies are designed to ensure that students who exhibit serious acts of misbehavior receive automatic and harsh punishment. Suspension, expulsion, and placement in alternative schools are common methods of such punishment. Polls show that both parents and teachers support zero tolerance policies (Rose & Gallup, 2000).

As reviewed later, many authorities on classroom discipline argue that schools place far too little emphasis on developing self-discipline or character and too much emphasis on the use of discipline, especially the use of punishment. That is, they fail to balance the two primary aims of discipline. For decades, authorities have argued that in emphasizing the *use* of discipline, schools simply teach obedience while failing to develop self-discipline. To be sure, it is clear that many educators and parents recognize that both the development of self-discipline and the use of discipline to correct misbehavior play important roles in classroom discipline. What is less clear, however, is whether schools devote far too much attention to correction, especially the use of punishment, and too little attention to developing self-discipline.

STOP AND REFLECT

Given limited time and resources, should schools focus primarily on teaching self-discipline with the aim of developing responsible citizens or on managing and correcting misbehavior with the aim of creating and maintaining safe and orderly schools? Can both aims be achieved simultaneously? If so, do they require the same or different strategies and techniques? For example, can correction and punishment be avoided by teaching self-discipline? To what extent is self-discipline taught by establishing clear and consistent rules and correcting misbehavior?

What Is Self-Discipline?

Self-discipline connotes internal regulation of one's behavior. It entails assuming responsibility for one's actions, understanding right from wrong, appreciating the importance of co-operative relationships, and inhibiting socially inappropriate behavior. It involves knowing what's right, desiring to do what is right, and *doing* what is right. Self-discipline reflects *internalization,* which is "taking over the values and attitudes of society as one's own so that socially acceptable behavior is motivated not by anticipation of external consequences but by intrinsic or internal factors" (Grusec & Goodnow, 1994, p. 4).

Internalization and, thus, self-discipline *develop* with age. Although it would be developmentally inappropriate for very young children to exhibit self-discipline, self-discipline certainly is a quality that all students should possess before they leave high school. As children develop, they interpret and add meaning to what happens in their lives. They construct their own values, goals, and standards, which tend to mirror those of other individuals who are significant in their lives, including their teachers. With age, they also increasingly monitor their own behavior and more consistently demonstrate self-directed behavior that is grounded in their own values, goals, and standards. Such consistency in the absence of external monitors, sanctions, and rewards is the hallmark of self-discipline. Thus, it is not uncommon for teachers to tend to think of students who are self-disciplined as those students who follow classroom rules without the teacher or other adults being present. In contrast, teachers also tend to think of students who *lack* self-discipline as those "you have to watch all the time." Indeed, a good litmus test of self-discipline in the classroom is whether or not students consistently behave when the teacher is out of the classroom or when a substitute teaches the class.

In addition to the term *self-discipline,* other terms are used, often interchangeably, when referring to the concept that behavior is regulated internally instead of externally. Among them, the most common are *responsibility, self-control, autonomy, character,* and *social and emotional learning.* As seen later, authors of popular models of classroom discipline tend to use these terms in arguing that the primary aim of classroom discipline, if not education in general, is to develop self-discipline. As also will be seen, some of these authors argue that the use of discipline and other means of external control, including the use of rewards, is *detrimental* to the development of self-discipline and contributes to increased behavior problems. These authors are not the first, however, to make these arguments. For several centuries American educators have questioned if *external* control is a wise and effective means of developing *internal* control of behavior.

STOP AND REFLECT

Before reading the following, reflect on what you believe to be the most critical elements of self-discipline. How did you develop self-discipline? What role did teachers and schools play in developing your character? Are schools, in general, successful in promoting self-discipline?

Self-Discipline as Responsibility and Self-Control

Many popular models of classroom discipline that advocate for the development of self-discipline and against the use of discipline are based on the classic writings of Rudolf Driekurs and William Glasser. Popular among educators in the 1970s and 1980s, their models of classroom discipline continue to have a profound influence on classroom discipline in many schools. Because of their impact on classroom discipline, their models will be highlighted later in separate chapters.

Dreikurs, author of *Discipline Without Tears* (Dreikurs & Cassel, 1972), *Logical Consequences* (Dreikurs & Grey, 1968), and several other books on classroom discipline, emphasized the need for each individual to experience social belonging, which he believed to be the key to self-worth. In Dreikurs's model, social belonging is dependent on a student acting in a *socially responsible* manner: Students cannot experience social belonging and feel good about themselves unless they cooperate and assume responsibility for their actions. Dreikurs argued that social responsibility is best taught using a democratic style of teaching, believing that: "The traditional autocratic approach of motivating children through pressure from without must be replaced with stimulation from within" (Dreikurs, 1968, p. 42).

Glasser, who remains a popular writer in education and psychiatry, best known for a model of classroom discipline he proposed in *Reality Therapy* (1965) and *Schools without Failure* (1969), views the teaching of *responsibility* as the key to classroom discipline and the development of responsibility as critical to feelings of self-worth. To Glasser, self-evaluation and a commitment to change one's behavior are the cornerstones of responsibility. In acting responsibly, students must reflect on and choose their behavior, which means they evaluate alternative behaviors and their consequences, and then choose to act in accordance with such self-evaluations. Glasser has been a harsh critic of schools, pointing out that common educational practices actually cause misbehavior and that, although schools preach self-discipline, they practice control of behavior. He asserts that educators often confuse conformity with responsibility, noting that responsibility is "something to which we give lip service but which we do not teach in school" (1969, p. 22). According to Glasser (1969), responsibility is a critical part of democracy and "Democracy is best learned by living it!" (p. 37).

Self-discipline as responsibility and self-control also is seen in more recent popular models of classroom discipline, many of which repeat the same arguments of Dreikurs and Glasser. For example, drawing mostly from the ideas of these two authors, *Positive Discipline* (Nelsen, Lott, & Glenn, 2000) and *Cooperative Discipline* (Albert, 1996) stress the importance of responsibility. Self-discipline as responsibility and self-control also is highlighted in the popular *Discipline with Dignity* model (Curwin & Mendler, 1999). In their widely disseminated book, *Discipline with Dignity,* Curwin and Mendler (1999) emphasize the critical importance of maintaining student dignity in matters of classroom discipline. They argue that student dignity can only be maintained if teachers teach students to be "self-responsible," which they regard as "the highest virtue of education" (p. 24). According to Curwin and Mendler, students value self-responsibility much more than behaving obediently in order to avoid punishment or receive rewards. They agree with Glasser that perceiving oneself as responsible is critical to one's dignity or self-worth.

Noting that there are two basic models of classroom discipline, the responsibility model and the obedience model, Curwin and Mendler (1999) criticize harshly those who adhere to the obedience model. As seen in the following quote, they argue that the obedience model not only insults the dignity of the individual but also is ineffective:

> We define obedience as following rules without question, regardless of philosophical beliefs, ideas of right and wrong, instincts and experiences, or values. A student "does it" because he is told to do it. In the short term, obedience offers teachers relief, a sense of power and control, and an oasis from the constant bombardment of defiance. In the long run, however, obedience leads to student immaturity, a lack of responsibility, an inability to think clearly and critically, and a feeling of helplessness that is manifested by withdrawal, aggressiveness, or power struggles. . . . We strongly believe that the training for obedience in schools is a personal and societal risk with dire potential consequences for everyone. Obedience, even when it "works," is not philosophically, psychologically, or sociologically defensible. Obedience models are far more interested in keeping students in line rather than maintaining their dignity. (Curwin & Mendler, 1999, pp. 23–24)

Thomas Gordon, founder of *Teacher Effectiveness Training* (1974, 2003), views *self-control* as the essence of self-discipline. Like all other authors mentioned previously, Gordon argues that in a democratic society children must be taught self-control. According to Gordon, traditional "obedience" models of classroom discipline that rely on the use of punishment not only fail to teach self-control but also cause antisocial behavior. As noted by Gordon (1989): "Disciplining kids does not produce disciplined kids, and I'll present the evidence for it. While it is true that obedient, fearful, submissive, and subservient kids are sometimes produced by adult-imposed discipline, truly self-disciplined youngsters are not" (p. 8). Gordon (2003) further notes that by not developing self-discipline in the early grades and by relying primarily on rewards and punishment to control behavior, educators create a nightmare for many high school teachers. This is because teacher-controlled rewards and punishment (with the possible exception of grades and suspension) are no longer effective. In the absence of their effectiveness and the lack of self-discipline, behavior problems should be expected.

Self-Discipline as Autonomy

Currently, perhaps the most vocal, and harshest, critic of the obedience model and advocate of self-discipline is Alfie Kohn. In *Beyond Discipline: From Compliance to Community,* Kohn (1996) not only attacks the obedience model of classroom discipline but also argues that most other models of classroom discipline are misguided obedience models in disguise.

Kohn (1996) warns, "These programs are merely packaged in such a way as to appeal to educators who are uncomfortable with the idea of using bribes and threats. The truth is what it has always been: a ruse is a ruse is ruse" (p. 53).

Kohn (1996) purports that nearly all models of classroom discipline equate self-discipline with the internalization of society's values—and that internalization of society's values should not be the aim of education. As noted by Kohn:

> When some people describe a student as self-disciplined, they mean only that she does what is expected when no adult is watching (or giving out rewards or punishments). The goal here is just to get the student to keep acting in ways that are acceptable to us, which amounts to trying to direct her behavior by remote control. (p. 83)

Consistent with the moral development theories of Jean Piaget (1932/1965) and Lawrence Kohlberg (1984), as well as other theories grounded in *constructivism,* Kohn (1996) believes that internalization of another person's values is not the same as the *self-construction* of values. He views self-construction of values as the key to *autonomy,* or true self-discipline. According to Kohn, a student should not adopt the values, beliefs, and expectations of others simply because the student feels compelled to do so, but rather because the student "knows and feels that it is the right thing to do" (p. 83). Thus, although Kohn is a strong advocate of developing self-discipline, he views it much differently than many others. To Kohn, the student must play an active, self-constructing role in the internalization process. Kohn and other constructivists believe that true internalization cannot occur simply by the direct teaching of values and specific behaviors. Instead, they argue forcefully that students must actively participate in the internalization process by being provided ample opportunities to practice collaborative social decision-making in schools—schools that Kohn refers to as *caring school communities.*

Although Kohn is perhaps the most vocal critic of the obedience model of classroom discipline and advocate of caring school communities that develop autonomy, he certainly is not the only one. For example, in *Beyond Behaviorism: Changing the Classroom Management Paradigm,* H. Jerome Freiberg (1999) argues that the obedience model, which he equates with the use of behavior modification techniques and the direct teaching of values and behavior, is a *teacher-centered* approach to classroom discipline and that a teacher-centered approach fails to teach self-discipline. Freiberg claims that it is only in *person-centered* learning environments, similar to Kohn's caring communities, that autonomy, or self-discipline, can be developed. According to Freiberg, "Self-discipline is built over time and encompasses multiple sources of experiences. It requires a learning environment that nurtures opportunities to learn from one's own experiences, including mistakes, and to reflect on these experiences" (p. 13). It is from such mistakes and experiences that a student develops a sense of autonomy.

Numerous other popular researchers and authors (e.g., DeVries & Zan, 1994; Noddings, 2002; Watson, 2003) also advocate a constructivist approach to classroom discipline and moral education in which caring classrooms and the development of autonomy receive center focus. They emphasize that the development of autonomy and moral responsibility depends on a classroom atmosphere in which mutual respect, cooperation, and caring are consistently practiced. In such an atmosphere "the teacher minimizes the exercise of unnecessary authority" (DeVries & Zan, 1994, p. 3). These authors also emphasize the critical role of moral reasoning, a caring climate, and supportive teacher–student relationship in the development of autonomy. They believe that students cannot experience true autonomy when their reasoning is based on the fear of punishment and the desire of rewards. As noted by DeVries, "Our extensive prison system attests to the fact that fear of punishment is an inadequate motivator of moral behavior" (DeVries & Zan, 1994, p. 29).

Self-Discipline as Character

Character represents one's disposition, personality, or continuity in behavior. Good character includes a wide variety of prosocial values and behaviors, including care, cooperation, respect, trustworthiness, honesty, and sensitivity to individual differences. Most of all, however, it entails self-discipline. With respect to character, self-discipline provides the moral strength necessary for one to exhibit each of the preceding values and virtues. Refraining from acting out in class or aggressing toward others requires self-discipline. But self-discipline also is required of such prosocial virtues as compassion, honesty, and loyalty. In acting prosocially, students must forgo their own egoistic, or self-centered, wants and desires and focus instead on the needs of others.

Character educators share the view that the teaching of responsibility, self-control, autonomy, or self-discipline should be a major aim of education. However, unlike in most models of classroom discipline, character educators place great emphasis on the *moral* dimension of self-discipline. To character educators, children need to develop what William Bennett (1995) calls a *moral compass* to help guide them in determining *when* and *why* a given misbehavior is wrong and self-discipline is important. Character educators also tend to differ from several of the previous authors, however, including Dreikurs, Glasser, Gordon, and Kohn, in another fundamental way: They are not critical of the "traditional" approach to the teaching self-discipline, which emphasizes the direct teaching of values and moral behavior and *use of discipline,* where appropriate (although nearly all reject the use of physical punishment). Whereas character educators reject an obedience model of discipline, they understand that character does not develop simply *within* the individual, but within the context of ongoing social interactions with peers and adults. This includes interactions in which students are taught right from wrong using not only student-centered instructional strategies advocated by constructivists but also teacher-centered, or traditional, instructional strategies such as highlighting values in curriculum lessons and rewarding good behavior. They also understand that it is difficult to develop character in schools that are uncaring and unsafe, and that the use of discipline often is necessary not only for purposes of safety but also to help teach self-discipline and maintain an environment that is conducive to learning and development.

Thomas Lickona, college professor, former public school teacher, and director of the Center for the 4th and 5th Rs (Respect and Responsibility), has written extensively on moral education and character education, including two popular books: *Educating for Character: How our Schools Can Teach Respect and Responsibility* (1991) and *Character Matters: How to Help Our Children Develop Good Judgment, Integrity, and Other Essential Virtues* (2004). To Lickona, and most other character educators, good character "consists of knowing the good, desiring the good, and doing the good—habits of the mind, habits of the heart, and habits of action" (Lickona, 1991, p. 51). Lickona further notes that the essence of good character is a combination of important virtues, or "dispositions to behave in a morally good way" (Lickona, 2004, p. 7). He gives ten essential virtues shared by societies and religions throughout the world: wisdom, justice, fortitude, self-control, love, a positive attitude, hard work, integrity, gratitude, and humility.

Kevin Ryan, professor, founding director of the Center for the Advancement of Ethics and Character at Boston University, and popular writer on character education, defines character similarly. In *Building Character in Schools: Practical Ways to Bring Moral Instruction to Life* (1999), Ryan and Karen Bohlin describe character as "knowing the good, loving the good, and doing the good" (p. 7), concluding that character "is very simply the sum of our intellectual and moral habits. That is, character is the composite of our good habits, or virtues, and our bad habits, or vices, the habits that make us the kind of person we are" (p. 9). Obviously, it is the good habits, or virtues, that character educators aim to inculcate in their students.

A final clear and succinct definition of character education is provided by Marvin Berkowitz, professor of character education at the University of Missouri–St. Louis. He defines character as "an individual's set of psychological characteristics that affect that person's ability and inclination to function morally. Simply put, character is comprised of those characteristics that lead a person to do the right thing or not to do the right thing" (Berkowitz, 2002, p. 48).

A wide spectrum of educators, parents, researchers, scholars, and religious, business, and community leaders, including Lickona, Ryan, Berkowitz, and representatives of many professional organizations (e.g., the National Education Association), recently established the Character Education Partnership (2004) for the purpose of advocating character education. The Character Education Partnership (2004) defines character as "knowing, caring about and acting upon core ethical values such as caring, honesty, fairness, responsibility, and respect for self and others" and character education as:

> . . . a national movement encouraging schools to create environments that foster ethical, responsible, and caring young people. It is the intentional, proactive effort by schools, districts, and states to instill in their students important core, ethical values that we all share such as caring, honesty, fairness, responsibility, and respect for self and others. Effective good character education is comprehensive; it is integrated into all aspects of classroom life, including academic subjects and infused throughout the school day in all areas of the school (playing field, cafeteria, hallways, school busses, etc.). It provides long-term solutions that address moral, ethical, and academic issues that are of growing concern about our society and the safety of our schools. (Character Education Partnership, 2002, p. 1)

STOP AND REFLECT

When we think about the kind of character we want for our children, it's clear that we want them to be able to judge what is right, care deeply about what is right, and then do what they believe to be right—even in the face of pressure from without and temptation from within. (Lickona, 1991, p. 51)

What do you believe are the core values, or virtues, of good character? As a teacher, to what extent should you be responsible for teaching values, virtues, character, or self-discipline?

Self-Discipline as Emotional Intelligence
or Social and Emotional Learning

In the 1990s, a new educational movement concerning classroom discipline, but particularly self-discipline, emerged in which emotion received much more attention than in the past. The *emotional intelligence,* or *emotion education,* movement was largely sparked by Daniel Goleman's best-selling book *Emotional Intelligence* (Goleman, 1995) and Howard Gardner's books and articles (e.g., Gardner, 1993) on his theory of multiple intelligences (which recognizes the importance of emotions in "interpersonal" intelligence and in "intrapersonal" intelligence). Based largely on these publications, numerous educational books and curricula were published that were designed to help teachers foster children's emotional intelligence or emotional development.

Emotional intelligence is defined as "the ability to perceive emotions, to access and generate emotions so as to assist thought, to understand emotions and emotional knowledge, and to reflectively regulate emotions so as to promote emotional and intellectual growth" (Mayer & Salovey, 1997, p. 5). As seen in this definition, emotional intelligence is an important part of self-discipline. Indeed, programs designed to promote emotional intelligence address many of the same issues, and use many of the same educational strategies and techniques, as those programs designed to develop self-control, responsibility, autonomy, or self-discipline.

Nearly all emotional intelligence programs attempt to promote both emotional and social intelligence. For this reason, the term *social and emotional intelligence,* or *social and emotional learning* (SEL), often is used to refer to emotional intelligence. SEL is defined as "the process of developing the ability to recognize and manage emotions, develop caring and concern for others, make responsible decisions, establish positive relationships, and handle challenging situations effectively" (CASEL, 2003, p. 1). Social and emotional learning programs target a combination of behaviors, cognitions, and emotions. They include many emotion education, moral education, and character education programs, as well as classroom discipline programs that focus on self-discipline. They also include programs designed to prevent school violence; drug, alcohol, and tobacco use; peer conflict; and sexual diseases and programs designed to promote mental and physical health, good character, and good citizenship (Zins, Elias, Greenberg, & Weissberg, 2000). To be considered an SEL program, a program must not be narrowly focused but be designed to address how children *think, feel,* and *act* (Elias et al., 1997). As such, obedience models of classroom discipline and lecture-based programs, in which students are *told* what to do, are not SEL programs (and are not effective). The goal of SEL programs is to develop a variety of important social and emotional competencies, such as the following (Payton, Wardlaw, Graczyk, Bloodworth, Tompsett, & Weissberg, 2000):

- *Awareness of self and others* (i.e., awareness of feelings, management of feelings, constructive sense of self, and perspective taking).
- *Positive attitudes and values* (i.e., personal responsibility, respect for others, and social responsibility).
- *Responsible decision making* (i.e., problem identification, social norm analysis, adaptive goal setting, and problem solving).
- *Social interaction skills* (i.e., active listening, expressive communication, cooperation, negotiation, refusal, and help seeking).

STOP AND REFLECT

Are there any other social and emotional competencies you should add to the foregoing list? Should the home or school be primarily responsible for helping children develop these competencies? What do teachers and parents do, or *should* do, to promote these competencies?

Why Development of Self-Discipline Should Be an Educational Priority

The general public agrees that the most important purpose of public education is "to prepare students to be responsible citizens" (Rose & Gallup, 2000, p. 48). Having socially responsible citizens—citizens who are self-disciplined and who require minimal external regulation—is of critical importance to our society. Obviously, self-discipline also is critically important, especially to teachers and students, because it reduces discipline problems in the classroom—problems that impact by disrupting learning and demand considerable time and effort from the teacher. Perhaps less obvious is that self-discipline also promotes (1) positive relations with others and a positive school climate, (2) academic achievement, and (3) self-worth and emotional well-being (Bear, Manning, & Izard, 2003). Each of these positive outcomes, as discussed here, benefits not just individuals and classrooms but also society in general.

Self-Discipline Promotes Positive Relations with Others and a Positive School Climate

A wealth of research in psychology shows that children prefer classmates who demonstrate self-discipline, or responsible behavior, as seen in their lack of aggression and antisocial behavior and their frequency of prosocial behavior (Rubin, Bukowski, & Parker, 1998). Students who frequently exhibit antisocial and aggressive behavior, such as fighting, bullying, lying, and stealing, tend to be rejected by their peers. Those who act prosocially tend to be popular among their peers and have closer friendships. This does not mean, however, that peers necessarily prefer those who never misbehave. Indeed, students who strictly pursue rule-following goals may be "teacher pets" but are not necessarily liked by their classmates (Wentzel, 1994). Conversely, peers who aggress toward others for the "right" reasons (e.g., in sports, in self-defense, or in the defense of victims of aggression) are seldom socially rejected and often quite popular among their peers (Bear & Rys, 1994).

Teachers also prefer students who demonstrate self-discipline and do not require constant supervision and external control. They report feeling closer to such students, especially those who display prosocial behavior rather than antisocial behavior (Birch & Ladd, 1998). In general, children who demonstrate self-discipline and act responsibly receive more social support from their teachers (Hughes, Cavell, & Willson, 2001), as well as from their peers (Wentzel, 1991). This helps promote an overall positive school environment. That is, students who feel supported by teachers and peers experience a sense of belonging to the school community (Osterman, 2000). Not only do these students feel cared about by others, but they also tend to reciprocate by caring about others in the community and acting accordingly. They display greater empathy for others, better conflict resolution skills, and reduced delinquency (Battistich, Schaps, Watson, Solomon, & Lewis, 2000). In sum, self-discipline contributes to the development of positive relationships with others and a positive school climate, which in turn motivate further responsible behavior.

Self-Discipline Fosters Academic Achievement

There is ample evidence that socially responsible behavior, character, or self-discipline, is related to academic achievement (Benninga, Berkowitz, Kuehn, & Smith, 2003; CASEL, 2003; Malecki & Elliott, 2002). Quite simply, children who respect others, care about their school community, and seldom demonstrate antisocial behavior tend to perform better academically. The relation between these behaviors and academic achievement is positive and reciprocal (Welsh, Parke, Widaman, & O'Neil, 2001). That is, self-discipline promotes academic achievement and academic achievement promotes self-discipline. This makes sense in that self-discipline and academic achievement share many of the same cognitive, social, and emotional processes, such as the ability to inhibit impulsive behavior and reflect on solutions to social and academic problems, the motivation to please others and to achieve internalized standards and social goals, and the anticipation of feelings of guilt or pride as outcomes of one's social and academic behavior.

The reciprocal relation between self-discipline and academic achievement has important implications for interventions. Not only does it mean that educators can improve academic achievement by fostering thoughts, feelings, and behaviors associated with self-discipline, but it also means that they can improve many aspects of self-discipline by emphasizing academics. Indeed, school interventions designed to foster social and emotional learning have been shown to produce gains in academic achievement and interventions designed to improve academic achievement have been shown to improve social and emotional learning (Elias et al., 1997). Some researchers argue, however, that there is more evidence supporting the positive effects of social interventions on academic achievement than of academic interventions on social behavior (Malecki & Elliott, 2002; Wentzel, 1993).

Not only are self-discipline and academic achievement reciprocally related to one another, but they also are reciprocally related to school climate and safety. Thus, by developing self-discipline and emphasizing academic success, educators help create school climates that are caring, safe, and conducive to learning. Conversely, by emphasizing positive school climates, educators help promote self-discipline and academic achievement.

Self-Discipline Contributes to Positive
Self-Worth and Emotional Well-Being

Children's overall self-worth, or self-esteem, is determined by many factors. One of the strongest determinants is self-perceptions of competence or adequacy in important domains of self-concept, including behavioral conduct (other domains are academics, social acceptance, physical appearance, and athletics) (Harter, 1999). Most children believe that "good" persons are largely defined by their behavioral conduct, or moral behavior, and, thus, are unlikely to perceive themselves positively when they understand that their behavior is "wrong" or inconsistent with their own personal standards. Not only do they feel good about their good behavior, but they also feel good about themselves in general. This is especially true when they believe moral behavior is important and they feel responsible for their good behavior, believing that their good behavior reflects their own choices and values. In turn, such positive feelings help motivate further good behavior, general emotional well-being, and achievement in other important areas of self-concept (Harter, 1999).

S T O P   A N D   R E F L E C T

Who's Responsible: Elementary, Middle, or High School Teachers?

In a course on classroom discipline taught by the author, it is not uncommon for experienced middle school and high school teachers to argue that although they should be responsible for preventing and correcting misbehavior, they shouldn't be responsible for developing self-discipline. That is, they often argue that self-discipline should be developed far earlier, and that remediation should be left to mental health and juvenile correction agencies and not to the schools. Elementary teachers often disagree with this perspective, although some argue that self-discipline should be in place before children enter school. Do you agree or disagree with these perspectives? To what extent should middle schools and high schools share in the responsibility of developing self-discipline?

Developing Self-Discipline: The Need for Comprehensive Classroom Discipline

Given its critical importance, how can teachers help students develop self-discipline in their classrooms or attain Jefferson's vision of a society of responsible citizens? To be effective, research suggests that classroom discipline programs must be comprehensive. Certainly, developing self-discipline should be an educational priority, but it should be only one part of a comprehensive program for *all* students. Comprehensive classroom discipline must also include *preventing misbehavior with effective classroom management and correcting misbehavior.* These three components apply to all students and to all classrooms. They are interrelated in that they influence one another in an ongoing, dynamic fashion, as explained here. They characterize effective classrooms *and* effective schools. As such, they can be viewed as components of both *classroom discipline* and *school discipline.*

There is a fourth aspect of discipline that is best viewed not necessarily as a component of classroom discipline because it does not apply to all classroom teachers and to all students: addressing serious and chronic behavior problems. Although certainly involved, individual teachers alone should not be responsible for this component of school discipline. It is a school responsibility shared by support staff and teachers with special training. This component of school discipline is more central to schools than individual teachers. It focuses on students who are at the greatest risk for serious and chronic behavior problems, including students with disabilities who require special provisions in developing and implementing interventions for misbehavior. It incorporates strategies and techniques for (a) preventing

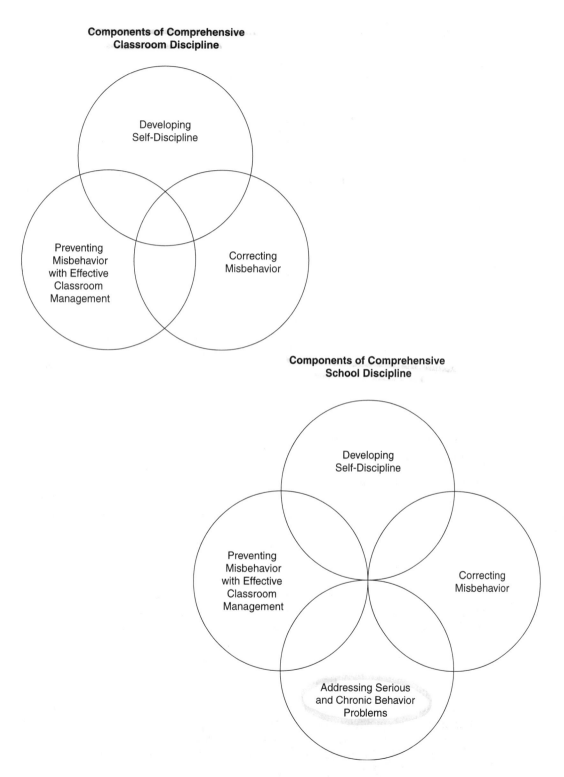

**Components of Comprehensive
Classroom Discipline**

Developing
Self-Discipline

Preventing
Misbehavior
with Effective
Classroom
Management

Correcting
Misbehavior

**Components of Comprehensive
School Discipline**

Developing
Self-Discipline

Preventing
Misbehavior
with Effective
Classroom
Management

Correcting
Misbehavior

Addressing Serious
and Chronic Behavior
Problems

serious and chronic behavior problems among highly at-risk students, (b) remediating serious and chronic behavior problems (including alternative and special education), and (c) preparing for and responding to crises and issues of school safety related to serious and chronic behavior problems.

Component 1: Developing Self-Discipline

Although certainly important in developing self-discipline, it is not sufficient that students simply acquire *knowledge* of what is right and wrong and know how to exhibit appropriate behavior. As argued earlier, students also need to develop social and emotional *competencies* that regulate their behavior in the absence of clear rules, adult supervision, external rewards, and the threat of punishment. Strategies and techniques for developing social and moral problem solving are the focus of Chapter 8. Students also need to develop emotions to help guide their decisions and behavior, especially the emotions of empathy, pride, and even guilt—an important emotion that underlies responsibility. Emotion-focused strategies and techniques for developing self-discipline are presented in Chapter 9. For schools to be successful in developing responsible citizens, social and emotional competencies need to be addressed in a deliberate and systematic fashion. Schools should not assume that students will learn these competencies on their own. Instead, schools must plan and implement lessons and activities and offer a wealth of opportunities for developing self-discipline throughout the school's curriculum, discipline policies, practices, and everyday interactions between teachers and students. By doing so, they prevent many behavior problems from occurring, allowing teachers to focus more on academic instruction while students assume greater responsibility for their own behavior.

Component 2: Preventing Misbehavior with Effective Classroom Management

Developing self-discipline helps prevent misbehavior, reducing the need for correction. However, another critical way to prevent misbehavior is by using strategies and techniques of effective classroom management. Research clearly shows that the greatest difference between effective and ineffective teachers with respect to classroom discipline lies not in the strategies and techniques they use to correct misbehavior, but in the strategies and techniques they use to *prevent* it (Brophy, 1996; Kounin, 1970). Few behavior problems exist in classrooms and schools characterized by key elements of effective classroom management. These elements include warm teacher–student relations, clear rules and fair consequences, developmentally appropriate and motivating academic instruction, favorable physical arrangements, and positive teacher–home communication.

It is important to note that although developing self-discipline and preventing misbehavior with effective classroom management are interrelated, they also comprise two distinct components of comprehensive classroom discipline. Unfortunately, most models of classroom discipline view them as one and the same as strategies and techniques for preventing misbehavior. To be sure, both components are preventive. That is, by developing self-discipline and employing effective classroom management, teachers avoid many behavior problems. However, many classroom management techniques, although effective in preventing misbehavior, contribute little to the development of self-discipline. Conversely, techniques for developing self-discipline do not necessarily impact classroom management. For example, teachers skilled in classroom management and who are proactive in their approach to misbehavior create classroom climates that are conducive to the development of self-discipline and academic learning but do not necessarily develop responsible behavior, autonomy, character, or other important aspects of self-discipline in their students. Conversely, teachers who are effective in developing self-discipline are not necessarily the most effective classroom managers. Thus, it makes sense to view the development of self-discipline and the prevention of misbehavior with effective classroom management as two distinct components of comprehensive classroom discipline. Strategies and techniques for preventing misbehavior with effective classroom management are the focus of Chapter 10.

Component 3: Correcting Misbehavior

Recall earlier in this chapter that discipline often is defined as the correction, or punishment, of misbehavior. Traditionally, with respect to classroom discipline the purpose of correction of misbehavior is twofold: (1) to help promote self-discipline and (2) to create and maintain safe, orderly, and positive learning environments. To be sure, when used wisely, correction fosters self-discipline and, thus, helps prevent future misbehavior. This is particularly true when the techniques used to correct misbehavior rely primarily on teaching and reinforcing appropriate behavior, thinking skills, and positive emotions. Situations calling for correction of misbehavior often provide excellent contexts in which social and emotional competencies can be developed.

The second purpose of correction—to create and maintain safe, orderly, and positive learning environments—is emphasized in the No Child Left Behind Act, zero tolerance policies, and the codes of conduct for most schools. Clearly, no teacher can avoid having to correct misbehavior. Unfortunately, many teachers must correct not only everyday acts of minor misbehavior but also more serious forms including acts of violence. Thus, using discipline, both positive and punitive forms, to correct misbehavior must be included as a critical component of comprehensive classroom discipline. Strategies and techniques for correction are interspersed throughout the book but receive primary focus in Chapters 11 and 12.

Addressing Serious and Chronic Behavior Problems

Fortunately, most misbehavior is not serious and can be prevented by developing self-discipline and using effective classroom management. Likewise, when misbehaviors do occur, typically they are responsive to the wise use of correction. Unfortunately, however, at one time or another nearly every teacher faces the challenge of teaching students who exhibit serious behavior problems, such as acts of violence, or who exhibit chronic behavior problems that are resistant to techniques for developing self-discipline and for preventing and correcting misbehavior. This is true even when schools make a special effort, as all schools should, to target students who are at the greatest risk for serious and chronic behavior problems and make sure they are provided additional services and supports as early as possible and before relatively minor acts of noncompliance and aggression evolve into behaviors that typically call for suspension or expulsion. When the preceding effort fails, schools need to provide *remediation*—educational and mental health services that are comprehensive, intensive, and sustained over time. Such services are not always best provided in regular classrooms but often require placement in alternative or special education settings. Hence, they are best viewed as a component of *school* discipline rather than *classroom* discipline.

One group of children who often require remediation, both academic and behavioral, is students with disabilities. Although the majority of students with disabilities do *not* exhibit serious or chronic behavior problems, certain categories of students with disabilities are at greater risk for such. Under the Individuals with Disabilities Education Act (IDEA), most of them qualify for special education services, in which intensive and sustained remediation is provided that targets not only their educational needs but also their social and emotional needs. They also qualify for special provisions under the act that govern the use of discipline, especially lengthy suspensions and expulsion. Because the majority of students with disabilities receive at least part of their instruction in the regular classroom, and federal law requires the participation of the regular classroom teacher in the development and implementation of interventions for behavior problems, it is imperative that all teachers be familiar with these special provisions and what otherwise is required of them under IDEA.

Although students with disabilities are at increased risk for exhibiting behavior problems, it should be emphasized that they certainly are not responsible for the majority of discipline problems. *Most students who are suspended and expelled are not students with disabilities.* Nevertheless, often these students have the same remedial needs as students who qualify for special education services. Suspension and expulsion do not meet these needs. Many of these students need remedial programs, provided either within their regular school or in an alternative school. Regardless of the setting, intensive intervention, or remediation, is required. Research shows that in order to have lasting effects, such programs for these students must be broad-based, comprehensive, and intensive (Bear, Webster-Stratton, Furlong, & Rhee, 2000). That is, schools, families, agencies, and communities must work together intensively in targeting multiple risk and protective factors that are linked to antisocial behavior.

Although the regular classroom teachers seldom play the primary role in the delivery of interventions for the students with serious and chronic behavior problems, they almost always play very important roles. Typically, they are the first ones to recognize the need for remediation and, thus, are counted on to refer students for needed services. Moreover, often they are members of intervention teams that must develop and implement strategies and techniques that address the behaviors of concern. Most of these strategies and techniques are the same ones that are presented in chapters on developing self-discipline and preventing and correcting misbehavior but they are delivered in a more frequent and systematic fashion for students with serious and chronic behavior problems.

S U M M A R Y   A N D   K E Y   P O I N T S

- There are two sides to, or definitions of, classroom discipline: *developing* self-discipline and *using* discipline to correct misbehavior.
- Self-discipline has always been a priority among educators in the United States and the general public. The development of self-discipline is highlighted in most models of classroom discipline, both old and new.

- Self-discipline connotes internal regulation of one's behavior. It entails assuming responsibility for one's actions, understanding right and wrong, appreciating the importance of cooperative relationships, and inhibiting socially inappropriate behavior. It involves knowing what's right, desiring to do what is right, and most importantly doing what is right. Self-discipline reflects internalization.

- The terms *responsibility, self-control, autonomy, character, emotional intelligence, social and emotional learning,* and *self-discipline* often are used interchangeably. Self-discipline is a critical component of character, emotional, intelligence, and social and emotional learning.
- Most federal and state initiatives, including the No Child Left Behind Act, focus more on correcting misbehavior and maintaining disciplined environments that are safe and conducive to learning than on developing self-discipline.
- Self-discipline is important because it helps prevent discipline problems, fosters academic achievement, promotes positive peer relations, and contributes to positive self-worth and emotional well-being.

- Many authors of popular models of classroom discipline claim that the use of discipline is detrimental to the development of self-discipline. Others disagree.
- The development of self-discipline is one component, arguably the most important component, of a comprehensive classroom discipline program. Two additional components are preventing misbehavior using effective classroom management and correcting misbehavior. Another aspect of discipline is addressing serious and chronic behavior problems. Because this aspect does not apply to all teachers and students, it is best viewed as an aspect of school, rather than classroom, discipline.

KEY TERMS AND CONCEPTS

Autonomy	Internalization	Self-discipline
Character	No Child Left Behind Act	Self-control
Character education	Prevention	Social and emotional learning
Correction	Remediation	
Emotional intelligence	Responsibility	

RECOMMENDED READINGS AND RESOURCES

Books on Developing Self-Discipline and Character

Bodine, R. J., & Crawford, D. K. (1999). *Developing emotional intelligence: A guide to behavior management and conflict resolution in schools.* Champaign, IL: Research Press.

Charney, R. S. (2002). *Teaching children to care: Classroom management for ethical and academic growth, K–8* (Rev. ed.). Greenfield, MA: Northeast Foundation for Children.

Damon, W. (Ed.) (2002). *Bringing in a new ear in character education.* Standford, CA: Hoover Institute Press.

DeVries, R., & Zan, B. (1994). *Moral classrooms, moral children: Creating a constructivist atmosphere in early education.* New York: Teachers College Press.

Elias, M. J., Zins, J. E., Weissberg, R. P., Frey, K. S., Greenberg, M. T., Haynes, N. M., Kessler, R., Schwab-Stone, M. E., & Shriver, T. P. (1997). *Promoting social and emotional learning: Guidelines for educators.* Alexandria, VA: Association for Supervision and Curriculum Development.

Lickona, T. (2004). *Character matters: How to help our children develop good judgment, integrity, and other essential virtues.* New York: Touchstone.

Noddings, N. (2002). *Educating moral people: A caring alternative to character education.* New York: Teachers College Press.

Ryan, K., & Bohlin, K. (1999). *Building character in schools: Practical ways to bring moral instruction to life.* San Francisco: Jossey-Bass.

Watson, M. (2003). *Learning to trust: Transforming difficult elementary classrooms through developmental discipline.* San Francisco: Jossey-Bass.

Zins, J. E., Weissberg, R. P., Wang, M. C., & Wahlberg, H. J. (2004). *Building academic success on social and emotional learning: What does the research say?* New York: Teachers College Press.

Websites for Character Education and Social and Emotional Learning

www.casel.org
 Website for the Collaborative for Academic, Social, and Emotional Learning (CASEL). Offers an electronic newsletter, excellent links to related sites, and reports and summaries of research and effective practices on promoting social and emotional learning.

www.character.org

> Website for the Character Education Partnership, a nonpartisan coalition of organizations and individuals dedicated to developing moral character and civic virtue. Contains general information about character and character education (including the "Eleven Elements of Effective Character Education"), a newsletter, resources, and links to other sites.

www.cortland.edu/www/c4n5rs

> Website for the Center for the 4th and 5th Rs. Includes general information and resources on character education. Disseminates articles and a newsletter on character education.

www.devstu.org

> Website for the Developmental Studies Center, the Child Development Project, and the Caring School Community, each dedicated to children's academic, ethical, and social development. This site provides research-supported information, resources, and curriculum materials on child development and education, with an emphasis on promoting self-discipline.

www.bu.edu/education/caec

> Website for the Center for the Advancement of Ethics and Character. Provides general information and curriculum resources on character education, including sample lessons.

www.charactercounts.org

> Website of Character Counts, a nonprofit, nonpartisan, coalition of schools, communities, and nonprofit organizations dedicated to teaching character education. Run by the Josephson Institute of Ethics, this is a good site for basic information and resources on character education, with a major focus on teaching the "six pillars of character": trustworthiness, respect, responsibility, fairness, caring, and citizenship.

www.goodcharacter.com

> Source of curricula and resources on character education, including free lessons and lesson plans for developing trustworthiness, respect, responsibility, fairness, caring, and citizenship.

www.ed.gov/about/offices/list/osdfs

> Website of the Office of Safe and Drug-Free Schools. Includes information on character education projects funded by the government's Partnerships in Character Education Program.

For additional resources on programs, strategies, and techniques for promoting self-discipline, character, and social and emotional learning, see Chapters 8 and 9.

Information on No Child Left Behind Act

www.nochildleftbehind.gov

> Government website for the No Child Left Behind Act of 2001.

For further information and resources on character education, the No Child Left Behind Act, and other current topics in education, check the websites of various national professional organizations in education.

> National Education Association (www.nea.org)
>
> Association for Supervision and Curriculum Development (www.ascd.org)
>
> National Parent Teacher Association (www.pta.org)
>
> National Association of Elementary School Principals (www.naesp.org)
>
> National Association of Secondary School Principals (www.nassp.org)
>
> National School Boards Association (www.nsba.org)
>
> National Parent Teacher Association (www.pta.org)

Also note that it is likely that the website for the department of education in your state, as well as websites for local school districts, include links, information, and resources on character education, the No Child Left Behind Act, and other topics of educational interest.

REFERENCES

Albert, L. (1996). *Cooperative discipline.* Circle Pines, MN: American Guidance Service.

Battistich, V., Schaps, E., Watson, M., Solomon, D., & Lewis, C. (2000). Effects of the Child Development Project on students' drug use and other problem behaviors. *Journal of Primary Prevention, 21,* 75–99.

Bear, G. G. (1998). School discipline in the United States: Prevention, correction, and long-term social development. *School Psychology Review, 27,* 14–32.

Bear, G. G., Manning, M. A., & Izard, C. (2003). Responsible behavior: The importance of social cognition and emotion. *School Psychology Quarterly, 18,* 140–157.

Bear, G. G., & Rys, G. S. (1994). Moral reasoning, classroom behavior, and sociometric status among elementary school children. *Developmental Psychology, 30,* 633–638.

Bear, G. G., Webster-Stratton, C., Furlong, M., & Rhee, S. (2000). Preventing aggression and violence. In

K. M. Minke & G. G. Bear (Eds.), *Preventing school problems—promoting school success: Strategies and programs that work* (pp. 1–69). Bethesda, MD: National Association of School Psychologists.

Bennett, W. J. (1995). *The moral compass.* New York: Simon & Schuster.

Benninga, J. S., Berkowitz, M. W., Kuehn, P., & Smith, K. (2003). The relationship of character education implementation and academic achievement in elementary schools. *Journal of Research in Character Education, 1,* 17–30.

Berkowitz, M. W. (2002). The science of character education. In W. Damon (Ed.), *Bringing in a new era in character education* (pp. 44–63). Stanford, CA: Stanford University Press.

Birch, S. H., & Ladd, G. W. (1998). Children's interpersonal behaviors and the teacher–child relationship. *Developmental Psychology, 34,* 934–946.

Brodie, F. M. (1974). *Thomas Jefferson: An intimate history.* New York: Bantam.

Brophy, J. E. (1996). *Teaching problem students.* New York: Guilford Press.

Character Education Partnership (2004). *Character education questions and answers.* Washington, DC: Author.

Collaborative for Academic, Social, and Emotional Learning (2003). *Safe and sound: An educational leader's guide to evidence-based social and emotional learning (SEL) programs.* Retrieved July 8, 2003, from the CASEL website: www.CASEL.org.

Curwin, R. L., & Mendler, A. N. (1999). *Discipline with dignity.* Alexandria, VA: Association for Supervision and Curriculum Development.

DeVries, R., & Zan, B. (1994). *Moral classrooms, moral children: Creating a constructivist atmosphere in early education.* New York: Teachers College Press.

Dreikurs, R., & Cassel, P. (1972). *Discipline without tears: What to do with children who misbehave.* New York: Hawthorn Books.

Dreikurs, R., & Grey, L. (1968). *Logical consequences: A handbook of discipline.* New York: Meredith Press.

Elias, M. J., Zins, J. E., Weissberg, R. P., Frey, K. S., Greenberg, M. T., Haynes, N. M., Kessler, R., Schwab-Stone, M. E., & Shriver, T. P. (1997). *Promoting social and emotional learning: Guidelines for educators.* Alexandria, VA: Association for Supervision and Curriculum Development.

Federal Register, March 13, 1995.

Finkelstein, B. (1989). *Governing the young: Teacher behavior in popular primary schools in 19th century United States.* New York: The Falmer Press.

Freiberg, H. J. (1999). Beyond behaviorism. In H. J. Freiberg (Ed.), *Beyond behaviorism: Changing the classroom management paradigm* (pp. 3–20). Boston: Allyn and Bacon.

Gardner, H. (1993). *Frames of mind: The theory of multiple intelligences.* New York: Basic Books.

Glasser, W. (1965). *Reality therapy.* New York: Harper & Row.

Glasser, W. (1969). *Schools without failure.* New York: Harper & Row.

Glasser, W. (1998). *The quality school* (3rd ed.). New York: Harper Perennial.

Goleman, D. (1995). *Emotional intelligence.* New York: Bantam.

Gordon, T. (1974). *TET: Teacher effectiveness training.* New York: David McKay Company.

Gordon, T. (1989). *Discipline that works: Promoting self-discipline in children.* New York: Plume.

Gordon, T. (2003). *Teacher effectiveness training.* New York: Three Rivers Press.

Grusec, J. E., & Goodnow, J. J. (1994). Impact of parental discipline methods on the child's internalization of values: A reconceptualization of current points of view. *Developmental Psychology, 30,* 4–19.

Gun-Free Schools Act of 1994. Public Law 103-382. 108 Statute 3907. Title 14.

Harter, S. (1999). *The construction of the self: A developmental perspective.* New York: Guilford.

Hughes, J. N., Cavell, T. A., & Willson, V. (2001). Further support for the developmental significance of the quality of the teacher–student relationship. *Journal of School Psychology, 39,* 289–301.

Hyman, I. A. (1990). *Reading, writing, and the hickory stick.* Lexington, MA: Lexington Books.

Kohlberg, L. (1984). *Essays on moral development: Vol. 2. The psychology of moral development.* New York: Harper & Row.

Kohn, A. (1996). *Beyond discipline: From compliance to community.* Alexandria, VA: Association for Supervision and Curriculum Development.

Kounin, J. (1970). *Discipline and group management in classrooms.* New York: Holt, Rinehart and Winston.

Lickona, T. (1991). *Educating for character: How our schools can teach respect and responsibility.* New York: Bantam.

Lickona, T. (2004). *Character matters: How to help our children develop good judgment, integrity, and other essential virtues.* New York: Touchstone.

Malecki, C. K., & Elliott, S. (2002). Children's social behaviors as predictors of academic achievement: A longitudinal analysis. *School Psychology Quarterly, 17,* 1–23.

Mayer, J. D., Salovey, P. (1997). What is emotional intelligence? In P. Salovey & D. Sluyter (Eds.), *Emotional development and emotional intelligence: Implications for educators* (pp. 3–31). New York: Basic Books.

Mayo, B. (1988). *Jefferson himself.* Charlottesville, VA: University Press of Virginia. (Original work published 1942).

National Education Goals Panel. (1994, August). *Data volume for the national education goals report, volume one: National data.* Washington, DC: Author.

Nelsen, J., Lott, L., & Glenn, H. (1993, 2000). *Positive discipline in the classroom.* Rocklin, CA: Prima.

Noddings, N. (2002). *Educating moral people: A caring alternative to character education.* New York: Teachers College Press.

Osterman, K. F. (2000). Students' need for belonging in the school community. *Review of Educational Research, 70,* 323–367.

Payton, J. W., Wardlaw, D. M., Graczyk, P. A., Bloodworth, M. R., Tompsett, C. J., & Weissberg, R. P. (2000). Social and emotional learning: A framework for promoting mental health and reducing risk behaviors in children and youth. *Journal of School Health, 70,* 179–185.

Piaget, J. (1965). *The moral judgment of the child.* Glenco, IL: Free Press. (Original work published 1932).

Public Agenda (1996). *Given the circumstances: Teachers talk about public education today.* New York: Author.

Rose, L. C., & Gallup, A. M. (2000). The 32nd annual Phi Delta Kappa/Gallup Poll of the public's attitudes toward the public schools. *Phi Delta Kappan, 82,* 41–66.

Rubin, K. H., Bukowski, W., & Parker, J. G. (1998). Peer interactions, relationships, and groups. In W. Damon (Series Ed.) & N. Eisenberg (Vol. Ed.), *Handbook of child psychology: Vol. 3. Social, emotional, and personality development* (5th ed., pp. 619–700). New York: Wiley.

Ryan, K., & Bohlin, K. (1999). *Building character in schools: Practical ways to bring moral instruction to life.* San Francisco: Jossey-Bass.

Six pillars of character: Developing moral values in youth. (1992). (Special issue). *Ethics: Easier Said Than Done, 19 and 20,* 34–88.

The White House. (2001). *No Child Left Behind.* Washington, DC: The White House.

Watson, M. (2003). *Learning to trust: Transforming difficult elementary classrooms through developmental discipline.* San Francisco: Jossey-Bass.

Webster's new world college dictionary (3rd ed.). (1996). New York: Macmillan.

Welsh, M., Parke, R. D., Widaman, K., & O'Neil, R. (2001). Linkages between children's social and academic achievement. *Journal of School Psychology, 39,* 463–482.

Wentzel, K. R. (1991). Social competence at school: Relation between social responsibility and academic achievement. *Review of Educational Research, 61,* 1–24.

Wentzel, K. R. (1993). Does being good make the grade? Social behavior and academic competence in middle school. *Journal of Educational Psychology, 85,* 357–364.

Wentzel, K. R. (1994). Relations of social goal pursuit to social acceptance, classroom behavior, and perceived social support. *Journal of Educational Psychology, 86,* 173–182.

Zins, J. E., Elias, M. J., Greenberg, M. T., & Weissberg, R. P. (2000). Promoting social and emotional competence in children. In K. M. Minke and G. G. Bear (Eds.), *Preventing school problems—Promoting school success: Strategies and programs that work* (pp. 71–99). Bethesda, MD: National Association of School Psychologists.

2 Discipline as Punishment

Issues and Controversies

- Why is punishment a popular strategy among teachers? Is its popularity justified?
- What are the general limitations to punishment?
- Should long-term suspension, expulsion, and a pervasive zero tolerance approach be viewed as harsh forms of punishment?

- Is it unfair or discriminatory when disciplinary policies result in disproportionate numbers of a racial or cultural group being paddled, suspended, or expelled?
- In what ways do effective and ineffective teachers differ in their use of punishment?
- Do the advantages of punishment outweigh the disadvantages?
- How might punishment be used wisely to help promote self-discipline and maintain classroom and school climates that are safe and conducive to learning?
- What are some positive alternatives to a reliance on the use of punishment to manage and correct behavior?

> Because children's wishes often conflict with those of their caregivers, the notion that children can or should be raised without using aversive discipline is utopian. (Baumrind, 1996, p. 409)

> What was once considered a schoolyard scuffle can now land a student in juvenile court or, even worse, in prison. In some instances this occurs regardless of age, intent, circumstances, severity of the act, or harm caused. (Advancement Project/Civil Rights Project, 2000, p. 12)

Nearly all educators would agree with the premise of Chapter 1 that the development of self-discipline *should* be a primary aim of education. However, most educators also would agree that there is another side to discipline that is of equal importance—a side that is much more controversial and emotionally laden—the *use of discipline* to correct misbehavior. Unfortunately, the use of discipline is commonly equated with *punishment*. And perhaps this is for good reasons: Throughout history, teachers always have relied on various forms of punishment, and today punishment remains the most common strategy for correcting misbehavior (Brophy, 1996). This is true despite continued criticism and controversy over its use and research showing that nonpunitive techniques often are more effective than punishment in reducing the recurrence of misbehavior. The purpose of this chapter is to discuss the criticisms and controversies surrounding the use of punishment. An attempt is made to present a balanced perspective toward the use of punishment, recognizing its limitations, advantages, and both good and bad reasons for its popularity.

Common Criticisms of Punishment

A frequent refrain among the critics of punishment is that it is ineffective and unethical. For example, here's what several authors of popular models of classroom discipline have said about the use of punishment in schools:

Rudolph Dreikurs, author of several classic books on classroom discipline, including *Logical Consequences* (Dreikurs & Grey, 1968) and *Discipline Without Tears* (Dreikurs & Cassel, 1972), states:

> *Punishment is only effective for those who don't need it.* . . . . Punishment does not influence behavior or "teach" anything today. (Dreikurs & Cassel, 1972, p. 60)

> [Punishment] belittles or demeans the child. . . . Denotes sin. . . . Implies that the child has no value. . . . Inevitably involves some moral judgment. (Dreikurs & Cassel, 1972, pp. 64–65)

Punishment teaches what not to do but fails to teach what to do. (Dreikurs & Grey, 1968, p. 22)

William Glasser, author of one of the most popular books, and models of classroom discipline, in the 1970s and 1980s *Reality Therapy* (Glasser, 1965) and several more recent popular books on school reform and school discipline (e.g., Glasser, 1986, 1998), notes:

Society and the schools mainly use punishment, and punishment doesn't work. (Glasser, 1969, p. 23)

Thomas Gordon, author of several popular books on discipline and developer of *Teacher Effectiveness Training* (1974, 2003), comments:

The bottom line is that today's parents and teachers are getting extremely bad advice from all the authors (and there are scores of them) who don't stand up against the use of punishment in our homes and schools. (Gordon, 1989, p. 33)

The mass of experimental evidence we have accumulated proves it: Punishing children will be hazardous to their mental health. To think otherwise is absurd. (Gordon, 1989, pp. 91–92)

Controlling and directing children and youth by the use of power—by punishment or threats of punishment and by rewards or the removal of rewards—robs children of the opportunity to become responsible. It keeps them locked into dependency and immaturity. (Gordon, 2003, pp. 249–250)

Gordon also cites research he believes proves that punishment *causes* a variety of deviant behaviors, including noncompliance and resistance, depression, psychosomatic ailments, eating disorders, alcoholism and drug addiction, and cheating. According to Gordon, "punishment is emotionally damaging to children." [As a result] "sick children grow up to be emotionally crippled, unproductive, antisocial, and often violent citizens" (Gordon, 1989, p. 92).

Lee and Marlene Canter (2001), authors of perhaps the most popular model of classroom discipline of all time, *Assertive Discipline,* note:

Canter

Punishment takes the form of criticism, humiliation or even physical pain. Teachers who try to curb disruptive behavior with punishment do so at the expense of student self-esteem and growth. Punishment breeds resentment. It does not encourage students to take responsibility for choosing appropriate behavior. (p. 63)

Jane Nelsen, Lynn Lott, and H. Stephen Glenn (1997), authors of *Positive Discipline,* state:

Any form of punishment or permissiveness is both disrespectful and discouraging. (p. 101)

Punishment has no place in the Positive Discipline classroom. (p. 102)

Teachers must take the first step to eliminate humiliation and punishment in order to create an environment that is nurturing, respectful, and conducive to learning. (p. 103)

One must wonder why punishment is the subject of such frequent and harsh criticism yet continues to be the strategy of choice for correcting misbehavior. To understand this irony it is necessary that we examine how authors, researchers, and practitioners have tended to define and view punishment differently. These differing definitions and viewpoints have helped create a great deal of confusion and misunderstanding among educators over the appropriate role of punishment in comprehensive classroom discipline.

What Is Punishment?

In psychology, the term *punishment* is used to refer to an event, or consequence, that follows a specific behavior and results in a decrease in the likelihood of that behavior recurring in the future (Martens, Witt, Daly, & Vollmer, 1999). Generally, the event or consequence that follows the specific behavior is aversive or unpleasant to the student. Note that what follows the behavior does not constitute punishment unless it is *effective* in decreasing the frequency of the behavior. Thus, punishment can include mildly unpleasant consequences, such as looking at a student in a way that conveys dissatisfaction ("the evil eye"), moving next to the student's desk, and verbally warning or mildly reprimanding a student. It also includes harsh consequences, such as beating, humiliating, or expelling a student from school. All of these corrective techniques follow the misbehavior, are typically unpleasant to students, and generally result in an immediate decrease in the misbehavior. Given the wide range of techniques that constitute punishment, and the fact that they decrease misbehaviors, it should come as little surprise that "punishment" is so popular.

The Common Mistake of Equating Punishment with Corporal Punishment and Emotional Maltreatment

Unfortunately, several popular writers in classroom discipline, including each of those noted previously, fail to accept the standard psychological definition of punishment—that punishment is something that follows a behavior and decreases its occurrence. Instead, when they refer to punishment, they are actually referring to harsh forms of punishment that often result in physical or serious emotional harm to the student. There is little disagreement among psychologists that such forms of punishment are inappropriate and unethical, especially in schools. To distinguish harsh forms of punishment that cause physical or emotional harm to students from nonharmful forms of punishment most psychologists use the terms *corporal punishment* and *emotional maltreatment* when referring to the former.

Most psychologists and experts in classroom discipline restrict the term *corporal punishment* to practices that intentionally cause physical pain or discomfort. For example, the National Association of School Psychologists (1988) views corporal punishment as "intentional infliction of physical pain, physical restraint, and/or discomfort upon a student as a disciplinary technique." Spanking or paddling is the most popular form of corporal punishment, with nearly all American adults reporting that they were spanked at one time or another during childhood (Greven, 1991, p. 1). About half of the American public views corporal punishment favorably (Gallup & Elam, 1988). Not only is it widely used in homes, but also twenty-two states do not ban its use in schools (Center for Effective Discipline, 2004). In several southern states corporal punishment is among the most common forms of correction (Maurer, 1990).

Irwin Hyman, director of the National Center for the Study of Corporal Punishment and Alternatives and the author of several popular books on school discipline and corporal punishment [e.g., *Reading, Writing and the Hickory Stick* (Hyman, 1990); *Dangerous Schools* (Hyman & Snook, 1999)], emphasizes that corporal punishment should not be limited to paddlings or other methods that intentionally cause physical pain but should include methods that are physically discomforting. Thus, he defines corporal punishment in the schools as "the infliction of pain or confinement as a penalty for an offense committed by a student" (Hyman, 1990, p. 10). According to Hyman, corporal punishment includes "preventing children from going to the bathroom, forcing children to assume uncomfortable postures for extended periods or to spend long durations in a time-out chair or confined space, and imposing painful physical drills" (Hyman & Snook, 1999, p. 31). (Hyman advises that the amount of time a student should spend in time-out should never be more minutes than the student's age. When the duration in time-out is longer, Hyman considers time-out to constitute "deprivation punishment," which he claims is one of the most common types of corporal punishment.) Not all authorities on classroom discipline agree with Hyman that corporal punishment includes not letting a child go to the bathroom and keeping a child in time-out for a period of time that exceeds his age. If one accepts Hyman's broad definition of corporal punishment, however, corporal punishment is extremely common not only in homes but also in most schools.

Despite its popularity in the homes of many Americans and in schools (primarily schools in southern states), only 13% of teachers and 28% of parents support the paddling of children in school (National Education Association, 1996). Moreover, nearly all leading professional associations in education and psychology (e.g., National Education Association, National Association of School Psychologists) oppose its use. Such opposition to the use of corporal punishment in school is not based on a lack of effectiveness. To be sure, corporal punishment often is quite effective in stopping a behavior, especially in the short term. Even the most difficult students stop misbehaving under the serious threat of a severe beating. The reason why most professional organizations and authorities on classroom discipline oppose the use of corporal punishment is based primarily on ethical and legal concerns and rightfully so. Chief among these concerns are respect for student dignity and individual rights and the negative outcomes associated with frequent and harsh corporal punishment.

Research shows that a host of serious negative outcomes are common among children and adolescents from homes in which corporal punishment is used, particularly when it is used in a frequent, harsh, unfair, and inconsistent manner. These outcomes include early juvenile delinquency (Farrington & Hawkins, 1991), depression and alcoholism (Holmes & Robins, 1987), and an increased likelihood that the child will demonstrate aggression toward others in the future (Strassberg, Dodge, Pettit, & Bates, 1994). The more harsh and severe is the punishment, the more negative are the outcomes.

It is important to note that punishment does not have to be physical to cause serious or lasting emotional harm. A steady diet of public fear, ridicule, humiliation, criticism, sarcasm, and denigration—either at home or school—can be just as damning as the frequent use of corporal punishment and more damning than the occasional use of corporal punishment. The same holds true with emotional neglect and social rejection, such as when teachers withdraw all forms of positive attention and social approval from students they do not like. Some authorities in classroom discipline consider practices such as these to be forms of *emotional maltreatment*. Hyman and Snook (1999) define emotional maltreatment as "any disciplinary or motivational practice that psychologically hurts children." Practices included under this definition are "humiliation, denigration, rejection, ignoring, isolation, excessive authoritarian discipline, sarcasm, put-downs, name-calling, ridicule, and bigotry" (p. 71).

The negative outcomes associated with corporal punishment and emotional maltreatment should be sufficient reasons why educators should refrain from their use. But there also are legal reasons why educators should think twice about using corporal punishment. On charges of child abuse, parents often file lawsuits against educators who bruise or emotionally traumatize students when using corporal punishment. In states in which corporal punishment in the schools is legal, parents rarely win such lawsuits unless the corporal punishment is determined to be excessive or malicious (in which case the offender may face criminal penalties) (Sales, Krauss, Sacken, & Overcast, 1999). However, even if the student is only slightly harmed (e.g., bruised), the offending educators may find themselves being legally classified by the local department of social services as "child abusers" (Hyman & Snook, 1999; Sales et al., 1999). In states in which corporal punishment in school is prohibited, parents are likely to win lawsuits pertaining to the use of corporal punishment irrespective of the harm caused (Sales et al., 1999).

STOP AND REFLECT

Emotional Maltreatment or Just Poor Choices of Punishment?

While working as a school psychologist, the following forms of punishment were witnessed by or reported to the author. Do you agree that each constitutes emotional maltreatment? What impact do you think these actions might have had on the students' self-concept, motivation, and behavior, as well as the climate of the classroom and school?

- A teacher asking her second-grade class to circle around a classmate and spit on him because he spit on another student.
- The coach of a high school soccer team refusing to speak to the leading scorer on the team for several weeks after he missed a penalty kick in a championship game.
- A high school gym teacher publicly ridiculing students in class for chewing gum and then making them wear chewing gum on their noses the remainder of the class.
- A first-grade teacher yelling and screaming at her students every day for the slightest misbehavior, as well as academic mistakes. Nearly half the students in the class were referred to the school psychologist by the teacher and parents because of social and emotional problems. School phobia, fear, and anxiety were found among most of the students, and nearly all showed little academic achievement that year.
- A teacher frequently referring to students (and not to their behavior per se) with demeaning labels such as "dumb," "stupid," and "hateful."
- A junior high school teacher clearly demonstrating her racial prejudice by first publicly reprimanding several Latino students for not knowing the answers to her questions and then never calling on them again (while not treating other students the same).

Sanitizing Punishment by Calling It Something Else

In criticizing punishment and failing to differentiate corporal punishment and emotional maltreatment from less harsh forms of punishment, most critics of punishment force themselves into the position of having to use another term to refer to unpleasant techniques for decreasing inappropriate behavior. Otherwise, they would be denouncing such common (and punitive) techniques as the "evil eye," moving near the student, calling a parent, or taking away a privilege (techniques that they themselves recommend!). Thus, in place of the term *punishment,* many writers and educators now use more pleasant-sounding terms intended to avoid images of a teacher *disciplining* students with corporal punishment. Two such terms used in several popular models of classroom discipline are *consequences* and *logical consequences.* Rudolf Dreikurs was the first to popularize the use of the term *logical consequences.* Dreikurs noted that logical consequences differed from punishment in that punishment is revengeful, abusive, "necessarily retaliatory rather than corrective" (Dreikurs & Cassel, 1972, p. 67), and results in "denigration of the violator" (Dreikurs & Cassel, 1972, p. 74). Whereas Dreikurs was correct in emphasizing that revenge, abuse, retaliation, and denigration have no place in classroom discipline, he was wrong in implying that these features necessarily characterize the use of all forms of punishment.

Following Dreikurs's lead, the term *consequence* is used in place of punishment in many other popular models of classroom discipline, including *Discipline with Dignity* (Curwin & Mendler, 1999), *Reality Therapy* (Glasser, 1965), and *Assertive Discipline* (Canter & Canter, 2001). It is apparent, however, that when these authors use the term *consequence* they are actually referring to mild forms of punishment. For example, each author recommends verbal warnings, reprimands, taking away privileges, and some form of time-out—each of which is a common type of mild punishment.

Zero Tolerance

In recent years, it has not been the use of mild forms of punishment, or even the use of corporal punishment, that has generated the greatest controversy with respect to classroom discipline. Instead, it has been the increasingly widespread use of suspension and expulsion. These two reductive techniques are designed to be punitive—to punish students for their misbehavior by removing them from the classroom or school for either a short number of days (i.e., suspension) or for the remainder of the school year or longer (i.e., expulsion). As with other types of punishment, they also are intended to decrease the likelihood that the student and others in the school will exhibit the behavior again. Additionally, they are intended to maintain a classroom environment that is safe and conducive to learning, such as when used in response to serious acts or threats of violence, possession of drugs or weapons, or chronically disruptive behavior.

In 1998 over 3 million students were suspended and 87,000 expelled (Advancement Project/Civil Rights Project, 2000). In Chicago alone, the number of expulsions increased from 14 during the 1992–1993 school year to 737 during the 1998–1999 school year. About 15% of students in regular education classes are suspended and/or placed in alternative education (U.S. General Accounting Office, 2001). These statistics are consistent with the results of public opinion polls that show that teachers and parents believe that disruptive students should be removed from the classroom. For example, a poll initiated by the National Education Association (Public Agenda, 1996) found that 88% of teachers and 73% of the public "think academic achievement would improve substantially if persistent troublemakers were removed from class."

STOP AND REFLECT

Do you agree that persistent troublemakers should be removed from class? In answering this question, assume the perspectives of all parties involved, including the student, classroom teacher, classmates, the principal, and the students' parents. If removed, where should they go? What behaviors do you believe warrant suspension or expulsion? How might suspension and expulsion be harsher than corporal punishment?

An increase in the use of suspension and expulsion can be attributed largely to many schools adopting what has become known as *zero tolerance policies,* as well as a more pervasive *zero tolerance approach* toward classroom discipline. It is important to distinguish rational and reasonable zero tolerance *policies* from a pervasive zero tolerance *approach* because it is the latter that is more harmful to the development of self-discipline and to school climate.

Zero Tolerance Policies

Nearly all schools now have zero tolerance policies on the possession of drugs, weapons, firearms, and acts of violence. In many cases these policies are fair and reasonable. That is, suspension and expulsion are administered judiciously with due consideration of the circumstances involved in the misbehavior (e.g., age of the student, intentions, prior history, etc.). Moreover, they are used as only one part of a comprehensive classroom discipline plan that emphasizes the use of preventive and positive corrective strategies.

In the late 1980s and early 1990s, zero tolerance policies were first applied to the possession of drugs and weapons on school property (Skiba & Peterson, 1999). Following the lead of several state legislatures, in 1994 Congress passed the Gun-Free Schools Act. This act mandates that schools expel any student for at least one year who possesses a gun on school property. Schools without such policies lose federal funding. It should be noted that under this law school authorities are granted discretion in determining a student's guilt and the appropriateness of expulsion. That is, expulsion is not absolute but at the discretion of school officials.

With the attention the mass media gave to the rash of multiple homicides in the schools during the mid and late 1990s, such as the shootings in Columbine, Colorado, there was widespread public support for states and local school districts to adopt zero tolerance policies. Indeed, from 1998 through 2001, polls showed that from 26% to 52% of parents feared for their children's physical safety at school (Gallup Organization, 2001) and that a clear majority of Americans (87%) supported zero tolerance policies (Rose & Gallup, 2001). Interestingly, such increased fears of school violence and support for zero tolerance policies came at a time when the U.S. government showed steady declines in actual school violence (Justice Policy Institute/Children's Law Center, 2000).

Largely in response to public pressure and the attention by the media to school violence, many states have extended the requirement of expulsion for the possession of guns to other behaviors thought to threaten school safety, such as possession of illegal drugs or alcohol, fighting, sexual harassment, and offensive touching. In many states, school administrators are granted little, if any, discretion in determining the consequences for the foregoing behaviors. Expulsion is automatic and cases involving the foregoing behaviors must be reported to the police. The message is clear: Drugs, weapons, and other criminal acts are not tolerated. Regardless of age, prior history, or circumstances involved, students who commit such acts risk expulsion and prosecution in court.

To be sure, zero tolerance policies toward behaviors that threaten the safety of others should be a part of comprehensive classroom discipline policies, as long as such policies are reasonable and administered fairly and judiciously. Such policies should apply only to the most serious disciplinary problems, however, with the punishment scaled in proportion to the seriousness of the misbehavior. They also should always be used only in combination with preventive and corrective techniques presented elsewhere in this book. Perhaps most importantly, if zero tolerance policies are to be beneficial to the student, they should not lead to the cessation of educational services. Fortunately, laws in many states require that when a student is expelled or suspended for a long period of time, educational services must continue, although in an alternative educational setting (Advancement Project/Civil Rights Project, 2000).

A Pervasive Zero Tolerance Approach to Classroom Discipline

Unfortunately, instead of adopting zero tolerance policies that are reasonable, judicious, and applied to a limited number of behaviors that truly threaten the welfare and safety of the school, many schools have adopted a *pervasive zero tolerance approach* to classroom discipline. Such an approach is based on the authoritarian view that punishment, consisting primarily of out-of-school suspension and expulsion, is the best strategy for creating safe and orderly schools. A zero tolerance approach advocates that all acts of misbehavior should be punished harshly, automatically, and without regard to the circumstances involved (Skiba & Noam, 2002; Skiba & Peterson, 1999).

Under a zero tolerance approach, students are removed from school for behaviors that teachers and administrators simply find "bothersome," including noncompliance, insubordination, and disruption (Advancement Project/Civil Rights Project, 2000). The intended purpose of the pervasive zero tolerance approach is to maintain consistency in disciplinary practices and send a message to students that violence and disruptive behavior will not be tolerated. Punishment, which most often commonly consists of suspension or expulsion, is invoked automatically, irrespective of the severity of the misbehavior and the circumstances involved, and without due consideration of the negative impact that harsh and unfair consequences have on the welfare of the offending student as well as the overall school climate (Hyman & Perone, 1998). Consistent with a zero tolerance approach, school codes of conduct have become "sentencing manuals," specifying a litany of misbehaviors and their automatic punishment (Curtis, Batsche, & Mesmer, 2000).

As a result of these practices, many students are suspended and expelled for offenses that in previous years would have resulted in mild, if any, punishment. For example, the national institutes, Harvard University's Advancement Project and the Civil Rights Project (2000) and the Justice Policy Institute/Children's Law Center (2000), and the Indiana

Education Policy Center (Skiba, 2000) reported the following cases of suspension and expulsion in the name of zero tolerance:

zero tolerance approach

- Suspending a student for writing a horror story.
- Suspending a student for failing to complete homework.
- Suspending students for unintentionally bringing nondangerous "weapons" to school, such as suspending a 6-year-old student for possessing toenail clippers; a kindergartener for bringing a toy ax to school, which was part of his Halloween costume; and a ninth grader for having sparklers in her book bag left over from the weekend.
- Suspending a high school sophomore for a "verbal attack" against a teacher, which consisted of the student jokingly announcing on the morning public address system that his French teacher was not fluent in French.
- Expelling a fifth grader who confiscated a razor blade from another student planning to use it in a fight.
- Suspending an honors student "indefinitely" for a fight—his first ever disciplinary referral.
- Suspending a fourth-grade girl for humming and tapping her desk ("defiance of authority").
- Suspending (but with the superintendent's recommendation of expulsion) a high school girl aspiring to be a medical doctor for possession of nail clippers.
- Suspending a 14-year-old girl for wearing one pants leg up, indicating "drug-related activity" although there was no evidence of drugs.

Following a zero tolerance approach to classroom discipline, many states now rely on the police to respond to misbehaviors that traditionally have been handled by the school. An increasing number of schools employ police or school resource officers to patrol hallways and enforce laws and school rules. Many schools also have adopted security and surveillance measures (including metal detectors, crisis drills, locker searches, and profiling of potential offenders), despite their questionable value in preventing school violence (Hoagwood, 2000; Hyman & Perone, 1998; Skiba, 2000). In a recent review of the effectiveness of school security measures, no research was found to support the effectiveness of metal detectors, locker searches, and surveillance cameras in reducing school violence (Skiba, 2000). In another study based on interviews of over 9,000 students ages 12–19 throughout the nation, Mayer and Leone (1999) used sophisticated statistical analyses to demonstrate that a zero tolerance approach consisting of increased use of metal detectors, locked doors, locker checks, and security guards often leads to more disorder in schools (Mayer & Leone, 1999). Increasing student awareness of school rules and using mild forms of punishment to enforce such rules were found to be more effective than security measures in reducing school violence.

In sum, in schools that follow a pervasive zero tolerance approach, zero tolerance has become equated with policies and practices "that punish all offenses severely, no matter how minor" (Skiba & Peterson, 1999, p. 373). Or, in the words of Kauffman and Brigham (2000, p. 278), zero tolerance "now means something stupid—getting tough on little things without allowing discretion in what to do about them." With respect to the effectiveness of the zero tolerance approach, Mayer and Leone (1999) concluded that "Creating an unwelcoming, almost jail-like, heavily scrutinized environment may foster the violence and disorder school administrators hope to avoid" (p. 349).

IMPLEMENTATION TIP

Multiple studies show that African American males are much more likely to receive corporal punishment and to be suspended or expelled than any other group of students, irrespective of socioeconomic status (Skiba, Michael, Nardo, & Peterson, 2002). (Note a lack of similar evidence that students of other ethnic backgrounds receive harsher punishment.) In your opinion, does such overrepresentation constitute racial discrimination? To what extent do you think such overrepresentation reflects the lack of sensitivity and acceptance of cultural differences among teachers who are predominantly white, middle class, and female?

To reduce overrepresentation in rates of suspension and expulsion of African American males, as well as other racial, ethnic, or cultural groups, and to otherwise be culturally responsive, the following suggestions are recommended (Day-Vines & Patton, 2003; Townsend, 2000):

- Make sure that the percentage of African American students (or any other racial, ethnic, or cultural group) who are suspended or expelled approximates the same percentage of students who are suspended or expelled in the general population (i.e., the percentage difference should not be more than 10%). If the rate is higher, school policies and practices should be examined to see if all students are treated equally for the same offenses. If necessary, policies and practices should be adjusted accordingly.
- Apply the "So What" test (Townsend, 2000). Teachers should ignore behaviors that bother the teacher but do not disrupt learning. For example, teachers should not always require that students sit quietly in their seats unless necessary for learning to occur. Before punishing a student for talking to others and for not sitting properly, the teacher should ask "*So what* if the student is talking quietly to others and has only one leg in his chair?"
- Examine your own attitudes, biases, beliefs, assumptions, and expectations, especially how they might differ from those of students and parents from other cultures. Ask yourself if you expect less of some students or treat students differently because of their race or background. Make sure that your actions convey that you hold high expectations for all students.
- Recognize that schools and many homes reflect different cultures. For example, from the perspective of many African American students, the culture of the school is one that best reflects white, middle-class norms in which they are expected to "act white" (Ogbu, 1992). As noted by Day-Vines and Patton (2003, p. 1), "These cultural differences are often competing and contradictory and may create distress for some students. Teachers must recognize that differences do not necessarily constitute deficiencies." (Kalyanpur & Harry, 1999)
- Focus more on prevention of behavior problems than on their correction. Make every effort to assure that students of all racial, ethnic, and cultural groups are presented with motivating instruction in a positive classroom environment. Use cooperative learning, peer tutoring, active learning, and other activities that allow for physical movement and social interaction.
- Strive to understand the cultural values, learning styles, and preferences of students from different racial, ethnic, and cultural groups. Make instruction culturally relevant. When appropriate, adopt instruction and classroom management practices to accommodate differences in cultural styles.
- Minimize linguistic barriers by familiarizing yourself with African American (or Latino, etc.) dialect. This would reduce the likelihood that you might misinterpret what a student says. It does not mean, however, that students should not be required to use Standard English, but that they should be taught to adapt their language, and behavior, to best fit a particular setting. As suggested by Day-Vines and Patton (2003, p. 1), "For best results, educators should use

(continued)

IMPLEMENTATION TIP *(continued)*

the language students bring to school as a springboard to teach Standard English in a manner that doesn't disparage their tongue."

- Focus on building a close positive relationship with each student, especially those who are at risk for suspension. Those with poor relations with teachers are at the greatest risk for suspension and dropping out of school.
- Encourage all students to actively participate in school activities, such as school clubs, organizations, and athletic teams. The more a student feels part of the school, the less likely the student will oppose school norms.
- Encourage all students to develop a cultural identity. Emphasize that their own culture values self-discipline, responsibility, honesty, trust, and similar values. Make frequent use of culturally diverse role models throughout the curriculum and make reference to such role models during everyday discourse with students.
- Build and strengthen collaborative partnerships with the student's family and community. Working with families and communities provides teachers with greater insights into cultural and other factors that account for a student's misbehavior, as well as strategies for addressing such factors.
- Examine schoolwide policies and practices that might contribute to students of diverse racial, ethnic, and cultural groups feeling unwelcome in the school community. This would include examining curricula, posters, music, art, and so on to ensure that they value cultural diversity.

STOP AND REFLECT

Do you agree with each of the preceding suggestions? Should they apply to *all* children—including Latinos, Asians, and whites—and not just to African American males? Why do you think the first suggestion might be the most controversial?

Limitations to the Use of Punishment

As noted previously, corporal punishment and emotional maltreatment have been shown to be associated with various negative outcomes, including physical and emotional harm, academic failure, and lawsuits. Similar negative outcomes are associated with suspension and expulsion (Bear, 2000). Additional limitations apply to all types of punishment (Bandura, 1986; Good & Brophy, 2000; Matson & Kazdin, 1981; Patterson, 1982)—limitations of which all educators should be keenly aware. Among them, the following are most relevant to the use of punishment in schools.

Punishment Teaches Students What *Not* to Do

Imagine the life of young children who are punished consistently at home for their misbehavior, rarely reinforced for good behavior, and given few opportunities to observe the prosocial behavior of others. In their homes, screaming, yelling, and physically aggressing are "normal" ways of getting what one desires and resolving interpersonal conflicts. That is, they come to believe that "everyone is doing it" and "it often works." Moreover, they fail to learn alternative ways of interacting. Unfortunately, many students who enter school with significant problems of aggression and noncompliance come from homes in which the preceding characteristics are common (Dishion, French, & Patterson, 1995). Through the process of punishment, these students learn what *not* to do, while failing to learn important prosocial skills. Although they may not lack knowledge of what is wrong, their knowledge is generally concrete, grounded in the simplistic understanding that you don't do things that might result in negative consequences to yourself. Such knowledge does little to guide prosocial behavior. With their parents' use of punishment as the primary strategy for "teaching" right from wrong, these children receive few lessons about why caring, kindness, respect, trust, honesty, and other prosocial values are important. Unfortunately, when punishment continues to be the primary strategy used in school, these children continue to miss opportunities to learn prosocial behavior, which is perhaps the greatest limitation to punishment. That is, punishment alone teaches neither prosocial behavior nor self-discipline. It simply teaches students to be quiet and docile in order not to be punished (Winett & Winkler, 1972).

The Effects of Punishment Often Are Short Term and Nonlasting

Students often respond to punishment, or the threat thereof, by immediately stopping their misbehavior. Although punishment typically has an immediate effect on misbehavior, too often the effect is nonlasting. This is particularly true when students believe that the punishment is easily avoidable ("I won't get in trouble if she doesn't see me do it"), tolerable ("If I get caught she'll probably just yell at me"), or when the rewards associated with the misbehavior are stronger than the punishment ("The worst that can happen if I continue to act out in class is that I'll get yelled at"). Such students behave appropriately when they figure that the chances of getting caught, and the severity of the resulting punishment, outweigh the personal gains that might be obtained from the misbehavior.

When teachers and staff are omnipresent and able to punish most acts of misbehavior, punishment can be quite effective in producing compliance. But even then the compliance is "grudging" compliance, not "willing" compliance (Brophy, 1996). Because grudging compliance is based on external control, it is short term. That is, the student grudgingly complies as long as surveillance and the threat of punishment are evident. As such, a zero tolerance or authoritarian approach to classroom discipline works, but only under prison-like conditions. When surveillance and the fear of getting caught are removed, there is little reason for students not to misbehave.

Punishment Teaches Students to Aggress toward and Punish Others

When children observe that verbal and physical aggression results in compliance from others, they learn that these two techniques are powerful ways to control and punish others. The effect of observing models is particularly powerful when the model is someone the student admires or is in a position of recognized authority (Bandura, 1986). As such, when parents, teachers, popular peers, or close friends punish others, students quickly learn that punishment not only is effective but also is an acceptable strategy for dealing with others. In observing frequent aggression and use of punishment, children learn not only how to aggress and punish others, but they also learn ways of *thinking* and *feeling* that support these behaviors.

④ **Punishment Fails to Address the Multiple Factors
That Typically Contribute to Student Misbehavior**

Far too often, punishment is used as the simple, short-term solution to a complex, long-term problem. With the exception of very young children (and some students with disabilities), very few students misbehave simply because they do not recognize wrongful behavior. There are many other factors that often account for misbehavior. Punishment addresses few, if any, of them. For example, a student with a temperament characterized by hyperactivity, impulsivity, and inattentiveness will be more difficult to teach. Among certain teachers (and parents), especially those lacking in tolerance, support, and effective teaching skills, this student is more prone to be punished. Increased punishment fails to promote prosocial behavior, often results in less time devoted to academics, and fosters social rejection (largely because prosocial skills are lacking and the student aggresses against others). In turn, academic failure often follows, as well as the eventual distancing of the student (and often the student's parents) from the school and the student from the normative peer group. Over time, the student drifts eventually toward peers who share (and reinforce) the values, beliefs, and behaviors associated with noncompliance and antisocial behavior. Punishment addresses few, if any, of these factors. For example, suspending a student for fighting does not address parenting and teaching skills, the lack of prosocial behavior, poor peer relations, academic failure, the child's thoughts and emotions, or the possible need for medication for impulsivity and poor attention. Because factors underlying a disciplinary problem remain intact when educators rely on punishment, any resulting improvements in behavior are not likely to last.

⑤ **Punishment Is Reinforcing**

Positive reinforcement and negative reinforcement are powerful strategies for increasing a student's behavior. Most educators understand the concept of positive reinforcement but too often incorrectly equate negative reinforcement with punishment. Positive reinforcement is commonly associated with the learning of desired behavior. That is, a student is praised or rewarded for good behavior, with the intent of increasing the frequency of a desired behavior. Positive reinforcement also accounts for the learning of *undesired* behavior, including the use of punishment. That is, those who use punishment often do so because its use is positively reinforced. For example, teachers are positively reinforced for using punishment when they are praised by an administrator for "not tolerating" any misbehavior. Likewise, many students are positively reinforced for punishing others when praised by their peers or parents for being "tough" and "not letting others push them around." The use of punishment also can be *self-reinforcing,* as when teachers or students feel a sense of power and control after using punishment to gain compliance from others.

In addition to the principle of positive reinforcement, the frequent use of punishment can be explained by *negative reinforcement.* When a behavior is irritating, bothersome, or aversive to another person and that person then uses punishment successfully to stop the behavior, negative reinforcement occurs. The use of punishment is *reinforced* because it stops or removes something that is undesirable to the person using it. Because punishment is reinforced, it is likely to be used again in the future when others who are perceived to be irritating confront the user. A good example of negative reinforcement in the classroom is a teacher yelling at students when they are noisy or disruptive. The misbehavior stops immediately as a consequence of the teacher's yelling. Satisfied that the bothersome behavior stops, at least temporarily, the teacher's yelling is reinforced and, thus, becomes a technique that is used again in the future in response to bothersome behavior. Note that whereas the teacher's behavior is reinforced (negatively), the student's behavior is punished. Typically, negative reinforcement works in combination with positive reinforcement in supporting the continual use of punishment as a frequent response to misbehavior.

⑥ Punishment Is Likely to Produce Undesirable Side Effects

As is true with adults, children and particularly adolescents resent attempts to externally control their behavior. This is especially true when punishment or the threat of punishment is the primary means of control. All students seek autonomy and dignity. Systematic attempts to stifle autonomy and dignity are likely to be met with resentment and resistance. Likewise, children and adolescents (and adults) are sensitive to issues of fairness and justice. They resent and resist punishment that they perceive to be undeserved or imposed in an unfair or unjust manner. When perceived accordingly, anger is often provoked, which in turn may trigger retaliation. Retaliation may consist of overt forms of aggression against the punisher or against others. Or it may consist of more subtle and passive forms of aggression, such as lack of cooperation and deliberate academic failure.

In addition to provoking anger, frequent and harsh punishment also is likely to trigger fear and avoidance. Fear is a very poor motivator of learning. As also is true with anger, fear often becomes associated with the person or activity that is the target. Few students like people and activities that they associate with fear and anger. To make matters worse, anger, fear, or a general disliking of a person or activity often generalizes to other people and activities. For example, students might fear and dislike a teacher who uses punishment frequently or unfairly and then come to dislike school in general. Likewise, students who are verbally reprimanded repeatedly or harshly for not raising their hand in science class are likely not only to refrain from class discussion in that class but also lose enjoyment toward science and perhaps school in general. Understandably, students tend to avoid people and activities associated with punishment and negative emotions. A serious consequence of such avoidance is reduced opportunities for teachers to influence students in positive ways. Closing the door to positive opportunities for developing self-discipline often opens the door to increased negative opportunities for students to engage in undesirable behaviors that are rewarded by others.

⑦ Punishment Often Creates a Negative Classroom Climate

Teachers who rely primarily on punishment to manage and correct behavior are on the constant lookout to "catch kids being bad." They repeatedly use warnings, threats, scoldings, removal from the classroom, and other forms of punishment to exercise their power and authority. Short-term compliance follows, but typically it is at the expense of developing self-discipline and a positive classroom climate that promotes academic achievement and prosocial behavior.

There is ample evidence in child development and education that such an *authoritarian* approach to discipline is not the best approach (Bear, 1998). Both learning and development are fostered best when teachers emphasize the use of positive techniques that create close teacher–student relations, reinforce appropriate behavior, and develop self-discipline.

Such a teaching style is referred to as *authoritative*. This style is discussed in Chapters 11 and 12. Although authoritative teachers hold high standards and expectations of student behavior and use punitive corrective techniques when their standards and expectations are not met, they use these techniques much less often than authoritarian teachers (Brophy & Mc-Caslin, 1992). In doing so, they help create a positive classroom climate.

STOP AND REFLECT

A Case Study

Maria was raised by her mother, a single parent who worked fifty hours weekly for minimum wages. Maria's older sibling also helped to care for her, especially when her mother worked. As a child, Maria was frequently and harshly reprimanded, often followed by a swift swat on the rear. Now that Maria is a teenager, her mother no longer beats her but yells, calls her a "failure," and threatens her with eviction from the home. As the third of five children, Maria quickly learned that the best way to get what she wanted and to defend herself among siblings and others in the community was to be verbally and physically aggressive. She also learned that verbal aggression is an effective way to stop her mother from yelling. Verbal and physical aggression and its supporting beliefs and values were modeled by others, reinforced, and rarely corrected. The opposite was true for prosocial behavior—it was rarely modeled or reinforced, and academic, social, and emotional support was generally lacking.

Now in high school, Maria has a history of academic difficulties, peer rejection, noncompliance, and aggression. Most recently, she was suspended for cursing at her teacher after being told to leave the classroom for disruptive behavior.

Reflect on Maria's difficulties and the factors that might have contributed to them. What factors do you think contributed most greatly? To what extent might punishment address her difficulties and the factors that contribute to them?

Given Its Many Limitations, Why Is Punishment So Popular?

In light of the preceding limitations, leading experts in psychology have repeatedly emphasized that *all* forms of punishment are inferior to nonpunitive techniques for teaching and increasing desired behaviors. These include the use of reinforcement (Skinner, 1971), modeling (Bandura, 1986), and developing moral reasoning (Kohlberg, 1984). As such, it is recommended that punishment be used only after the systematic use of alternative, nonpunitive techniques fails to reduce inappropriate behavior. Moreover, it is recommended that when punishment is used, it only be used in combination with these techniques.

Despite their many limitations, different forms of punishment are used frequently in the schools to correct misbehavior, including the use of corporal punishment, public humiliation, expulsion, and other harsh types of punishment. When one includes milder types of punishment that are used much more often, such as verbal reprimands, it is clear that few, if any, students go through school without experiencing individual or group punishment, whether or not it is deserved. Both the worst and best teachers mete out punishment. And they do so for both the worst and best reasons. These reasons are discussed next.

Reasons Why Ineffective Teachers Use Punishment

Alfie Kohn (1996), a popular author in education and vocal critic of the use of punishment and rewards in schools, gives the following reasons why punishment is a popular strategy among teachers and parents. Note that, unlike many other critics, Kohn does not limit punishment to corporal punishment but includes any intervention technique that is unpleasant to the student and decreases misbehavior.

1. It is easy to use, requiring little skill or thought.
2. It yields immediate changes in behavior.
3. It is what others who are important, including administrators and parents, expect teachers to do.
4. It is what we learned from our parents and teachers—to punish others.
5. It makes the user feel a sense of power and control.
6. Its use is supported by the common belief that bad behavior should not go unpunished— that justice must be served.
7. Teachers feel that they are negligent if they do nothing when a student misbehaves and that they have to do something in response to a misbehavior.

Kohn offers some good reasons why punishment is used too often, especially by teachers who are generally ineffective in managing classrooms and developing self-discipline. Unfortunately, he implies that all teachers who use punishment are simpleminded, uncaring individuals driven by control, power, and revenge and who punish students because they are told to do so and know of no other alternatives. To be sure, these features often characterize ineffective teachers. But in criticizing punishment with a broad brush, Kohn and others fail to differentiate undesirable and desirable types of punishment. They fail to explain why punishment is a strategy used not only by uncaring and ineffective teachers but also by the most caring teachers who are quite effective in balancing the use of discipline with positive techniques for developing self-discipline and correcting misbehavior.

Reasons Why Both Effective and Ineffective Teachers Use Punishment

Research shows that outstanding teachers, as judged by administrators, peers, or students, do not refrain from the wise use of mild forms of punishment. It is not the use of punishment per se that differentiates these teachers from those judged to be poor classroom managers. Instead, what best differentiates effective and ineffective teachers is that the former are much more likely to *prevent* behavior problems (Brophy, 1996). Moreover, when behavior problems do occur, effective teachers do not view disciplinary encounters as occasions to use punishment but as *opportunities* to help students learn appropriate behavior and develop self-discipline. When punishment is used, it is used only in combination with techniques designed to teach appropriate, or replacement, behaviors and to develop self-discipline. Effective classroom teachers are certainly well aware of the many limitations of punishment and use punishment sparingly, but they also are aware that there are some good reasons for the appropriate use of punishment in their classroom and school. These reasons follow.

"Class, who can tell me what I have preserved in this jar?
No, it's not a pig or a baby cow...it's the last student
who got caught cheating on one of my tests!"

Copyright 1996 Randy Glasbergen. www.glasbergen.com

Despite the Best Preventive Efforts by Teachers and Parents, at One Time or Another Students Misbehave, and Some Exhibit Serious Forms of Misbehavior. Effective teachers prevent most behavior problems by addressing multiple factors that influence student behavior. For example, they ensure that academic tasks are motivating and not frustrating, hold clear and high expectations, demonstrate sincere concern and care, and often encourage and reinforce positive behaviors. However, there are many factors that determine classroom behavior that teachers have limited influence over. A prime example is reinforcement from peers. Another is the lack of support from home. When such factors are prevalent, prevention often is difficult and of limited effectiveness. Because all behavior problems cannot be prevented, even the best teachers have to respond to acts of misbehavior *after* they have occurred.

Nearly all teachers routinely face "normal" acts of misbehavior, such as students talking and getting out of their seats without permission. Almost every student exhibits these behaviors at one time or another. Many teachers also face more serious discipline problems—behaviors deemed problematic due to their frequency and severity. This includes repeated acts of "normal" misbehavior that cause minor disruption in the classroom (e.g., talking when not allowed, not attending, getting out of one's seat, etc.), as well as less common but often more serious disciplinary problems that cause greater disruption or harm to others. What types of disciplinary problems are most common? Studies show that the most common reasons for referring students to the office for disciplinary action are disobedience, classroom disruption, defiance, physical fighting, tardiness, absenteeism or cutting class, tobacco use, vandalism of school property, student use of alcohol, verbal abuse of teachers, and theft (Heaviside, Rowand, Williams, & Farris, 1998; Skiba, Peterson, & Williams, 1997).

Teachers also should expect disciplinary problems that constitute criminal offenses, especially teachers of middle school and high school students. In the age group 12–18, about

2.7 million crimes occurred at school in 1997. The largest number of crimes involve theft or vandalism. Homicide, the crime to which many schools have responded with the adoption of a zero tolerance approach, is extremely rare, with the odds of about 1 in 2 million that a child will be killed in school (Justice Policy Institute/Children's Law Center, 2000). Although homicides are extremely rare, threats of violence with a weapon are more common. For example, between 7% and 9% of high school students report being recently threatened or injured with a weapon by classmates and about 13% report being in a physical fight at school (U.S. Department of Education and Justice, 2003). A much greater number of adolescents (about 50%), however, report *threatening* to hit another student (Gottfredson, 1987). Indeed, although most do so relatively infrequently, nearly all students exhibit antisocial and aggressive behavior during the normal course of development, particularly during adolescence (Moffitt, 1993). As concluded by Kauffman (2001) on reviewing the past four decades of research on the prevalence of behavior problems, "Most children and youth exhibit seriously troublesome behavior at some time during their development" (p. 49).

The majority of students who exhibit seriously troublesome behavior only do so occasionally. Only a small percentage of students are responsible for a high number of crimes and disciplinary problems. For example, with respect to criminal behavior, about half of all crimes are committed by 5% to 6% of adolescents and young adults who begin their antisocial activities at an early age (Moffitt, 1993). Across grades, the average school should expect about 2% to 9% of its students to exhibit misbehavior that is serious enough to warrant the psychiatric diagnosis of "conduct disorder" and 6% to 10% to warrant the diagnosis of "oppositional defiant disorder" (Doll, 1996; McMahon & Wells, 1998). A common characteristic of students with these two disorders is the lack of self-discipline, as seen in frequent violations of rules, disobedience, and a general desire to seek immediate gratification with little consideration of the negative impact of one's misbehavior on others.

Teachers cannot necessarily expect to count on others to educate students with the most serious behavior problems. For example, despite the preceding statistics, less than 2% of these students receive special education services based on their emotional and behavioral problems (Kauffman, 2001). Moreover, the majority of students with serious emotional and behavioral problems not only fails to receive special education services but also fails to receive any type of mental health treatment (U.S. Congress, Office of Technology Assessment, 1991). Thus, not only should teachers expect to face minor everyday behavior problems exhibited by nearly all children, but they should also expect to face the more serious behavior problems of students who qualify for special education and require mental health treatment but receive neither.

To be sure, teachers, parents, and students are well aware that discipline is a serious problem in many schools. Over the past two decades every annual Gallup poll of the public's attitudes toward public education has found the "lack of discipline/more control" to be among the top three problems facing public schools (Rose & Gallup, 2003). Most years it has been rated the number one problem. And parents are not too happy about the way schools handle discipline problems: 70% give schools a "C" or lower in this area (Elam et al., 1996), and 54% question teachers' decisions in matters of classroom discipline (National Education Association, 1996). The view among parents that the lack of discipline in school is a national problem is also echoed in the sentiments of teachers and students. When asked what is the greatest obstacle to teaching or learning, both teachers and students cite discipline problems (MetLife, 2001). Interestingly, the second major obstacle that students give is "teachers not knowing students as individuals" and the second concern by teachers is "students with problems such as hunger, poverty or troubled families."

STOP AND REFLECT

Are All Kids Bullies?

Among the issues of school violence and zero tolerance is that of bullying—an issue that has gained great attention among the media, educators, and legislatures. For sure, bullying is a serious problem, especially because victims of bullying are at high risk of experiencing academic, emotional, social, and behavioral difficulties (Elias & Zins, 2004). Unfortunately, many schools and states (fifteen states have legislation on bullying) have poor definitions of bullying, no definition at all, or definitions that are inconsistent with the perspectives of researchers and authorities on the topic of bullying (Furlong, Morrison, & Greif, 2003; Limber & Small, 2003). It should come as no surprise then that some surveys show that nearly all kids are "bullies." For example, one published research study (Hoover, Oliver, & Hazler, 1992) reported that 77% of junior high and high school students are victims of bullying during school hours. It is not uncommon to find articles in newspapers and magazines (as well as school reports) indicating an even higher rate. A more realistic rate is that of 8%, as reported by the U.S. Departments of Education and Justice (DeVoe et al., 2003). Such high incidence rates happen when bullying is viewed as including all forms of verbal teasing and mild forms of common aggression such as pushing and shoving. An unfortunate consequence of such findings is that schools often respond to the alarming and misleading statistics with a zero tolerance approach in which harsh punishment is used to "correct" forms of "bullying" that characterize nearly all children at one time or another, such as teasing.

One way to help avoid an overresponse to bullying is to define bullying appropriately. A good definition, which is consistent with the perspective of most researchers and experts on the topic, is offered by the U.S. Department of Education (1998). Bullying is defined as "intentional, repeated hurtful acts, words or other behavior, such as name-calling, threatening and/or shunning committed by one or more children against another. The victim does not intentionally provoke these negative acts, and for such acts to be defined as bullying, an imbalance in real or perceived power must exist between the bully and the victim. Bullying may be physical, verbal, emotional, or sexual in nature" (p. 1).

Note that key features of this definition are *intentionality, repeated acts over time,* and *a relationship of an imbalance in power.*

Using the foregoing definition, what specific behaviors might be included and excluded as bullying? What role do you think punishment should play in a comprehensive approach to bullying? How might it be used in combination with techniques that emphasize the development of self-discipline and the prevention of all forms of aggression and violence?

Punishment Is Not Only Expected from Teachers, but It Is Also Required of Them. For many discipline problems, particularly those that might result in harm to others, the classroom teacher has little or no choice but to use punishment. In nearly all schools, policies mandate that teachers punish students as a consequence of certain rule violations. Rarely are these policies developed arbitrarily or out of a sense of revenge and power. Instead, they are designed to help maintain an orderly environment that is conducive to learning. As noted in the previous chapter, the goal of creating and maintaining a safe, orderly, and positive learning environment is seen in national educational initiatives such as the federal No Child Left Behind Act, which implies that discipline should be external, imposed by teachers and other staff. Teachers who fail to punish students for serious violations of a school's code of conduct are likely to be punished themselves via reprimands or even dismissal.

③ ***At Least in the Short Term, Punishment Is Effective in Decreasing Undesirable Behavior.*** A wealth of research shows that when used appropriately, mild punishment is an effective and humane strategy for decreasing the strength of misbehavior (Kauffman, 2001). Many punitive corrective techniques are not only effective in bringing about immediate changes in behavior but also are easy to use. Recall that short-term effectiveness and ease of use were cited by Kohn (1996) as shortcomings of punishment. Are they necessarily shortcomings? When an eighth-grade teacher is presenting a motivating lesson to twenty-five or more students and a student gets out of his or her seat and harasses a classmate despite several frequent warnings and disciplinary actions, the teacher has little time to engage in peer mediation, problem solving, or positive reinforcement of appropriate behavior (at least not at that time). Under such circumstances it would be quite reasonable and fair to remove the student from the classroom and place him or her in time-out or in-school suspension. Of course, positive corrective techniques should be implemented first in combination with mild punishment in order to promote more lasting changes in behavior. But in situations such as this one, punishment seems quite appropriate for correcting misbehavior and restoring classroom order.

④ ***Punishment Deters Others from Misbehaving and Helps Establish an Environment Conducive to Learning.*** Rules and punitive consequences routinely function as social sanctions that transmit standards of behavior. They educate students as to what is right and wrong. By observing the consequences of misbehavior, students learn what behaviors are expected of them. A wealth of research demonstrates that just as students tend to repeat behaviors performed by others when the respective behaviors are rewarded, they also tend to inhibit behaviors performed by others when the behaviors result in punishment (Bandura, 1986). Observing the punishment of others, especially when the punishment is perceived by the observer to be reasonable and fair, serves as a strong means of deterring misbehavior.

When the social group supports rules, social sanctions against violating them become a more powerful deterrent against misbehavior than punishment per se. That is, most students refrain from violating school rules, especially ones governing serious acts of misbehavior, not out of fear of punishment but out of concern about what their peers, teachers, and parents will think about them if they were to violate such rules. For example, research shows that a major characteristic of schools in which there are few behavior problems is that students perceive the school as having clear and fair rules (Mayer & Leone, 1999). In these schools, sanctions are unambiguous. This does not mean that these schools use harsh forms of punishment or use punishment as their primary means of discipline. Instead, they use punishment, particularly milder forms, but focus primarily on achievement, use of reward structures, student–teacher relations, and helping students feel a sense of belonging and community (e.g., Duke, 1989; Gottfredson, Gottfredson, & Hybl, 1993; Mayer & Leone, 1999).

An awareness of social standards and social sanctions is often related to appropriate behavior, but it is not sufficient for acceptance and internalization of such standards. That is, it is very unlikely that standards conveyed in rules and consequences will be adopted as personal standards unless students value such standards and social approval from others. This is only likely to occur in social contexts that are positive and supportive and in which punishment, when used, is used in a fair and judicious manner.

When Used Wisely, Punishment Helps Foster the Development of Self-Discipline. When used wisely, punishment sends the message to students that certain behaviors are socially unacceptable, and not because some rule or authority says so but because of the negative impact they have on the self and others. Whether or not this message is heard depends on the manner by which punishment is delivered. It is not heard when the punishment is perceived to be overly harsh or unfair, or when it is delivered out of revenge, for the purpose of control, or in an autocratic and uncaring manner. In such cases the student focuses on the punishment, not the message. Reasons underlying the punishment are not heard and, thus, are unlikely to be processed. Punishment fosters self-discipline best when it is used in the context of a supportive relationship, with the focus of the disciplinary encounter being on how the misbehavior impacts others, not just the student. The process of promoting self-discipline during disciplinary encounters by focusing on the needs and welfare of others and not on punishment per se is called *induction* (Hoffman, 2000). Both theory and research support the effectiveness of induction in promoting self-discipline and prosocial behavior.

Induction is particularly effective when it is combined with firm controls, clear expectations of socially responsible behavior, flexibility in disciplinary practices based on mitigating circumstances, and consideration of the child's perspective (Baumrind, 1996; Hoffman, 2000). When used together with induction, punishment promotes self-discipline by helping children develop personal standards of behavior that are not based simply on calculated risks of getting caught. Such personal standards develop over time as social standards become internalized or adopted as one's own. With increased student internalization, teachers are able to appeal to both personal and social standards—a strategy that is more likely to have a lasting impact on behavior than the use of punishment alone.

In addition to sending a message to the student that the misbehavior is serious business, punishment also can help inform parents of the seriousness of their child's misbehavior. For example, administrators report that suspension often serves as an opportunity to garner the support of parents as well as community agencies (Morrison & Skiba, 2001). In such situations, suspension is most effective when it coincides with the administrator's belief that the student does not need punishment per se but needs support and services from others to help the student improve in behavior.

IMPLEMENTATION TIP

How to Reduce the Use of Punishment

Punishment is much less necessary when teachers emphasize its alternatives. Foremost among alternatives to the use of discipline, especially punishment, is *prevention*. Two critical and interrelated components of comprehensive classroom discipline address prevention: developing self-discipline and preventing misbehavior with effective classroom management. Strategies and specific techniques for these two components are the focus of Chapters 8, 9, and 10. General recommendations for focusing on prevention as an alternative to punishment follow:

- Teach students social and moral problem-solving skills and emotional competencies that they can use to prevent and resolve interpersonal problems.
- Develop moral emotions, especially those associated with caring and responsibility. This would include empathy and feelings of guilt or remorse over wrongdoing.
- Develop and maintain positive teacher–student relations and a classroom climate that is safe, pleasant, and conducive to teaching and learning. Demonstrate warmth, support, and caring toward all students, while showing sensitivity to individual and cultural differences. Expect and encourage students to do the same toward you and their classmates.
- Establish and maintain close communication with each student's parents and work hard to garner their support.
- Provide academic instruction and activities that motivate learning.
- Praise and reinforce desired behaviors, thoughts, and emotions. Do so frequently and strategically.
- Be fair and consistent in rules and consequences. Establish predictable procedures and routines.
- Frequently monitor student behavior and respond quickly to signs of misbehavior.

In addition to preventing misbehavior, when correcting misbehavior be sure to use the following general strategies either alone or in combination with more punitive or reductive techniques (as discussed in Chapter 11):

- Positively reinforce desired behaviors.
- Provide realistic expectations and ample models of desired behaviors.
- View disciplinary incidents as opportunities for students to learn self-discipline.
- Above all, ask yourself, "What am I teaching the student other than obedience, compliance, and not to get caught?"

SUMMARY AND KEY POINTS

- Punishment includes a wide range of techniques used to decrease the likelihood that a given misbehavior will recur. These techniques range from mild verbal reprimands and warnings in response to everyday misbehavior in the classroom to harsh practices such as corporal punishment and expulsion.
- The use of harsh punishment, especially corporal punishment and forms of emotional maltreatment, often result in social, emotional, and behavioral problems among children. Unfortunately, these techniques continue to be used in some classrooms.
- Zero tolerance refers to the automatic punishment, typically consisting of suspension or expulsion, of students who exhibit certain acts of misbehavior. Most schools have adopted reasonable zero tolerance policies that apply to serious acts of misbe-

havior. Unfortunately, some schools have adopted an unreasonable zero tolerance approach to school discipline in which security and surveillance are widely employed and a wide variety of misbehaviors, including those that pose no serious threat to the safety of others, are punished harshly, automatically, and without regard to the circumstances involved.

- All teachers should be aware of the limitations of punishment. Punishment:
  - informs students what not to do but fails to teach desirable behavior and why students should not misbehave (other than to avoid punishment).
  - produces effects that often are short term and nonlasting.
  - teaches students to aggress toward and punish others.

- fails to address the multiple factors that typically contribute to misbehavior.
- often reinforces the very behavior targeted for punishment.
- is likely to produce undesirable side effects, including resentment, retaliation, and avoidance.
- often creates a negative classroom climate by encouraging teachers to "look for problems" instead of looking for opportunities to reinforce appropriate behavior and develop self-discipline.

■ Ineffective teachers use punishment too often and for the wrong reasons. Effective teachers, however, use punishment sparingly and only in combination with other more positive techniques for developing self-discipline and for preventing and correcting behavior problems.

■ Although there are poor reasons why punitive corrective techniques are popular in schools, there also are some good reasons:

- Despite the best preventive efforts by teachers and parents, at one time or another all students

misbehave and some exhibit serious forms of misbehavior.

- Punishment is not only expected from teachers, but also it is required of them.
- At least in the short term, punishment is effective in decreasing undesirable behavior.
- Punishment deters others from misbehaving and helps establish an environment that is conducive to learning.
- When used wisely, punishment helps foster the development of self-discipline.

■ It is unrealistic to expect educators to avoid the use of punishment. It is realistic, however, to expect teachers to place much greater emphasis on more positive techniques for developing self-discipline and for preventing misbehavior. Such an emphasis characterizes the most effective classroom teachers and schools.

KEY TERMS AND CONCEPTS

Corporal punishment	Positive corrective techniques	Zero tolerance approach
Emotional maltreatment	Positive reinforcement	Zero tolerance policies
Induction	Punishment	
Negative reinforcement	Reductive techniques	

RECOMMENDED READINGS AND RESOURCES

Books on the Controversial Use of Punishment in Classroom Discipline

Butchart, R. E. (1998). *Classroom discipline in American schools: Problems and possibilities for democratic education* (pp. 19–49). Albany: State University of New York Press.

Freiberg, H. J. (1999). Beyond behaviorism. In H. J. Freiberg (Ed.), *Beyond behaviorism: Changing the classroom management paradigm* (pp. 3–20). Boston: Allyn and Bacon.

Hyman, I. A., & Snook, P. A. (1999). *Dangerous schools.* San Francisco: Jossey-Bass.

Kohn, A. (1996). *Beyond discipline: From compliance to community.* Alexandria, VA: Association for Supervision and Curriculum Development.

Kohn, A. (1999). *Punished by rewards: The trouble with gold stars, incentive plans, A's, praise, and other bribes.* New York: Houghton Mifflin.

Readings on Zero Tolerance and Its Implications

Ayers, W., Dohrn, B., & Ayers, R. (2001). *Zero tolerance: Resisting the drive for punishment.* New York: New Press.

Advancement Project/Civil Rights Project. (2000). *Opportunities suspended: The devastating consequences of zero tolerance and school discipline policies.* Cambridge, MA: Harvard University.

Casella, R. (2001). *At zero tolerance: Punishment, prevention, and school violence.* New York: Peter Lang Publishing.

Skiba, R. J., & Noam, G. G. (2002). *Zero tolerance: Can suspension and expulsion keep schools safe?: New directions for youth development.* San Francisco: Jossey-Bass.

Townsend, B. L. (2000). The disproportionate discipline of African American learners: Reducing school suspensions and expulsions. *Exceptional Children, 66,* 381–391.

Recommended Guides and Readings on Bullying and School Violence

Coloroso, B. (2003). *The bully, the bullied, and the bystander: From preschool to high school. How parents and teachers can help break the cycle of violence.* New York: HarperResource.

Dwyer, K., & Osher, D. (2000). *Safeguarding our children: An action guide.* Washington, DC: U.S. Departments of Education and Justice, American Institutes for Research. Available www.ed.gov, www.ideapractices.org, and http://cecp.air.org.

Dwyer, K., Osher, D., & Warger, C. (1998). *Early warning, timely response: A guide to safe schools.* Washington, DC: U.S. Department of Education. Available www.ed.gov, www.ideapractices.org, and http://cecp.air.org.

Elias, M. J., & Zins, J. E. (2004). *Bullying, peer harassment, and victimization in the schools.* Binghamton, NY: Haworth Press.

Juvonen, J., & Graham, S. (2001). *Peer harassment in school: The plight of the vulnerable and victimized.* New York: Guilford.

Olweus, D. (1994). *Bullying at school: What we know and what we can do.* Malden, MA: Blackwell Publishing.

Osher, D., Dwyer, K., & Jackson, S. (2003). *Safe, supportive, and successful schools step by step.* Longmont, CO: Sopris West.

For Information and Resources on School Violence and Bullying

www.ed.gov/about/offices/list/osdfs
The U.S. Department of Education's website for the Office of Safe and Drug-Free Schools. An excellent source for the most recent statistics on school violence. Also contains useful fact sheets and other practical information on school violence and safety.

www.bullying.com
Contains useful list of published books on bullying.

For information on the use of corporal punishment, including court cases and advice to teachers and parents on the use of discipline:

www.stophitting.com (Center for Effective Discipline)

For additional resources on strategies, and techniques for preventing bullying and school violence, see Chapters 8, 9, 10, and 13.

REFERENCES

Advancement Project/Civil Rights Project. (2000). *Opportunities suspended: The devastating consequences of zero tolerance and school discipline policies.* Retrieved from Harvard Law School Web site: http://www.civilrightsproject.harvard.edu/research/discipline/opport_suspended.php.

Bandura, A. (1986). *Social foundations of thought and action: A social cognitive theory.* Englewood Cliffs, NJ: Prentice-Hall.

Baumrind, D. (1996). The discipline controversy revisited. *Family Relations, 45,* 405–414.

Bear, G. G. (1998). School discipline in the United States: Prevention, correction, and long-term social development. *School Psychology Review, 27,* 14–32.

Bear, G. G. (2000). School suspension and expulsion. In *Encyclopedia of Psychology.* Washington, DC: American Psychological Association.

Brophy, J. E. (1996). *Teaching problem students.* New York: Guilford Press.

Brophy, J. E., & McCaslin, M. (1992). Teachers' reports of how they perceive and cope with problem students. *Elementary School Journal, 93,* 3–68.

Canter, L., & Canter, M. (2001). *Assertive discipline: Positive behavior management for today's classroom.* Santa Monica, CA: Canter & Associates.

Center for Effective Discipline (2004). *Discipline and the law.* Retrieved January 14, 2004, from www.stophitting.com/laws/legalInformation.php.

Curtis, M. J., Batsche, G. M., & Mesmer, E. M. (2000). Implementing the IDEA 1997 amendments: A compelling argument for systems change. In C. F. Telzrow & M. Tankersley (Eds.), *IDEA amendments of 1997: Practice guidelines for school-based teams* (pp. 383–410). Bethesda, MD: National Association of School Psychologists.

Curwin, R. L., & Mendler, A. N. (1999). *Discipline with dignity.* Alexandria, VA: Association for Supervision and Curriculum Development.

Day-Vines, N. L., & Patton, J. M. (2003). *No Child Left Behind: Now what do we need to do to be culturally responsive?* Retrieved January 10, 2004, from Training and Technical Assistance Center at the College of William and Mary website: www.wm.edu/TTAC/articles/legal/nowwhat.htm.

DeVoe, J. F., Peter, K., Kaufman, P., Ruddy, S. A., Miller, A. K., Planty, M., Snyder, T. D., & Rand, M. R. (2003). *Indicators of school crime and safety: 2003.* U.S. Departments of Education and Justice. Washington, DC. Available: http://nces.ed.gov.

Dishion, T. J., French, D. C., & Patterson, G. R. (1995). The development and ecology of antisocial behavior. In D. Cicchetti & D. J. Cohen (Eds.), *Developmental psychopathology, Vol. 2: Risk, disorder, and adaptation* (pp. 421–471). New York: John Wiley.

Doll, B. (1996). Prevalence of psychiatric disorders in children and youth: An agenda for advocacy by school psychology. *School Psychology Quarterly, 11,* 20–47.

Dreikurs, R., & Cassel, P. (1972). *Discipline without tears: What to do with children who misbehave.* New York: Hawthorn Books.

Dreikurs, R., & Grey, L. (1968). *Logical consequences: A handbook of discipline.* New York: Meredith Press.

Duke, D. L. (1989). School organization, leadership, and student behavior. In O. C. Moles (Ed.), *Strategies to reduce student misbehavior.* Washington, DC: U.S. Department of Education.

Elam, S. M., Rose, L. C., & Gallup, A. M. (1996, September). The 28th annual Phi Delta Kappa/Gallup poll of the public's attitudes toward the public schools. *Phi Delta Kappan,* 41–58.

Elias, M. J., & Zins, J. E. (2004). *Bullying, peer harassment, and victimization in the schools.* Binghamton, NY: Haworth Press.

Farrington, D. P., & Hawkins, J. D. (1991). Predicting participation, early onset and later persistence in officially recorded offending. *Criminal Behaviour and Mental Health, 1,* 1–33.

Furlong, M. J., Morrison, G. M., & Greif, J. L. (2003). Reaching an American consensus: Reactions to the special issue on school bullying. *School Psychology Review, 32,* 456–470.

Gallup, A., & Elam, S. M. (1988). The 20th annual Gallup poll of the public's attitudes toward the public schools. *Phi Delta Kappan, 70,* 33–40.

Gallup Organization. (2001). Gallup poll topics: A–Z. Children and Violence [Online]. Available: www.gallup.com.

Glasser, W. (1965). *Reality therapy.* New York: Harper & Row.

Glasser, W. (1969). *Schools without failure.* New York: Harper & Row.

Glasser, W. (1986). *Control theory in the classroom.* New York: Harper & Row.

Glasser, W. (1998). *The quality school: Managing students without coercion.* New York: Harper & Row.

Good, T. L., & Brophy, J. E. (2000). *Looking in classrooms* (8th ed.). New York: Longman.

Gordon, T. (1974). *TET: Teacher effectiveness training.* New York: David McKay Company, Inc.

Gordon, T. (1989). *Discipline that works: Promoting self-discipline in children.* New York: Plenum.

Gordon, T. (2003). *TET: Teacher effectiveness training.* New York: Three Rivers Press.

Gottfredson, D. C., Gottfredson, G. D., & Hybl, L. G. (1993). Managing adolescent behavior: A multi-year, multischool study. *American Educational Research Journal, 30,* 179–215.

Gottfredson, G. D. (1987). American education—American delinquency. *Today's Delinquent, 6,* 5–70.

Greven, P. (1991). *Spare the child: The religious roots of physical punishment and the psychological impact of physical abuse.* New York: Knopf.

Gun-Free Schools Act of 1994. Public Law 103-382. 108 Statute 3907. Title 14.

Heaviside, S., Rowand, C., Williams, C., & Farris, E. (1998). *Violence and discipline problems in U.S. public schools: 1996–97* (NCES 98-030). Washington, DC: U.S. Department of Education, National Center for Education Statistics.

Hoagwood, K. (2000). Research on youth violence: Progress by replacement, not addition. *Journal of Emotional and Behavioral Disorders, 8,* 67–70.

Hoffman, M. L. (2000). *Empathy and moral development: Implications for caring and justice.* New York: Cambridge Press.

Holmes, S. J., & Robins, L. N. (1987). The influence of childhood disciplinary experience on the development of alcoholism and depression. *Journal of Child Psychology and Psychiatry, 28,* 399–415.

Hoover, J. H., Oliver, R., & Hazler, R. J. (1992). Bullying: Perceptions of adolescent victims in the Midwestern USA. *School Psychology International, 13,* 5–16.

Hyman, I. A. (1990). *Reading, writing, and the hickory stick.* Lexington, MA: Lexington Books.

Hyman, I. A., & Perone, D. C. (1998). The other side of school violence: Educator policies and practices that may contribute to student misbehavior. *Journal of School Psychology, 3,* 7–27.

Hyman, I. A., & Snook, P. A. (1999). *Dangerous schools.* San Francisco: Jossey-Bass.

Justice Policy Institute/Children's Law Center. (2000). School house hype: Two years later. Available: www.cjcj.org.

Kalyanpur, M., & Harry, B. (1999). *Culture in special education: Building reciprocal family-professional relationships.* Baltimore, MD: P. H. Brookes.

Kauffman, J. M. (2001). *Characteristics of emotional and behavioral disorders of children and youth.* Columbus, OH: Merrill Prentice Hall.

Kauffman, J. M., & Brigham, F. J. (2000). Editorial: Zero tolerance and bad judgment in working with students with emotional or behavioral disorders. *Behavioral Disorders, 25,* 277–279.

Kohlberg, L. (1984). *Essays on moral development: Vol. 2. The psychology of moral development.* New York: Harper & Row.

Kohn, A. (1996). *Beyond discipline: From compliance to community.* Alexandria, VA: Association for Supervision and Curriculum Development.

Limber, S., & Small, M. (2003). Laws and policies to address bullying in U.S. schools. *School Psychology Review, 32,* 445–455.

Martens, B. K., Witt, J. C., Daly III, E. J., & Vollmer, T. R. (1999). Behavior analysis: Theory and practice in educational settings. In C. R. Reynolds & T. B. Gutkin (Eds.), *Handbook of school psychology* (pp. 638–663). New York: Wiley.

Matson, J. L., & Kazdin, A. E. (1981). Punishment in behavior modification: Pragmatic, ethical, and legal issues. *Clinical Psychology Review, 1,* 197–216.

Maurer, A. (1990). Corporal punishment in the public schools. *The Humanistic Psychologist, 19,* 30–47.

Mayer, M. J., & Leone, P. E. (1999). A structural analysis of school violence and disruption: Implications for creating safer schools. *Education and Treatment of Children, 22,* 333–356.

McMahon, R. J., & Wells, K. C. (1998). Conduct problems. In E. J. Mash & R. A. Barkley (Eds.), *Treatment of childhood disorders* (2nd ed., pp. 111–207). New York: Guilford.

MetLife, Inc. (2001). *The MetLife survey of the American teacher, 2001: Key elements of quality schools.* Available: www.MetLife.com/companyinfo.

Moffitt, T. E. (1993). Adolescence-limited and life-course–persistent antisocial behavior: A developmental taxonomy. *Psychological Review, 100,* 674–701.

Morrison, G. M., & Skiba, R. (2001). Predicting violence from school misbehavior: Promises and perils. *Psychology in the Schools, 38,* 173–184.

National Association of School Psychologists. (1988). *Supporting paper on corporal punishment position statement.* Washington, DC: Author.

Public Agenda (1996). *Given the circumstances: Teachers talk about public education today.* New York: Author.

Nelsen, J., Lott, L., & Glenn, H. S. (1997). *Positive discipline in the classroom.* Rocklin, CA: Prima Publishing.

Ogbu, J. (1992). Understanding cultural diversity and learning. *Educational Researcher, 21,* 5–14.

Patterson, G. R. (1982). *Coercive family process.* Eugene, OR: Castalia.

Rose, L. C., & Gallup, A. M. (2001, September). The 33rd Annual Phi Delta Kappa/Gallup Poll of the Public's Attitudes Toward the Public Schools. *Phi Delta Kappan, 83,* 41–48.

Rose, L. C., & Gallup, A. M. (2003, September). The 35th Annual Phi Delta Kappa/Gallup Poll of the Public's Attitudes Toward the Public Schools. *Phi Delta Kappan, 84,* 41–46.

Sales, B. D., Karauss, D. A., Sacken, D. M., & Overcast, T. D. (1999). The legal rights of students. In C. R. Reynolds & T. B. Gutkin (Eds.), *The handbook of school psychology* (3rd ed., pp. 1113–1144). New York: John Wiley.

Skiba, R. J. (2000). *An analysis of school disciplinary practice.* (Policy Research Rep. No. SRS2). Bloomington, IN: Indiana Education Policy Center.

Skiba, R. J., Michael, R. S., Nardo, A. C., & Peterson, R. L. (2002). The color of discipline: Sources of racial and gender disproportionality in school punishment. *The Urban Review, 34,* 317–342.

Skiba, R. J., & Noam, G. G. (2002). *Zero tolerance: Can suspension and expulsion keep schools safe?: New directions for youth development.* San Francisco: Jossey-Bass.

Skiba, R., & Peterson, R. (1999). The dark side of zero tolerance: Can punishment lead to safe schools? *Phi Delta Kappan, 80,* 372–382.

Skiba, R. J., Peterson, R. L., & Williams, T. (1997). Office referrals and suspension: Disciplinary intervention in middle schools. *Education and Treatment of Children, 20,* 295–315.

Skinner, B. F. (1971). *Beyond freedom and dignity.* New York: Knopf.

Strassberg, Z., Dodge, K. A., Pettit, G. S., & Bates, J. E. (1994). Spanking in the home and children's subsequent aggression toward kindergarten peers. *Development and Psychopathology, 6,* 445–461.

Townsend, B. L. (2000). The disproportionate discipline of African American learners: Reducing school suspensions and expulsions. *Exceptional Children, 66,* 381–391.

U.S. Congress, Office of Technology Assessment. (1991). *Adolescent health* (OTA-H-468). Washington, DC: U.S. Government Printing Office.

U.S. Department of Education. (1998). Preventing bullying: A manual for schools and communities. Washington, DC: Author.

U.S. Department of Education and U.S. Department of Justice. (2003). *2003 Annual Report on School Safety.* Washington, DC: Authors.

U.S. General Accounting Office (2001). *Student discipline: Individuals with disabilities education act. Report to the Committees on Appropriations, U.S. Senate and House of Representatives.* Washington, DC: Author. Available: www.gao.gov.

Winett, R. A., & Winkler, R. C. (1972). Current behavior modification in the classroom: Be still, be quiet, be docile. *Journal of Applied Behavior Analysis, 5,* 499–504.

3

Critical Issues

Changing Perspectives on Governing Students and Developing Character

GUIDING QUESTIONS

- What basic philosophies or approaches to classroom discipline are most consistent with your own beliefs?

- In general, how has classroom discipline changed over the centuries? How is it different today? What societal and educational factors account for the differences?

- Were children exposed to less or more violence and punishment in the past than today?

- How has religion influenced classroom discipline, including the teaching of values, developing self-discipline, and correcting misbehavior?

- How does classroom discipline today reflect the philosophies of John Locke, Jean-Jacques Rousseau, and John Dewey?

- Should public schools be responsible for teaching morals and values?

- What is *character?* Is it best viewed as a trait? To what extent is character situationally determined? What are the goals of character education? What educational strategies are best for developing character?

- Should character education, as taught in the first half of the twentieth century, now be an educational priority? If so, what might be the obstacles to the implementation and effectiveness of character education programs?

> No person has a fully developed moral character until there has been a transfer of the seat of authority from without to within himself; a moral man obeys himself. Each child in every grade should be steadily helped towards self-direction and self-government. Effective means to this end are: appeals to initiative and resourcefulness, the development of such a sense of honour as will preserve order without surveillance, and some form of organisation designed to quicken and exercise the sense of responsibility. To trust a child tends to make him trustworthy. (From *Course of Study and Syllabuses in Ethics, English, History, and Civics for the Elementary and High Schools of the City of New York,* 1905. Cited in Spiller, 1909, pp. 286–287)

> The first condition of effective discipline is respect for the authority of the teacher. If this respect be sufficiently strong, the whole problem clears up and the solution is comparatively simple. To permit children to grow up in a constant attitude of disrespect for authority is to commit the gravest of pedagogical crimes. Legitimate responsibility must always be equalized by legitimate authority; authority must always be checked by responsibility. The law endows the teacher with sufficient authority to enforce every requirement for which he is legally and morally responsible. The vital question is how to assert this authority effectually over one's pupils. (Bagley, 1908, p. 93)

There are few issues of classroom discipline that are new to educators in the twenty-first century, including the critical issue of how to balance the aim of developing self-discipline with the need to correct misbehavior. In historical perspective, this chapter examines this issue and other critical issues of classroom discipline. Three basic and traditional philosophical approaches to classroom discipline are explored: *authoritarian, permissive,* and *moderate.* These approaches appeared at the onset of education in the United States, and the popularity of each approach has waxed and waned over the years. In addition to examining traditional approaches to classroom discipline, including corresponding techniques for developing self-discipline and correcting misbehavior, the chapter explores what teachers over the years have perceived to be the general societal factors that contribute to behavior problems.

Character education, which emerged in the early twentieth century as a moral education alternative to nearly three centuries of religious education in public schools, is reviewed, and basic techniques associated with indirect and direct methods of character education are discussed. In viewing the different traditional approaches to classroom discipline and character education, a goal of this chapter is to challenge readers to reflect on their own philosophies of classroom discipline. Another goal is to examine the different societal factors and changing societal perspectives that have influenced classroom discipline over the years and that largely explain why certain strategies and techniques of classroom discipline are, and are not, used today.

Early Approaches and Methods of Classroom Discipline

Three Basic Approaches

When education first began in seventeenth-century colonial America, three basic approaches to discipline, each reflecting different perspectives about children and adolescents, were evident: *authoritarian, permissive,* and *moderate.* To a large degree, each of these three approaches has continued to exist throughout the history of American education.

Authoritarian Approach.   The predominant approach toward discipline was the *authoritarian* approach. Held by evangelical Protestants who constituted the vast majority of the colonists, this approach was based on the strong belief that the primary aim of education is to govern children and to teach them to obey authority—which at the time meant primarily the authority of God but also that of parents and teachers (Greven, 1977; McClellan, 1999). It also was believed that children are born evil and that adult authorities must shape them into good, or moral, citizens. Consistent with these beliefs, parents and teachers demanded strict suppression of any signs of assertiveness, independence, disobedience, or self-pleasure. Obedience was rigorously enforced by external means of control, especially the use of corporal punishment and constant adult supervision. Although most parents felt unconditional love for their children, they readily used corporal punishment in the name of love to teach obedience to authority. They felt that this was their duty and moral responsibility, and not to do so was considered sinful (Morgan, 1966).

Although later largely stripped of its religious basis and the harsh use of corporal punishment, the authoritarian, or "tough love," approach to discipline and governing children has always been popular in public schools. Today it is perhaps best seen in those schools that rely primarily on corporal punishment, suspension, and expulsion, not only for correcting misbehavior but also with the misguided assumptions that this approach prevents misbehavior and develops self-discipline.

Permissive Approach.   Not all Protestants shared the authoritarian view toward discipline that was held by evangelical Protestants (Greven, 1977; McClellan, 1999). The genteel class, a small group of upper-class Protestant Americans, followed a more *permissive* approach. They believed that children (particularly *their* children) were inherently good and viewed God as kind and forgiving. Few children of the upper class attended school; most were schooled at home by tutors. As is true today, a major reason for home schooling was to avoid exposure to what was believed to be the undesirable influences of those in the public schools. Although corporal punishment was used to correct disciplinary problems, such punishment was typically the primary responsibility of servants. It was believed that the use of punishment by parents (or teachers) would harm the parent–child (or teacher–child) relationship. Instead of frequent corporal punishment, parents and teachers used moral reasoning, encouragement, and modeling of appropriate behavior in teaching desired values.

Although a permissive approach later became popular in the 1960s and 1970s when many schools refrained from the direct teaching of values and were hesitant to infringe on students' rights, there has been no period in American history when the permissive approach has been more popular than the authoritarian approach (or the moderate approach). However, over the years many individual teachers, as well as a few private and public schools, have certainly followed what best can be described as a permissive approach in which teacher control and direction are minimal and student self-direction, self-esteem, and expression of creativity are more highly valued.

Moderate Approach. A third and more balanced and moderate approach to discipline was held among another small group of parents (Greven, 1977; McClellan, 1999). Instead of viewing God as demanding and repressive, as was viewed by those who embraced the authoritarian approach, these parents and teachers shared the permissive view that God is accepting and understanding. Their relations with children mirrored this view. However, children were clearly taught to respect authority, and punishment was among the techniques used for this purpose (with the use of corporal punishment decreasing over the years). The ultimate goal of education and discipline was not to teach blind obedience but to foster a sense of autonomy and independence anchored in reasoning, regulation of one's emotions, and virtuous behavior. Thus, there was a balance between fostering autonomy and teaching respect for authority. Although this more moderate and balanced approach was held by the minority in the seventeenth century, it became more prevalent in the eighteenth century and particularly in the nineteenth and twentieth centuries.

Most theoretical models of school discipline that are popular today are consistent with the moderate and balanced, or authoritative, approach. Such models recognize the need to balance the student's need for autonomy with the need to learn to respect authority. They also recognize the need of teachers and schools to exert their authority, when appropriate.

Early Methods of Classroom Discipline: A Focus on Corporal Punishment and Direct Instruction

Given the predominance of the authoritarian approach in early America, few schools were pleasant places for students to learn. Seriously lacking in training, unrestricted by laws and the rights of students, and guided by the belief that fear and shame are effective motivators of good behavior, teachers reverted to whatever methods they so desired to exert their authority. In doing so, they did not spare the use of harsh punishment and public ridicule. In front of many schools was a whipping post, used largely to beat the evil out of misbehaving boys (girls rarely misbehaved, particularly in school). Harsh discipline in the schoolhouse mirrored harsh discipline imposed on children at home, as well as harsh discipline used throughout society (McClellan, 1999).

One major reason why corporal punishment was widely used was because schools were held accountable for the behavior of their students. Similar to the emphasis on accountability seen today, as reflected in the No Child Left Behind Act of 2001, teachers of colonial America were expected to govern, or control, their students. Interestingly, despite the unregulated use of harsh punishment, some schools still had serious problems with class-room discipline. In his observations of schools in Massachusetts in 1837, Horace Mann documented that about 400 schools in the state were temporarily closed for disciplinary reasons. Moreover, he observed that 328 floggings occurred in one week in a school of about 250 students! (Baker & Rubel, 1980; cited in Crews & Counts, 1997, p. 55). Obviously, the unrestricted use of the harshest of methods of discipline was not always effective—not unlike the overuse of suspension and expulsion today.

Although teachers used corporal punishment to correct misbehavior and to instill fear and shame among students, the primary method of moral instruction in colonial America was the *direct teaching* of religious values and moral virtues. Religion permeated all aspects of instruction, for it was believed that a student acquired self-discipline by memorizing Biblical scriptures and church doctrines. Educators believed strongly that by drilling moral knowledge into the minds of their pupils and by instilling fear and shame, they became "moral" and responsible citizens. It was not until several centuries later that this belief was proven wrong.

STOP AND REFLECT

Compare and contrast the preceding three basic approaches to discipline with those seen in homes and schools today. In what ways are these approaches reflected in discipline in boot camps, alternative schools, private schools, home schools, public schools, as well as in the homes of children with and without behavior problems? Which approach is most consistent with the general views of society toward children and adolescents? Which approach is most consistent with your own philosophy?

Challenges and Alternatives to the Harsh Authoritarian Approach

Early Challenges: Locke, Rousseau, Jefferson, and the Enlightenment

Reliance on harsh punishment and memorization of scripture in moral education and class-room discipline softened in the late eighteenth century and early nineteenth century (McClellan, 1999). This change was consistent with the arguments of Thomas Jefferson, Thomas Paine, Benjamin Franklin, and other founding fathers that the primary aim of education in America was not to teach religion per se but *to develop responsible, self-disciplined citizens.* They believed that individuals would learn and choose to adopt moral values and virtuous behavior through the learning and practice of habits of self-discipline, the development of moral reasoning, and by observing models of virtuous behavior. Although they surely viewed religion as important in one's life, they did not see it as playing the *primary* role in moral education. The burden of morality was to fall on the individual, not the church or state. Public education was to play a critical role in developing self-discipline and in preserving democracy. Thus, there was a slow and steady shift from a strict authoritarian approach to a more moderate approach that balanced aspects of the authoritarian approach with those of the permissive approach.

For sure, habits of virtue, the Puritan work ethic, and obedience to adults continued to be directly taught. And, as before, corporal punishment was often used to correct misbehavior. However, corporal punishment was used less and was no longer seen as being sufficient for the teaching of self-discipline. The recognized ideal with respect to teaching self-discipline was not to teach blind obedience to authority, to inculcate a pervasive fear of punishment, or to stifle evil hedonistic impulses. Instead, Jefferson and others envisioned that public schools were to help children overcome self-interest through the cultivation of industry, duty, and a moral instinct of care (Mayo, 1942/1988). Benjamin Franklin noted that the principal ingredients for the learning of self-discipline were *student practice, good student–teacher relations, and a motivating curriculum* (Travers, 1980)—sound advice that one finds in most modern-day texts on classroom discipline, including this one.

The ideas of Jefferson, Paine, and Franklin reflected the philosophy of their time, the *Enlightenment period* (also called the Age of Rationalism or the Age of Reason). With respect to parenting and education, the Enlightenment period is perhaps best represented in the philosophies of John Locke, an English philosopher, and Jean-Jacques Rousseau, a French philosopher. Because both of these philosophies greatly influenced moral education and psychological theory and continue to be reflected in models of classroom discipline today, some of their revolutionary ideas relevant to classroom discipline are summarized next.

Locke's Philosophy of Moral Education: Shaping Behavior and Reason. The following ideas of John Locke were revolutionary at the time and widely read by eighteenth-century American educators. It is remarkable that many of these ideas are widely recognized today as "best practices" in classroom discipline. The quotes that follow are from John Locke, as cited by Gay (1964) in *John Locke on Education:*

1. *It is primarily education, "9 parts of 10," that determines if a person is "good or evil"* (p. 20). Locke believed that the key to shaping the reasoning and behavior of an individual was education.
2. *Corporal punishment "has no educational function of any sort; it does not get at the roots of misbehavior; it fosters disgust with learning rather than pleasure in it; it encourages either blind rebellion or slavish obedience, both undesirable traits in children and adults"* (p. 33). Although Locke endorsed mild corporal punishment, when necessary and especially when children are young, he strongly opposed its overuse, referring to it as the "usual lazy and short way" to bring about a change in behavior.
3. *Educators should respect children's "innocent folly, playing, and childish actions" and the "faults of their age"* (p. 40). Locke noted that whereas reasoning should be used, it should be "suited to the child's capacity and apprehension. Nobody can think a boy of three or seven years old should be argued with, as a grown man" (p. 65). To Locke, developmental differences were to be appreciated.
4. *Good habits are to be learned and developed through modeling and frequent practice.* Locke recognized that children learn by watching others and by practicing what they observe.

5. *Mental development is related to physical health.* Locke noted that children require warm clothing, good diet, exercise, fresh air, sufficient sleep, and "no wine or strong drink" (p. 25). Locke was well aware that education, including moral education, is much more difficult when the basic needs of children are not met.

6. *Although children have a "duty" to learn, they also need to be motivated to learn.* According to Locke, children must be presented with "variety and freedom," for they "hate to be idle" (p. 95). They learn best when what is taught is not "made a burden to them, or imposed on them as a task" (p. 55). To Locke, motivation was determined by both the child and the teacher.

7. *Rewards and punishments gain power by becoming linked to emotions.* Locke stated that "Esteem and disgrace are, of all others, the most powerful incentives to the mind, when once it is brought to relish them. If you can once get into children a love of credit, and an apprehension of shame and disgrace, you have put into them the true principle, which will constantly work, and incline them to the right" (p. 36). Although Locke often is viewed as emphasizing behavior and reasoning, he clearly recognized the important role of emotions in behavior.

8. *Kindliness is superior to punishment.* Way ahead of his time, Locke understood the limitations of punishment.

Rousseau's Philosophy of Moral Education: Importance of Emotions.   Like Locke, Jean-Jacques Rousseau emphasized the role of reasoning in moral behavior, but he placed much greater importance on emotions and free expression. His most famous book, *Emile* (1762/1993), had a revolutionary impact on the use of discipline. In this book, Rousseau asserted the following:

1. *Children are born good, or kind, but become aggressive and self-centered by living in corrupt societies.* As noted by Rousseau, "God makes all things good; man meddles with them and they become evil" (Rousseau, 1762/1992, p. 5).

2. *The role of education in a democratic society is to encourage children's reasoning and emotional expression.*

3. *Harsh and direct methods of instruction are ineffective.* Rousseau noted that there was a "continual outcry against the established method, but no attempt to suggest a better way" (p. 1). He believed that he suggested a better way.

4. *Experiencing is much more important than direct instruction in all areas of learning, including the learning of self-discipline.*

5. *The roots of moral behavior lie in emotions. Feeling* what is right is much more important than *knowing* what is right. As noted by Rousseau, "If you would inspire young people with a love of good conduct avoid saying, 'Be good'; make them feel the value of goodness and they will love it" (p. 5).

6. *Not all students are alike: They differ in many important ways.* As such, educators are to be cognizant of individual differences. One important difference recognized by Rousseau was age. Like Locke, Rousseau believed that young children were not to be taught the same as adolescents—a practice that was common at the time.

7. *Spontaneity and creativity are as important, if not more important, than reasoning.* As such, educators should devote more time to fostering spontaneity, creativity, curiosity, and the expression of feelings of the heart. These qualities are repressed in classroom environments that emphasize direct teaching and teacher control.

__Limited Influence of the Enlightenment on Classroom Discipline.__   Influenced by Locke, Rousseau, Jefferson, Paine, Franklin, and other writers of the Enlightenment, the rigid, authoritarian, direct approach to transmitting moral values and governing students fell out of favor as the primary and singular method of moral education. Many teachers began to recognize that there were other more democratic and kinder ways by which self-discipline, viewed as the key to democracy, could be taught. Not all agreed, however, with certain methods advocated by Jefferson and other followers of Locke and Rousseau. In particular, many questioned the more permissive viewpoint of Rousseau that an emphasis on nurture and reasoning would result in a free and moral individual (McClellan, 1999; Raichle, 1977–78). Indeed, whereas in most schools the use of harsh corporal punishment decreased, the development of reasoning or emotions never took hold as the primary aim of moral education (McClellan, 1999). Thus, most eighteenth- and nineteenth-century educators refused to depart from the predominantly authoritarian methods of moral education that prevailed in the seventeenth century in which teacher control and the direct teaching of values were emphasized (Finkelstein, 1989). Consequently, the more moderate ideas of Jefferson and other revolutionists, which balanced the authoritarian and permissive approaches, met much resistance. Often they were seen as contributing to an erosion of traditional Protestant values. As such, they were not embraced by many educators until the end of the nineteenth century (Travers, 1980).

STOP AND REFLECT

Reflect on the revolutionary ideas of Locke and Rousseau. Which ideas are most consistent with your own? How are these ideas reflected in educational practices seen in today's schools? Why do you think many educators over the years have resisted some of these ideas?

Same Approaches But Different Methods

Although certainly less harsh and strident, the religious-oriented authoritarian approach toward moral education and discipline continued as the *predominant* approach as educators entered the nineteenth century (McClellan, 1999; Raichle, 1977–78). However, different methods now were being used. Many educators believed that to prepare America's youth for democracy and to stem what was perceived to be increasing violence as the country expanded westward, society needed to insist on self-restraint, uncompromising virtuous behavior, and cultural conformity (Kaestle, 1984; McClellan, 1999). Self-discipline, or self-governance, was still the ultimate goal, but many educators argued that this goal was best achieved, not the *democratic way* but the *old-fashioned way,* with an emphasis on teaching religion and obedience, as well the frequent use of punishment (although less physically harsh).

Instead of teaching specific church doctrines (which now were taught in Sunday school), students were directly taught moral and religious nonsectarian principles shared by Protestant religions (McClellan, 1999). This resolved much disagreement among the Protestant religions over which church doctrines their children were to memorize in school.

Greater emphasis was now placed on principles and themes that united, rather than splintered, various Protestant religions.

The Secular Textbook

Instead of specific church doctrines and the Bible, textbooks such as William Holmes's McGuffey reading series were used to teach traditional (i.e., Protestant) values such as truth, honesty, industry, thrift, duty, love of God and America, and respect. First appearing in the 1830s, the McGuffey series was used throughout most of the nineteenth century and into the twentieth century (Cremin, 1980). Children were taught to read "good" books—those that developed virtues and taught children to avoid vices. The texts continued to cover religious (i.e., Protestant) content similar to that covered earlier in the eighteenth century. What differed was that for the first time these texts reflected an orchestrated, institutional effort on the part of schools nationwide to ensure that the same nonsectarian morals, values, and religious beliefs were taught to all children in public schools. Unfortunately, this did not include children of color, especially African Americans and American Indians, who were commonly portrayed in textbooks as inferior to whites. As in earlier centuries, the morals and values taught in these textbooks were uniform and rigid. So, too, were the instructional methods employed by teachers. In sum, rigid methods were used to teach rigid values for the ultimate purpose of developing self-governed, self-disciplined, and rigid individuals.

STOP AND REFLECT

Although colonial teachers experienced discipline problems in their classrooms, such problems were not nearly as serious or frequent as those experienced by today's teachers. Which of the following factors do you think contributed most to the absence of serious discipline problems during colonial times: religion, fear of God and parents, use of corporal punishment and harsh discipline, classroom management, absence of adolescents in the schools, community support and unity, suppression of children's emotions, strict codes of discipline, a curriculum that emphasized moral values, close teacher–student relations, parent support, different role models, or small schools?

Alternatives to Corporal Punishment

In general, methods used to correct disciplinary problems continued to soften throughout the second half of the nineteenth century and into the twentieth century, as greater attention was directed toward children's emotional well-being (Raichle, 1977–78). Led by a coalition of moral and school reformers, both educators and parents questioned if punishment, fear, shame, and ridicule were appropriate methods of discipline. Many began to understand that an atmosphere characterized by punishment, obedience, fear, and shame was detrimental to the development of self-discipline (Crews & Counts, 1997). At times, challenges to these practices resulted in mass student and parent protests, the forced firing of teachers, and even physical assaults on teachers (Kaestle, 1984).

Despite the questioning of the use of harsh methods of classroom discipline and the abolishment of corporal punishment in several states, harsh punishment continued to be used in most schools throughout the nation. For example, in 1887 Horace Mann reported that "Adults thought of punishment lightly, spoke of it with amusement, and inflicted it liberally" (Raichle, 1977–1978, p. 357). Although Mann himself preferred more humanitarian methods, he thought corporal punishment was necessary for controlling classroom behavior. Mann also believed that improved teacher training was the answer to the problem of the overuse of punishment.

Many educators sought alternatives to corporal punishment as a means of controlling and correcting misbehavior. They often turned to grades and comments on report cards as a means of control, but most believed that such methods were less effective than corporal punishment. Suspension helped fill the void. The U.S. Commissioner of Education (1887–1888) endorsed school suspension, recommending that it be used in place of, or in conjunction with, corporal punishment (Raichle, 1977–78). However, some educators rejected this recommendation, recognizing that children with behavior problems were better off in school than on the street. Thus, another option emerged: special schools taught by specially trained teachers. Special schools (a blend of today's alternative education and special education schools) served both to punish and to remediate what was perceived to be a rapidly growing number of children with behavior problems, including those often referred to as "incorrigibles"— youth who lacked self-discipline and resisted old-fashioned methods of classroom discipline.

Changing Demographics and Pressure to Change Classroom Discipline

Adolescents Enter the Schools

The perception that behavior problems were increasing in the late nineteenth century was accurate. A major factor that contributed to an increasing number and severity of behavior problems was a rapidly growing number of adolescents in the schools. Among the approximately 80% of children who attended public schools during the nineteenth century, only about 10% pursued an education beyond elementary school (Raichle, 1977–78). Although thirty-one states had compulsory education laws by 1890, few included adolescents. Those adolescents who did stay in school were motivated to do so in order to gain admission into college. Very few remained in high school if their performance, academic and moral, was not promising with respect to college entry. This was beginning to change, however, as more and more states began to make education compulsory for more and more adolescents, primarily for the purpose of preparing them for work in a modern industrialized society. High school enrollments doubled every decade from 1890 to 1940 (McClellan, 1999). And with each decade, adolescents had more leisure time and financial resources. Thus, for many adolescents academics became less of a priority.

Although relatively few adolescents completed high school, the large number entering high school greatly influenced classroom discipline in several ways. First, they placed increased demands on the curriculum, which had previously emphasized moral education. Moral education was no longer seen as a major part of the school curriculum, particularly in high school. Instead, emphasis was placed on teaching academics and vocational skills (McClellan, 1999). The increasing age of students and the industrialization of America pressured

"At your age, Tommy, a boy's body goes through changes that are not always easy to understand."

Copyright 1996 Randy Glasbergen. www.glasbergen.com

schools not only to modify the curriculum for teaching self-discipline but also to reconsider how to best correct discipline problems. Given increased prosperity, mobility, and proximity to adolescent peers with different beliefs and values and a growing emphasis on democratic ways of thinking, it should come as no surprise that for the first time in American history a large number of students across the nation no longer accepted authority without questioning. They were more independent and many "claimed to be hard-boiled, heavy-drinking, and daring" (Crews & Counts, 1997, p. 65).

Teachers now faced many of the same everyday problem behaviors faced by teachers today. For example, in the 1930s and 1940s truancy was the most common discipline problem (Crews & Counts, 1997). Other common problems were "talking, chewing gum, making noise, running in the hallways, getting out of place in line, wearing improper clothing, and not putting paper in wastebaskets" (Crews & Counts, 1997, p. 69; Goldstein, Apter, & Harootunian, 1994). More serious behavior problems were beginning to gain widespread attention—in both school and society at large. A survey of 915 teachers revealed the following top twenty "kinds of delinquents or problem types" (Germane & Germane, 1930, p. 143): theft, lack of interest, disobedience, selfishness, poor sportsmanship, lying, cheating, mischievousness, discourtesy, lack of self-control, stubbornness, disregard for property, antisocialism, bullying, near-incorrigibleness, truancy, unadjustment, noncooperativeness, irresponsibility, and quarrelsomeness. Not unlike today, teachers reported that in the upper grades the "lack of interest" was the greatest problem. Based on descriptions provided of students by teachers, Germane and Germane (1930) described the problem as follows:

> Child naturally lazy; no ambition; no ideals; failing in history, hence discouraged with school; a bluffer; home indifferent; disliked anything in the nature of study; thought he knew it all; lack of self-respect; lack of self-reliance; smarty; a general mischief maker; had not learned to obey; resented authority; indifferent; irresponsible; curriculum unsuited to needs of pupil; interested only in manual work; a born mechanic but no student; wanting to play all the time; not made to work at home. (pp. 153–154)

As in nearly every period before (and after) the early twentieth century, increasing problems of classroom discipline mirrored increasing crime in society and a perceived moral decay of the nation. For example, in a 1935 book on character education, McKown reported the following disturbing statistics: 1,200% increase in crime over the past 45 years; a 350% increase in murder since 1900; 50 times more homicides annually than in Great Britain; 400 policemen murdered in one year (1934); and 3,000 lynchings during the past 35 years. He also noted that the two largest groups of criminals were 19- and 18-year-olds.

It is intriguing that teachers not only cited many of the same behavior problems but also attributed them to many of the same factors that teachers mention today. For example, in Germane and Germane's (1930) survey, teachers ranked the child's "past environment" as the primary cause of disobedience followed by "moral concepts lacking," "had not been taught to think," "environment of self-control lacking," "wrong habits formed from associates," "pampered, petted, spoiled," and "naturally impulsive and emotional" (p. 146). Germane and Germane posited that 97% of cases of criminality could be avoided if the home, school, and community worked together in providing proper guidance to all children.

STOP AND REFLECT

Compare and contrast the foregoing factors that were thought to contribute to discipline problems and crime with factors that you think influence discipline problems and crime today. What factors do you believe contribute most to discipline problems and to their absence? Do you agree with Germane and Germane that 97% of cases of criminality could be avoided if the home, school, and community worked together?

More Religious and Cultural Diversity

In addition to the increasing age of students, increasing religious and cultural diversity had a significant impact on classroom discipline, especially on the moral education curriculum. Unlike the impact of the increasing age of students, the impact of greater diversity in religion and culture was not limited to high schools. From the mid-nineteenth century through the early twentieth century, which was a period of early industrialization, there was a rapidly increasing number of immigrants who did not share the same religious beliefs of the Protestant majority. Among the largest group of immigrants during this period was the Irish Catholics. Often they were presented (with other non-Protestants) in textbooks as threats to American democracy. Although not a threat to democracy, they were a threat to the standard method of teaching values, which was the direct teaching of the Protestant religion. Catholics presented a great challenge to established methods of moral education because they strongly objected to the teaching of Protestant-specific values and religious beliefs (McCellan, 1999). Some schools attempted a compromise, ensuring that either general Christian values would be taught rather than Protestant-specific values, or that both Protestant- and Catholic-specific values would be taught. Most attempts at compromise failed.

Instead of trying to force a meshing of divergent beliefs, Catholics argued that they should be allowed to establish their own schools. In these schools Catholicism would be taught, preferably at public expense (McClellan, 1999). If Protestants had their schools, why shouldn't Catholics? Only a few school systems agreed to fund Catholic schools (those that did insisted that religion be taught only before or after school). Because of the lack of compromise over how self-discipline (i.e., religion) was to be taught, an extensive Catholic parochial school system emerged throughout the United States near the turn of the century, particularly in large cities. Indeed, in 1884 American bishops ordered *all* parishes to form their own schools and for Catholic children to attend them.

Catholics were not the only group growing in numbers. In 1911, half of the students in thirty-seven of the nation's largest cities were children of parents not born in America (Rippa, 1997). Unlike early immigrants, most of these were not from western and northern Europe but were instead from southern and eastern Europe, differing from the earlier immigrants in language, culture, and customs. Such increased diversity posed problems similar to those first presented by the surge of Irish Catholics, but on a much larger scale. No longer were Catholics the only sizable group to challenge Protestant teachings in moral education. Additional religious and cultural groups were asking why the Protestant belief system was the sole basis of moral education in the schools—in violation of the Constitution.

Thus, schools were forced to reexamine their role in moral education. It had become increasingly clear that many of the traditional methods of teaching self-discipline were no longer appropriate in a religiously and culturally diverse and industrialized society. In particular, it was evident that religious education, and the direct methods of instruction associated with it, could no longer serve as the basis for teaching self-discipline. What rose in its place was character education.

STOP AND REFLECT

Early Racial Discrimination and Hypocrisy

Many Catholics and other religious groups chose to create separate schools, and despite their separation from others, they became assimilated into mainstream American society. However, nonwhite racial groups rarely had a choice. Foremost among them were African Americans and American Indians. Few received any formal education, particularly in the South, until the end of the Civil War and the end of slavery. Thereafter, and until the 1954 Supreme Court decision of *Brown v. Board of Education,* separate, and greatly unequal, schools were created for African Americans and American Indians.

Separate schools were consistent with the popular belief that nonwhites were inferior and could not be either civilized or assimilated into society. As noted by educational historian Lawrence Cremin (1980), "The assumption was that white immigrants were assimilable and indeed needed to be assimilated as rapidly as possible. Clearly, however, the assumption of the dominant white community with respect to blacks and Indians, and indeed with respect to all peoples of color, was that they were unassimilable" (p. 245).

Was the practice of separation consistent with educational efforts to teach children the value of freedom, democracy, and other moral values? With respect to both the past and present, what impact might separate schools have on classroom discipline and children's moral development?

Character Education

The Need for a New Foundation for Developing Self-Discipline: Character Education

Entering the twentieth century there was intense discussion and debate among educators over how to develop self-discipline in schools with marked diversity in a modern, industrialized society. The role of religion in moral education had drastically declined. Moral and religious content in school readers decreased from 100% prior to 1786 to 50% between 1786 to 1825, and to 5% in the early 1900s (McKown, 1935, p. 74). Instead of teaching morals that defined the moral Protestant, schools began teaching *character traits* that defined the moral American citizen. Thus, come the twentieth century, character education had replaced religious education as the primary approach to moral education. To be sure, religious values continued to be cherished in homes, communities, and public schools, and they were clearly embedded in character education. However, no longer were moral values synonymous with religious values, particularly those of Protestants. The character education movement began near the end of the nineteenth century and peaked in the 1920s and 1930s. It reemerged in the 1990s as a popular and influential force in classroom discipline. Today, many of the strategies and techniques now used for character education are the same as those developed in the early nineteenth century.

What is character? John Dewey, educational philosopher and leading spokesperson on character education at the turn of the century, defined character as:

> that body of active tendencies and interests in the individual which make him open, ready, warm to certain aims, and callous, cold, blind to others, and which accordingly habitually tend to make him acutely aware of and favorable to certain sorts of consequences, and ignorant of or hostile to the consequences. . . . The genuinely moral person is one in whom the habit of regarding all capacities and habits of self from the social standpoint is formed and active. Such a person forms his plans, regulates his desires, and hence performs his acts with reference to the effect they have upon the social groups of which he is a part. (Dewey & Tufts, 1910, pp. 255–256)

McKown (1935), author of a textbook on character education, *Education for Character,* offered a more concise definition of character as "the sum total of an individual's inner traits as represented in his conduct" (p. 1). Note that these definitions do not differ greatly from more recent definitions of character given in Chapter 1. By 1935 every state required the teaching of character education and at least seventeen had an organized character education program in place (McKown, 1935). The primary aim of these programs was indoctrination. Schools were to imbue in students the democratic beliefs, values, and virtues that characterized the good and responsible citizen. Traditional moral education, without its emphasis on religion, was thus combined with *citizenship education.*

As is true today, most character education programs emphasized the teaching of specific values and virtues, such as respect, responsibility, and honesty. The ones targeted for character education varied somewhat from school to school, but in general there was little public debate over which values and virtues *should* be taught. Germane and Germane (1930) found the following fifteen virtues to be representative of what both elementary and high school teachers hoped to imbue in their students: accuracy, cleanliness, fairness, thrift, cooperation, courtesy, creative thinking, honesty, industry, initiative, obedience, patriotism, punctuality, self-control, and sportsmanship. There was intense debate, however, over *how* values were to be taught. Whereas many character educators chose to continue using the same methods of instruction used traditionally in religious education, other educators advocated major changes in the methods of instruction. Foremost among these advocates of change was John Dewey and the Progressive educators.

STOP AND REFLECT

Is Moral Behavior Situational, or Is It a Character Trait?

Perhaps no other single study in psychology has had more impact on character education than that of Hugh Hartshorne and Mark May of Columbia University. In the 1920s they studied 10,000 children to see if moral knowledge necessarily translated into moral conduct (Hartshorne & May, 1928, 1929). Their *studies of deceit* consisted of multiple contrived opportunities for students to cheat on class and homework assignments and in athletic contests and party games. Students also were administered measures in which they self-reported lying and stealing.

Results showed that honesty tended to be related positively to intelligence, emotional stability, resistance to suggestion, academic achievement, teacher ratings of good behavior, and a positive classroom climate. Honesty tended to be related negatively to age (older children were less honest; however, fifth graders were the least honest), family background (less honest children tended to come from homes characterized by lower socioeconomic conditions, more parental discord, less "culture and refinement," poor parental discipline, and an "impoverished type of community"), nationality of parents, and movie attendance (those who went to the movies more often than once a week tended to cheat more than those who went less often). Hartshorne and May also found a tendency for classmates to associate with those with similar characteristics. For example, cheaters associated with cheaters. Finally, they found that honesty was unrelated to gender, physical condition, religious affiliation, Sunday school attendance, and membership in organizations claiming to teach honesty. These latter findings seriously challenged popular methods of character education that directly taught children to recognize right from wrong.

Perhaps Hartshorne and May's most important finding with respect to character education, however, was that moral behavior depended more on the *situational context* than on moral knowledge. That is, *their studies of deceit found little evidence supporting the existence of a global character trait.* As concluded by Hartshorne and May (1929, p. 411): "The results of these studies show that neither deceit nor its opposite, 'honesty,' are unified character traits, but rather specific functions of life situations. Most children will deceive in certain situations and not in others." As such, teachers were told not to view a student as "honest" or "dishonest" by nature since deceit was found to be normal and largely explained by basic principles of learning, such as reinforcement and punishment. This finding cut right into the heart of popular theories of child development and methods of teaching character education, causing psychologists and educators to rethink their positions that character is a trait that can be developed by directly teaching moral knowledge and habits of good behavior. It should be noted that more sophisticated statistical analyses of Hartshorne and May's data were later conducted by Burton (1976), which showed that the relation between moral knowledge and behavior was much stronger (correlation = .46) than Hartshorne and May concluded (Burton, 1976). However, the damage had already been done to traditional methods of moral and character education.

Do you think behavior is primarily a reflection of one's character traits or of situational factors? How might your own beliefs about character and its roots influence your philosophy and practice of classroom discipline?

Dewey's Progressive Education and Its Implications for Character Education

John Dewey was the primary founder of the Progressive education movement, which emphasized the importance of the active participation of students in the learning process. Dewey advocated *learning by doing,* as proposed by Rousseau two centuries earlier. Progressive education's influence on character education increased as the character education movement advanced from the early 1900s to the 1930s, 1940s, and 1950s. Consistent with the research findings of Hartshorne and May, progressive educators viewed moral values as relative to situational contexts and not as absolutes. For example, they believed that it did little good to teach children to always value telling the truth given that lying is the moral thing to do in certain situational contexts (such as saving someone's life). They believed that because social contexts are constantly shifting, children needed to learn flexibility in thinking. This position called for a radical change in methods of character education: No longer were the *direct* teaching of morals, values, and codes of good character to be the primary focus of character education. Instead, teachers were to use *indirect* methods.

Direct Methods of Character Education.   Lecture and memorization were the primary methods of direct instruction used by character educators during the 1900s, as well as by religious and moral educators before then, particularly those who adhered to the authoritarian approach to classroom discipline. While the popularity of direct methods peaked in the 1920s, these methods received increasingly intense criticism from philosophers, psychologists, and character educators, and especially from progressive educators. These individuals challenged not only the methods of direct instruction but also their aim, which many saw as simply developing specific character traits grounded in *knowing* right from wrong based on rewards and punishment. Reminiscent of Jefferson's teachings, progressive educators argued that the aim of character education was *progress in democracy,* not the development of egoistic, self-centered individuals. Helping others and seeking justice out of a sense of personal and social responsibility were viewed as much more important than abiding by an externally imposed set of inflexible standards designed to govern each individual's personal life. Other limitations of the direct approach to teaching self-discipline also became evident: It failed to teach students *why* one should follow conventional rules, it did not tolerate cultural diversity, it stifled individual autonomy, and it failed to equip students with skills necessary to solve social and moral problems in which values conflict or rules are unclear (McClellan, 1999). Moreover, as shown in Hartshorne and May's studies of deceit, direct methods were simply ineffective.

Although progressive education discouraged reliance on the use of direct methods of moral education, many character education programs continued to embrace them. This was particularly true in the first several decades of the twentieth century before Dewey's progressive education gained popularity (McClellen, 1999). Common direct methods of the time were memorization and recitation of slogans, pledges, oaths, and verses; writing stories, essays, and poems; making posters and bulletin boards; reading values-rich curricula; developing projects; and performing good deeds. Using these methods, children were directly taught traditional values and virtues believed to characterize the ideal American citizen. Although greater in variety, these methods differed little from those used by moral educators in the eighteenth and nineteenth centuries.

A new direct method for promoting character development did appear, however. Children were taught *codes of conduct.* Codes of conduct were developed or adopted by nearly every school board as a means of promoting good citizenship. Unlike codes of conduct that exist in nearly all schools today, however, such codes emphasized virtues and values, not simply rules and consequences. *Grades for citizenship* also were now included on the report card. The codes of conduct and citizenship grades reflected the traditional values and virtues that were shared by diverse religious and cultural groups. The *Children's Morality Code,* published in 1917 under sponsorship by the Character Education Association, strongly influenced what appeared in school codes and on report cards across the nation (McClellan, 1999). This code presented *ten laws of right living:* self-control, good health, kindness, sportsmanship, self-reliance, duty, reliability, truth, good workmanship, and teamwork. For each law, specific social skills were listed that children pledged to follow. Many schoolwide programs focused on teaching such laws, virtues, or character traits.

In addition to the preceding methods, many high schools required courses on citizenship. To assist teachers of these courses, commercially produced curriculum materials from major publishers were made widely available. Included were texts with accompanying teacher manuals and student workbooks. A variety of written materials was used to present students with information on citizenship and values, including bibliographies of popular people who exhibited important character traits, lists and descriptions of traits (or "laws of conduct") for each month, and descriptions of social problems to be solved. Many schools focused on a specific virtue each month, such as responsibility in September, honesty in October, and so on. Not unlike in many schools today, such virtues were emphasized in readings, writing assignments, hallway posters, and assemblies.

The direct teaching of character education began the first day children entered school and continued until students finished their schooling. Knowledge about character permeated the entire curriculum and school climate (Leighton, 1926). Direct methods made character education concrete and easy to teach. They also were consistent with traditional methods of teaching in general. As such, direct methods were particularly appealing to those educators who desired to teach character without having to change the way they had always been teaching moral education.

Indirect Methods of Character Education.   In using indirect methods of character education, students were no longer told to solve social problems by recalling the correct way a good citizen would behave. Instead, they were challenged to think creatively, to be open-minded, and to self-determine how to act in given situations by applying the scientific method to real-life social problems. No longer was a correct solution necessarily one that was derived from authority or social conformity, but one that was self-determined, democratic, just, based on reason, and led to positive outcomes for the individual *and* society. Students were now encouraged to question rules and decisions that were arbitrarily determined by authority and to attend to social and political issues instead of focusing on themselves. Civility in behavior was still demanded, but progressive educators sought to grant more individual freedoms.

Lectures and textbooks in citizenship classes and social studies that taught inflexible codes of conduct, values, and virtues were replaced by class discussions of civic responsibilities, duties, rights, and how to solve social problems (McClellan, 1999). The goal of the use of indirect methods was to promote the integration of reasoning, behavior, and emotions

(McKown, 1935). Similar to class meetings seen today, many schools added the *homeroom* period for the explicit purpose of arranging a specific time for discussion of personal, social, and school issues pertaining to character. During homeroom period, teachers encouraged students to discuss current concerns and issues, provided guidance to students, and publicly recognized good character.

Progressive educators understood that *peers* could be used to help transmit society's values (McClellan, 1999). Peer influence was recognized as a powerful factor in teaching values. Clubs, both inside and outside of school, became extremely popular, such as the Boy Scouts, Campfire Girls, and school-organized clubs. In addition to school clubs, other extracurricular activities were promoted to develop self-discipline and character, including service learning and team sports. Such peer-oriented activities were used by advocates of both direct and indirect methods, but the focus of instruction differed: Instead of focusing on learning codes of conduct, pledges, and specific virtues, as was the case with direct instruction, advocates of indirect instruction used the peer group to teach group problem solving, debate, discussion, and cooperation.

The following advice given to teachers in McKown's 1935 text *Character Education* perhaps best summarizes how the Progressive's indirect approach differed from the traditional direct approach:

- "Reasoning should be stressed, excessive moralizing avoided."
- "Solutions to particular problems should be applied and generalized."
- "The child's point of view must be understood and appreciated." (pp. 160–161)

STOP AND REFLECT

Character Education Partnership's Eleven Principles of Character Education

As noted previously, many of the methods and techniques of character education used in the early twentieth century are very similar to those used by character educators today. To help guide schools in their choice of methods and techniques the Character Education Partnership offers the following key elements of an effective character education program. An effective character education program:

1. Promotes core ethical values as the basis of good character.
2. Defines "character" comprehensively to include thinking, feeling, and behavior.
3. Uses a comprehensive, intentional, proactive, and effective approach to character development.
4. Creates a caring school community.
5. Provides students with opportunities for moral action.
6. Includes a meaningful and challenging academic curriculum that respects all learners, develops their character, and helps them to succeed.
7. Strives to foster students' self motivation.
8. Engages the school staff as a learning and moral community that shares responsibility for character education and attempts to adhere to the same core values that guide the education of students.
9. Fosters shared moral leadership and long-range support of the character education initiative.

(continued)

S T O P   A N D   R E F L E C T   *(continued)*

10. Engages families and community members as partners in the character-building effort.
11. Evaluates the character of the school, the school staff's functioning as character educators, and the extent to which students manifest good character.

To what extent are these principles consistent with methods presented in this chapter that were used by character educators much earlier in history? To what extent are they seen in schools with which you are familiar?

Note. From "CEP's Eleven Principles of Effective Character Education" by T. Lickona, Eric Schaps, and Catherine Lewis, 2003. Copyright 2003 by the Character Education Partnership. Reprinted with permission.

"Progressive" Methods of Correcting and Preventing Misbehavior

Declining Use of Punishment.   While methods of teaching moral values were changing in the early twentieth century, so too were the methods of classroom management and correction of misbehavior. Although punishment, including corporal punishment, was used widely throughout the first half of the twentieth century, it was used more sparingly than previously. More teachers were beginning to understand its many shortcomings (Raichle, 1977–78). For example, writing to teachers, Germane and Germane (1930) pointed out that a problem with punishment is that a child might simply learn not to get caught. They noted that if a boy is punished for stealing, "He has learned that it is a mistake to get caught. He is sorry that he was not more cunning and next time will be wary in his theft. If he does practice honesty, it will be because it is policy to do so. He is still dishonest at heart"(p. 15). As in other textbooks of the day and consistent with a moderate approach to classroom discipline, Germane and Germane did not tell teachers to entirely avoid the use of punishment but instead to use it infrequently and in combination with reinforcement.

In using punishment to correct misbehavior, alternatives to corporal punishment were becoming popular. Referred to today as time-out and in-school suspension, misbehaving students were removed from regular classrooms and sent to another setting within the school. For the most serious offenses, students were suspended and expelled. For students who continued to display serious behavior problems in the classroom, *last chance schools* were created (Crews & Counts, 1997; Cubberley, 1934). These highly structured alternative schools offered one last chance for the student's behavior to improve before the student was expelled or sent to a state-run *industrial school* for incorrigible students. By the 1930s, one in 350 school-age youths in America was placed in an industrial school. The majority of students placed in these schools were males, a disproportionate number (13%) being African American, and many were of low intellectual functioning (Crews & Counts, 1997; Cubberley, 1934). For students with the most chronic and serious behavior problems, separate institutions for juvenile delinquents were developed. Educators viewed these institutions as a point on the extreme end of the continuum of educational programs for disruptive youth.

Positive Alternatives to Punishment.   In general, teachers of the twentieth century were much more humanitarian in their approach to correcting misbehavior. Trained in education and psychology, most teachers knew of alternatives to use of punishment. In a survey in which 917 teachers were asked what should be done with a child who was disobedient, the following recommendations were given (Germane & Germane, 1930, p. 147). Note that such recommendations are similar to those found in textbooks today.

1. Individual or group discussion
2. Appeal to reason, honor, pride, etc.
3. Call attention to the group rules violated
4. Let the student solve the problem after discussion
5. Coercion (included time-out and suspension)
6. Focus on the behavior in a class or group project
7. Have the student consult with others
8. Require reading of materials related to the problem
9. Win student's confidence
10. Use kindness
11. Assign duties that demand honor and honesty
12. Cooperate with parents
13. Develop interest in wholesome activities
14. Assign constructive work
15. Appeal to fair play
16. Encourage and praise good behavior
17. Withhold privileges
18. Show interest in the student
19. Demonstrate care and trust
20. Isolate the student

Consistent with progressive education, teachers understood that the frequent use of reinforcement was preferred over punishment and that they could prevent most behavior problems by providing warm and supportive student–teacher relationships and a caring and well-managed classroom. Textbooks informed teachers of these and other research-supported practices for preventing behavior problems. For example, Germane and Germane (1930) recommended the following preventive strategies:

- *Begin early.* Teachers were told that the first five years of life were critical to character formation. The role of the school was to build on the positive qualities taught by parents and "to destroy, or supplant with right whatever has been done for bad" (p. 172).
- *Use good classroom management as a means of preventing behavior problems.* Teachers were instructed to ensure that lessons were motivating and developmentally appropriate. Student failure was to be avoided because it causes a variety of emotional and behavioral problems, including: "sullenness, stubbornness, indifference, irritability, lack of self-control, selfishness, intolerance, jealousy, and inferiority" (p. xii). To prevent failure, teachers were encouraged to present an attractive physical environment, adopt motivating curriculum materials, arrange for the efficient use of time, reduce opportunities that foster behavior problems, and avoid preaching and lecturing (McKown, 1935).

■ *Apply a "case study method" when handling an individual student's problem behaviors.* Teachers were instructed to examine each child as an individual, recognizing that factors that explain problem behaviors vary from child to child. The purpose of analyzing the cause(s) of each individual's behavior problems was to design and implement individualized methods of discipline. It was understood that the same form, or intensity, of corrective discipline is not effective with all children.

■ *Work cooperatively with the home and community.* Germane and Germane noted, "The significance of the socializing influence of such institutions as the home, church, press, theater, clubs, and local or community government is not minimized. Each of these is indispensable" (p. xvi). The authors also offered an innovative idea for the time: a *parent–teacher organization* in each school that would meet every other week after school.

Such recommendations were certainly progressive in the early 1900s. Today they are also supported by research and are among the practices found in schools that are the most effective in developing discipline and in preventing and correcting misbehavior. To be sure, character education in the early 1900s reflected a culmination of improvements in classroom discipline that many progressive educators such as Locke, Rousseau, and Jefferson wrote about earlier but that only a few schools had implemented. As a separate movement in education, it also resulted in many revolutionary changes that have had a lasting impact on classroom discipline.

STOP AND REFLECT

Reflect on the preceding positive, alternative, and preventive strategies as well as the punitive ones presented earlier. Which ones are consistent, or inconsistent, with strategies and techniques seen in schools today? Which ones do you support?

SUMMARY AND KEY POINTS

■ Three basic approaches to classroom discipline emerged in colonial America: authoritarian, permissive, and moderate. To one extent or another, each can be seen in classrooms of every century. In general, schools have become less authoritarian and more moderate.

■ Led by philosophers John Locke and Jean-Jacques Rousseau, the Enlightenment influenced moral education. Discipline became less physically harsh, and children's reasoning and emotions were increasingly recognized as being important.

■ Throughout the nineteenth century many educators and parents continued to question if punishment,

fear, shame, and ridicule were appropriate methods of discipline. As corporal punishment became less harsh in the second half of the nineteenth century, schools increasingly turned to grades, suspension, and placement in special schools as strategies for controlling and correcting misbehavior.

■ Behavior problems increased in the second half of the nineteenth century as the nation became industrialized and the student population became older. At the turn of the century, religious education was problematic as it became evident that a religiously and culturally diverse student population should not be taught the Protestant, or any other, religion.

■ Since the early nineteenth century, two methods of character education have remained popular: the traditional direct method and the progressive indirect method. The direct method mainly includes strategies that have traditionally been used to teach self-discipline (e.g., memorization and recitation). The more "progressive" indirect method teaches social decision-making and social problem-solving skills and provides students with ample opportunities to practice democratic and prosocial behavior.

■ Unlike previous periods in history, progressive character educators placed much greater emphasis not only on alternatives to punishment but also on the continued importance of *preventing* behavior problems by developing self-discipline and other character traits. In preventing behavior problems, progressive educators emphasized the importance of the student–teacher relationship, the classroom climate, early intervention, classroom management, individual differences, and home–school relations.

KEY TERMS AND CONCEPTS

Authoritarian approach
Character education
Dewey, John
Direct methods of character education
Hartshorne and May's studies of deceit

Indirect methods of character education
Locke, John
Moderate approach
Moral education

Permissive approach
Progressive education
Religious education
Rousseau, Jean-Jacques

RECOMMENDED READINGS AND RESOURCES

Books on the History of Moral Education, Character Education, and Classroom Discipline

Butchart, R. E., & McEwan, B. (Eds.), *Classroom discipline in American schools: Problems and possibilities for democratic education* (pp. 19–49). Albany: State University of New York Press.

Crews, G. A., & Counts, M. R. (1997). *The evolution of school disturbance in America: Colonial times to modern day.* Westport, CT: Praeger.

Finkelstein, B. (1989). *Governing the young: Teacher behavior in popular primary schools in 19th century United States.* New York: Falmer Press.

McClellan, B. E. (1999). *Moral education in America: Schools and the shaping of character from colonial*

times to the present. New York: Teachers College Press.

Books on the Moral Education Philosophies of Dewey, Locke, and Rousseau

Dewey, J. (1991). *The child and society & the school and the curriculum.* Chicago: University of Chicago Press.

Dewey, J. (1997). *Experience and education.* New York: Free Press.

Gay, P. (1964). *John Locke on education.* New York: Teachers College Press.

Rousseau, J-J. (1992). *Emile.* Boston: Tuttle Publishing. (Original work published 1762).

REFERENCES

Bagley, W. C. (1908). *Classroom management: Its principles and technique.* New York: Macmillan.

Burton, R. V. (1976). Honesty and dishonesty. In T. Lickona (Ed.), *Moral development and behavior: Theory, research, and social issues* (pp. 173–197). New York: Holt, Rinehart and Winston.

Cremin, L. A. (1970). *American education: The colonial experience, 1607–1783.* New York: Harper and Row.

Cremin, L. A. (1980). *American education: The national experience, 1783–1876.* New York: Harper and Row.

Crews, G. A., & Counts, M. R. (1997). *The evolution of school disturbance in America: Colonial times to modern day.* Westport, CT: Praeger.

Cubberley, E. P. (1934). *Public education in the United States.* Boston: Houghton Mifflin.

Dewey, J., & Tufts, J. H. (1910). *Ethics, 72,* 55–256.

Finkelstein, B. (1989). *Governing the young: Teacher behavior in popular primary schools in 19th century United States.* New York: Falmer Press.

Gay, P. (1964). *John Locke on education.* New York: Teachers College Press.

Germane, C. E., & Germane, E. G. (1930). *Education for character.* New York: Silver, Burdett and Company.

Goldstein, A., Apter, B., & Harootunian, B. (1994). *School violence.* Englewood Cliffs, NJ: Prentice Hall.

Greven, P. (1977). *The Protestant temperament: Patterns of child-rearing, religious experience and the self in early America.* New York: American Library.

Hall, G. S. (1911). *Educational problems* (Vol. 1). New York: D. Appleton.

Hartshorne, H., & May, M. A. (1928). *Studies in the nature of character: Vol. I: Studies in deceit.* New York: Macmillan.

Hartshorne, H., & May, M. A. (1929). *Studies in the nature of character: Vol. II: Studies in service and self-control.* New York: Macmillan.

Kaestle, C. F. (1984). Moral education and common schools in America: A historian's view. *Journal of Moral Education, 13,* 101–111.

Leighton, J. A. (1926). *The individual and the social order.* New York: Appleton and Company.

Lickona, T. (2004). *Character Matters: How to help our children develop good judgment, integrity, and other essential virtues.* New York: Touchstone.

Lickona, T., Schaps, E., & Lewis, C. (2003). *CEP's eleven principles of effective character education.* Washington, DC: Character Education Partnership.

Mayo, B. (1988). *Jefferson himself.* Charlottesville, VA: University Press of Virginia (Original work published 1942).

McClellan, B. E. (1999). *Moral education in America: Schools and the shaping of character from colonial times to the present.* New York: Teachers College Press.

McKown, H. C. (1935). *Character education.* New York: McGraw-Hill.

Morgan, E. S. (1966). *The Puritan family.* New York: Harper & Row.

Raichle, D. R. (1977–78). School discipline and corporal punishment: An American retrospect. *Interchange, 8,* 71–83.

Rippa, A. (1997). *Education in a free society: An American history.* New York: Longman.

Rousseau, J- J. (1993). *Emile.* Boston: Turtle Publishing. (Original work published 1762).

Spiller, G. (1909). *Report on moral instruction and on moral training.* London: Watts & Co.

Travers, P. D. (1980, Summer). An historic view of school discipline. *Educational Horizons,* 184–187.

4

Critical Issues

Causes of School Violence, the Legal Rights of Students, and Problems of Character Education

GUIDING QUESTIONS

- What factors might lead a nation to stop teaching values and character education?
- With increasing pressure to teach academics, can schools afford to devote sufficient time to the teaching of self-discipline or character? Should they?
- In what ways have schools failed to adjust to the needs of culturally diverse students? How has this affected classroom discipline?
- How has increased enrollment in private schools, and the more recent increase in home schools, affected discipline in the public schools?
- What basic rights do students, teachers, and schools have with respect to classroom discipline?
- What role, if any, should teachers play in the teaching of values in a culturally diverse society?
- What student, classroom, school, and societal factors best account for violence and behavior problems in the school?

> By the end of the 1970s, moral education had reached a historic low point in the nation's public schools. What had for more than three centuries been a central responsibility of the school had now become both peripheral and problematic. (McClellan, 1999, p. 78)

> In the absence of a specific showing of constitutionally valid reasons to regulate their speech, students are entitled to freedom of expression of their views. (Justice Fortas speaking for the majority in the 1969 Supreme Court case of *Tinker v. Des Moines*)

Reflection on critical issues of classroom discipline continues in this chapter, with an emphasis on issues that arose in the second half of the twentieth century and that continue to apply to schools today. Perhaps the greatest issues of classroom discipline during this period concerned increasing school violence, a greater recognition of the legal rights of students, and less emphasis on character education. It is important to note that these three issues were not necessarily causally related. That is, greater student rights and decreased character education may not have caused increased school violence. However, it is likely that many of the same societal and school factors greatly influenced each of these issues. Such factors are examined in this chapter, with an emphasis on their implications for classroom discipline.

Increasing Behavior Problems and Decreasing Character Education

Problems of the Day

As American educators entered the second half of the twentieth century, they faced behavior problems daily, albeit few were serious. The majority of students respected the authority of their teachers. With the exception of fistfights, school violence was rare. Other than fistfights, the most prevalent discipline problems were stealing, running in the halls, chewing gum, speaking out of turn, throwing spitballs, inattention, truancy, and smoking (Reese, 1995). A 1956 survey conducted by the National Education Association revealed that teachers viewed only 1% of students as discipline problems and 95% of students as *exceptionally well behaved or reasonably well behaved* (Reese, 1993, p. 358). Nevertheless, the survey indicated an increasing concern among teachers about discipline. There were valid reasons for such concern. As a harbinger of times to come, congressional hearings were being held in the 1940s on the increasing rate of juvenile delinquency (Reese, 1995). The hearings indicated that students were beginning to bring weapons to school, especially to urban high schools that now were characterized by ethnic and racial tension. J. Edgar Hoover, director of the FBI, expressed a fear of a teen crime wave (which, he noted, included girls).

As is true today, gangs could be found in many schools, particularly ethnic neighborhood gangs in large cities. Most gangs were comprised of teenage males in families that had recently immigrated from throughout the world. In northern cities, a large number of gang members were from African American families that had recently migrated from the South in search of employment. Many of the immigrants and African Americans were unskilled, transient, and living in poverty. As noted by Hampel (1986):

> Children living in slums grew up more rapidly than their rural and suburban counterparts: exposure to and participation in domestic strife, street violence, drugs, sex, and other experiences initiated ghetto youth to adulthood at an early age. The rawness of the streets affected the schools. In the mid 1950s, teachers in the largest systems reported four times as many assaults as rural school teachers. (pp. 75–76)

But it was not just an increase in the number of urban students living in poverty and attending school that contributed to increased behavior problems, including school violence. As had influenced classroom discipline in the first half of the nineteenth century when high school attendance became compulsory, an ever growing number of working-class adolescents were remaining in school. By 1940, 73% of 14- to 17-year-olds were in school, compared to 11% in 1900 (Hampel, 1986). It is clear that working-class adolescents were not the only misbehaving students, however. Educational historian Robert Hampel (1986) notes that "teenagers of all social classes showed increased affection for cigarettes, beer, fast and loud cars, louder music, faster dancing, and necking parties—rowdiness that took place off campus" (p. 78). Times were changing.

In general, teachers found students to be less respectful, more disruptive, and more difficult to relate to. This new kind of student gradually changed the composition of many American high schools. In prior decades, working-class youth were the primary responsibility of the military, employers, and institutions other than the school (Reese, 1995). Now they were primarily the responsibility of the public schools. The number of students of diversity and of the working class continued to grow steadily in the 1960s and 1970s, particularly in large cities. Few schools adjusted to their needs, resulting in frequent failure among both students and schools.

Methods of the Day: Progressive + Traditional

A Combination of Direct and Indirect Strategies.   Progressive educators never succeeded in replacing the traditional direct methods of classroom discipline of the past with their indirect methods of developing self-discipline. Instead, a moderate and balanced approach tended to exist. Most schools that had experimented with the indirect teaching strategies advocated by the progressives decided to return to their traditional, and authoritarian, practices of classroom discipline (Hampel, 1986; McClellan, 1999). In the minds of many educators, reliance on the use of indirect strategies did not make classroom discipline any more effective. Indeed, the term *progressive* became associated with schools that opposed an authoritarian approach to discipline and *failed* to control their students because their approach was too permissive (Hampel, 1986). Only a few schools, mostly private and elementary, considered themselves as model progressive schools. For sure, many educators did use methods associated with progressive education, but not to the extent that the progressive movement had hoped. Thus, most educators tended to employ a *combination* of direct and indirect methods.

Democracy Taught But Not Practiced.   Although many teachers in the 1940s and 1950s were authoritarian in their approach to classroom discipline, especially in high schools, they tended to be less coercive than in the past. Fewer relied upon corporal punishment to obtain obedience (Hampel, 1986; McClellan, 1999). It was clear that progressive education did have some influence on education: In general, schools were more pleasant and efficient places to learn and teach (Butchart, 1998). Due to progressive education, schools demonstrated greater concern about the physical and emotional health of students; teaching was less rigid, with a greater variety of teaching techniques being employed; the curriculum was much more expansive; and students were given a much greater choice of extracurricular activities.

It was clear, however, that the teacher was still the controlling authority in the classroom. Contrary to the student-centered philosophy of progressives, high school students rarely questioned a teacher's authority, much less expressed how they actually felt. *Teachers preached democracy and egalitarianism, but they did not practice it.* High schools were larger, and more impersonal. Hampel offered the following characterization of discipline in the typical American high school of the 1940s and 1950s:

> Paternalistic control was firmly in place in the 1940s. From the castle-style architecture of the school to the hall pass required of a student to walk through the fortress of virtue, the institution powerfully reminded teachers and students alike that submissiveness and propriety were expected. As one textbook warned, "The school must not be merely a pleasant place in which pupils will be encouraged or permitted to establish through practice whatever predisposition they bring to it." (pp. 21–22)

STOP AND REFLECT

Looking back on the changing composition of American schools, particularly urban high schools, what might schools have done differently to adjust to the needs of the working-class and culturally diverse students and to prevent increasing behavior problems and school violence?

A Gradual Decline in Character Education

For sure, schools continued to teach character education in the 1940s and 1950s using a combination of direct and indirect strategies. However, a gradual decline in character education was occurring. This gradual decline can be attributed primarily to two factors: (a) increased emphasis on the teaching of academics, especially science and math, and (b) challenges to the teaching of morals, values, and character.

Increased Emphasis on Academics.   An increased emphasis in teaching academic and cognitive skills was the primary factor leading to a gradual decline in character education in the 1940s, 1950s, and early 1960s (McCellan, 1999). Educators still recognized the importance of character, but character education was no longer their top priority. Not unlike today, teachers and parents were much more concerned about grades, test scores, and preparing students to enter college and the workforce. Likewise, society in general was more concerned about schools addressing weaknesses in science and mathematics education, especially because the Russians had beaten the United States to space. As a result, teachers had to devote more time to teaching academic skills, especially math, science, and social studies (particularly about the evils of communism and the superiority of capitalism). Such time often came from that devoted previously to character education.

Challenges to the Teaching of Morals, Values, and Character.   Coinciding with the increased emphasis on academics, a backlash was occurring against the teaching of topics related to social and emotional adjustment. This included character education. These topics now were perceived to be academically unchallenging (Hampel, 1986). Moreover, parents and teachers began to question if public schools *should* address the social, emotional, and moral aspects of children's development (McClellan, 1999). While for decades educators had debated the role of religious education in the schools, now they debated the role of character education. Character education was associated with moral education, and too often moral education was equated (incorrectly so) with religious education. Many believed that morality, values, and religion were private matters best left to the home and church. Thus, many parents began to question the content of character education programs. Such questioning became much more intense in the 1960s and 1970s. Educators were beginning to think that it was safer for them to teach students about the value of democracy (and the evils of communism) than the value of morality.

STOP AND REFLECT

To what extent do academics today take precedence over character education or other programs for developing self-discipline? Do you believe an emphasis on academics and accountability has contributed to school violence and discipline problems? Should character education be a priority in education? Why, and why not?

Rapid Decline in Character Education and an Increase in Alternative Models of Classroom Discipline

In the 1960s and 1970s school discipline problems, juvenile crime, and concerns about school safety increased steadily. Reese (1995) cited a 1964 survey showing that teachers estimated 3% of students were discipline problems. Although relatively low compared to today, this represented a 200% increase over the previous decade. A 1975 report by a U.S. Senate subcommittee entitled *Our Nation's Schools—A Report Card* (1975) gave America's schools an "A" in school violence and vandalism based on a survey of crime in schools between 1970 and 1973. This report, which received substantial media attention, showed that school violence no longer was limited largely to fistfights but also now included brutal assaults on teachers and students, rapes, extortion, burglaries, thefts, and use of weapons. Assaults on students had increased 85.3% and assaults on teachers had increased 77.4%. Vandalism was the most common crime, with 90% of the nation's schools reporting broken glass and windows.

Reflecting the increase in school violence, security guards and police now appeared in many urban high schools. An 1976 National Public Radio program on school violence began with the prophetic announcement "Violence and vandalism in schools are problems that won't go away . . . they seem to have reached crisis proportions" (cited by Reese, 1995, p. 361). The high rate of school violence never did go away, although it stabilized in the 1970s. Reasons for a moral decay in the nation's schools did not differ greatly from those heard today. Blame was attributed to "youth culture, liberalism, radical professors, poverty, declining family values, racism, peer groups, Communists, arbitrary teachers or school administrators, an irrelevant curriculum, spoiled baby boomers, large class or school size . . ." (Reese, 1995, p. 359). The nation itself was divided over controversial moral issues, especially civil rights and the Vietnam War. Following the 1954 Supreme Court decision of *Brown v. Board of Education of Topeka,* which brought an end to racial segregation in public schools, racial strife was common. Protests, both peaceful and violent, over civil rights, integration, and the war were common. Protests were against the war and the American government and in support of marijuana, civil rights, and sexual freedom. Such protests were often witnessed by students who spent hours daily watching television. Many high school students joined in these protests and carried their protests to the doors of their schools.

Together with parents, students questioned if authoritarian and nondemocratic disciplinary practices violated their constitutional rights. Protests and challenges were largely sparked by two general factors: (a) a perspective of personalism, permissiveness, and relativism and (b) increased recognition of individual rights by the courts. These factors contributed to increased problems of school discipline and to the precipitous decline in character education. It was clear that a new type of student was emerging in the schools—one who did not hesitate to challenge authority—the type of student in many classrooms today.

Increased Personalism, Permissiveness, and Cultural Relativism

The 1960s and 1970s marked the rise of *personalism,* characterized by a focus on individual rights and freedom, self-worth, self-respect, self-dignity, and autonomy (Lickona, 1991). The rights and pleasures of the individual were of primary concern, often superseding commitments to the community, church, and family. On the positive side, America's focus on individual rights increased civil rights for minorities, women, and individuals with disabilities. These groups included students. On the negative side, at least as viewed by many schools, the focus on individual rights encouraged students and parents to question policies and practices of social institutions, including schools, that were viewed as restricting or infringing on individual rights (Lickona, 1991). Reminiscent of the Revolutionary period, it was widely held that authority could and should be challenged, especially when it conflicted with individual rights or the will of the people.

Changes in the values, beliefs, and behavior of American youth also were fostered by changes in the values, beliefs, and behavior of their parents. Childrearing practices were much more permissive than in the past, as parents strived to ensure that their children did not experience the same hardships that they and their parents had experienced (McClellan, 1999). Popular parenting guides of the period, such as those written by Dr. Benjamin Spock, encouraged a more permissive, emotion-focused, and less coercive style of childrearing (Hampel, 1986). Instead of receiving a spanking for misbehavior, children were much more likely to have privileges withheld or to be the focus of a family discussion. In general, children were freer to express themselves verbally and emotionally at home, with less fear of punishment. These freedoms soon extended to the school.

A focus on individual rights was expressed in the increased use of drugs and alcohol, not only at home but also in school. In reviewing the history of education in high schools in the 1960s and 1970s, Hampel (1986, p. 89) reported a 135% increase in alcohol-related offenses between 1960 and 1973 and that approximately 10% of high school students were "stoned during a typical school day." Students did not lack plenty of negative role models, ranging from characters on television and in the movies to political leaders in the highest offices who were found guilty of lying, cheating, and breaking laws. With increased media coverage, it was clear to all students that criminal acts and immorality were widespread.

In a climate of increased personalism and permissiveness, parents and educators questioned the authority of schools to dictate which values were to be taught. Many believed that values were *culturally relative* and should not be determined by a local school board, curriculum, administrators, or teachers. Who was to say that one person's, or culture's, values were better than another's, or necessarily "moral"? Cultural relativists argued that there were few, if any, universal values—that values are relative to one's culture or to a given situation. Consequently, schools became less concerned about teaching character education and more concerned about not offending cultural, ethnic, and racial groups, as well as individual parents. Out of a sense of compromise and tolerance of differing viewpoints, many schools thought it best not to teach values and character education at all. Thus, schools tended to either neglect character education or adopt programs that emphasized cultural relativism. *Values clarification,* to be reviewed later in this chapter, quickly became the approach of choice among educators who supported an approach of cultural relativism.

STOP AND REFLECT

What Factors Does Research Show to Be the Primary Determinants of Aggression and Antisocial Behavior?

Educators today continue to face frequent disciplinary problems, including problems of school violence. Unlike ever before, however, in recent decades researchers have provided schools with a

(continued)

S T O P   A N D   R E F L E C T *(continued)*

greater understanding of the multiple factors that contribute to the presence, and relative absence, of aggression and other types of antisocial behavior, ranging from noncompliance to violence. These factors explain not only why students differ in behavior, but also why classrooms and schools differ with respect to discipline problems. They can best be conceptualized as falling into three general categories: (1) home/community/peer, (2) classroom/school, and (3) individual child. Note that factors within each category often influence factors in the other two categories. For example, just as a student's thoughts, emotions, and behavior affect the teacher–child relationship, so too does the teacher–child relationship affect a student's thoughts, emotions, and behavior. Likewise, whereas the peer group can certainly influence a student or a school, so too can a student or school influence the peer group. As such, the relation between factors is complex and *reciprocal,* not one way. Thus, changing one factor in a positive way is also likely to have a positive influence on other factors (e.g., by improving teacher–student relations, student behavior improves). Perhaps, more importantly, research shows that the effects of these factors are cumulative—the greater the number of factors, the greater the risk for aggression and violence (Hawkins, Catalano, & Miller, 1992; Reid & Eddy, 1997). A major implication of this finding is that schools can best prevent and respond to violence, aggression, and other behavior problems by targeting as many of the contributing factors as feasible (Bear, Webster-Stratton, Furlong, & Rhee, 2000). Is it rarely sufficient to focus on a single factor (e.g., the home, the child's specific behavior, the classroom climate).

In reviewing the following factors, reflect on how schools might target each one. What ones might schools target, especially in programs that focus on developing self-discipline and preventing misbehavior?

Factors Related to Aggression and Antisocial Behavior

I. *Home/Community/Peer Factors*
- Parenting skills and practices
- Emotional attachment to parents
- Parental values, beliefs, and expectations
- Supervision and monitoring of behavior
- Degree of academic support
- Parental expectations
- Mental health of parents
- Criminality of parents
- Family stressors (e.g., drugs, alcohol, poverty, divorce, large family size)
- Models of aggression in the home and community
- Communication between parents and child
- Consistency, or lack thereof, in values or expectations between home and school
- Degree of exposure to violent behavior (including TV, CDs, and video games)
- Being a victim of aggression or bullying
- Availability and use of weapons and drugs
- Community crowding, norms, values
- Norms, values, beliefs among peers that support aggression
- Peer rejection

II. *Classroom/School Factors*
- Teacher/school expectations, goals, commitment
- Use of proactive or preventive classroom management
- Degree to which deliberate attempts are made to teach self-discipline
- Relationship between student(s) and teacher

- Physical environment
- Curriculum and instruction
- Motivational strategies
- Disciplinary policies and practices (e.g., fairness, consistency, degree of use of punishment)
- Class and school size
- School and classroom climate
- Home–school communication and collaboration
- Staff qualifications and skills

III. *Individual Child Factors*

- Previous history of antisocial behavior or exposure to risk factors listed earlier
- Social skills (including communication skills, behavioral deficiencies, and prosocial skills)
- Belonging to a gang
- Academic achievement, commitment, and aspirations
- Social problem-solving and information-processing skills
- Personal beliefs, attitudes, and values (especially those that support aggression and risk-taking behavior)
- Temperament (e.g., impulsive versus reflective style)
- Self-efficacy, or self-confidence, in performing appropriate behavior
- Assumption of responsibility for one's actions
- Moral reasoning
- Regulation of emotions, especially anger
- Empathy and sympathy regarding others
- Feelings of pride, shame, and guilt
- Feelings of depression, loneliness, rejection
- Self-concept, including self-perceptions of oneself in important domains (e.g., academics, behavior, peer relations, athletics, physical appearance) and perceptions of support from others (especially parents, friends, peers, and teachers)
- Nutrition, sleep, and effects of medication
- Attention-deficit/hyperactivity disorder
- Alcohol and drug use
- Biological factors, especially neuropsychological deficits (likely causes: maternal substance abuse, smoking; poor prenatal nutrition; pre- or postnatal exposure to toxic agents, such as lead; brain insult during delivery; genetically inherited differences; nutrition; lack of stimulation or affection; child abuse and neglect)

Note: "Preventing aggression and violence," by G. G. Bear, C. Webster-Stratton, M. J. Furlong, and S. Rhee. In *Preventing School Problems—Promoting School Success: Strategies and Programs That Work* (p. 6), by K. M. Minke and G. G. Bear (Eds.), 2000, Bethesda, MD: National Association of School Psychologists. Copyright 2000 by the National Association of School Psychologists. Reprinted with permission of the publisher.

Increased Recognition of Student Rights by the Courts

Another impetus for the rapid decline in character education was increased litigation, and threats thereof, by parents and students. In 1962 the Supreme Court ruled that nondenominational prayer in public schools was unconstitutional, and in 1963 it ruled the same about Bible reading. Parents who objected to prayer and Bible reading by the public schools as a method of moral education now had a strong legal basis for their objections. There were other

Supreme Court cases that had an even greater impact on discipline in the schools, however—those concerning students' constitutional rights to freedom of speech and expression and to procedural due process.

Freedom of Speech and Expression.   Several Supreme Court cases in the 1960s addressed freedom of speech and expression in the public schools. With respect to school discipline, the most monumental decision was the 1969 Supreme Court case of *Tinker vs. Des Moines.* The Court ruled that students have the constitutional right to freedom of speech and expression in school. In this specific case the Court ruled that students had the right to wear black armbands in protest of the Vietnam War, but the ruling extended to other expressions of protest. The ruling helped end years of unquestionable and limitless authority of educators over students. It was now made clear by courts that students have some of the same fundamental and constitutional rights as adults and that schools are to respect these rights. In particular, students have the right of free expression, unless it can be shown that such expression *materially and substantially disrupts school discipline or interferes with the constitutional rights of others.* The decision sent several additional messages to schools (Hampel, 1986; Sales, Krauss, Sacken, & Overcast, 1999):

- Schools cannot stifle a student's democratic rights simply for the sake of control and order.
- Schools are to encourage, or at least accept, diversity of opinions and beliefs.
- The burden of proof in litigation concerning rules and regulations that might interfere with a student's rights rests with the school, not the student.
- Schools are to proceed judiciously, and on a case-by-case basis, in matters involving disciplinary procedures that might violate basic constitutional rights.
- The democratic process is not only to be taught but also *practiced* in school.

These messages certainly apply to schools today. That is, largely as a result of *Tinker v. Des Moines* and other court cases in the 1960s and 1970s, students have the constitutional right to express their values and beliefs in class discussions and other communications with teachers and students, as well as in what they wear. Legally schools can neither prevent nor punish such expression, unless the school can convince a court that such behavior materially and substantially disrupts school discipline or otherwise interferes with the rights of others. Thus, although schools have the legal right to punish students for obscene, vulgar, or disruptive language and attire, they do not have the right to punish students for questioning or protesting school rules, policies, and procedures or otherwise expressing themselves in a peaceful and nondisruptive fashion.

Additional court cases during this period granted students more specific rights related to the freedom of expression. Indeed, there were more court cases against school practices between 1969 and 1978 than during the previous fifty years, with 48% (compared to 19% before 1969) decided in favor of the parent or student (Hampel, 1986). Thus, it became evident that schools no longer could unilaterally and arbitrarily dictate students' clothing, hair length, or what students read and wrote. When schools could not demonstrate that refusal to recite the Pledge of Allegiance or wearing long hair or blue jeans interfered with learning, safety, or order, they were forced to change their codes of conduct out of recognition of the

**"My lawyer says I can sue the school
because they're violating my right to be stupid."**

Copyright 1996 Randy Glasbergen. www.glasbergen.com

student's constitutional rights. Schools were required to make codes of conduct more clear to students and to their parents, especially if the rules and consequences in the code of conduct involved basic personal freedoms (Sales, Krauss, Sacken, & Overcast, 1999). Due to these court cases, schools today must show that rules are for the purpose of preventing disruption of the educational process and for maintaining an orderly learning environment and not simply for controlling the personal lives of students.

Right to Due Process.   In 1974 the U.S. Supreme Court made it clear that the constitutional right to procedural due process applies not just to adults but also to children. *Due process* consists of establishing and adhering to official procedures that ensure that citizens are not denied their legal rights, especially their right to confront their accuser and the accusations levied against them. In the landmark case of *Goss v. Lopez* the Court ruled that it is a violation of a student's constitutional rights for a school to employ punitive practices that deny the student a public education without due process of law. In this case the punitive practice was suspension for up to ten days. As a result of *Goss v. Lopez,* schools no longer can arbitrarily or unfairly suspend a student without the potential of litigation. Due process procedures are required, consisting of oral or written notice of the charges against the student, an explanation of evidence supporting the charges, and the opportunity for the student (but not necessarily the parents or legal counsel) to question the charges and present his or her position. Typically, due process procedures should occur before the student is removed from school. An exception to this requirement, however, is when a student presents an immediate danger to self or others. In such circumstances, the student can be removed immediately from school and due process procedures would take place as soon as possible. Because due process procedures often vary across states and school districts, teachers should be aware of the procedures in the school in which they are employed.

End of Character Education in the Public Schools

In a climate of personalism, permissiveness, cultural relativism, and litigation, it is perhaps understandable why character education was in full retreat in the 1970s. Educators were unsure as to what values and aspects of character should be taught and many feared protests and litigation if they systematically taught any values at all. Moreover, with an ever increasing emphasis on academics, many found less time to devote to character education. To be sure, during the 1960s and 1970s many teachers continued to teach values and character, but they did so in schools and communities that no longer viewed character education as an educational priority and in some that viewed it as a liability. Thus, if parents wanted their children in schools in which character education was a priority, and many still did, they had to look outside the public schools. Indeed, private school enrollment, particularly in evangelical and fundamentalist Christian schools, grew rapidly in the late twentieth century, beginning in the mid-1960s (Reese, 1995). Many parents saw this as the solution to the perceived moral decay of the public schools. Although there was little evidence that character, moral, or religious education *caused* the absence of school violence, this did not matter to parents: They believed that private schools emphasized self-discipline, controlled classroom behavior, and provided their children with an environment that was safe and conducive to learning.

Regaining Control of Classrooms

With the demise of character education and rapidly escalating problems of school discipline in the 1970s, schools looked in two directions for help—directions that they continue to look today. First, schools looked to the courts for legal guidance as to which practices could be used to correct behavior problems without risking lawsuits. Second, they looked to new educational models for guidance on how to teach and develop self-discipline as well as to manage and correct misbehavior.

Guidance from the Courts

The Right of Schools to **Reasonable** ***Rules and Regulations.***   Teachers and school administrators demanded that, just as students were being granted increased rights, they too be given rights and authority to maintain effective control (Hampel, 1986). Courts responded by making it clear that schools, as well as individual teachers, have a broad legal right to regulate student behavior for the purpose of maintaining a safe and orderly environment. Courts recognized the right of local school boards, superintendents, and principals to dictate rules regulating student behavior, as long as the constitutional rights of students are not violated. The same right is granted to individual teachers with respect to classroom discipline. Teachers are cautioned, however, not to make rules or use disciplinary practices that are inconsistent with other rules and regulations established by the school or district (*Eisner v. Stanford Board of Education,* 1971).

Court decisions in the 1960s and 1970s placed limits on school rules and regulations, requiring that they be *reasonable.* These limits apply today. To be judged *reasonable:*

> school regulations must be within the authority of the school and reasonably related to the goal of maintaining order and discipline in the educational system . . . giving due regard to

all the circumstances surrounding the nature of each event and the age, health, and mental condition of the student. (Sales, Krauss, Sacken, & Overcast, 1999, p. 1123)

Reasonableness is not limited to matters of safety and potential disruption, however. Courts have ruled that whereas students have the right to express unpopular and controversial views, schools have the right and responsibility to teach socially appropriate behavior (e.g., Supreme Court decision of *Bethel v. Fraser,* 1986). Thus, from a legal standpoint it is reasonable for schools to disallow lewd, obscene, and offensive speech, clothing, and symbols. Likewise, it is reasonable for schools to assume editorial control over school-sponsored student newspapers.

STOP AND REFLECT

Are School Uniforms Reasonable? Effective? A Violation of Student Rights?

With respect to the rights of students and the legitimate authority of schools, one of the most controversial issues of the 1960s and 1970s was hair length. Federal circuit courts tended to split on this issue (National School Boards Association, 1995). That is, about half ruled that schools could not dictate a student's hair length, particularly when it could not be shown that long hair materially and substantially disrupted schooling or the rights of others. These courts tended to view restrictions on hair as a more serious infringement on individual freedom than restrictions on clothing, especially since students cannot change their hair as easily as their clothing on entering and leaving school. The other half of the courts, however, tended to rule that no constitutional rights were involved in the matter of hair length and that school boards, not courts, should govern school policies. Thus, these courts ruled in favor of the schools. The Supreme Court refused to hear these cases.

A more recent controversial issue pitting student rights against school authority is the issue of school uniforms. Many schools have mandated school uniforms, arguing that they reduce discipline problems and improve self-esteem and learning. Indeed, a survey of 755 principals found that that although 71% did not require uniforms in their schools, the majority nevertheless believed that school uniforms reduce peer pressure and improve the image of the school, school discipline, school spirit, learning, and school safety (National Association of Elementary School Principals, 2000).

Although few court cases have yet emerged on the issue of school uniforms, legal advice on this matter appears split. Attorneys who believe that schools can mandate uniforms tend to argue that (1) there is no constitutional right protecting one's appearance and (2) schools have the right to set reasonable rules. These attorneys also emphasize, however, that the case for school uniforms is strongest when schools can show that uniforms improve learning and school discipline. For example, court rulings have indicated that schools have a stronger case for uniforms when they can show that gangs exist in a school and that their members wear certain clothing. Such schools can thus argue that by requiring uniforms, they are reducing school violence and improving learning (National School Boards Association, [NSBA], 1995).

Other attorneys strongly oppose school uniforms, however, siding in favor of the rights of students and arguing that there is little, if any, evidence that uniforms influence school discipline or learning. To them, wearing school uniforms is an authoritarian solution to problems of school violence that does not address any of the true determinants of good and bad behavior.

S T O P   A N D   R E F L E C T *(continued)*

It is likely that the same courts that split on the issue of hair length in the 1970s will split on the issue of school uniforms in the coming years. However, there is an increasing tendency for courts to be more conservative than in the 1970s and to rule that decisions about uniforms are best left to school boards and not to the courts (NSBA, 1995).

What does the research say about school uniforms? Plenty of principals and parents claim improvements in discipline, self-esteem, and learning (U.S. Department of Education, 2003). Indeed, in its *Manual on School Uniforms* the U.S. Department of Education (2003) claims the following "potential benefits of school uniforms":

- Decreasing violence and theft—even life-threatening situations—among students over designer clothing or expensive sneakers
- Helping prevent gang members from wearing gang colors and insignia at school
- Instilling students with discipline
- Helping parents and students resist peer pressure
- Helping students concentrate on their school work
- Helping school officials recognize intruders who come to the school

Although few empirical studies have been conducted, those that have been conducted have not supported claims of improved learning and behavior (Brunsma, 2002; Brunsma & Rockquemore, 1998).

In light of the foregoing, do you believe that uniforms should be required in schools? What might be the perspectives of parents, teachers, and students on this issue?

Reasonable *Consequences.*   Courts have also granted schools considerable leeway in determining the consequences of violations of rules and regulations, as long as the constitutional rights of students are not violated. As noted again by Sales et al. (1999):

> During school hours a teacher has the authority to punish a student for any behavior that is detrimental to the order and best interests of the school and for the breach of any rule or regulation that is within the power of the school to adopt. It is not necessary for the school to formally adopt and publish rules and regulations. (p. 1135)

Thus, as supported by court cases during the 1960s and 1970s, as well as before and since then, it *is* reasonable for a school to punish students for almost any type of behavior that materially and substantially disrupts school discipline or interferes with the constitutional rights of others. Such behavior may occur on school grounds or off of school grounds during school-sponsored activities (e.g., field trips, extracurricular events). This would include behaviors that are harmful to self and others, as well as more common and minor disruptive behaviors such as not obeying the teacher, truancy, and teasing others. It is *not* reasonable, however, to punish students for failing to obtain good grades, for violations of school rules committed by their parents (e.g., parents refusing to sign a homework notebook or not allowing their child to participate in a given activity), and for most behaviors that do not substantially disrupt school discipline or the constitutional rights of others (Sales et al., 1999).

In 1977, the Supreme Court, in the case of *Ingraham v. Wright,* ruled that schools have the right to use corporal punishment, as long as it is not abusive and excessive. The Court determined that the Eighth Amendment against cruel and unusual punishment does not apply to the school's use of corporal punishment against students. Since then, most courts in states in which corporal punishment is permitted by law have supported the use of corporal punishment and have granted educators immunity against resulting lawsuits. In the case of *Garcia v. Miera,* however, a court ruled that school officials *are* liable for damages if their use of corporal punishment is *so grossly excessive as to be shocking to the conscience.* In this case the principal caused severe welts and bruises and a 2-inch scar from a cut on one leg. It is important to note that in states in which corporal punishment is prohibited (twenty-eight states), teachers have no legal right to use it regardless of the harm it causes. In states in which corporal punishment is allowed, it behooves teachers to be well aware of local school board policies governing its use (as well as to seriously question its effectiveness).

In sum, courts in the 1960s and 1970s made it clear that students have certain constitutional rights in school but that there are limits to such rights. In particular, the constitutional rights of an individual student are not to interfere with school discipline or the rights of others. Likewise, courts made it clear that teachers and administrators also have certain rights, especially the right to maintain safe and orderly schools, and to teach socially appropriate behavior. They have the right to punish students, including the use of corporal punishment, suspension, and expulsion, as long as the punishment is reasonable and due process procedures are followed. Under such conditions, school officials are generally immune from civil lawsuits. Such immunity does not apply, however, when their actions result in a clear violation of the constitutional rights of others. Overall, courts have sent the message to educators that the legal system is likely to be on their side when discipline is used in a judicious and reasonable manner.

STOP AND REFLECT

On investigating the use of corporal punishment, suspension, and expulsion in a local school, a child advocacy group discovers that Latinos are twice as likely as other students to be paddled, suspended, and expelled. In your opinion, would this reflect a violation of civil rights? Should the offending school officials be liable for civil damages?

Guidance from Models of Classroom Discipline

Despite protests in the 1960s and 1970s against the teaching of values, morals, and character, many educators were not content with the void created by the demise of character education (McClellan, 1999). Although primarily concerned about managing behavior problems, including acts of violence, they saw the need to return to the American tradition of teaching character, including self-discipline. They sought new alternatives, preferably ones that would not generate protests and complaints from parents and the community. What emerged to fill the void was an assortment of new models of moral education and classroom discipline. The earliest to gain popularity was a radically different model of moral education called *values clarification*—a model that emphasized that values are culturally relative and that students should not be indoctrinated in the values of others.

Values Clarification.   In 1966, Louis Raths, professor of education at New York University, and two of his graduate students, Sydney Simon and Merrill Harmin, proposed the theory of *values clarification* in their book *Values and Teaching.* Throughout the late 1960s and into the early 1980s, Simon and others published a flurry of books and materials to guide teachers in helping students clarify their own values. According to Raths and colleagues, the root of most discipline problems was not that students fail to recognize right from wrong but that they fail to *choose* among often competing values. They purported that character education methods of the past are ineffective because they fail to emphasize *student choice* and *autonomy.* Moreover, they argued that the situation in the 1960s was worse than ever before because values and moral education were being widely neglected in the public schools.

To Raths, Harmin, and Simon (1966), behavior is determined by values based on certain beliefs that individuals hold about issues in a variety of areas, including character, money and success, academic achievement, and friendship. An aim of values clarification was to guide students in developing beliefs into values. According to values clarification, a belief develops into a value only if it is:

- chosen freely
- chosen from among alternatives
- chosen after thoughtful consideration of the consequences of each alternative
- prized and cherished
- publicly affirmed
- acted on in reality
- acted on repeatedly across settings and time

Up to this point, few, if any, of the preceding ideas sound radical or inconsistent with theory and research in developmental psychology (although educators may question the emphasis on student autonomy). What was radically different from methods of the past, however, was that in clarifying values, teachers were to be nondirect, nonindoctrinative, and nonjudgmental. Teachers were to respect each individual student's right to choose his or her own values. Consistent with the philosophy of cultural relativism that characterized the 1960s and 1970s, teachers were instructed that it is morally wrong to force their own values on students, particularly in a culturally diverse society. To do so was viewed as hypocritical. As noted by Simon (1976, p. 136), "none of us has the 'right' set of values to pass on to other people's children." Thus, in contrast to an authoritarian approach to classroom discipline, teachers were to be more permissive (this was more true in respect to teaching values than in correcting misbehavior, however, since values clarification was not an approach to managing and correcting behavior).

In values clarification, the primary role of the teacher was to help students clarify their own values, whatever they might be. This was done best by facilitating individual and small group exploration. As *facilitators,* value educators were to promote reflection and exploration of each student's values by applying the counseling skills of active listening. Such skills included open-ended questioning, listening, paraphrasing, summarizing, acceptance, and respect. More importantly, teachers were to use *clarifying responses.* Clarifying responses avoided moralizing, criticizing, interrogating, and evaluating; placed responsibility on the student; and stimulated thought and reflection among individual students. As noted by Raths et al. (1966), "They are *not* appropriate for drawing a student toward a predetermined answer. They are *not* questions to which the teacher has an answer already in mind" (p. 54).

In values clarification teachers often were given a list of thirty-five questions to draw from in helping students clarify their values (e.g., "Is this something that you prize?" "How did you feel when that happened?" "Did you consider any alternatives?" "Do you value that?"). To make implementation easy, teachers were provided with a wide array of easy-to-use teaching materials including student worksheets, simulations, role-plays, discussion activities, guide books, and filmstrips. Students ranked competing values, judged values along a continuum, examined their values during role-play activities, and explored how their personally chosen values might be applied in specific situations.

According to Raths et al. (1966), the values clarification process entailed applying the scientific method to personal and social problems. As such, students were to identify a value conflict, consider factors that contributed to the value conflict, brainstorm alternative solutions, critically evaluate alternatives and their consequences, and choose an action that reflects *prized* or *cherished* values. It was assumed that the values clarification process would lead to improvements in behavior.

STOP AND REFLECT

Is it possible *not* to convey one's own values in the classroom? With respect to developing classroom discipline, what might be the educational implications of an extreme position of cultural relativism in which values are not taught? What might characterize a more balanced approach to teaching values in which a teacher is sensitive to cultural and individual differences yet teaches basic values that are shared across cultures and/or derived from the U.S. Constitution?

Values clarification made several important contributions to moral education and classroom discipline. First, it reminded educators that schools should not neglect the more personal and cultural aspects of character development. Values clarification emphasized the critical importance of personal and social responsibility and individual choice in a democratic society. It also respected individual and cultural differences in values. Second, values clarification emphasized that schools need to teach the *process* by which students come to make important decisions. It is not sufficient that students simply be told what values they should hold and how they should behave. Third, values clarification encouraged educators to question the authoritarian approach to classroom discipline and to reflect on how teacher–student relations could be improved. Fourth, although values clarification did not offer effective strategies for changing or teaching values, which would be against its philosophy, it did offer educators some useful strategies to help students become more self-aware and committed to values they already hold. When used in combination with other strategies and techniques for developing social and emotional competence, such activities may be useful in developing self-discipline and preventing misbehavior.

Despite its contributions, values clarification fell out of favor in the early 1980s for a variety of reasons. First, with increasing discipline problems in the schools, educators became much more concerned about maintaining order and control than about developing values or any other aspect of character. Raths et al. (1966) made it clear that values clarification was not a system of classroom management, not therapy, and not for students with serious emotional problems. Likewise, as noted by Raths (1976), values clarification was not appropriate for behavior problems "whose causes lie outside of value issues" (p. 8). Thus, values clarification was not intended to address most of the behavior problems that teachers faced in the 1960s and 1970s. Unfortunately, many educators incorrectly expected otherwise and were disappointed in values clarification's lack of effective outcomes. The harshest critics (e.g., Goble & Brooks, 1983) claimed that not only did it fail to improve student behavior but also that it contributed to, or caused, increased disciplinary problems by encouraging students to question authority. For sure, values clarification was too permissive, humanistic, and democratic for those educators who cherished their authority.

Second, many educators began to question the philosophy of cultural relativism on which values clarification was based. As noted by Lickona (1991), values clarification "took the shallow moral relativism loose in the land and brought it into the schools" (p. 11). Teachers were told that they were not to teach their own values but to accept the personal values held by any individual student. Unfortunately, many students chose values based on self-interest and not on respect of others. Third, values clarification had a weak theoretical foundation and little, if any, research to support its effectiveness. Many of the classroom materials designed to help teachers develop their students' values presented students with trivial exercises that were not guided by supporting research.

STOP AND REFLECT

Reemergence of Character Education

Reflect on the mistakes made by values clarification that eventually led to its demise, especially its lack of demonstrating effectiveness in improving observable behavior, an emphasis on student choice in determining values, and the use of trivial exercises for fostering values clarification (and student self-esteem). To what extent might these same mistakes apply today to character education or other schoolwide programs for developing self-discipline with which you are familiar?

Alternative Models of Classroom Discipline

As values clarification fell in popularity, a variety of alternative models to character education and values education gained in popularity. Developed in the 1960s and 1970s, several of these models should be considered *classic* models of classroom discipline and moral education. This is not necessarily because of their quality or definitive components but because of their enduring and broad influence on classroom discipline.[1] These models can be placed along a continuum with respect to their emphasis in promoting self-discipline, particularly autonomy, and in managing and controlling classroom behavior.

At one end of the continuum would be values clarification and another model of moral education that first became popular in the late 1970s and 1980s—the *cognitive-developmental approach to moral education* as advocated by Jean Piaget (1932/1965) and Lawrence Kohlberg (1984; Power, Higgins, & Kohlberg, 1989). Instead of helping students clarify their values, as was the case in values clarification, the primary role of teachers of the cognitive-developmental approach is to facilitate growth through stages of moral reasoning, primarily by means of class discussions of moral dilemmas and establishing a "just community" in which students take an active role in the school government and discipline. Although their methods and techniques differ, both values clarification and the cognitive-developmental approach share the traditional educational aim of developing individuals who are socially responsible and autonomous. Neither has much interest in managing and controlling student behavior, believing that authoritarian techniques are unnecessary when their own (more permissive) approach is implemented. Many aspects of the cognitive-developmental approach continue to be popular today and can readily be seen in current programs in character education and social and emotional learning (as will be seen in Chapter 8).

Falling elsewhere along the continuum are models traditionally viewed as models of classroom discipline (as opposed to models of moral education). *Assertive discipline* (Canter, 1976; Canter & Canter, 2001) falls at the other end of the continuum. This is not necessarily because the approach is more authoritarian but because its philosophy and techniques fail to focus on the development of self-discipline and autonomy. Instead, the emphasis is on managing and controlling student behavior. In the middle of the continuum are Rudolph Dreikurs's (1968) model of *logical consequences,* or *discipline without tears* (Dreikurs & Cassel, 1972) and William Glasser's (1965) *reality therapy.* These two models are more balanced in perspective, providing teachers with strategies for developing self-discipline *and* for managing and correcting behavior problems. *Assertive discipline,* Dreikurs's model, and Glasser's *reality therapy* are reviewed in the next three chapters. These models were chosen for review because of the important issues they address. They also were chosen because each has had a lasting impact on classroom discipline and has remained popular over the years. More importantly, they were chosen because when they are viewed together there are few, if any, key concepts and strategies that these three classic models do not cover, as can be seen in Table 4.1.

---

[1]Although many other authors and researchers made important contributions to classroom discipline in the 1960s and 1970s, few proposed a model of classroom discipline or moral education that became popular among educators. An exception, however, was Thomas Gordon's (1970, 2003) *Teacher Effectiveness Training* (TET), which provided teachers with many practical and effective strategies for enhancing teacher–student communication and helping students develop social problem-solving skills. Very few of these strategies were unique to TET and the model per se failed to have a lasting impact on classroom discipline. Thus, it is not considered here as a classic model of classroom discipline.

TABLE 4.1   Key Concepts and Strategies of the Classic Models of Dreikurs, Glasser, and Canter and Canter That Can Be Found in Other Popular Models of Classroom Discipline

	Dreikurs	Glasser	Assertive Discipline (Canter & Canter, 2001)	Cooperative Discipline (Albert, 1996)	Positive Discipline (Nelsen et al., 1997)	Discipline with Dignity (Curwin & Mendler, 1999)
Key Concepts						
Meeting Student's Psychological Needs of:						
Social Belonging	✓+	✓+	✓	✓+	✓+	
Self-Worth (including respect and dignity)	✓+	✓+	✓	✓+	✓+	✓+
Student Choice and Responsibility	✓	✓+	✓–	✓+		✓+
Mistaken Goals as Determinants of Behavior (e.g., attending, revenge, power)	✓+	✓	✓–	✓+	✓+	✓+
Developing Self-Discipline	✓+	✓+	✓–	✓	✓	✓+
Teacher Assertion and Control	✓–	✓	✓+	✓–	✓–	✓
Key Strategies						
Democratic Teaching	✓+	✓+	✓–	✓	✓+	✓+
Encouragement or Supportive Feedback	✓+	✓+	✓+	✓+	✓+	✓+
Teaching Social Problem-Solving Skills	✓	✓+	✓	✓	✓+	✓+
Teaching Values and Moral Reasoning	✓+	✓+	✓–	✓	✓	
Establishing Positive Teacher–Student Relations	✓+	✓+	✓+	✓+	✓+	✓+
Modeling	✓	✓	✓	✓	✓	✓+
Prevention via Classroom Management	✓+	✓+	✓+	✓+	✓+	✓+
Prevention via Avoidance of Academic Failure	✓	✓+	✓–	✓	✓	✓
Teacher–Parent Communication	✓+	✓	✓	✓+	✓	✓+
Class Meetings and Sense of Community	✓+	✓+	✓–	✓+	✓+	✓–
Logical and Natural Consequences	✓+	✓	✓	✓+	✓+	✓+
Positive Confrontation (e.g., challenging excuses)	✓	✓+	✓	✓	✓	✓+
Matching Corrective Techniques with Student's Goals	✓+	✓–	✓–	✓+	✓+	✓–
Systematic Recording of Behavior	✓–	✓–	✓+	✓–	✓–	✓–
Discipline Plans and Hierarchies	✓–	✓–	✓+	✓–	✓–	✓
Contingent Praise and Rewards	✓–	✓	✓+	✓–	✓–	✓
Punitive or Corrective Consequences	✓–	✓	✓+	✓	✓–	✓
Functional Behavioral Assessment	✓	✓	✓	✓	✓	✓

✓+ = Major element in the model.   ✓ = Recognized as important and is addressed.   ✓– = Receives little, if any, attention.

The Positive Classroom (Jones, 1988)	Various "Models" of Classroom Management Based on Applied Behavior Analysis*	Teacher Effectiveness Training (Gordon, 2003)	Developing Emotional Intelligence (Bodine & Crawford, 1999)	Responsive Classroom and Teaching Children to Care (Charney, 2002)	Love & Logic (Fay & Funk, 1995)	Developmental Discipline (Watson & Ecken, 2003)
✓	✓–	✓	✓	✓+	✓	✓+
✓	✓–	✓+	✓	✓+	✓+	✓+
✓	✓	✓+	✓+	✓+	✓+	✓+
✓–	✓–	✓–	✓–	✓–	✓–	✓–
✓	✓–	✓+	✓+	✓+	✓+	✓+
✓	✓+	✓–	✓–	✓–	✓	✓–
✓	✓–	✓+	✓	✓+	✓	✓+
✓	✓+	✓+	✓+	✓+	✓+	✓+
✓	✓	✓+	✓+	✓+	✓	✓+
✓	✓–	✓	✓+	✓+	✓	✓+
✓+	✓	✓+	✓+	✓+	✓+	✓+
✓+	✓+	✓	✓+	✓+	✓	✓+
✓+	✓+	✓+	✓	✓+	✓–	✓+
✓+	✓+	✓+	✓	✓	✓–	✓+
✓	✓–	✓+	✓	✓+	✓	✓+
✓	✓–	✓+	✓+	✓+	✓	✓+
✓	✓	✓	✓+	✓+	✓+	✓
✓	✓	✓	✓	✓–	✓	✓
✓–	✓–	✓–	✓–	✓–	✓–	✓–
✓	✓+	✓–	✓–	✓–	✓–	✓–
✓	✓+	✓–	✓–	✓–	✓	✓–
✓+	✓+	✓–	✓–	✓	✓–	✓–
✓	✓+	✓–	✓	✓	✓	✓–
✓	✓+	✓	✓–	✓	✓	✓

*For example: Alberto & Troutman (2003); Kerr & Nelson (2002); Martella, Nelson, & Marchard-Martella (2003)

SUMMARY AND KEY POINTS

■ In the 1940s and 1950s, behavior problems were common but few were serious. Students respected authority, and teachers demonstrated their authority. Times were changing, however, as a greater diversity of students entered and stayed in school.

■ Most teachers blended direct and indirect methods of character education. However, very few schools were models of progressive education. Instead, progressive education often was associated with schools that failed to control their students.

■ Two major factors contributed to the decline in character education in the 1940s and 1950s: pressure on teachers to teach academic subjects and challenges from parents concerning the role of education in the teaching of morals and values.

■ Crime and violence increased drastically in school and society throughout the 1960s and 1970s, an era characterized by personalism, permissiveness, and relativism.

■ Courts increasingly recognized the individual rights of students. No longer could schools arbitrarily stifle the right of students to free speech and expression.

■ Courts recognized the right of schools to use discipline, when reasonable, to punish students for almost any type of behavior that materially and substantially disrupts classroom discipline or interferes with the constitutional rights of others.

■ Courts ruled that schools could continue to use corporal punishment and that suspension and expulsion were reasonable consequences as long as due process procedures were followed.

■ In response to increased discipline problems and school violence and the void in the teaching of self-discipline caused by the demise of character education, schools turned not only to courts for help but also to new models of classroom discipline.

■ One of the first models to gain popularity was values clarification, which was grounded in a philosophy of cultural relativism. Teachers were not to teach values, or impose their own values on students, but were to help each student clarify his or her personal values.

■ Although values clarification remained popular for about a decade, it failed to meet the needs of teachers, especially those concerned about managing and correcting behavior problems. Thus, teachers turned to a variety of other models of classroom discipline that emerged in the 1960s and 1970s.

KEY TERMS AND CONCEPTS

Authoritarian schools
Cognitive-developmental approach
Compulsory education
Cultural relativism
Eisner v. Stanford and teachers' rights

Garcia v. Miera and corporal punishment
Goss v. Lopez and due process rights
Ingraham v. Wright and corporal punishment

Personalism and permissiveness
Reasonable consequences
Tinker v. Des Moines and freedom of expression
Values clarification

RECOMMENDED READINGS AND RESOURCES

Books on the History of Moral Education,
Character Education, and School Discipline

Butchart, R. E. (1998). Punishments, penalties, prizes, and procedures: A history of discipline in U.S. schools. In R. E. Butchart & B. McEwan (Eds.), *Classroom discipline in American schools: Problems and possibilities for democratic education* (pp. 19–49). Albany: State University of New York Press.

Hampel, R. L. (1986). *The last little citadel: American high schools since 1940.* Boston: Houghton Mifflin.

McClellan, B. E. (1999). *Moral education in America: Schools and the shaping of character from colonial times to the present.* New York: Teachers College Press.

Recommended Books for an Overview of Popular Models of School Discipline

Charles, C. M. (2002). *Building classroom discipline.* Boston: Allyn and Bacon.

Wolfgang, C. H. (2001). *Solving discipline and classroom management problems: Methods and models for today's teachers.* New York: John Wiley.

Recommended Books on Legal Issues in Education and Classroom Discipline

Alexander, K., & Alexander, M. D. (2005). *American public school law* (6th ed.). Belmont, CA: Wadsworth.

Irons, P. H. (Ed.) (2000). *May it please the Court: Courts, kids, and the Constitution: Live recordings and transcripts of sixteen Supreme Court oral arguments on the constitutional rights of students and teachers.* New York: New Press.

Mazin, L., Hestand, J., & Koester, R. (1998). *An educator's legal guide to stress-free discipline and school safety.* Bloomington, IN: National Educational Service.

Oakstone Legal and Business Publishing Staff (2003). *Deskbook encyclopedia of American school law, 2004.* Wayne, PA: Center for Education and Employment.

Raskin, J. B. (2003). *We the students: Supreme Court decisions for and about students.* Washington, DC: CQ Press.

Yudof, M. G., Kirp, D., Levin, B., & Moran, R. (Eds.) (2002). *Educational policy and the law* (4th ed.). Belmont, CA: Wadsworth.

Books and Resources on School Uniforms

Brunsma, David L. (2004). *What the school uniform movement tells us about American education: A symbolic crusade.* Lanham, MD: Scarecrow Education.

U.S. Department of Education (2003). *Manual on school uniforms.* Available www.ed.gov/updates/uniforms.

Books on Models of Classroom Discipline (in Table 4.1)

Albert, L. (1996). *Cooperative discipline.* Circle Pines, MN: American Guidance Service.

Alberto, P. A., & Troutman, A. C. (2003). *Applied behavior analysis for teachers* (6th ed.). Columbus, OH: Merrill Publishing.

Bodine, R. J., & Crawford, D. K. (1999). *Developing emotional intelligence: A guide to behavior manage-* ment and conflict resolution in schools. Champaign, IL: Research Press.

Charney, R. S. (2002). *Teaching children to care: Classroom management for ethical and academic growth, K–8* (Rev. ed.). Greenfield, MA: Northeast Foundation for Children.

Curwin, R. L., & Mendler, A. N. (1999). *Discipline with dignity.* Alexandria, VA: Association for Supervision and Curriculum Development.

Fay, J., & Funk, D. (1995). *Teaching with love and logic: Taking control of the classroom.* Golden, CO: Love and Logic Press.

Gordon, T. (2003). *TET: Teacher effectiveness training.* New York: Three Rivers Press.

Jones, F. (1988). *Positive classroom discipline.* Santa Cruz, CA: Fredric H. Jones & Associates.

Kerr, M. M, & Nelson, C. M. (2002). *Strategies for addressing behavior problems in the classroom* (4th ed.). Upper Saddle River, NJ: Merrill Prentice-Hall.

Martella, R. C., Nelson, J. R., & Marchand-Martella, N. E. (2003). *Managing disruptive behaviors in the schools.* Boston, MA: Allyn & Bacon.

Nelsen, J., Lott, L., & Glenn, H. (2000). *Positive discipline in the classroom.* Rocklin, CA: Prima.

Watson, M. (2003). *Learning to trust: Transforming difficult elementary classrooms through developmental discipline.* San Francisco, CA: Jossey-Bass.

Websites for Information on Legal Issues in Classroom Discipline and Education

www.findlaw.com
Searchable directory for finding law cases of interest at the state and federal levels.

www.nea.org
Website for the National Education Association.

www.nsba.org
Website for the National School Boards Association.

www.aclu.org
Website for the American Civil Liberties Union.

www.naesp.org
Website for the National Association of Elementary School Principals.

www.nassp.org
Website for the National Association of Secondary School Principals.

REFERENCES

Bear, G. G., Webster-Stratton, C., Furlong, M., & Rhee, S. (2000). Preventing aggression and violence. In K. M. Minke & G. G. Bear (Eds.), *Preventing school problems—Promoting school success:*

Strategies and programs that work (pp. 1–69). Bethesda, MD: National Association of School Psychologists.

Bethel School District v. Fraser, 106 S. Ct. 3159 (1986).

Brown v. Board of Education, 347 U.S. 483 (1954).

Brunsma, D. L. (2002). *School uniforms: A critical review of the literature.* Bloomington, IN: Phi Delta Kappa.

Brunsma, D. L., & Rockquemore, K. A. (1998). Effects of student uniforms on attendance, behavior problems, substance abuse, and academic achievement. *Journal of Educational Research, 92* (1), 53–62.

Butchart, R. E. (1998). Punishments, penalties, prizes, and procedures: A history of discipline in U.S. schools. In R. E. Butchart & B. McEwan (Eds.), *Classroom discipline in American schools: Problems and possibilities for democratic education* (pp. 19–49). Albany: State University of New York Press.

Canter, L. (1976). *Assertive discipline: A take charge approach for today's educator.* Santa Monica, CA: Lee Canter and Associates.

Canter, L., & Canter, M. (2001). *Assertive discipline: Positive behavior management for today's classroom.* Santa Monica, CA: Canter and Associates.

Dreikurs, R. (1968). *Psychology in the classroom: A manual for teachers.* New York: Harper & Row.

Dreikurs, R., & Cassel, P. (1972). *Discipline without tears: What to do with children who misbehave.* New York: Hawthorn Books.

Eisner v. Stanford Board of Education. 440 F.2d 803 (2nd Cir. 1971).

Garcia v. Miera. 817 F2d 650 (10th Cir. 1987).

Goble, F., & Brooks, B. D. (1983). *The case for character education.* Ottawa, IL: Green Hill Publishers.

Glasser, W. (1965). *Reality therapy.* New York: Harper & Row.

Goss v. Lopez (1974). 95 S. Ct. 729, 419 U.S. 565 (1974).

Hampel, R. L. (1986). *The last little citadel: American high schools since 1940.* Boston: Houghton Mifflin.

Hawkins, J. D., Catalano, R. F., & Miller, Y. (1992). Risk and protective factors for alcohol and other drug problems in adolescence and early adulthood: Implications for substance abuse prevention. *Psychological Bulletin, 112,* 64–105.

Ingraham v. Wright. 97 S. Ct. 1401, 430 U.S. 651 (1976).

Kohlberg, L. (1984). *Essays on moral development: Vol. 2. The psychology of moral development.* New York: Harper & Row.

Lickona, T. (1991). *Educating for character: How our schools can teach respect and responsibility.* New York: Bantam.

McClellan, B. E. (1999). *Moral education in America: School and the shaping of character from colonial times to the present.* New York: Teachers College Press.

National Association of Elementary School Principals (2000). *Survey of school principals reports positive effects of school uniforms.* Abstract retrieved January 5, 2003 from www.naesp.org.

National School Boards Association (1995). *Legal guidelines for curbing school violence.* National School Boards Association, Council of School Attorneys. Alexandria, VA: Author.

Our Nation's Schools—A Report Card: "A" in School Violence and Vandalism. (1975). Preliminary Report of the Subcommittee to Investigate Juvenile Delinquency Based on Investigations, 1971–1975, Senator Birch Bayh, Chairman, to the Committee on the Judiciary, United States Senate (Washington, DC: Government Printing Office).

Piaget, J. (1965). *The moral judgment of the child.* Glenco, IL: Free Press. (Original work published 1932).

Power, F. C., Higgins, A., & Kohlberg, L. (1989). *Lawrence Kohlberg's approach to moral education.* New York: Columbia University Press.

Raths, L. (1976). Freedom, intelligence, and valuing. In National Education Association (Eds.), *Values concepts and techniques* (pp. 10–17). Washington, DC: Author.

Raths, L., Harmin, M., & Simon, S. (1966). *Values and teaching.* Columbus, OH: Charles E. Merrill.

Reese, W. J. (1995). Reefer madness and a *Clockwork Orange.* In D. Ravitch and M. A. Vinovskis (Eds.), *Learning from the past.* Baltimore: The Johns Hopkins University Press.

Reid, J. B., & Eddy, J. M. (1997). The prevention of antisocial behavior: Some considerations in the search for effective interventions. In D. M. Stoff, J. Breiling, & J. D. Maser (Eds.), *Handbook of antisocial behavior* (pp. 343–356). New York: Wiley.

Sales, B. D., Krauss, D. A., Sacken, D. M., & Overcast, T. D. (1999). The legal rights of students. In C. R. Reynolds & T. B. Gutkin (Eds.), *The handbook of school psychology* (pp. 1113–1144). New York: John Wiley.

Simon, S. B. (1976). Values clarification vs. indoctrination. In *Values, concepts, and techniques* (pp. 136–143). Washington, DC: National Education Association.

Tinker v. Des Moines Ind. Comm. Sch. Dist., 393 U.S. 503 (1969).

U.S. Department of Education (2003). *Manual on school uniforms.* Retrieved January 5, 2003 from www.ed.gov/updates/uniforms.

5

Goals, Encouragement, and Logical Consequences

Dreikurs's Model of Classroom Discipline

GUIDING QUESTIONS

- How do feelings of self-worth and social belonging relate to classroom discipline?
- Do students misbehave on purpose? Is misbehavior driven by goals? If so, what are the goals?
- Is it important to consider a student's goal(s) when preventing and correcting misbehavior?

- Should the classroom teacher assume the role of "counselor" for the purpose of gaining insight into a student's misbehavior?

- How does praise differ from *encouragement?* How does punishment differ from *natural* and *logical consequences?* Do the differences really matter?

- What role might class discussions play in preventing and correcting behavior problems?

- How do Dreikurs's views differ from those of earlier educators?

Traditional teaching methods where the autocratic teacher was a boss who used force, pressure, competition and the threat of punishment are now out-dated; even the pupils themselves do not accept this kind of leadership any more. If they are not given the opportunity to get involved in a participatory classroom democracy they either rebel in class, or at home, or against society in general.

Many teachers have decided to change their autocratic ways and try the democratic approach. However, because there was no one to teach them the new skills of becoming democratic leaders, they have become permissive anarchists. Their classrooms have become chaotic. Their pupils do what they want, learn what and when they want, care nothing for the needs of others, have little respect for the teacher, school or friends. Both teacher and pupil have become discouraged.

We know that when children are discouraged they misbehave, have no respect for order, and learn very little. These classrooms of laissez-faire anarchy are producing a generation of tyrants whose prime aim and value is to do their own thing with no social awareness or consideration of their responsibility to contribute to society. (Dreikurs & Cassel, 1972, p. 12)

As seen in the preceding passage from *Discipline Without Tears* (Dreikurs & Cassel, 1972), Rudolph Dreikurs supported democratic teaching methods, believing that authoritarian teaching methods were outdated and ineffective. However, he also believed that democratic teaching methods used in the 1960s, which he perceived as being too permissive, were "producing a generation of tyrants" (p. 12). According to Dreikurs, permissiveness and chaos resulted because teachers did not know how to teach democracy correctly. Teachers needed to be taught *new* democratic methods of preventing and correcting discipline problems, and Dreikurs claimed to offer them. Dreikurs and colleagues wrote many books for teachers and parents on democratic teaching and classroom discipline, which became the basis of the Dreikurs model of classroom discipline, often referred to as "democratic discipline." Among these books were *Encouraging Children to Learn: The Encouragement Process* (Dinkmeyer & Dreikurs, 1963), *Psychology in the Classroom: A Manual for Teachers* (Dreikurs, 1968), *Logical Consequences: A Handbook of Discipline* (Dreikurs & Grey, 1968), *Discipline Without Tears: What to Do with Children Who Misbehave* (Dreikurs & Cassel, 1972), and *Maintaining Sanity in the Classroom: Classroom Management Techniques* (Dreikurs, Grunwald, & Pepper, 1982). Dreikurs's model of classroom discipline, as presented in these writings, is the focus of the present chapter. His key concepts are reviewed and critiqued, especially those that continue to be seen in more recent models of classroom discipline.

Teachings and Philosophy of Dreikurs

Dreikurs's writings were based primarily on the earlier psychoanalytic writings of Alfred Adler, a colleague of Sigmund Freud in Vienna, Austria. As a psychotherapist, professor of psychiatry, and director of the Alfred Adler Institute of Chicago, Dreikurs applied many of Adler's ideas to the schools. Central among these ideas are (1) the primary goal of behavior (and misbehavior) is social belonging, (2) biased perceptions often account for misbehavior, (3) self-discipline is the key to democracy, (4) individual differences in personality are important, and (5) goals and functions explain why students misbehave.

① The Primary Goal of Behavior (and Misbehavior) Is Social Belonging

Drawing from Adler's theory of personality, Dreikurs argued that behavior is self-determined, or driven by purposeful goals. The most fundamental goal is to experience a sense of *social belonging,* or social acceptance. Individual happiness and success in all areas of life, including academics and classroom behavior, depend on meeting this basic goal, or need. Social belonging is thus viewed as the primary motivator of behavior and as the key to self-worth, or self-esteem. When the natural goal of social belonging is not achieved, feelings of inferiority result, which, in turn, lead to feelings of low self-worth and various maladaptive and disruptive behaviors.

② Biased Perceptions Often Account for Misbehavior

Another key theoretical concept of Adlerian psychology is that an individual's behavior is determined by how the individual *perceives* reality—the individual's own subjective perceptions and interpretations of the world. Unfortunately, perceptions and interpretations are often wrong or biased. According to Dreikurs (1968), "all the goals of children's misbehavior are the result of the child's 'faulty logic.' His faulty private logic is only his perception of reality" (p. 42). For example, when not asked to play in a game, students may perceive this as an act of social rejection. In turn, they get angry and seek revenge or socially withdraw. In reality, however, no social rejection may have been intended.

Because all students have biased perceptions and interpret social situations incorrectly, educators should expect them to make mistakes in their choices and behavior. That is, their choices and behaviors are not always based on reality. Of course, this also applies to adults, although to a lesser degree because social perceptions and reasoning mature with age. Adler and Dreikurs argued that mental health problems are common among individuals who frequently seek goals based on subjective biases, rather than reality.

③ Self-Discipline Is the Key to Democracy

Dreikurs believed that all individuals cherish a sense of autonomy. He also argued that in a democratic society *self-discipline* and autonomy are critical. Self-discipline is defined as "discipline without imposed authority by any individual, but imposed by the individual himself and by that of the group; the development of intelligent self-control rather than blind obedience because of fear" (Dreikurs, 1968, p. 22). Agreeing with the philosophy of John Dewey and other progressive educators, Dreikurs posited that unless students learn to be responsible for their own behavior, they cannot be successful in a democratic society. He understood that teaching self-discipline and democracy is a challenge, especially when society grants all individuals, including students, certain freedoms and rights. As noted by Dreikurs and Cassel (1972), however, "Our dilemma is that children are gaining freedom without learning an accompanying sense of responsibility" (p. 14).

④ Individual Differences in Personality Are Important

To Dreikurs, teachers should expect students to differ in their attitudes, beliefs, values, and behaviors. Dreikurs believed that an understanding of individual differences among students, including the *causes* of individual differences, is important to teachers. He proposed that only with such an understanding can teachers best address the current needs and behavior of their students. Thus, Dreikurs encouraged teachers to learn about their students' personalities by observing them, talking to them, listening to them during class discussions, and having them write about themselves. However, like other psychoanalytic therapists, Dreikurs believed that personality was developed by age 6. As such, he purported that there are *limits* to what teachers can do to change a student's personality.

Dreikurs also recognized that families play a key role in meeting the need for social belonging and in the development of a child's personality. He stressed the importance of a positive family atmosphere and good parenting skills. Interestingly, he also stressed that the family constellation is a key factor in children's feelings of belonging, as well as in their general personalities. He advised teachers and parents that birth order largely determines a child's personality, as well as the likelihood that the child may feel inferior. To Dreikurs, whether or not a child is the first, middle, or last child in the family group determines social challenges, competition, and parental treatment. Although Dreikurs was correct in emphasizing individual differences in personality, his psychoanalytic emphasis on birth order is not particularly helpful, nor is it supported by research.

⑤ Four Simple Goals Explain Why Students Misbehave

Believing that every behavior has a purpose, Dreikurs argued that the purpose of most classroom behavior is to gain social acceptance, either from the teacher or from peers. Most students learn that the best way to gain social acceptance is by conforming to social norms, including school rules, and by getting along with others. Because their need for social acceptance is met, these students are well behaved and socially adjusted. Unfortunately, too many other students perceive (correctly or incorrectly) that their teachers or peers do not like them. Dreikurs purported that these students become discouraged and seek other maladaptive goals based on the misperception and poor logic that they will help them be socially accepted and feel worthwhile. Although maladaptive, these goals nevertheless serve to help buffer many students from feelings of inferiority, at least in the short term.

Dreikurs argued that four goals explain why students, but especially those under age 10, misbehave in the classroom: (1) to gain attention, believing that attention is necessary for self-worth and that the best way to gain attention is by misbehaving; (2) to demonstrate power and superiority, believing control over others enhances feelings of self-worth; (3) to seek revenge, thinking that they can feel more significant by "paying others back" for hurting them; and (4) to socially withdraw, hoping that others will leave them alone (which allows them to conceal deficiencies and inadequacies, real or imagined, that contribute to low self-worth). Each goal can be seen in one of two forms of destructive behavior, an active destructive form or a passive destructive form, as described next:

Goal 1: Attention Seeking

Active destructive form = *"nuisance"* behaviors that frequently describe the class clown, such as showing off, constantly asking questions, acting tough, and engaging in minor mischief.

Passive destructive form = *"laziness"* behaviors that require others' assistance or attention, such as underachievement, lack of effort, anxiety, being bashful or fearful, untidiness, eating difficulties, and speech impediments.

Goal 2: Power and Superiority

Active destructive form = behaviors of the *"rebel,"* or one who argues, contradicts, bullies, lies, disobeys rules, dawdles, and displays temper tantrums.

Passive destructive form = behaviors of the *"stubborn"* child, or one who is lazy, disobedient, and forgetful.

Goal 3: Revenge

Active destructive form = *"vicious"* behaviors, such as stealing, "bed-wetting," and acts of violence and delinquency.

Passive destructive form = behaviors of *"violent passivity,"* such as in sullen and defiant behavior.

Goal 4: Social Withdrawal

(This does not exist in active destructive form according to Dreikurs.)

Passive destructive form = *"hopeless"* behaviors, including "stupidity," social withdrawal, and low self-esteem.

Dreikurs noted that these four goals are hierarchical in the sense that when the first one does not work, students revert to the next one in the sequence. Thus, if students do not obtain attention, they seek power, and if they do not obtain power, then they seek revenge. If revenge fails, they give up and experience self-defeat and low self-esteem. Dreikurs also noted there are times when well-adjusted students share these goals but achieve them in constructive ways. This is particularly true with the goal of attention getting, in which most students learn that they can gain attention in positive ways such as by doing well academically and by exhibiting prosocial behavior.

Whereas attention getting is the most common goal, revenge is the goal that is most destructive to other people, and social withdrawal is the goal that is most destructive to oneself. According to Dreikurs, students who seek revenge pose the greatest problem, both scholastically and behaviorally. They are violent and brutal or sullen and defiant. Those who socially withdraw also present a significant problem. Instead of acting out, they give up all hope; expecting only failure and defeat, they refuse to even try to succeed socially or academically. Dreikurs referred to such feelings of hopelessness as an *inferiority complex.*

STOP AND REFLECT

What might be the practical implications of the foregoing central ideas in Dreikurs's model of classroom discipline? How might they influence classroom practice?

Strategies for Developing Self-Discipline and for Preventing and Correcting Misbehavior

Democratic Teaching

With respect to preventing behavior problems, Dreikurs shared many of the views of progressive educators. He emphasized the importance of democratic education, believing that the best way to teach democratic thinking and promote self-discipline is by using indirect, rather than direct, methods of teaching. Like many other writers of the period, Dreikurs stressed that both permissive and authoritarian (or "autocratic") styles of teaching are harmful to the development of democratic thinking and autonomy, as well as to learning in general. He advocated a balanced and moderate approach. In defense of this position, Dreikurs (1968) cited a classic and intriguing study by Kurt Lewin and colleagues (Lewin, Lippitt, & White, 1939).

The study examined the social climate created by three different leadership styles—autocratic, democratic (or moderate), and laissez-faire (or permissive). These three styles characterized adults who supervised boys in a Boys' Club. As predicted, discipline problems were worst under laissez-faire leadership. Somewhat surprising was the finding that boys were well behaved under *both* democratic and autocratic leadership. However, students in the democratic and autocratic groups differed markedly in behavior when adults were absent. When the adults were absent, students in the autocratic group exhibited the most behavior problems, including fighting, and the fewest prosocial behaviors. Such differences in behavior continued when students left the group. Perhaps most intriguing was that Lewin found that when autocratic leaders tried to shift from an autocratic to a democratic style, "Bedlam broke loose" (Dreikurs, 1968, p. 73). This tended to last for at least a week until the students adjusted to the new style. Dreikurs concluded that this important study demonstrated that "Whenever children move from an autocratic environment into a democratic setting, they tend to run wild, to abuse their freedom, because they have not learned to rely on their inner restraint when the outside pressure failed to force them into submission" (p. 73). Accordingly, teachers were to expect the transition from authoritarian to democratic leadership in the classroom to be difficult at first but worthwhile in the long run.

Dreikurs also argued that although teachers have the moral responsibility to help students develop self-discipline, they do not have the right to impose their will on students or to punish and threaten them. As democratic leaders, they are to guide and motivate students.

He contrasted democratic teachers to autocratic, or traditional, teachers with the following respective descriptors (Dreikurs & Cassel, 1972): leader versus boss, friendly voice versus sharp voice, invitation versus command, influence versus power, winning cooperation versus demanding cooperation, "I tell you what I will do" versus "I tell you what you should do," selling ideas versus imposing ideas, guidance versus domination, encouragement versus criticism, acknowledgment of achievement versus faultfinding, helping versus punishing, discussion versus "I tell you," "I suggest, and help you decide" versus "I decide, you obey," and shared responsibility of team versus sole responsibility of boss (p. 18).

Democratic teachers teach students to think and behave in a manner consistent with democracy. Hence, they encourage students to be responsible for their own behavior and for that of the group. Unfortunately, Dreikurs did not provide much guidance as to which specific methods of teaching and curriculum work best for teaching self-discipline. However, he did highlight a variety of qualities and skills that characterize effective democratic teachers (Dreikurs & Cassel, 1972). Dreikurs argued that these characteristics are the key to preventing many behavior problems and developing self-discipline. As will be seen in later chapters, research supports his argument. The qualities of effective democratic teachers highlighted by Dreikurs are:

- Warmth and friendliness
- Sense of humor
- Sincere interest in each child
- Self-confidence in teaching and discipline
- Excellent classroom management and organizational skills (e.g., instruction is planned before class begins, students are grouped to maximize learning)
- Shows respect toward all students by listening and demonstrating empathy
- Is impartial and doesn't show favoritism
- Is always encouraging
- Fosters democratic decision making through group discussions and active participation of students in important classroom decisions
- Gives sincere recognition of effort
- Involves all students in chores and responsibilities

STOP AND REFLECT

Read the following quote by Dreikurs:

> One cannot influence anybody unless one has first established a friendly relationship. This fundamental premise is often neglected. Most difficulties with students are the logical outgrowth of disturbed relationships between child and adult. The same child who seems unmanageable to one teacher may be, and often is, cooperative with another. If a good relationship exists, serious disturbances of cooperation hardly ever arise. (Dreikurs, 1968, p. 59)

What characteristics of teachers do you believe best reflect "a good relationship" with students?

Development and Prevention through Encouragement

Dreikurs believed that chief among the preceding teacher characteristics is *encouragement,* defined as the process of accepting "the child as worthwhile, regardless of any deficiency," and assisting the student in "developing his capacity and potentialities" (Dreikurs & Grey, 1968, p. 56). Encouragement consists of respecting all individual students and supporting their development regardless of their race, culture, backgrounds, shortcomings, and behaviors. It means helping students feel capable, competent, worthwhile, and responsible for their own behavior. It also means showing care and a personal interest in each student. Encouragement is critical to preventing behavior problems, motivating learning, and enhancing self-esteem. It also is an effective strategy for correcting misbehavior. Encouragement, unlike praise, is best used when students experience frustration or failure, as opposed to success. Dreikurs was quite critical of the use of praise, arguing that praise often is ineffective because it fosters dependency on adults. Moreover, when praise is not forthcoming students experience a sense of failure. As noted by Dreikurs:

> Praise can be terribly discouraging. If the child's efforts fail to bring the desired amount of praise he may assume either that he isn't good enough or that what he has to offer isn't worth the effort and so he gives up.
>
> If a child has set exceedingly high standards for himself, praise may sound like mockery or scorn, especially when his efforts fail to measure up to his own standards. In such a child, praise only serves to increase his anger with himself and his resentment at others for not understanding his dilemma. (Dreikurs & Cassel, 1972, p. 55)

Dreikurs also differentiated encouragement from the use of rewards, while opposing the latter. He strongly objected to the use of rewards and punishment, viewing both of them as outdated strategies that *discourage* self-discipline and learning. To Dreikurs, discouragement is the root of most behavior problems: Rewards are bribery, and students do not like being bribed but want to experience *self-satisfaction* with their accomplishments. Self-satisfaction is viewed as the key to self-discipline and democracy. Dreikurs believed that rewards and praise stifle self-satisfaction and convey a lack of trust and respect. Moreover, he argued that rewards and punishment are no longer as effective as they were in the past when a strictly authoritarian style of teaching prevailed.

When teachers use encouragement, they show support and "faith in the child" by focusing on the inappropriateness of the present behavior and not on the student's past. Likewise, in using encouragement, teachers highlight effort, not outcomes; emphasize each student's strengths and interests; and view mistakes as learning experiences, not failures. It is in this manner that encouragement fosters self-confidence, self-discipline, and self-worth. Some examples of verbal *encouragers* that Dreikurs presented in his books are: "I'm so glad you enjoy learning," "How nice that you could figure that out for yourself. Your skill is improving!" and "Isn't it nice that you can help?" (Dreikurs, 1971, p. 73).

Dreikurs recommended that teachers use encouragement not only to promote self-worth but also to develop the following individual competencies and values. He believed these competencies and values characterize the "well-adjusted" student:

- Respects rights of others
- Is tolerant of others

- Is interested in others
- Co-operates with others
- Encourages others
- Is courageous
- Has a true sense of own worth
- Has a feeling of belonging
- Has socially acceptable goals (Dreikurs & Cassel, 1972, p. 33)

Dreikurs argued that teachers must avoid *discouragement*, which Dreikurs believed was the source of most discipline problems. As noted earlier, teachers are to avoid rewards, but more importantly they are to avoid ridicule, punishment, and other negative practices commonly employed by authoritarian teachers. This includes practices that promote competition, such as grading. In competitive activities, more students lose than win. Consequently, more students experience a sense of failure, and resulting low motivation, than a sense of self-worth. Interestingly, Dreikurs (1968) also claimed that competition is undemocratic.

STOP AND REFLECT

Do you agree with Dreikurs that praise, rewards, punishment, and competition *discourage* appropriate behavior? Under what, if any, conditions, might this occur?

Strategies for Correcting Discipline Problems

Although encouragement is a powerful strategy for improving behavior, Dreikurs realized that there are times when students need more than encouragement. When encouragement fails to prevent misbehavior from recurring, Dreikurs advised teachers to first identify whether the misbehavior is motivated by a desire for attention, power, revenge, or social withdrawal. He believed that "a teacher needs to understand the psychodynamics of a child and talk with him about his mistaken concepts and attitudes in order to help him to overcome his deficiencies. Getting psychological information and conveying to the child the insight that the teacher was able to gain is an essential part of her function" (Dreikurs & Grey, 1968, p. 57).

Thus, Dreikurs recommended that teachers, in a nonthreatening and supportive manner, confront a misbehaving student, while pointing out that the student's identified maladaptive goal interferes with being socially accepted. The teacher is then to apply procedures designed to correct the misbehavior. These two steps are explained next.

Step 1: Identify and Confront Maladaptive Goals.   In attempting to identify which maladaptive goal is the cause of a given misbehavior, the teacher is not to ask *why* the student misbehaved. Instead, the teacher should ask *for what purpose* did the student act the way he or she did. According to Dreikurs, there is a subtle, yet important, difference between *why* and *for what purpose*. Whereas the former focuses on the student's past, the latter focuses on present intentions. According to Dreikurs, teachers can influence a student's intentions, but not past behavior.

Probing about the purpose of the misbehavior is not to be done at the same time that the misbehavior occurs, however. According to Dreikurs, talking about the problem then is ineffective. Instead, the teacher is to ask about the purpose of the misbehavior later during a *private counseling situation* or in a *classroom discussion* (Dreikurs & Cassel, 1972, p. 42). Dreikurs and Cassel offered the following example of confronting a student for his misbehavior during a private counseling situation:

TEACHER: Do you know why you did———(whatever the misbehavior was)?

STUDENT: No (and at an aware level he probably honestly means it).

TEACHER: Would you like to know? I have some ideas that may be helpful. Would you be willing to listen?

STUDENT: O.K. (usually children will be interested).

TEACHER: (in a nonjudgmental and unemotional way poses all the following four questions; only one guess at a time)

1. Could it be that you want special attention?
2. Could it be that you want your own way and hope to be boss?
3. Could it be that you want to hurt others as much as you feel hurt by them?
4. Could it be that you want to be left alone? (p. 42)

Dreikurs suggested the following corrective procedures for behaviors related to each of the four goals of misbehavior.

For Misbehavior Motivated by

Attention getting: Ignore a student who seeks attention in destructive ways. Don't argue or show annoyance. Be firm. When the student behaves constructively, give attention.

Power: Recognize that the student does have power but avoid a power struggle. Respect the student and seek the student's assistance and agreement.

Revenge: If a student upsets you, don't show it. Apply natural consequences but not punishment (since it fosters more revenge). Try to get a peer to help the student and try to show the student that he is liked. "Do the unexpected" (Dreikurs & Cassel, 1972, p. 44)

Social withdrawal: Try to make the student feel worthwhile. Praise the student for effort and try to convince the student that you're there to help. Seek assistance from classmates. Don't support negative self-statements.

STOP AND REFLECT

In correcting a student's misbehavior, when is it best to refrain from talking about the problem until later? When are Dreikurs's private counseling situations and class discussions most appropriate? Do you agree that "why" questions should be avoided? Do you agree with Dreikurs's recommendations for dealing with behaviors motivated by attention, revenge, power, and social withdrawal?

Step 2: Use Natural and Logical Consequences.   Dreikurs credited the eighteenth-century French philosopher Jean-Jacques Rousseau and the nineteenth-century English philosopher Herbert Spencer for his own ideas on punishment and consequences. He was a harsh critic of the use of punishment, preferring the use of what he and Spencer called *natural consequences* and *logical consequences*. Dreikurs argued that every behavior has a consequence, and that consequences are of two kinds—natural and logical. *Natural consequences* are consequences "denoting the natural results of ill-advised acts" (Dreikurs, 1968, p. 63). In the classroom, natural consequences are the direct result of the student's own actions. According to Dreikurs, teachers do not control natural consequences. Examples of natural consequences are a student injuring himself as a result of running in the halls or being rejected by his peers because of his deviant behaviors (e.g., bullying, bragging). Dreikurs believed that self-discipline is largely learned from natural consequences.

In contrast to natural consequences, *logical consequences* are consequences that are arranged by teachers or other adults (Dreikurs, 1968, p. 65). They are logically related to the behavior being corrected. What differentiates logical consequences from punishment is the intent or motive behind the act. According to Dreikurs (1968), logical consequences are intended to help students learn self-discipline, whereas punishment is "necessarily retaliatory rather than corrective" (p. 67) and intended to harm or control the child. Punishment is "administered with anger, abuse, or denigration of the violator" (Dreikurs & Cassel, 1972, p. 74). Thus, Dreikurs believed that if a teacher intends to inflict pain or to autocratically control a student, the act is one of punishment.

Dreikurs argued that logical consequences have certain advantages over punishment. He argued that, unlike punishment, logical consequences focus on the present, allow for student choice, respect the student, separate the deed from the doer, convey understanding, acceptance and support (not anger), encourage learning, are consistent with democratic (not autocratic) governance, and have "no element of moral judgment" (Dreikurs & Cassel, 1972, p. 64). Dreikurs gave the following examples of the appropriate application of natural and logical consequences:

Behavior problem	*Consequence*
Doesn't complete homework	Gets a zero (natural) or is given detention (logical)
Receives a poor grade	Fails (natural) or is given tutoring (logical)
Defaces property	Has to clean the property (logical)
Gets out of seat	Chair is removed (logical)
Is disobedient	Given in-school suspension (logical)

Dreikurs recommended that logical consequences be used for behaviors motivated by getting attention and natural consequences be used for behaviors motivated by power or revenge. Neither consequence is to be used for social withdrawal.

The Importance of Class Meetings

For purposes of prevention and correction, but particularly the former, Dreikurs (Dreikurs & Cassel, 1972) recommended that teachers hold a weekly class discussion lasting approximately 30 minutes. Class discussions serve to teach listening skills, help students understand themselves and their classmates, and to encourage students to help one another and experience a sense of shared responsibility for classroom behavior. In this manner, they provide lessons and practice in democratic thinking.

The teacher chairs the initial class meetings (posting agreed-upon rules of conduct and reminding students to follow them), with students quickly assuming responsibility for conducting the meetings after observing how they are run. According to Dreikurs, meetings should focus on five issues: (1) good things that happened during the previous week, (2) how students can improve the following week, (3) personal problems, (4) responsibilities, and (5) future plans (Dreikurs & Cassel, 1972). These five topics and points made by students about each topic are written on the board. Discussion is limited to six minutes for each topic. When misbehavior is a topic of concern, the discussion is to center on the goals of misbehavior. More importantly, they are to be constructive, supportive, and nonconfrontational. Dreikurs noted that class discussions help classmates realize that their classmates might have problems similar to theirs, including feelings of inferiority.

In the following example given by Dreikurs, one can see how a class discussion might serve to both prevent and correct behavior problems by focusing on improvements in class behavior, personal problems, responsibilities, and future plans.

> The class has agreed that playing ball near the school windows is not allowed. Billy does so and breaks a window. The class decides at the discussion period that Billy should forfeit part of his allowance over a period of time to pay for the window. In this way, Billy learns to respect property and to realize why he should not play near the windows. (Dreikurs & Cassel, 1972, p. 83)

Dreikurs strongly advocated the use of class discussions, believing that discussions among peers are much more effective in changing an individual's values than are discussions between a teacher and student. Moreover, he believed that class discussions are invaluable in teaching and practicing democracy.

Critique of Dreikurs's Model of Classroom Discipline

Although Dreikurs's ideas were perceived by educators as being progressive, very few of them were new. He credited Adler for his emphasis on the importance of social belonging and self-worth and on how the goals of attention getting, power, revenge, and social withdrawal often interfere with their development. He credited Dewey for his ideas on democratic teaching, Spencer for his distinction between punishment and consequences, and Rousseau for his emphasis on the use of encouragement. Although Dreikurs borrowed these ideas from others, he was the first to incorporate them into a coherent approach for developing self-discipline and for preventing and correcting misbehavior. Unfortunately, Dreikurs seldom cited theory and research to support his ideas and the practices he recommended. To be sure, there was research and much more now, supporting most of his ideas. But to Dreikurs, as well as to developers of more recent variations of his model (e.g., *cooperative discipline* [Albert, 1996], *positive discipline* [Nelsen, Lott, & Glenn, 2000]), research and theory appear to be of little importance in developing a model of classroom discipline.

TABLE 5.1   What the Research Says about Dreikurs's Ideas

Although not all, many of Dreikurs's ideas and recommended strategies are supported by research (to be reviewed in later chapters). In brief, here's what the research says about his key ideas.

Supported by Research:

- The role of self-perceptions of social belonging in determining overall feelings of self-worth and behavior.
- The influence of biased perceptions and individual differences in misbehavior.
- The importance of self-discipline in behavior.
- The role of goals in determining behavior, including the goals of gaining attention, demonstrating power and superiority, seeking revenge, and socially withdrawing.
- The effectiveness of democratic teaching and leadership in developing self-discipline.
- The importance of teacher encouragement and supportive teacher–student relations in preventing misbehavior.
- *How* a student is encouraged or praised often more important than what is actually said.
- The many limitations to the use of punishment and rewards, but particularly the former.
- The influence of natural and logical consequences in determining behavior.
- The usefulness of class meetings, discussions, and peer influence in developing self-discipline and in preventing and correcting misbehavior.

Not Supported by Research:

- The importance of birth order in determining behavior and the belief that personality is fixed by age 6.
- The idea that all misbehavior can be explained by the four goals of gaining attention, demonstrating power and superiority, seeking revenge, and socially withdrawing.
- The idea that praise and rewards, in general, are ineffective.
- The idea that *all* forms of punishment are ineffective and unethical.

Although intuitively appealing, Dreikurs's explanations as to *why* students misbehave are rather simplistic and inconsistent with a wealth of research. Reflecting his psychoanalytic background, he links misbehavior to personality (fixed by age 6), birth order, and four personal goals. Undoubtedly, students often do misbehave to gain attention, to seek revenge, and to experience a sense of power and superiority over others. But there are many other explanations of misbehavior, including impulsivity, lack of social problem-solving and decision-making skills, lack of social skills, poor regulation of emotions, immature moral reasoning, and multiple external factors associated with schools, teachers, peers, homes, and communities. With the exception of teacher–student relations, Dreikurs devotes little attention to these factors.

Dreikurs's model also assumes that students know *why* they misbehave, and that if teachers act like psychotherapists and probed sufficiently, they can unlock students' inner secrets to their misbehavior and know how to intervene effectively. There is little research to support these assumptions. To claim, as did Dreikurs, that bed-wetting is revengeful, speech impediments and eating difficulties are attention-getting behaviors, arguing and dawdling are motivated by power, and "stupidity" is due to a sense of inadequacy, is simply indefensible, particularly in the absence of supporting research and theory. Such assumptions and claims are likely to lead to poorer rather than better understanding of behavior and interventions.

Dreikurs's legacy lies in his distinguishing encouragement from rewards and praise and punishment from logical and natural consequences. Today, many teachers continue to be taught these distinctions in popular models of classroom discipline. Dreikurs deserves much credit for pointing out that the manner by which students are rewarded, praised, or punished is often more important than the rewards, praise, or punishment per se. That is, Dreikurs's approach is correct in noting that praise can be damming when delivered insincerely, rewards are not needed when students are intrinsically motivated, and punishment is likely to be ineffective (especially in the long term) when it is too harsh or delivered out of anger. Likewise, it is wise to warn teachers of the limitations and dangers of the systematic use of rewards, praise, and punishment to control student behavior. Unfortunately, however, instead of simply warning teachers of the limitations of rewards, praise, and punishment, and advising teachers in their judicious, ethical, and effective use, Dreikurs recommended that they be abolished and replaced by "new" methods—methods that are essentially the same as those that good teachers have been using for years, including the use of rewards, praise, and punishment (or "encouragement" and "consequences").

Although Dreikurs tried to distinguish encouragement from praise and rewards, the distinction is subtle, if not confusing. For instance, he gave the following examples of praise compared to encouragement. Upon receiving good grades, a teacher would use encouragement by saying "I'm so glad you enjoy learning" instead of praising the student by saying "I'm so proud of you for getting good grades." For behaving on the school bus during a class trip, a teacher is to provide encouragement by saying "We all enjoyed being together on the school bus" but would not praise the student by saying "I'm proud of you for behaving so nicely on the school bus" (Dreikurs & Cassel, 1972, p. 56). Again, these distinctions are very subtle, confusing, and of undemonstrated value in practice. Moreover, Dreikurs's advice against the use of praise is simply inconsistent with theory and research in developmental and educational psychology. That is, there is no research showing that a teacher stifles self-satisfaction or motivation by conveying that he or she is proud of a student (or, more importantly, of a student's *effort* and *work*). Instead, both theory and research highlight the importance of pride in achievement and behavior and show that teacher praise fosters, rather than stifles, feelings of self-worth (Bear, Minke, Griffin, & Deemer, 1998).

As illustrated in examples presented earlier in this chapter, Dreikurs's distinction between punishment and natural and logical consequences is confusing and misleading. In fairness to Dreikurs, it should be emphasized that he was correct in pointing out limitations to the use of punishment and deserves much credit for bringing these limitations to the attention of educators. It is unfortunate, however, that he advised teachers to avoid *all* forms of punishment. And it is confusing that in their place he recommended the use of logical consequences consisting of the same methods of punishment that good teachers have used for centuries (e.g., verbal reprimands, taking away privileges).

Dreikurs's model is far from being comprehensive, and it focuses much more on elementary school students than those in higher grades. Although it highlights the role of prevention and offers some useful ideas on the correction of everyday discipline problems, it provides very little guidance to teachers regarding how to deal with more serious behavior problems. For example, in a chapter entitled "Conflict Solving and How to Deal with Tyrants," Dreikurs and Cassel (1972) recommended empathy, active listening, respect, understanding the child's motives, and teaching the decision-making process. Such advice is hardly sufficient for dealing with school violence and other serious problems of discipline.

Despite the preceding limitations, several features of Dreikurs's model appealed to teachers in the 1960s and 1970s and continue to do so today. First, Dreikurs's model is student centered, highlighting the importance of social acceptance, self-worth, and self-discipline in learning and behavior. Second, it provides teachers with insight as to why students often misbehave and offers suggestions for changing behavior based on such insight. Third, it emphasizes the critical role of positive teacher–student relations in developing self-discipline. Fourth, it challenges the traditional authoritarian approach to classroom discipline with its emphasis on student control and encourages teachers to be democratic in their teaching by providing students with ample opportunities to learn and practice self-discipline and self-governance. For these good reasons, Dreikurs's model will always remain one of the classic models of classroom discipline.

SUMMARY AND KEY POINTS

According to Dreikurs:

- Autocratic (or authoritarian) and permissive styles of teaching contribute greatly to behavior problems in the classroom and to a variety of societal problems.
- *Democratic education,* which focuses on the development of self-discipline, is the best method for developing self-discipline and for preventing behavior problems.
- Teachers have the moral responsibility to help students develop self-discipline. They do not have the right to impose their will on students or to punish and threaten them.
- In order to meet the needs of students, teachers must gain insight into the personalities of students and the goals of their behavior.
- *Social belonging* is the primary goal of behavior and is central to overall self-worth.
- Students who fail to experience a sense of social belonging turn to other maladaptive goals while misunderstanding that these goals will lead to social acceptance and feelings of self-worth. These goals are attention getting, revenge, power (or superiority), and social withdrawal. They are the major reasons why students misbehave.

- When correcting misbehavior, teachers must identify and confront the student's maladaptive goal. This is best done in a private counseling situation or in a classroom discussion.
- Punishment, praise, and rewards should never be used because they are harmful to learning and to the development of self-discipline. Instead, teachers are to use *encouragement, natural consequences,* and *logical consequences.*

Additional key points:

- Although his terminology is misleading and his approach too psychoanalytic to many educators, Dreikurs made many important and lasting contributions to the field of classroom discipline.
- Dreikurs's model of classroom discipline is best seen today in two popular models: Albert's *cooperative discipline* (Albert, 1996) and *positive discipline* (Nelsen, Lott, & Glenn, 2000). Many more models emphasize the importance of major concepts in Dreikurs's model, especially the importance of supportive teacher–student relations, encouragement, natural and logical consequences, classroom meetings, and a democratic style of teaching.

KEY TERMS AND CONCEPTS

Active and passive forms of goal
seeking
Attention getting as a goal
Classroom meetings
Cooperative discipline

Democratic teaching
Encouragement
Logical consequence
Natural consequence

Power, or superiority, as a goal
Revenge as a goal
Social belonging as a goal
Social withdrawal as a goal

RECOMMENDED READINGS AND RESOURCES

Books on Dreikurs's Model of Classroom Discipline and Recent Models Based Primarily on Dreikurs's Work

Albert, L. (1996). *Cooperative discipline.* Circle Pines, MN: American Guidance Service.

Albert, L. (1996). *Cooperative discipline implementation guide.* Circle Pines, MN: American Guidance Service.

Dreikurs, R., & Cassel, P. (1972). *Discipline without tears: What to do with children who misbehave.* New York: Hawthorn Books.

Dreikurs, R., & Grey, L. (1968). *Logical consequences: A handbook of discipline.* New York: Meredith Press.

Dreikurs, R., Grunwald, B. B., & Pepper, F. C. (1982). *Maintaining sanity in the classroom: Classroom management techniques.* New York: Harper & Row.

Nelsen, J., Lott, L., & Glenn, H. (2000). *Positive discipline in the classroom.* Rocklin, CA: Prima.

REFERENCES

Albert, L. (1996). *Cooperative discipline implementation guide.* Circle Pines, MN: American Guidance Service.

Bear, G. G., Minke, K. M., Griffin, S. M., & Deemer, S. A. (1998). Achievement-related perceptions of children with learning disabilities and normal achievement: Group and developmental differences. *Journal of Learning Disabilities, 31,* 91–104.

Dinkmeyer, D., & Dreikurs, R. (1963). *Encouraging children to learn: The encouragement process.* Upper Saddle River, NJ: Prentice-Hall.

Dreikurs, R. (1968). *Psychology in the classroom: A manual for teachers.* New York: Harper & Row.

Dreikurs, R., & Cassel, P. (1972). *Discipline without tears: What to do with children who misbehave.* New York: Hawthorn Books.

Dreikurs, R., & Grey, L. (1968). *Logical consequences: A handbook of discipline.* New York: Meredith Press.

Dreikurs, R., Grunwald, B. B., & Pepper, F. C. (1982). *Maintaining sanity in the classroom: Classroom management techniques.* New York: Harper Collins.

Lewin, K., Lippitt, R., & White, R. K. (1939). Patterns of aggressive behavior in experimentally created "social climates." *Journal of Social Psychology, 10,* 271–299.

Nelsen, J., Lott, L., & Glenn, H. (2000). *Positive discipline in the classroom.* Rocklin, CA: Prima.

6

Responsible Choices and Confrontation

Glasser's Model of Classroom Discipline

GUIDING QUESTIONS

- What psychological needs do students have that should be of concern to educators? Do educators have a responsibility to meet these needs?

- Is misbehavior best viewed as a *choice* made by the student?

- Is it harmful for students to feel guilty after they misbehave? Is it wrong for teachers to try to induce guilt?

- How do the teacher–student relationship and the overall school atmosphere influence student behavior and the development of social responsibility?
- Are class meetings an effective means of addressing issues of classroom discipline?
- In correcting misbehavior, when should confrontation be used?
- What impact do teaching and the curriculum have on discipline problems?
- In what ways are Glasser's philosophy, strategies, and techniques similar to those of Dreikurs and to those that characterized earlier educators in the history of classroom discipline?

> No one is more aware of the problems of failing children than those who work in the schools. Almost every teacher and administrator I have spoken to in the past several years has been disturbed, puzzled, and in many cases disheartened over the increasing numbers of children who seem to be totally recalcitrant to the school process. They are rebellious, they do not read, they are unmotivated, they are withdrawn, they are apathetic. They seem to be impossible to educate. *The major problem of the schools is a problem of failure.* (Glasser, 1969, pp. 6–7)

> As I stated in the beginning of the chapter, school children should have some part in making the rules of their school. They do not decide, however, whether or not rules, once established, should be enforced. They may choose to disobey the rules; this choice is open to all. But they then have to accept the consequences of their choice. If my suggestions for discipline are taken totally out of context and represented as "Follow our rules or be kicked out," they make no sense. Rules should be reasonable; they should be changed when conditions change; they should, when possible, be decided upon jointly by faculty and students; and they should be enforced. (Glasser, 1969, p. 193)

William Glasser began his lengthy and productive career in education and psychology working with children and adolescents who were experiencing a wide range of social and emotional problems. Like Dreikurs, he was a practicing psychotherapist. In addition to a private practice, he devoted eleven years to helping adolescent girls with conduct disorders at a private residential school. Drawing largely from these experiences, in 1965 Glasser wrote his classic book *Reality Therapy* in which he challenged many of the practices that mental health professionals and educators were using with children and adolescents. In particular, he questioned Freudian-based therapeutic practices, such as focusing on children's past experiences and helping them gain "insight" into the reasons for their misbehavior. Reality therapy offered an alternative approach that Glasser believed could be used by mental health workers, teachers, and parents.

In 1969 Glasser published *Schools Without Failure,* which quickly became one of the most widely read books on education. In this book Glasser applied principles of reality therapy to the schools, particularly schools in inner cities, and argued forcefully that most mental health problems among children and adolescents could be prevented by preventing school failure. Discipline problems were viewed as an outcome of school failure and as a common indicator of mental health problems. Hundreds of thousands of teachers received in-service training in reality therapy and many more read his books and applied his teachings to practice. As seen in this chapter, much of his teachings, philosophy, and strategies for classroom discipline continue to be popular today, especially Glasser's emphasis on psychological needs, choice and responsibility, social problem solving, the role of academic failure in classroom discipline, class meetings, and the use of confrontation when correcting misbehavior. Glasser continues to write on issues of education and classroom discipline and has offered more recent theories or models of educational reform. However, with respect to classroom discipline, it is his early ideas that have had the most lasting impact on actual practice.

Teachings and Philosophy in Glasser's Reality Therapy

The philosophy underlying Glasser's reality therapy model of classroom discipline can be gleaned from *Reality Therapy* (Glasser, 1965) and *Schools Without Failure* (Glasser, 1969), although in neither book does Glasser claim to propose a model of classroom discipline per se. In the first book he proposes a new type of *therapy* that can be used by teachers and parents, as well as psychologists and counselors. In the second book he addresses the more general issue of schools failing to meet the academic, social, and emotional needs of students. Together, however, the two books provide the basis for his model of classroom discipline.

Glasser argues that a major aim of schools should be to help meet the psychological needs of all children and adolescents. He believes that too many schools not only fail to recognize the importance of this aim but also fail to adopt practices to help achieve it. As a result of these failures, teachers should expect to face not only everyday *discipline incidents* but also more frequent and more serious *discipline problems*. Reality therapy offers educators a model for preventing and correcting both discipline incidents and discipline problems. The model was built on a philosophy of education that sounds much like that of earlier progressive educators. With respect to student behavior, Glasser balances the needs and democratic rights of students with those of teachers. He offers much insight into teacher- and school-related factors that often contribute to student failure and discipline problems. Central among these factors is the quality of the teacher–student relationship. Glasser argues that in order to develop self-discipline and prevent discipline problems it is critical that teachers attend to the *psychological needs* of their students and recognize the important roles of *choice and responsibility* in the development of self-discipline. These two concepts are central to his philosophy and are reviewed next. After reviewing these two concepts, Glasser's strategies for developing self-discipline and for preventing and correcting discipline problems are presented.

Children's Psychological Needs

According to reality therapy, all individuals have two basic *psychological needs.* The first is *relatedness,* or to love and be loved. The second is *self-worth,* or to feel worthwhile. Relatedness and self-worth are intertwined: A student who fails to experience relatedness is unlikely to feel worthwhile and a student who does not feel worthwhile is unlikely to relate well to others. These two needs are central to one's self-identity and overall self-esteem and, thus, to self-discipline. When these needs are not met, discipline problems are likely to evolve. When not met over time, more serious academic, social, and emotional problems are likely, including dropping out of school, social withdrawal, suicide, school violence, and juvenile delinquency.

In helping students feel a sense of relatedness and positive self-worth, Glasser emphasizes that teachers (and parents) must demonstrate warmth, care, and support. As such, from the standpoint of both psychological needs and teaching strategies, Glasser clearly recognizes the role of emotions in mental health and classroom behavior. To be sure, with respect to classroom behavior Glasser believes emotions are of secondary importance when it comes to prevention and correction. How students actually act is of greatest importance. To Glasser, when behaviors improve, so do emotions. He asserts that students cannot feel good about themselves until *after* they stop engaging in irresponsible behavior. Once students decide to change their behavior and do so, they will feel more worthwhile. In turn, their behavior will continue to improve. In this sense, feeling worthwhile is viewed as both a motivator and an outcome of good behavior as well as success in school and life.

STOP AND REFLECT

In addition to the critical needs of relatedness and feeling worthwhile, what needs do you think students have that teachers should address? How about feelings of autonomy? How about self-perceptions of competence in important areas of one's self-concept, such as in academics, behavioral conduct, sports, peer relations, and physical appearance? Recent research shows that self-perceptions in these areas are a major determinant of overall self-worth or self-esteem. Should children's needs in these areas also be addressed by educators? If so, how might they be addressed?

② Choice and Responsibility

Like Dreikurs, Glasser highlights the role of personal needs in human behavior, but he is perhaps best known for emphasizing the roles of *choice* and *responsibility* in developing self-discipline (including feelings of self-worth) and in preventing and correcting misbehavior. According to Glasser, students often fail to meet their own needs because of the way they act. That is, they act in ways that interfere with their own needs and the needs of others, and they *choose* to do so. *Their choice* to exhibit behaviors that violate societal norms prevents them from developing and maintaining close relations with others. Because they choose to misbehave, they should assume responsibility for the negative consequences that typically follow misbehavior. Glasser recognizes that poverty, poor parenting, and a host of other individual and environmental factors influence student misbehavior, but he maintains that misbehavior almost always reflects a personal choice: Students *choose* to cheat, lie, steal, bully others, disrupt the classroom, and so forth.

According to Glasser, responsibility for behavior rests with the individual student, but schools have a social responsibility to help them make the right choices. This is best done within the context of a supportive teacher–student relationship and within a school atmosphere in which responsibility and democratic decision making are directly and indirectly taught and practiced. As described by Glasser (1969), it is necessary that students are taught in a "nonpunitive, open, honest, problem-solving environment in which children can live a moral life, not just pay lip service to it. In schools without such an environment, morality and responsibility will be only words for most children" (p. 186).

With respect to responsibility, Glasser believes that guilt is a major motivator of moral behavior. That is, many students and adults refrain from moral transgressions out of the anticipation of feelings of guilt. According to Glasser, guilt also is instrumental in correcting misbehavior: Students are unlikely to change their misbehavior unless it becomes apparent to them that such behavior is inconsistent with how they *should* behave according to societal and internalized standards and norms. Hence, guilt occurs when students recognize that they are responsible for doing something that they should not have done. Glasser argues that the induction of guilt, when used within a context of a supportive relationship, is healthy and need not be avoided. Not only does guilt or the anticipation of guilt help students behave in accordance with moral standards and values, but also, in turn, it helps protect their sense of self-worth. As noted by Glasser (1965):

> Happiness occurs most often when we are willing to take responsibility for our behavior. Irresponsible people, always seeking to gain happiness without assuming responsibility, find only brief periods of joy, but not the deep-seated satisfaction which accompanies responsible behavior. (p. 29)

STOP AND REFLECT

In general, is guilt healthy? When are feelings of guilt harmful or helpful in the development of self-discipline? What do teachers do to inculcate guilt in students? What role did guilt play in your own moral development?

Strategies for Developing Self-Discipline and for Preventing and Correcting Misbehavior

In addition to insight as to why misbehavior occurs, reality therapy provides educators with a wealth of thoughtful strategies for developing self-discipline and for preventing and correcting misbehavior. Many of the strategies are general ones, consisting of basic principles of classroom and school effectiveness. Others are more concrete, specific, and useful. As noted previously, these strategies can be seen in many other popular models of classroom discipline.

Strategies for Preventing Discipline Problems

> Unless we can provide schools where children, through a reasonable use of their capacities, can succeed, we will do little to solve the major problems of our country. (Glasser, 1969, p. 6)

In reality therapy, Glasser argues that nearly all behavior problems in school could be prevented and self-discipline promoted, if educators adhered to the following:

Create and Maintain a Warm, Positive, and Supportive Relationship with Each Student. In reality therapy, Glasser asserts that behavior problems are inevitable whenever a student's two basic needs, relatedness and self-worth, are not met. He also argues that schools cannot count on these needs being met at home or in the community. Consequently, in many instances, teachers are the best ones to meet the psychological needs of children and adolescents. And the best method is conveying warmth and support. In addition to helping meet psychological needs of students, warmth and support promote a relationship of trust and mutual respect that fosters social, moral, and academic growth. Like Dreikurs, Glasser believes that warmth and support characterize a democratic style of teaching, as opposed to the traditional authoritarian style.

Teach Students Social Problem Solving and Responsibility. Glasser strongly endorses the *social-problem-solving process,* in which students are taught to *identify* a social problem, *discuss* its importance, *brainstorm* reasonable alternative solutions, *make a commitment to a chosen solution,* and *implement* the solution chosen. As described later, Glasser developed the social-problem-solving classroom meeting for the purpose of teaching and practicing the social-problem-solving process. He views this process as superior to "the present process of blindly obeying (or breaking) rules and unthinkingly echoing back right (or wrong) answers to questions raised by others" (Glasser, 1969, p. 37). In addition to teaching students how to apply the social-problem-solving process in the context of classroom discussions about social problems, Glasser encourages teachers to guide students through the social-problem-solving process whenever they *correct* student misbehavior.

Teach Values, Including Moral Values. Glasser has never refrained from endorsing the teaching of moral values, or indoctrination. Indeed, he believes that *it is the school's social responsibility to do so*. As such, democratic and moral values should permeate the school atmosphere and should be taught using both direct and indirect methods of instruction. In response to advocates of the cultural relativism viewpoint that all values are culturally relative and, thus, values should not be taught, Glasser suggests that the teaching of moral values should be restricted to those moral values with which few, if any, citizens would disagree. As such, he strongly recommends that real-life discipline problems in the classroom concerning moral values, such as lying, bullying, cheating, and stealing, be discussed. They are to be discussed openly and honestly and in the context of social-problem-solving classroom meetings. During these discussions, teachers are to help students come to understand the importance of responsible behavior and acting in accordance with one's values.

STOP AND REFLECT

To answer the argument that problems of morality belong strictly to the home or church, I can say only that I believe that, whatever the effectiveness of the home and church, when a problem of morality exists in school, the school should not avoid it. (Glasser, 1969, p. 189)

Do you agree or disagree with Glasser's opinion? What problems of morality should be discussed in school?

Provide Opportunities for Students to Participate in Democratic Decision Making and Governance.   Consistent with the philosophies of Dewey and progressive educators, Glasser believes that "Democracy is best learned by living it!" (1969, p. 37). He argues that students of all ages should be granted ample opportunities to experience and practice democracy. As such, students should have a voice in determining classroom rules and consequences, as well as the curriculum. Having a voice does not mean that they are to decide on the rules, consequences, and curriculum, but only that their input is solicited and respected. Students also are to have an active voice and to assume a major responsibility in solving social problems in the classroom. As described later, classroom meetings are critical to teaching and *living* democracy.

Use Motivating Teaching Methods and Curricula.   In *Schools Without Failure,* as well as in his more recent writings, Glasser (1969) stresses that the *key* to preventing school failure, including discipline problems, is the use of teaching methods and curricula that are relevant, stimulating, and above all, not boring. *How* and *what* teachers teach are viewed as having the greatest influence on student behavior. Accordingly, it is foolish for teachers to expect students to behave during lengthy lectures and boring projects. Such practices invite behavior problems and should be avoided. In contrast, the use of a variety of stimulating methods of teaching helps prevent misbehavior as well as academic failure.

Avoid Educational Practices That Might Result in Labeling.   Practices that stigmatize students as failures are to be avoided because they block students from feeling worthwhile. This includes grading practices and grouping students homogeneously according to ability. Glasser believes that mixed-ability groupings are best for academic achievement, as well as for social and emotional development. According to Glasser, all students learn best from one another when in mixed groups. In homogeneous groups the learning and self-worth of low-achieving students suffer. Glasser recognizes, however, that there often is a need for some homogeneous reading groups (after second grade) and for special or alternative placements for a small number of students with serious social and emotional problems.

hetero vs. homo. grouping

Classroom Meetings: A Strategy for Preventing and Correcting Discipline Problems

Although Glasser offered many strategies for preventing and correcting discipline problems, the *classroom meeting* is perhaps his most popular contribution to classroom discipline. Glasser was not the first to recommend that teachers hold class meetings in which the teacher and students discuss various topics of importance, including problems of behavior. For years teachers had held similar class meetings. Much earlier in the twentieth century progressive educators began the homeroom concept in high schools for the same purpose. Dreikurs, who wrote at about the same time as Glasser, also endorsed classroom meetings. Glasser expanded the concept, however, recommending that classroom meetings be held daily and be of three types: (1) the social-problem-solving meeting, which focuses on student behavior, (2) the open-ended meeting, which focuses on intellectually important subjects, and (3) the educational-diagnostic meeting, which involves student understanding of academic lessons. All three provide teaching and practice in democratic decision making. Because the social-problem-solving classroom meeting is the one that focuses on issues of classroom discipline, it will be discussed here.

Glasser argues that all schools should teach students how to solve social problems (as well as understand that many social problems are difficult to solve), while noting that few schools do so. The social-problem-solving meeting is to help fill this void. Social-problem-solving classroom meetings are to address both individual and group problems, such as teasing, tardiness to class, failure to complete classwork and homework, and so forth.

In solving individual and group social problems, students are taught the following social-problem-solving steps:

1. **Identify the problem.** (What exactly happened? What is the problem we need to discuss and solve?)
2. **Discuss its importance to the class.** (Why is this a problem? How does it influence everyone involved, including the class?)
3. **Brainstorm alternative solutions.** (What are some good solutions to this problem?)
4. **Make a commitment to the solution chosen.** (Do you agree that the best solution should be chosen?)
5. **Implement the solution.** (How can we apply this solution? Do we need a plan? If so, what should the plan look like?)

During classroom meetings, students are to be seated in a circle so that everyone can see one another. Meetings should last 10 to 30 minutes for children in lower grades and 30 to 45 minutes for children in higher grades. The duration of a meeting is less important than its regular occurrence and the pertinence of the problems discussed. The role of the teacher is to lead and facilitate discussion, while remaining nonjudgmental and ensuring that the classroom atmosphere is nonfaultfinding and nonpunitive. Such an atmosphere is necessary to help students feel confident about their ability to solve social problems. Students are encouraged to confront the socially inappropriate behavior of their peers in an open and honest fashion. Although the teacher is to remain nonjudgmental, the teacher is to encourage students to judge the behavior of their peers, especially behaviors that interfere with the needs and rights of others. Glasser understood that students often respond better to criticism and guidance from peers than from adults.

Social-problem-solving meetings teach students how to solve problems, remind them of their individual and group responsibilities, and provide a means by which individual and group behavior can be monitored. Feedback from students should be constructive and should include social reinforcement of appropriate behavior. Glasser (1969) made the following observations of a social-problem-solving class meeting that centered on a classmate who was a bully:

> First, often the solution to the problem of such a child lies not so much in coming up with an exact answer, but in the discussion itself. . . . Second, after he is discussed several times, discussion of the bully might be avoided. Unless he does something worthwhile or constructive, he is not talked about; if he does something constructive, it is mentioned. This technique removes the attention that he is getting through aggressive behavior and focuses on constructive, positive action. The teacher might say, "There is no sense talking about Johnny because he is doing the same thing everyone is complaining about. Let's wait until we talk about

something else he might do that the class would like." Johnny, hearing this and needing attention, will often improve his behavior.

It is important, therefore, in class meetings for the teacher, but not the class, to be nonjudgmental. The class makes judgments and from these judgments works toward positive solutions. (pp. 130–131)

Strategies for Correcting Discipline Problems

To be sure, Glasser emphasizes that most behavior problems can be prevented, including everyday, or normal, discipline incidents and less common, but more serious, discipline problems. However, he is well aware that both discipline incidents and discipline problems arise in all classrooms, including those of the best teachers, and that the classroom meeting is not the best context for correcting misbehavior. To Glasser, misbehavior is irresponsible behavior and is not to be tolerated. Thus, according to reality therapy, teachers are to correct misbehavior not only for the purpose of maintaining an atmosphere conducive to learning but also for the purpose of helping to develop self-discipline. When classroom meetings are inappropriate or ineffective in correcting a student's misbehavior, teachers are to take a more confrontational approach.

Facing Reality with Confrontation.   Disciplinary encounters are to be handled in a calm, firm, supportive, yet somewhat confrontational style guided by the problem-solving process. For example, the teacher would use the following steps:

1. When the student misbehaves, the teacher directs the student to stop and redirects the student's attention (e.g., "Let's stop talking to Carlos and get back to work").
2. If the behavior continues, the teacher confronts the student, asking the student first to *identify* the misbehavior (e.g., "What are you doing?").
3. The teacher then asks the student to *evaluate* the misbehavior and make a value commitment not to do it again (e.g., "Is that something that you should do? Do you think you should keep doing it?").
4. Next, the teacher requires the student to make a corrective plan for preventing the behavior from happening again (e.g., "What can you do next time to make sure the same thing doesn't happen?").
5. If the misbehavior is repeated, the teacher firmly tells the student that the behavior must stop and reminds the student of the commitment to stop the misbehavior and of the corrective plan made.
6. If the misbehavior continues, in-class time-out is used.
7. If the misbehavior continues, in-school time-out or in-school suspension is used.
8. If the misbehavior continues, out-of-school suspension is used.
9. If the foregoing are unsuccessful, the student is referred to placement in an alternative education program.

Teachers are to focus on present behavior, not past behavior, and not on excuses for the misbehavior. Although they are to ask "What are you doing?" they are to avoid asking "Why?" (recall that Dreikurs also opposed why questions). Teachers are not to lecture, dictate, or preach. Glasser believes that engaging in these common practices does little to teach responsibility for one's actions because the teacher, not the student, makes a value judgment about the behavior (e.g., "Stealing is wrong. Here's the punishment"). Glasser believes that it is the student's, and not the teacher's, responsibility to make a value judgment about a misbehavior. Teachers are not to allow students to relinquish their responsibility. Thus, they shouldn't hesitate to confront, or challenge, a student's misbehavior, making it clear that the misbehavior is wrong. To Glasser, moral values are not relative: An effective teacher recognizes right from wrong and has a social obligation to teach students the same. Teachers are not encouraged to lecture, dictate, or preach, but they also should not allow wrongful acts to go unchallenged.

Confrontation is appropriate when students deny reality, which includes responsibility for their misbehavior. In reality therapy, facing reality is critical to behavior change. Before students can make a commitment to changing behavior, they first have to recognize that the behavior is wrong and accept responsibility for the wrongful act. In developing a plan for improving behavior, students are to think of alternatives and evaluate them. When necessary, the teacher provides assistance. It is critical, however, that the individual student, not the teacher, choose among the alternatives, make a value judgment about the chosen alternative, and commit himself or herself to changing the behavior. Where appropriate (e.g., with repeated offenses), the plan is to be presented as a written contract between the teacher and student. However, a written plan is developed only if the student makes a commitment to change his or her behavior. The teacher is to hold the student to his or her committed course of action. Excuses for failing to adhere to the commitment are not to be accepted. As stated by Glasser, "Finally, and this is the keystone of Reality Therapy, when a child makes a value judgment and a commitment to change his behavior, no excuse is acceptable for not following through. This is discipline" (Glasser, 1969, p. 23).

If the student fails to follow the written plan, negative consequences will follow. As noted earlier, Glasser understood that changes in behavior generally precede changes in attitudes and values. Thus, teachers are to be persistent in making sure changes in behavior occur for the purpose of not only improving present behavior but also producing more lasting changes in behavior by influencing the student's attitudes and values.

Regardless of the offense and the student's response to correction, the teacher is to exhibit unwavering support and acceptance of the individual student. Although it is appropriate for the teacher to judge a behavior to be wrong and to challenge the student's choice to misbehave, the teacher nevertheless should convey that the student is still "lovable." As also emphasized by Dreikurs, it is the student's behavior, not the student as a person, that the teacher does not like.

STOP AND REFLECT

Read and reflect on the following quote from Glasser. Do you agree with the importance he places on a student's making a value judgment about a behavior in order for a change in behavior to occur? How about his view toward the necessity that students "must suffer the consequences" of misbehavior?

To help a presently failing child to succeed, we must get him to make a value judgment about what he is now doing that is contributing to his failure. If he doesn't believe that what he is doing is contributing to his failure, if he believes his behavior is all right, no one can change the child now. He must then suffer the consequences of his refusal to change his behavior. Neither school nor therapist should attempt to manipulate the world so that the child does not suffer the reasonable consequences of this behavior. But we should not give up; accepting failure is not a reasonable consequence. (Glasser, 1969, p. 21)

Using Discipline but Not Corporal Punishment. Glasser supports the use of punitive corrective techniques but avoids the use of the term *punishment,* preferring the term *discipline.* To Glasser, punishment and discipline differ. However, he never makes it exactly clear how they differ except that, unlike discipline, punishment consists of the arbitrary infliction of pain following an undesirable behavior. Glasser clearly opposes the use of *corporal punishment,* believing it to be ineffective and a barrier to constructive and collaborative social problem solving. To Glasser, punishment produces fear, and fear is ineffective in motivating students to change their behavior. He also strongly objects to public ridicule and sarcasm, equating them with corporal punishment. Glasser notes that these strategies might be effective in producing short-term changes in behavior, but they rarely produce lasting improvements. Glasser recognizes that reinforcement of appropriate behavior is a much more effective strategy for changing behavior. In contrast to punishment, Glasser argues that discipline "asks only that a student evaluate his behavior and commit himself to a better course" (Glasser, 1969, p. 23). "Reasonable" consequences also are appropriate, but especially when a student refuses to accept responsibility for his or her behavior and make a commitment to change. This distinction is similar to that made by Dreikurs in distinguishing punishment from natural and logical consequences, reflecting an attempt to sanitize punishment by calling it something else.

Although Glasser is against corporal punishment, he advocates for other common forms of punishment (or what he simply refers to as consequences). For example, Glasser supports removal of students from the classroom as a consequence of misbehavior. Depending on the chronicity and severity of their misbehavior, students are sent to a time-out place within the class where they reflect on the plans they committed to; an in-school suspension room elsewhere in the building; or out-of-school suspension. If removed from the classroom and sent to the principal for in-school or out-of-school suspension, the principal is to respond in a nonpunitive, problem-solving manner. Glasser recommends that a student's return to the classroom be a topic of discussion at a classroom meeting, because the student's behavior affected the entire class, not just the misbehaving student.

Control Theory: Glasser's More Recent Version of Reality Therapy

In 1986, Glasser published *Control Theory in the Classroom.* Unfortunately, the book, or new model of classroom discipline, offers teachers few ideas that have not already been presented in his previous works. An exception is that instead of the two basic needs, as Glasser presents in reality therapy, five are now proposed. Relatedness and the need to feel worthwhile are collapsed into one need, *to belong and love,* and added are the following needs: *to survive and reproduce, to gain power, to be free,* and *to have fun.* Among these needs, to gain power is seen as the greatest source of behavior problems. Glasser (as cited in Brandt, 1987) notes:

> I believe that the need for power is the core—the absolute core—of almost all school problems. Even the good students don't feel all that important in school, and the students who receive poor grades certainly can't feel important from the standpoint of academic performance. So they say to themselves, "I won't work in a place in which I have no sense of personal importance, in which I have no power, in which no one listens to me." Literally no one in the world who isn't struggling for bare survival will do intellectual work, unless he or she has a sense of personal importance. (p. 658)

Unlike in his previous writings, Glasser does not make it exactly clear how the need for power, or how any of the other needs, relates to teaching and classroom discipline, although he links the need for power to student motivation. The central theme of control theory is that school practices, especially *how* and *what* teachers teach, are responsible for a student's sense of power. If a student fails to meet his or her need for power in a constructive way, such as in academic success, the student will meet it in destructive ways. Typically, this is done by acting out. Recall that Dreikurs also viewed power, or superiority, as a maladaptive goal that often leads to misbehavior.

In control theory Glasser continues to argue, as he did forty years ago in previous publications, that students *choose* to behave or misbehave. However, he places much greater emphasis on the responsibility of schools in determining student behavior. To be sure, as in reality therapy, the focus of control theory is on the individual: Individuals act to fulfill their five needs and their actions are self-determined rather than determined by the environment. But whereas students can control their own actions, so too can schools control student behavior by preventing school failure. This theme is similar to the basic theme presented much earlier by Glasser in *Schools Without Failure:* Schools can prevent failure by creating a caring, noncoercive atmosphere and by adopting practices that meet each student's needs for power and belonging.

With the exception of general strategies for preventing school failure, such as the use of "learning teams" (i.e., cooperative learning) that receives much attention in control theory, very little in control theory is specific to classroom discipline. Unfortunately, as concluded by Charles (2002), control theory and Glasser's more recent books on quality schools and educational reform (Glasser, 1998a, 1998b) can best be described as "old wine in new bottles," offering few new ideas on classroom discipline.

Critique of Glasser's Reality Therapy

Glasser offers educators many excellent suggestions for classroom discipline as well as school reform. Although reality therapy does not provide a comprehensive model of classroom discipline, which it was not designed to do, it has greatly impacted the way many teachers think about and practice classroom discipline. Like Dreikurs, Glasser borrows many of his ideas from progressive educators that preceded him, arguing that motivating teaching and curriculum, caring teachers, and democratic practices in the classroom are the keys to preventing classroom discipline problems. Few of his ideas are new to education. What appealed to many teachers in the 1960s, and continues to do so today, is Glasser's emphasis on students needing to assume responsibility for their own actions, as well as the actions of the class. To be sure, teachers are to share responsibility for the behavior of the class, as emphasized in Glasser's more recent writings, especially the responsibility of helping teach students to make the right choices and to follow through with them. When discipline problems occur, they are to provide systematic guidance in social problem solving, confront the behavior using a problem-solving approach, strive to obtain a commitment from the misbehaving students to change their behavior, and implement a behavior improvement plan, when necessary. If the plan is not adhered to, punitive consequences are to follow. Thus, responsibility for changing behavior is certainly shared. However, much emphasis is placed on the student's responsibility or self-discipline.

In addition to his emphasis on responsibility and choice, Glasser is perhaps best known for classroom meetings. In the 1960s, 1970s, and 1980s many teachers adopted this strategy and many continue to use it today. It provides students with the opportunity to participate in democratic decision making, experience a sense of classroom community, and solve social problems cooperatively. The classroom meeting reflects Glasser's balanced approach to classroom discipline in which both teachers and students share responsibility for developing self-discipline and for preventing and correcting misbehavior.

Unfortunately, Glasser does not always present his ideas in a practical and useful manner. When reading *Reality Therapy* and *Schools Without Failure,* teachers have to struggle to tease out practical and relevant classroom strategies and techniques. It also is likely that many teachers question Glasser's idea (shared by Dreikurs) that teachers are to function as therapists who counsel individual students in developing values and personal decision-making skills. Indeed, it is questionable if many teachers have adequate training to perform this role effectively. Likewise, it is questionable if many teachers, especially in the upper grades, have adequate time to fill this role.

As is true with most models of classroom discipline, little empirical research has been published on the effectiveness of reality therapy. The few studies that have been published have yielded mixed results, with most showing that reality therapy has no effects on the achievement and attitudes of students or on the attitudes of teachers (Emmer & Aussiker, 1990). More encouraging results were found in a study that looked at the effects of class meetings. Marandola and Imber (1979) found that class meetings are effective in reducing arguing among students. Despite the lack of research on reality therapy, recent theory and research support many of the basic strategies and techniques incorporated into the model, as will be seen in later chapters. This includes the importance of supportive teacher–student relations in which the teacher demonstrates care and warmth but also holds high expectations and standards regarding appropriate behavior, the effectiveness of teaching social problem solving in both individual and group contexts, the critical role of motivating teaching and curricula in preventing discipline problems, the importance of teaching students to be responsible for their own choices and behavior, and the value of targeting students' thoughts, feelings, and behavior when attempting to prevent and correct behavior problems.

SUMMARY AND KEY POINTS

- Like Dreikurs and progressive educators who preceded him, Glasser argues that classroom discipline should emphasize the development of self-discipline and the prevention of discipline problems.
- In reality therapy, Glasser asserts that the two basic psychological needs of children and adolescents that motivate behavior are relatedness and self-worth. In his later writings he adds the needs of survival, power, freedom, and fun.
- In reality therapy, Glasser places great emphasis on the role of choice and responsibility in behavior. Thus, when students misbehave they should assume responsibility for their behavior and accept the consequences.
- For developing self-discipline and preventing misbehavior, Glasser emphasizes the importance of warm and supportive teacher–student relations; teaching social problem solving, responsibility, and values; the active involvement of students in democratic decision making and governance; the use of motivating teaching methods and curricula; and the avoidance of grouping, grading, and other practices that result in labeling.
- Social-problem-solving classroom meetings are of central importance in Glasser's model of classroom discipline. They help teach social problem solving, remind students of their individual and group responsibilities, and provide a means by which the class can monitor and respond to the behavior of classmates.
- Glasser believes that discipline problems are to be confronted in a calm and firm manner. In confronting misbehavior, the teacher is to encourage students to reflect on their values and behavior and to make a commitment to change their behavior.
- Although Glasser is against corporal punishment and often equates it with the term *punishment,* it is clear that he endorses many traditional forms of punishment (or what he calls discipline). He supports reasonable punitive consequences, including time-out and suspension.
- Since first publishing *Reality Therapy* and *Schools Without Failure* in the 1960s, Glasser has published many other books on school reform and discipline and offered new classroom models. Although his more recent writings place much emphasis on the responsibility of schools in preventing school failure, for the most part they present the same important concepts Glasser introduced in his first two classic books.
- Although there is a lack of research on the effectiveness of Glasser's model of classroom discipline per se, ample theory and research support the strategies and techniques that he recommends.

KEY TERMS AND CONCEPTS

Class meetings	Discipline incidents versus	Reality therapy
Choice in behavior	discipline problems	Relatedness
Confrontation	Glasser, William	Responsibility and choice
Control theory	Guilt	Self-worth
Democratic governing	Personal needs	Social-problem-solving process

RECOMMENDED READINGS AND RESOURCES

Glasser, W. (1965). *Reality therapy.* New York: Harper & Row.

Glasser, W. (1969). *Schools without failure.* New York: Harper & Row.

Glasser, W. (1986). *Control theory in the classroom.* New York: Harper & Row.

Glasser, W. (1998a). *The quality school: Managing students without coercion.* New York: Harper & Row.

Glasser, W. (1998b). *The quality school teacher.* New York: HarperCollins.

REFERENCES

Brandt, R. (March, 1987). On students' needs and team learning: A conversation with William Glasser. *Educational Leadership,* 38–45.

Charles, C. W. (2002). *Building classroom discipline.* Boston: Allyn and Bacon.

Emmer, E., & Aussiker, A. (1990). School and classroom discipline programs: How well do they work? In O. C. Moles (Ed.), *Student discipline strategies: Research and practice* (pp. 129–167). New York: State University of New York Press.

Glasser, W. (1965). *Reality therapy.* New York: Harper & Row.

Glasser, W. (1969). *Schools without failure.* New York: Harper & Row.

Glasser, W. (1986). *Control theory in the classroom.* New York: Harper & Row.

Glasser, W. (1998a). *The quality school: Managing students without coercion.* New York: Harper & Row.

Glasser, W. (1998b). *The quality school teacher.* New York: HarperCollins.

Marandola, P., & Imber, S. C. (1979). Glasser's classroom meeting: A humanistic approach to behavior change with preadolescent inner-city learning disabled children. *Journal of Learning Disabilities, 12,* 383–387.

CHAPTER

7

Assertive Discipline

From "Take Charge" to "Be Positive"

GUIDING QUESTIONS

- Do teachers have the right to be assertive and control behavior? With respect to classroom discipline, should this be their primary aim?
- What does assertive discipline teach students? To what extent does it teach self-discipline?

128

- How does assertive discipline differ from Dreikurs's and Glasser's models of classroom discipline? How does its basic philosophy compare to that of other approaches to classroom discipline used in previous centuries?
- In what basic ways does the 1976 version of assertive discipline differ from the most recent 2001 version? Was the 1976 model much more than names on the board and marbles in a jar?
- How is the 2001 version of assertive discipline a "positive" approach to classroom discipline?
- Which techniques of assertive discipline are of most value to the classroom teacher?

"An assertive teacher is one who clearly and firmly expresses her wants and feelings to the children and is prepared to back up her words with actions. She clearly tells the children what behavior is acceptable and which is unacceptable. The assertive teacher recognizes the fact that she has wants and needs and has the right to get them met in the classroom." (Canter, 1976, p. 30)

"Supportive feedback is the sincere and meaningful attention you give a student for behaving according to your expectations. Its use motivates students to choose appropriate behavior and creates a positive atmosphere in the classroom that will allow cooperative relationships to flourish. Supportive feedback must become the most active part of your classroom discipline plan." (Canter & Canter, 2001, p. 41)

When *Assertive Discipline: A Take Charge Approach for Today's Educator* (Canter, 1976) was first introduced in 1976, it stood in marked contrast to, and in reaction to, the models of Dreikurs and Glasser. Instead of an emphasis on democratic decision making, feelings of positive self-worth and social belonging, and the prevention of behavior problems, emphasis was placed on the systematic use of rewards and punishment to correct and control misbehavior. Reminiscent of earlier centuries, the role of the teacher in assertive discipline was to govern behavior, not to develop self-discipline. Just as the student-centered models of Dreikurs and Glasser emphasized the responsibility of students, the teacher-centered model of assertive discipline emphasized the responsibility and duty of teachers. With discipline problems and school violence escalating at the time, teachers demanding the legal *right to use discipline,* and the growing popularity of behavior modification, it is no wonder that many teachers turned to assertive discipline in the 1970s as an alternative to the student-centered approaches of Dreikurs and Glasser. Since then, Canter and Associates has continued to produce books, films, and in-service training programs that have remained popular among educators in the United States and in many other countries. They have sold over 2 million books and trained over 1.5 million teachers (Canter & Canter, 2001).

It should be emphasized that just as assertive discipline responded to the needs of teachers in the 1970s, over the years it also has responded to many of its critics. This has resulted in a much less assertive and more balanced and positive approach to classroom discipline. Unfortunately, some educators continue to think of the 1976 version of the model when they think of assertive discipline, and many continue to rely on the punitive techniques emphasized in that version. For this reason in this chapter the 1976 version of assertive discipline is first presented and critiqued followed by the 2001 version. This provides not only a comparison of the two different versions but also a segue to the remaining sections of the book on evidence-based strategies and techniques for developing self-discipline and for preventing and correcting misbehavior.

The 1976 Take Charge
Version of Assertive Discipline

Assertive discipline began with the premise that students are not the only members of the school community with rights. Teachers also have their rights! Chief among them were the rights to establish and maintain order and routine in the classroom, to demand appropriate behavior from students, and to seek and receive assistance from principals, parents, and others. Although Canter avoided use of the term *authoritarian,* it is clear that he endorsed an authoritarian, or autocratic, approach to classroom discipline. He believed that teachers had given up their rights in the 1960s and 1970s by failing to be sufficiently assertive when faced with disrespectful and ill-behaved students. Consequently, students and parents no longer respected teachers as they had in the past.

To earn back students' respect it was believed that teachers needed a "new" kind of training—training that empowered them to *take charge* of their students. Canter (1976) grounded his philosophy in *assertiveness training,* which was popular in psychology during the time. Assertive teachers are those who make their expectations about classroom behavior clear to students. They are firm and punitive when necessary. An assertive teacher is one who is "prepared to back up her words with actions" (p. 30) and who "lets the child know that she means what she says and says what she means" (p. 9).

Canter (1976) believed that too many teachers lacked assertiveness and skills in classroom management and classroom discipline. Too many were either nonassertive or hostile. Both of these styles were viewed (and correctly so) as equally ineffective. Canter argued that to be effective, teachers had to respond assertively to discipline problems. Canter presented the following examples of the nonassertive, hostile, and assertive styles when responding to a chronically disruptive and disobedient sixth grader:

Nonassertive Response
The teacher states, "You never talk to me like that again. Get to work." The child just sits there and does nothing. The teacher does not back her words up with an appropriate limit setting follow-through consequence.

Hostile Response
The teacher angrily grabs the child and shouts, "Keep your big filthy mouth shut. If you open your mouth again I'll slap it shut."

Assertive Response
The teacher firmly states, "You never talk back to me again! Now you have a choice, get to work immediately or I will suspend you this instant!" (pp. 42–43)

The purpose of assertive responses was for teachers to express their disapproval of inappropriate behavior and to make clear to students what behavior was expected of them. To be sure, the teaching style is direct and authoritarian. Although Canter emphasized that teachers always should remain "cognizant of the students' needs for warmth and positive support" (p. 10), the 1976 version of assertive discipline included few, if any, indirect or democratic methods advocated by Dreikurs and Glasser that focused on developing positive teacher–student relations and self-discipline.

S T O P   A N D   R E F L E C T

Examine the examples used by Canter (1976) to describe the nonassertive, hostile, and assertive responses to a student who disrupts the classroom and refuses to obey the teacher. Can you distinguish how an assertive response differs from a hostile response? Drawing from the approaches of Dreikurs and Glasser, how might the foregoing assertive statements be reframed to be less hostile and more constructive? Which, if any, of the foregoing responses reflects the discipline styles of teachers you have known or your own style?

Canter (1976) believed that to be assertive, teachers must look out for their own wants, needs, and rights, which were viewed as one and the same. Undoubtedly, this philosophy was teacher centered: Assertiveness was valued among teachers, yet stifled among students. Assumingly, only teachers had the right to be assertive in the classroom. Students were not taught to be assertive, although it was highly likely that many learned to be assertive, hostile, and punitive by observing their teachers practice the 1976 techniques of assertive discipline.

It should be noted that although the 1976 approach of assertive discipline was teacher centered, it also recognized that students had their rights. But such rights were quite limited and served the purpose of justifying the authority of the teacher. As such, students had the "right" to have a teacher who was controlling and manipulating, and they had the "right" to "choose how to behave and know the consequence that will follow" (Canter, 1976, p. 8).

"Take Charge" Techniques of Assertive Discipline

The 1976 model of assertive discipline used a variety of disciplinary techniques that teachers have been using for years, including eye contact, hand gestures, physical proximity, "I-messages," and verbal warnings to prevent and correct behavior problems. Greater attention is given to the systematic application of behavior modification, however, particularly to the use of two types of behavioral techniques: reinforcement and punishment. Although both types always have been advocated, it is the latter that is most commonly associated with the 1976 model of assertive discipline, and rightfully so.

Canter (1976, 1993) presented assertive discipline as a model program of the systematic application of behavior modification to problems of classroom discipline. But, as correctly noted by several critics (e.g., Render, Padilla, & Krank, 1989), the 1976 model relied heavily on techniques that behaviorists preferred the least: punitive techniques. Rewards, or reinforcement, were of secondary importance. Despite this legitimate criticism, it is difficult to deny that assertive discipline represented the systematic application of behavior modification as used by millions of teachers at the time. Textbooks on classroom discipline routinely presented assertive discipline as the classic example of behavior modification applied to the schools (and many continue to do so).

As seen in previous chapters, the use of reinforcement and punishment certainly was not new to educators. What was new in the 1976 model of assertive discipline, however, was linking these techniques to the philosophy of assertiveness and delivering them in a structured, systematic fashion that teachers could easily follow. Consistent with the practice of behavior modification, teachers were taught to pinpoint specific behaviors that bothered them and to target these behaviors for change. Teachers listed bothersome behaviors in the classroom for all students to see (teachers were instructed to list no more than five). For example, during the first day of school, the 1976 version advised teachers to make their demands and rules clear by posting rules in the classroom, such as: Follow directions, don't back talk, work independently, complete all assignments, no stealing, no cursing or swearing, tell the truth, no screaming, and so forth (Canter, 1976, p. 63). Violators of the rules were to be corrected immediately.

Correcting Misbehavior with the Broken Record, Names on the Board, and the Discipline Hierarchy.   In addition to posting rules in the classroom, the consequences for each rule infraction were to be made clear to students and their parents. Students were to make a copy of the teacher's classroom rules and take it home and have their parents sign it. In the 1976 version they also were told to keep the copy on their desks. When the teacher posted the rules, students were told that violations of the rules would not be tolerated. The teacher was to write the following on the board:

1. The first time you do not follow directions, shout out, or bother someone, I will put your name on the board.
2. If you again choose to disrupt, I will put a check next to your name. One check equals an additional ten minutes after school.
3. If you get your name and more than two checks on the board during the day, I will call your parents. (Canter, 1976, pp. 127–128)

Millions of teachers across the country followed the preceding steps, which became equated with assertive discipline. In addition to names and checks on the board, assertive discipline offered a variety of other punitive techniques designed to reduce or eliminate undesirable behaviors. For example, it was recommended that the initial assertive response to students who failed to obey directions or class rules should be the "Broken Record." In using this technique the teacher would sound like a record stuck on the same words, repeating them over and over. As noted by Canter (1976), "When you learn to speak as if you were a broken record, you will be capable of expressing your wants and needs, and ignore all sidetracking manipulations of the students" (p. 79). The Broken Record was recommended when students failed to listen or assume responsibility for their behavior. The record was to be repeated no more than three times during a disciplinary encounter.

If the Broken Record did not work, teachers were to revert to other punitive techniques arranged in a hierarchy, called the *discipline hierarchy,* from mild to severe. Teachers were advised to first give a warning before writing names and checks on the board. If this did not stop the misbehavior, more aversive consequences (i.e., types of punishment) were to be employed, including time-out in another classroom, after-school detention, withholding a privilege or preferred activity, calling the parents (and requesting that they punish the student), and tape recording the behavior and showing the behavior to the student's parents. For the most serious rule infractions, suspension was recommended. Assertive discipline opposed corporal punishment, however.

Regardless which type of punishment was used, the 1976 version of assertive discipline emphasized the importance of assertive teachers being firm, consistent, and following through with promises to punish (which were differentiated from threats). It was important that teachers were prepared and planned ahead. Thus, in correcting misbehavior teachers were to have a plan that included five punitive consequences, and they were not to deviate from the plan. As emphasized by Canter (1976), "The first, and only, Commandment of *Assertive Discipline* is this: *"Thou shalt not make a demand thou art not preparest to follow-through upon!"* (p. 74).

Reinforcing Good Behavior with Marbles in a Jar and Other Rewards. Assertive and punitive techniques were at the core of the 1976 model. To be fair, however, assertive discipline also strongly recommended, and continues to recommend, more positive strategies (now called *positive assertions* and *positive consequences*). Teachers were urged to balance the use of limit-setting assertions with positive assertions. Consistent with basic principles of reinforcement, it was understood that rewards increase the frequency of appropriate behaviors and decrease the frequency of inappropriate behaviors. In the 1976 model, however, it was made clear that the systematic use of rewards benefited the *teacher:* It enhanced the teacher's self-esteem and created a more favorable working environment for the *teacher.*

The following positive consequences, or rewards, were recommended (and continue to be): teacher attention, positive notes or phone calls to parents, awards, special privileges, material consequences, and home follow-through (special privilege from home). Assertive discipline also offered several creative reinforcement games for elementary school classrooms, which remain in the most recent model. The most popular among them is Marbles in a Jar. After students were told about the name on the board and check system, they were then told the following:

> I also have a responsibility to all of you to let you know that I like it when you do what I want, and when you contribute to a positive classroom environment. Thus, I have here an empty jar, and a bag of marbles. Each marble that goes in the jar will earn the entire class 30 seconds of free choice, to be collected at the end of each day. The more you follow the class rules, the more marbles you will earn. Do you have any questions as to the behavior I want? What will I do if you do not do what I want? What will I do if you do what I want? (Canter, 1976, p. 138)

Like Names on the Board, Marbles in a Jar quickly became another signature technique of assertive discipline. In the 1980s there were many school districts in which these two games were being used to control and manage classroom behavior.

Seeking Help from Principals and Parents. If the foregoing techniques failed to work, teachers reverted to another component of their discipline plan: seeking assistance from the principal or the student's parents. Teachers were not to hesitate to send students to the principal or to call their parents. Teachers are still encouraged to do so but in a more positive manner. In the 1976 version use of these two techniques was viewed as one of the rights of assertive teachers, and they were to assert this right when necessary. Thus, when communicating with the principal and parents, teachers had to be assertive and use many of the same

strategies they used with their students. For example, the Broken Record was highly recommended. Thus, if the principal was reluctant to suspend a student, the teacher had to repeat over and over to the principal that the student needed to be suspended. Likewise, in a
meeting with the parents of a misbehaving student, the teacher had to repeat over and over
that parent cooperation (i.e., discipline) was needed. As was true when teachers corrected a
student's behavior in the classroom, collaboration was not a recommended strategy. The
teacher knew what was needed and, in acting assertively, told parents what they were to do.

STOP AND REFLECT

I wish teachers did not need to use negative consequences at all. I wish all students came to school
motivated to learn. I wish all parents supported teachers and administrators. But that's not the reality
today. Many children do not come to school intrinsically motivated to behave. Their parents have
never taken the time or don't have the knowledge or skills to teach them how to behave. Given these
circumstances, teachers need to set firm and consistent limits in their classrooms. However, those
limits must be fair, and the consequences must be seen as outcomes of behaviors that students have
chosen. (Canter, 1993, p. 101)

Do you agree with Canter regarding the primary cause of misbehavior and that the best way
to address a disciplinary problem is with firm and consistent limits and consequences? In general,
what are your reactions to the techniques of assertive discipline presented so far? What do you think
are the advantages and disadvantages of the model?

Critique of the 1976 Model of Assertive Discipline

Canter (1976) created one of the first models of classroom discipline that was commercially
produced and mass-marketed. Few, if any, classroom discipline programs have obtained the
same degree of popularity. Similar to authoritarian approaches of the past, assertive discipline differed markedly from character education and the models of classroom discipline by
Dreikurs and Glasser, which focused on *preventing* behavior problems and *developing* character, values, democratic thinking, or self-discipline. Assertive discipline addressed none of
these themes but focused exclusively on *correcting* everyday behavior problems. The *take
charge* approach resonated with teachers of the late 1970s, 1980s, and 1990s (as well as
many teachers today) who wanted to hear that *teachers,* not students, must control the classroom and that this can easily be done by using a few simple behavior modification techniques. Other popular models of the period might have talked about correcting discipline
problems, but few showed teachers how to do it in a concrete and systematic fashion. Assertive discipline filled this void.

Nearly all the criticisms of the 1976 model of assertive discipline are ones you would
predict after having read the previous chapters, particularly about the limitations of relying
primarily on the use of punishment and rewards. In addition to the lack of long-term effectiveness and issues of ethics and fairness, a major criticism concerned the primary function
of the teacher and education in general: Is it to control and govern students or to teach self-
discipline? The 1976 model of assertive discipline taught compliance out of fear of punish-

ment and the promise of rewards. It taught students little more. Although its methods were certainly less harsh than those common in the eighteenth and nineteenth centuries, its philosophy and goals were the same: Teachers must control and govern students. As such, students learned to behave to avoid punishment (i.e., the public humiliation of having their names written on the board, losing recess, or having their parents called) or to earn rewards (i.e., marbles in a jar). They learned little else. As noted by several researchers who presented a comprehensive review of the model, "The Canters ignore children's needs and do not discuss how to balance the teacher's need for control with the child's need for independence, nor how to encourage children's participation in decision making" (Render et al., 1989, p. 622).

As was true with behavior modification in general, assertive discipline was not about teaching self-discipline, responsibility, values, and moral reasoning. Nor did it appear to be about caring teachers and a trusting teacher–student relationship. These were valid criticisms of assertive discipline (see Kohn, 1996; Render et al., 1989). But to be fair, Canter (1976) never claimed these important purposes and goals in the 1976 model. Assertive discipline promised it would put teachers in charge of their classrooms, and in many ways it delivered on its promise.

Canter (cited by Render et al., 1989) reported that about 90% of teachers and administrators who completed assertive discipline training felt more empowered in correcting discipline problems and that they enjoyed their jobs more. Canter also reported additional evidence, derived primarily from unpublished dissertations, showing that assertive discipline dramatically reduced behavior problems in the classroom, at least in the short term. Unfortunately, such reports of effectiveness were open to valid criticism. Comprehensive reviews of the literature on the effectiveness of assertive discipline failed to find many studies supporting its use. Not one study of assertive discipline (including the more recent 1992 and 2001 models) has been published that meets common research standards (e.g., use of a comparison group, random assignment of students, use of reliable and valid measures of behavior change). Over a dozen studies of less scientific rigor have been published, with most of the evidence showing that assertive discipline has no effects, or mixed and negative aspects, on student behavior and attitudes (Emner & Aussiker, 1990; Render et al., 1989). As concluded by Render et al. (1989), "It is obvious that there is an incredible lack of systematic investigation regarding the effectiveness of assertive discipline" (p. 616).

In response to such critics, Canter (1989) agrees that there is "nothing new" about assertive discipline but argues that research in behavior modification and classroom management supports the techniques used in the model, particularly clear expectations and rules, and combining praise and rewards with the loss of privileges and other punitive techniques. Although Canter is correct, he fails to recognize the many limitations of the systematic use of punishment and rewards to correct behavior, particularly when not combined with more student-centered strategies and techniques for fostering self-discipline.

The 1992 and 2001 Versions of Assertive Discipline: Be Positive!

Largely in response to their critics, Canter and Canter revised the 1976 model in 1992 and again in 2001. Whereas they continue to argue that teachers have the right to be assertive and to use behavior modification techniques to manage and control student behavior, the rhetoric is much softer. As in the 1976 version, in the more recent versions nearly all of the techniques for classroom discipline entail the systematic use of positive reinforcement and punishment. Fortunately, however, much less emphasis is placed on the latter. Positive reinforcement now receives primary emphasis, which is reflected in the change in title of the program. *Assertive Discipline: Positive Behavior Management for Today's Classroom* (1992, 2001) replaced *Assertive Discipline: A Take Charge Approach for Today's Educator* (Canter, 1976). The result is a kinder, gentler, and more positive approach to classroom discipline.

Assertive Discipline's Positive Behavior Management

In preventing and correcting misbehavior, teachers now are strongly encouraged to rely primarily on a variety of types of reinforcement, including material rewards and special privileges, and on social reinforcement from teachers, peers, and parents. As in the 1976 model, teachers also should use common techniques of classroom management (to be reviewed in Chapter 10), including redirecting behavior, catching misbehavior early before it escalates, physical proximity, circulating about the classroom, and so forth. Gone, however, are many of the punitive corrective techniques that characterized the early version of assertive discipline, including Names on the Board. Canter and Canter (2001) now caution teachers not to monitor misbehavior by putting names and checks on the chalkboard because "some individuals have misinterpreted the use of names and checks on the board as a way of humiliating students" (p. 72). In the place of writing names on the board, teachers now are advised to record the names of offending students more discretely in a record book or on a clipboard.

To be sure, Canter and Canter (1992, 2001) still believe that assertive teachers should not refrain from using punitive corrective techniques (note that they avoid the term *punishment*). However, consistent with research on the effectiveness of punishment, they now wisely advise teachers to use punitive corrective techniques only in combination with reinforcement and only after more positive techniques fail. As noted by Canter and Canter (2001), "Effective behavior management is defined by a balance between structure (rules and limits) and a genuine effort to reach out and establish cooperative relationships (i.e., by using reinforcement)" (p. 21). To achieve this balance, Canter and Canter advise teachers to implement a three-part discipline plan, which they claim helps promote self-discipline. The three parts are (1) clear rules, (2) supportive feedback, and (3) corrective actions. The plan should be posted in the classroom and thoroughly explained. Additionally, the teacher should directly teach the plan using verbal instruction and modeling, ensuring that all students understand it.

Clear Rules.   Canter and Canter recommend that classroom rules be few in number, observable, and ones that would apply throughout the school day. Teachers are encouraged to solicit suggested rules from their students. Rules are differentiated from routine procedures (e.g., entering and leaving the room, organizing one's desk, going to gym, etc.) and general policies (e.g., using the pencil sharpener, going to the bathroom, etc.). However, rules, procedures, and policies should be directly taught to all students. Three rules that they recommend are:

- Follow directions.
- Keep hands, feet, and objects to yourself.
- Use appropriate school language: no put-downs, teasing, or bad language.

Supportive Feedback. Canter and Canter (2001) emphasize that supportive feedback should be the most important part of any classroom discipline plan. They correctly note that supportive feedback increases appropriate behavior, decreases inappropriate behavior, fosters positive teacher–student and student–student relations, and helps enhance self-esteem. Instead of focusing on misbehavior, as was largely true in the 1976 version, the new assertive teacher actively monitors, reinforces, and publicly highlights instances of appropriate behavior. The teacher positively repeats what behaviors are expected from students by publicly recognizing and socially reinforcing those who behave. For example, on observing two students listening and raising their hands to be called on, the teacher would comment before the class, "I appreciate the way Mary is listening and raising her hand." A similar comment would then be repeated for the second student. Canter and Canter call this *behavioral narration* and recommend that teachers use it every time they give a direction during the first two weeks of school, every third time during the second two weeks, and every fourth or fifth time thereafter.

In addition to using praise, assertive teachers are encouraged to recognize desirable behavior with a positive note or phone call to a student's parents, with special privileges, or with a tangible reward (e.g., stickers). They caution teachers, however, to use tangible rewards sparingly—only on occasions that students tend to be most disruptive, such as before vacations. Teachers also are encouraged to create a system for monitoring, teaching, and recognizing good behavior classwide. Suggested techniques are the old Marbles in a Jar and a Positive Behavior Bulletin Board to display the points needed and earned for a classwide reward.

IMPLEMENTATION TIPS

Canter and Canter (2001) provide a number of positive techniques that can be used to show interest in students and demonstrate care. Among them are the following (p. 183):

- Greet your students by names as they enter the classroom.
- Stop to chat with them in the hallway, in the cafeteria, at recess, before class.
- Make a point of initiating conversations.
- Monitor and modify your tone and body language to convey openness and friendly concern.
- Show your interest and give complete attention when your students are talking to you.
- Smile and show a sense of humor.
- Take a student interest inventory at the beginning of the year to learn about your students' favorite activities.
- Call a student after a bad day to discuss how you might have a better day tomorrow.
- Call a student after a good day and compliment her on her success.
- Send get-well notes, or call home if a student is sick.
- Attend school activities: plays, dances, athletic events. Don't forget to mention a student's accomplishment the next day as you greet her at the door.

Here are some additional techniques that were provided by Patti Bear and numerous other classroom teachers enrolled in courses on classroom management taught by the author (and his wife, Patti):

- Shake hands and have personal comments for students as they leave at the end of the day.
- Make positive phone calls or send positive e-mails home to parents on a regular basis.

(continued)

IMPLEMENTATION TIPS *(continued)*

- Send letters home that showcase positive details of a field trip, focusing on the good behavior of the students and thanking parents for raising polite children.
- Place a quick note of appreciation to students, written on Post-it Notes and left on their desk when they leave the room. Better yet, mail students thank-you cards.
- Advertise the Student of the Week with a poster outside of the class. Include the student's interests, hobbies, and goals.
- Take pictures of students at work, at play, at school activities (concerts, etc.). Make doubles and send copies home or put them on PowerPoint slides to share with the class and others.
- Record positive quotes from students and use them in the context of class discussion.
- Send postcards to welcome new students to the class, to wish students good luck on an important test or in a sports event, for example, and to thank students for acts of kindness to others.
- Display newspaper articles of students' accomplishments.
- Send the student to the principal with a "confidential" note informing the principal of the student's improved behavior or any other major accomplishment.

STOP AND REFLECT

In developing the 1976 model, Canter argued that increased behavior problems in the schools called for a more assertive and punitive approach to classroom discipline. Interestingly, with continued, if not increased, behavior problems and school violence, Canter and Canter (2001) now argue that teachers must be more positive. Were they wrong in 1976 calling for a "take charge" authoritarian approach to increased behavior problems? Are they correct now in advocating for a more positive approach? Is one approach better than the other for all students?

Corrective Actions.   Canter and Canter (2001) still recommend that teachers develop their hierarchy of *corrective* (i.e., punitive) *actions* and communicate it clearly to students. They argue that corrective actions not only are necessary for effective classroom management but also are necessary for developing self-discipline. They recommend the following discipline hierarchy:

> *First offense:* Issue a reminder. For example: "Marshall, you should be at your desk right now. That's a reminder."
>
> *Second or third offense:* Immediately provide a corrective action, or consequence, that is easy to use, such as requiring the student to wait one minute after class, changing the student's seat, sending the student to time-out, or writing about the misbehavior in a behavior log or journal in which the student explains why he or she misbehaved and what alternative actions he or she will take in the future.
>
> *Fourth offense:* Call the parents or send a note home.
>
> *Fifth offense:* Send the student to the principal, which should result in counseling, a parent conference, or suspension.

For serious misbehavior, such as fighting and severe class disruption, the hierarchy is invoked but the student should be immediately removed from the classroom. This is referred to as the *severe clause* on the discipline hierarchy. Regardless of where the corrective action is placed within the hierarchy, it is never to be physically or psychologically harmful.

Critique of the 1992 and 2001 Versions

Overall, the recent model is kinder and gentler than the 1976 model and more consistent with research. Unlike in the 1976 model and consistent with the models of Dreikurs and Glasser, Canter and Canter (1992, 2001) now emphasize that a warm and supportive relationship with a student is important, especially if the teacher is attempting to influence or change a student's behavior. For example, in dealing with difficult students, Canter and Canter now emphasize the importance of showing empathy and concern, gaining insight as to why the student exhibits the problem behavior, and meeting with the student in a one-to-one problem-solving conference to help the student plan how to improve his or her behavior. While being caring and supportive, the teacher must make it clear what behaviors are expected from the student and that the teacher believes the student will meet those expectations. These ideas, similar to those of Dreikurs and Glasser, depart greatly from the 1976 model.

Although much improved, the new assertive discipline model remains open to criticisms that are commonly voiced against the systematic use of rewards and punishment to control behavior. Moreover, the model still relies on a limited number of simplistic techniques for behavior change: use of positive techniques such as social, material, and activity rewards to increase desirable behavior and use of punitive techniques such as response cost, time-out, contacting parents, sending the student to the principal, and suspension to decrease desirable behavior. Because these techniques often produce short-term improvement in behavior, they appeal to many teachers. Unfortunately, other behavioral techniques that have been shown to foster self-discipline, particularly self-management, receive little, if any, attention in assertive discipline. More importantly, with the exception of cursory attention given to encouraging students to use social problem-solving skills, students' thoughts and emotions also receive little attention. Thus, it is unclear how self-discipline or the following claim is achieved simply with supportive feedback: "If you recognize a student's compliance with your directions, the student will be motivated to repeat his performance in order to be recognized again. Over time, however, the student will internalize the rules and no longer need your supportive feedback to comply. He will have learned to manage his behavior on his own" (p. 115). In addition to giving scant attention to social and emotional competencies, the model largely neglects other multiple factors that contribute to misbehavior as well as to the development of self-discipline. The emphasis continues to be more on correction than on other necessary components of comprehensive classroom discipline.

In sum, although the 2001 version is much more attractive than the 1976 version, there is no evidence that the model teaches self-discipline. Nevertheless, it does provide teachers a nicely packaged program of practical techniques that often are effective in bringing about short-term improvements in behavior. Although certainly not sufficient for developing self-discipline, at times such techniques are valuable, and often necessary, in creating and maintaining a safe, orderly, and positive classroom climate.

SUMMARY AND KEY POINTS

- When first developed in 1976, assertive discipline was based on principles of assertiveness training and behavior modification. According to its authors, Canter and Canter, teachers had the right to be assertive and to control student behavior using punitive and positive techniques of behavior modification.
- Largely in response to critics, the 1992 and 2001 versions of the model are much less punitive. The "take charge" approach of the 1976 version was replaced with a gentler, kinder, and "positive" approach to behavior management.
- In placing greater emphasis on positive techniques than in earlier models, teachers now are encouraged to prevent behavior problems by reinforcing appropriate behavior with positive recognition, directly teaching specific desirable behaviors, and developing a positive relationship with each student that is characterized by care, respect, and support.
- At the core of the 2001 version is a three-part discipline plan that teachers implement, which is comprised of clear rules, supportive feedback, and corrective actions.
- The model continues to focus on the management and control of behavior. It is unclear how the model develops self-discipline, as claimed by the authors. Nevertheless, the model is very popular among teachers, largely because it provides teachers with many practical techniques for managing and correcting student behavior.

KEY TERMS AND CONCEPTS

Names on the Board	Corrective actions	Positive recognition
Assertive, hostile, and nonassertive responses	Lee Canter and Marlene Canter	Supportive feedback
Behavioral narration	Positive assertions	Marbles in a Jar
Broken Record	Positive consequences	Discipline hierarchy

RECOMMENDED READINGS AND RESOURCES

Canter, L., & Canter, M. (1992, 2001). *Assertive discipline: Positive behavior management for today's classroom.* Santa Monica, CA: Canter and Associates.

For additional books, videotapes, curriculum packages, training workshops, and other resources see www.canter.

net. For examples and testimonials on the implementation of assertive discipline, use most search engines on the Web to find schools that are currently implementing assertive discipline.

REFERENCES

Canter, L. (1989). *Assertive discipline: A response.* Santa Monica, CA: Lee Canter and Associates.

Canter, L. (1993). Assertive discipline—More than Names on the Board and Marbles in a Jar. In A. Woolfolk (Ed.), *Readings and cases in education psychology* (pp. 99–103). Boston: Allyn and Bacon.

Canter, L. (1976). *Assertive discipline: A take charge approach for today's educator.* Santa Monica, CA: Lee Canter and Associates.

Canter, L., & Canter, M. (1992, 2001). *Assertive discipline: Positive behavior management for today's classroom.* Santa Monica, CA: Canter and Associates.

Emmer, E. T., & Aussiker, A. (1990). School and classroom discipline programs: How well do they work? In O. C. Moles (Ed.), *Student discipline strategies: Research and practice* (pp. 129–165). Albany, NY: State University of New York Press.

Kohn, A. (1996). *Beyond discipline: From compliance to community.* Alexandria, VA: Association for Supervision and Curriculum Development.

Render, G. F., Padilla, J. M., & Krank, H. M. (1989). Assertive Discipline: A critical review and analysis. *Teachers College Record, 90,* 607–630.

8 Developing Social and Moral Problem Solving and Self-Discipline

GUIDING QUESTIONS

- In what ways are social and moral problem solving related to self-discipline?
- Is *how* students think more important than *what* they think?
- What social and moral problem-solving skills and processes, or lack thereof, best account for desired and undesired behavior?
- What strategies and techniques are most effective in developing social and moral problem-solving skills?

- How does modeling influence behavior? How can modeling be used to develop social and moral problem-solving skills?
- How might techniques for developing social and moral problem solving be used during disciplinary encounters?
- In what areas of the general curriculum might social and moral problem solving best be taught?
- How might social and moral problem solving be fostered within the context of everyday teacher–student and student–student social interactions?

> No one doubts, theoretically, the importance of fostering in school good habits of thinking. But apart from the fact that the acknowledgment is not so great in practice as in theory, there is not adequate theoretical recognition that all which the school can or need do for pupils, so far as their *minds* are concerned . . . is to develop their ability to think. (Dewey, 1916/1944, p. 152)

> **JIMINY CRICKET:** "You see, the world is full of temptations. They're the wrong things that seem right at the time. But even though the right things may seem wrong sometimes, sometimes the wrong things may be right at the wrong time or vice versa. Understand?"
>
> **PINOCCHIO:** "No, but I'm going to do right." (Disney, *Pinocchio,* 1940)

Since the early 1900s educators have understood that if a true aim of education is to develop self-discipline, characterized by autonomous and responsible behavior, it is not sufficient to teach children *what* to think: They also must be taught *how* to think. Thus, it is now commonly recognized that in addition to acquiring moral knowledge, students also need to develop thinking *processes,* or skills, that are required to solve social and moral problems. The field of psychology that is devoted to the study of cognitive processes related to social and moral behavior is referred to as *social cognition,* or *social cognitive psychology.* Researchers in social cognition have provided educators with much insight into the thought processes that help explain common acts of antisocial and prosocial behavior. They have successfully identified thought processes that differentiate aggressive and noncompliant students from those who tend to exhibit self-discipline. To a lesser extent, they have identified thought processes that tend to differentiate students who often act prosocially from those who seldom do so. Researchers also have discovered that many of the same processes help explain why individuals behave inconsistently over time and across situations. To be sure, researchers in social cognition recognize the critical influences of situational, biological, and emotional factors in behavior. But consistent with their theoretical perspective they focus on how children *think* about social and moral problems, believing this to be the single most important factor in behavior.

The strategies and techniques presented in this chapter draw from research and theory in social cognition, particularly the classical works of Albert Bandura (1986; 1997) on modeling and self-regulation; George Spivack and Mryna Shure (Spivack, Platt, & Shure, 1976; Spivack & Shure, 1982) on interpersonal cognitive problem solving; Kenneth Dodge (Coie & Dodge, 1998; Crick & Dodge, 1994) on social information processing; and Lawrence Kohlberg (1984; Power, Higgins, & Kohlberg, 1989), Martin Hoffman (2000), and Larry Nucci (2001) on moral and social conventional reasoning. Whereas these researchers and theorists emphasize different aspects of social cognition, they all share an interest in understanding the thought processes that students use to solve social and moral problems.

Fortunately for educators, research and theory in social cognition have been translated into practical strategies and techniques that they can use. These strategies and techniques are widely used in character education and social and emotional learning programs to develop self-discipline. They also can be used during disciplinary encounters for the same purpose. The target of these strategies and techniques is the thought behind the behavior—the thinking skills, or the processes of thinking, that determine or influence behavior. This includes specific cognitive processes commonly taught as social problem-solving skills, such as identifying a social problem, thinking of goals and alternatives, evaluating alternatives, and implementing a plan. It also includes more general, or global, reasoning processes that focus on issues of fairness, justice, caring, and the welfare and rights of others. These processes are referred to as moral reasoning. Both specific problem-solving skills and more global types of moral reasoning are highlighted in this chapter. It is for this reason that the term *social and moral problem solving* is used.

Social Cognitive Components of Self-Discipline

TEACHER: What would you do if someone bumped into you or shoved you in the hall, and no teachers were looking?

AGGRESSIVE ERIC: I would either shove him back, or say, "What do you think you're doing?"

IMPULSIVE ZACH: I would probably bump or shove him back.

PROSOCIAL GINA: I would keep on walking or I might say, "Excuse me!"

TEACHER: Why would each of you do what you just decided you would do?

AGGRESSIVE ERIC: Because he started it.

IMPULSIVE ZACH: I usually do stuff like that without thinking much, and then I get into trouble. I would probably first shove the guy and then I might stop and think: "That was stupid. Why did I do that?"

PROSOCIAL GINA: Maybe it was an accident—the person wasn't paying attention or someone else bumped into him. It would be dumb to try to make a big deal out of it.

TEACHER: What are some other things you could do in a situation like this one? Give me some good alternative solutions.

AGGRESSIVE ERIC: You could keep on walking. You could give him a mean look. You could tell him to apologize. You could push him against the wall, or you could wait and get him after school.

IMPULSIVE ZACH: You could distract him by saying something like, "What class are you going to?" or "Hey, nice shove." That might make him laugh. Or you could say, "Do you want me to shove you back? Well, I'm not because it's really not worth getting into trouble."

PROSOCIAL GINA: You could just smile or look at him like, "Are you stupid or something? Do you really want to get suspended?" or you could ask "What did I do?"

TEACHER: Okay, thinking of these and any other solutions, what do you think you *should,* or *ought,* to do? Tell me what you ought to do, and *why.*

AGGRESSIVE ERIC: Yep, that's what you should do. You should shove him back. Like I said, he started it. I'm not going to let someone push me around. I don't want others to think I'm a wimp. I wouldn't want to get caught and be suspended, but it's a stupid rule to say that you can't protect yourself. That's my own business.

IMPULSIVE ZACH: I know what I'm supposed to do. That's not the problem. The big problem is doing it! You should ignore him or do whatever you can to avoid getting him mad or to avoid a fight, but that's not easy. Even if I did stop and think, I might think, "Well, others are going to laugh *at* me if I don't push him back." You shouldn't do it because you'll get into trouble and it's just not right for people to go around the hall shoving one another and fighting.

PROSOCIAL GINA: You should make sure it doesn't result in an argument or fight. Someone might get hurt or into trouble. I wouldn't want to hurt anyone and wouldn't want them to hurt me. I also wouldn't want others to think that I'm the kind of person who can't control myself or stay out of trouble. Besides, I just don't want to be that kind of person.

Most classrooms have students like Eric, Zach, and Gina—students who think differently about social and moral problems. Such differences in thinking often translate into differences in behavior, especially when adults are not around. For example, in light of the differences in thinking just presented, it is quite likely that in the absence of the high risk of getting caught (e.g., knowing that an adult is not watching), Eric and Zach would shove the student back. Eric's reaction would be consistent with his mind-set "you don't let others push you around" and his perception that someone was trying to do just that. Moreover, given his self-centered perspective, it is likely that Eric would voice no remorse or responsibility for his behavior. Although Zach's behavior would likely be the same as Eric's, it is guided by a different style of thinking, or the *lack* of thinking, which is related to his impulsivity. Unlike Eric, Zach knows what he *should* do but recognizes that he often fails to engage in any reflection before responding. And, unlike Eric, however, it is likely that Zach would regret and feel responsible about his behavior, as reflected in the concern he voiced about others. In contrast to Eric, Gina did not interpret any hostile intention on the part of the student who shoved her. To her, his behavior was accidental. And, in contrast to Zach, Gina did not respond impulsively but stopped and thought (even for a split second) about the situation. She thought that you should not shove someone back, especially if that person did not intend to shove you, because someone might get hurt and getting into fights is likely to harm her reputation, induce feelings of guilt, and affect her self-concept (reasons that are uncommon in early elementary school but prevalent thereafter).

As reviewed here, social cognitive processes reflected in the verbal responses of Eric, Zach, and Gina largely account for differences in behavior between different students, as well as differences in behavior within individual students across different situations (e.g., when peers are present). To guide educators in helping students develop social and moral problem-solving skills, it helps to think of social and moral problem solving as comprising four general components (Bear, Manning, & Izard, 2003): (1) perceiving that a social or moral problem exists, (2) determining what one *ought* to do, (3) deciding what you will do after weighing values, goals, and alternatives, and (4) having the motivation and self-confidence to actually do it. Within each of these four components, biases, deficits, and deficiencies in social cognitive processes often explain why some children and adolescents often exhibit aggression and antisocial behavior, and why many others do the same in certain situations.

Component 1. Perceiving That a Social or Moral Problem Exists

Biases and Deficits in Reading Social Cues.   When faced with social or moral problems, students first encode and interpret, or "read," visual and verbal social cues (Crick & Dodge, 1994). How they read social cues strongly influences their subsequent thoughts, emotions, and behavior (Eisenberg, 2000; Hubbard, Dodge, Cillessen, Coie, & Schwartz, 2001). As seen in Eric's responses to the shoving incident, aggressive and disruptive students are more likely than others to overly interpret the intentions of others as being hostile. This *hostile attributional bias* is especially prevalent in ambiguous social situations (Zelli, Dodge, Lochman, & Laird, 1999), when it is unclear exactly what is happening and why. Aggressive students also tend to overlook mitigating cues, which contributes to their hostile bias (Dodge & Tomlin, 1987). For example, whereas Gina considered that the other person did not intend to bump into her, Eric and Zach did not consider this mitigating circumstance.

Another factor that contributes to a hostile bias and to general inaccuracies in encoding and interpreting information is the presence of memory and retrieval deficits. Ordinarily, in a given situation a student reads social cues, compares them to cues already stored in memory, quickly assesses what the problem might be while guessing why the problem exists, compares the present social situation with previous ones ("What happened last time I was in this situation? Was I successful? Should I do the same thing I did before again?"), and considers the importance of the social situation to the self and to others ("Is this important to others or me?"). Whereas this characterizes the thought processes of most students in most situations, it does not characterize students who tend to get into the most trouble. Habitually aggressive and noncompliant students tend to react impulsively, skipping these guiding questions, forgetting about consequences of their behavior and alternative solutions, and quickly retrieving from memory thoughts that lead to their misbehavior ("Don't let others push you around").

Cognitive Scripts that Support Antisocial Behavior.   In reacting impulsively, many antisocial students often fail to engage in the components of social and moral problem solving that typically follow the encoding and interpretation of social cues (Crick & Dodge, 1994). Instead, they draw impulsively from existing and well-established *cognitive scripts* (or schemas) stored in memory that support their misbehavior (Burks, Laird, Dodge, Pettit, & Bates, 1999; Zelli et al., 1999). Grounded in personal beliefs, attitudes, and values, these cognitive scripts are analogous to the script in a film, repeated over time, telling students what to do and what to expect in a given situation (e.g., "hit others when threatened," "don't let others push you around," "obey rules only if you think you might get caught") (Huesmann, 1988). Because the self-centered, noncompliant, and aggressive behaviors of these students are often reinforced (i.e., they get what they want), the cognitive scripts that support the misbehavior become well established and continue to guide future misbehavior. This makes it difficult for educators to change both the scripts and the misbehavior.

Social and Moral Insensitivity.   A final factor related to encoding and interpreting social cues that contributes not only to aggression and noncompliance but also to the lack of prosocial behavior is social and moral insensitivity. Some students simply fail to recognize the important social and moral issues in a given situation—issues that call for either prosocial behavior or for an inhibitory response. Such lack of social and moral awareness can be explained not only by social cognitive deficits in the reading of social cues but also by emotional deficits, especially deficits in empathy, sympathy, and guilt (Hoffman, 2000). As will be seen in the next chapter on emotions, it is empathy, sympathy, and anticipated guilt that often arouse students to social and moral reflection or to immediate prosocial action. When these emotions are lacking, problems are likely to arise.

As is true with all other social cognitive processes, encoding and interpreting social cues are influenced not only by cognitive and emotional factors but also by a variety of situational factors (Crick & Dodge, 1994; Eisenberg & Fabes, 1998). These include the clarity of the circumstances involved (e.g., it is clear to Eric that the other student shoved him intentionally), the saliency of the situation to the individual (e.g., Eric had been shoved by this student many times before), emotional and physical closeness with others involved (e.g., the other student is someone Eric dislikes), peer pressure (e.g., peers encourage Eric to retaliate), and the presence or absence of adult supervision (e.g., no teachers are monitoring the halls).

Component 2. Determining What One Ought to Do

Thinking of Alternatives and Consequences.   On recognizing that a social problem exists, students typically begin to think of alternative responses to the situation (Crick & Dodge, 1994; Elias et al., 1997). Alternative responses are culled from memory, or a novel response is generated if the situation requires one. In either case, research shows that compared to other students, antisocial students tend to think of solutions that are inferior in both quantity and quality. Their solutions tend to be fewer in number (Slaby & Guerra, 1988) and to be more atypical, maladaptive, and aggressive (Rubin, Briem, & Rose-Krasnor, 1991). Perhaps more problematic is that they view their qualitatively inferior, and often immoral, alternatives as acceptable ones (Boldizar, Perry, & Perry, 1989; Crick & Ladd, 1990). Thus, they are quick to generate and accept poor solutions with little reflection on their consequences and impact on others. In short, the evaluation process is short-circuited.

Moral Reasoning.   A critical part of the evaluation process is moral reasoning—the ability to decide what one *ought* to do based on issues of fairness, justice, and the rights and welfare of others (Bear, Richards, & Gibbs, 1997). Research on sociomoral reasoning has been guided primarily by Kohlberg's (1984) cognitive developmental theory of moral development. This popular theory asserts that moral reasoning is the strongest single determinant of morally responsible behavior. Moral reasoning is viewed as progressing through six global and qualitatively distinct stages in an invariant order. This means that individuals do not skip stages but move from Stage 1 to Stage 2, Stage 2 to Stage 3, and so forth. Few, however, proceed past Stage 4. Each stage reflects increased maturity of cognitive development and social perspective taking (Colby & Kohlberg, 1987). Only the first four apply to school-age children and adolescents (and are the only stages consistently supported by research). Using language useful to educators, Gibbs, Potter, and Goldstein (1995) labeled these stages:

Stage 1—Power: Might makes right; Stage 2—Deals: You scratch my back, I'll scratch yours; Stage 3—Mutuality: Treat others as you would like to be treated; and Stage 4—Systems: Are you contributing to society? These four stages are described in Table 8.1.

TABLE 8.1   Stages of Moral Reasoning

Immature Level	**Mature Level**
Stage 1—Power: Might Makes Right. Reasoning is characterized by three core beliefs: The moral significance of an action resides in its inherent goodness or badness; authority figures dictate what is right or wrong; and punishment is an inevitable consequence of wrongdoing. Once students learn that lying, stealing, or hurting someone is wrong, no further justification is needed to establish the moral status of such actions. Moreover, authority figures, not cooperating individuals, determine standards of right or wrong— at least those not already self-evident. This means that right action is construed as deference to a superior power. Morally good means doing what one is told by a powerful authority—someone older, bigger, stronger, or more prominent. Stage 1 core beliefs also translate into the idea that you get what you want if you're powerful enough.	*Stage 3—Mutuality: Treat Others As You Would Like to Be Treated.* Conventional moral reasoning begins with Stage 3, a major advancement from the two preconventional stages. It is at this stage that most preadolescents and early adolescents discover that moral decisions based on individual self-interest are flawed. For one thing, there is no reliable way to resolve disagreements when one-on-one negotiations break down. For another, increasing social awareness promotes a more comprehensive view of the moral domain. Stage 3 reasoning coordinates colliding individual perspectives and, as a consequence, constructs reference points outside the two-party framework. Moral decisions are now based on shared values and norms. One manifestation of such thinking is that one should abide by the golden rule by putting oneself into another person's shoes. Another is that good intentions as well as actions must be considered when judging the moral transgressions of others.
Stage 2—Deals: You Scratch My Back, I'll Scratch Yours. Individuals reasoning at Stage 2 no longer believe punishment to be an inevitable consequence of transgression. Given their improved perspective taking they recognize that punishment is dependent on situational variables. Judgments continue to be concrete, pragmatic, and individualistic, but right and wrong are construed in a situational context. *If* you get caught, and who catches you, determines whether the behavior is right or wrong. The fundamental operating philosophy is now naive, instrumental hedonism—the belief that every individual has the right to pursue his or her own best interests. Making a deal is important in that it allows two individuals to advance their respective self-interests simultaneously. Moreover, one person should help another because the favor will be returned. The same notions of instrumental exchange apply to aggressive actions: If one is hit, one should hit back.	*Stage 4—Systems: Are You Contributing to Society?* Evolving in adolescents, Stage 4 reasoning widens the reference group still further. Just as individual needs were subordinated to the values of limited reference groups during the transition to Stage 3, these values, in turn, are subordinated to or integrated into the laws and ideals of society as a whole. Individuals reasoning at Stage 4 act out of the conviction that without laws and authorities to enforce them, competing self-interests (Stage 2) and limited group loyalties (Stage 3) would erode the social fabric and society would break down. It is in the best interest of everyone, then, to be law abiding. The Stage 4 perspective is "generally that of a societal, legal, or religious system that has been codified into institutionalized laws and practices" (Colby & Kohlberg, 1987, p. 28). For some individuals, however, Stage 4 reasoning may be grounded in religious law rather than secular.

Note: From "Sociomoral Reasoning and Behavior," by G. G. Bear, H. C. Richards, and J. C. Gibbs. In *Children's Needs II: Development, Problems, and Alternatives* (p. 16), by G. G. Bear, K. M. Minke, and A. Thomas, 1997. Bethesda, MD: National Association of School Psychologists. Copyright 1997 by National Association of School Psychologists. Reprinted with permission of the publisher.

In general, less mature forms of moral reasoning, particularly reasoning consistent with Stages 1 and 2, have been shown to be associated with a variety of behavior problems, particularly among adolescents (for whom immature moral reasoning is no longer developmentally normal). This includes disruptive and aggressive behavior in the classroom (Bear, 1989; Manning & Bear, 2003) and risk-taking and delinquent activities in the community (e.g., violence, theft, substance abuse, and early sexual behavior; Hubbs-Tait & Garmon, 1995; Kuther, 2000; Palmer & Hollin, 2001; Taylor & Walker, 1997). A certain element of Stage 2 moral reasoning also has been shown to characterize students in the early elementary grades who are aggressive and disruptive and also are socially rejected by their peers (Bear & Rys, 1994; Manning & Bear, 2002). This element is a self-centered hedonistic perspective in which students are overly concerned about the consequences of their actions on *themselves,* while being much less concerned about the psychological consequences of their actions on *others.* Although developmentally normal among students in early elementary school, this same element of Stage 2 reasoning, rather than Stage 2 moral reasoning per se, accounts for chronic aggression and antisocial behavior among many adolescents (Barriga, Landau, Stinson, Liau, & Gibbs, 2000). For example, in a school survey of seventh to eleventh graders, aggressive and violent students were more likely than other students to endorse the following two attitude items: "If someone threatens you, it is okay to hit that person," and "It feels good when I hit someone" (Cornell & Loper, 1998). In another survey of over 800 students in two "average" middle schools, approximately one quarter voiced reasoning similar to that reflected in the preceding items (Giancola & Bear, 2003). They believed it was all right to break school rules and the law if you don't get caught, to bully others to get respect, and to break rules and the law to be popular.

Whereas immature moral reasoning, particularly that reflecting a self-centered, hedonistic perspective, is associated with aggressive and disruptive behavior, moral reasoning characterized by a concern about the needs of others (found in Stages 3 and 4, and to a lesser extent within Kohlberg's Stage 2) is associated with the inhibition of antisocial behavior (Manning & Bear, 2002) and the presence of prosocial behaviors such as sharing and helping (Miller, Eisenberg, Fabes, & Shell, 1996), cooperative play (Dunn, Cutting, & Demetriou, 2000), and conflict resolution (Dunn & Herrera, 1997).

STOP AND REFLECT
Cultural Differences in Moral Reasoning

In general, research shows that individuals of all cultures progress through Kohlberg's first four stages of moral reasoning, as described in Table 8.1, in the same invariant order (Stage 1 before Stage 2, etc.). However, both within and across cultures not all individuals obtain the same highest stage, nor do they progress at the same rate. Thus, individual and cultural differences in moral reasoning are quite common. For example, in studying differences in moral reasoning, emotions, and classroom behavior of students in the United States and Japan, the author and colleagues (Bear, Manning, Shiomi, & Kurtz, 2004) interviewed over 200 fourth and fifth graders in each country and asked them why they should not engage in each of eight classroom misbehaviors (e.g., "Why shouldn't you hit others?" "Break in line?" "Break a promise?" "Tease others?"). A major difference emerged between countries in the responses to these questions.

American students were much more likely to respond with reasoning consistent with Kohlberg's Stage 2. That is, they were likely to focus on getting caught and punished (e.g., "You might get into trouble"). In contrast, this type of response was rare among Japanese students. Japanese students were much more likely to focus on the impact of their behavior on others and the importance of maintaining positive relations with others (Stage 3). These findings are consistent with research by others that American teachers and parents are much more likely than Japanese teachers and parents to highlight punishment during disciplinary encounters instead of the impact of misbehavior on others (Tsuchida & Lewis, 1996; Zahn-Waxler, Friedman, Cole, Mizuta, & Hiruma, 1996).

What stages of moral reasoning do you find more common among students? What cultural differences in homes, schools, and society might explain the foregoing cultural differences in moral reasoning? Do you think these differences might help explain why Japanese students tend to exhibit fewer behavior problems?

Component 3. Deciding among Competing Values, Goals, and Alternatives

Competing Values and Goals.   As succinctly put by Zach, "I know what I'm supposed to do. That's not the problem. The big problem is doing it!" Many students (and adults) share this sentiment. That is, they recognize what is right but, nevertheless, decide not to act accordingly (Component 3) or decide to act accordingly but fail to do so (Component 4). Multiple factors, including social cognitive, emotional, and situational ones, determine the consistency, or lack thereof, between social and moral reasoning and social and moral behavior. With respect to social cognitive factors, inconsistency between reasoning and behavior often can be attributed to impulsivity, as reflected in Zach's response, or to different values and goals competing with one another (Erdley & Asher, 1998; Nucci, 2001; Turiel, 1998). For example, in a given social situation the value or goal of pleasing the classroom teacher may be preempted by the goal of gaining peer approval or simply getting to do what one wants to (despite knowing that it is not the right thing to do). When the author asked his son, Adam, in the second grade, "Why did you leave the classroom and go out to recess when you knew that you weren't allowed to because you were being punished for not completing your homework?" Adam responded (with tears in his eyes), "I would rather play outside than stay in the room and do homework." Unfortunately, although developmentally appropriate in second grade, such reasoning characterizes many adolescents (including at times Adam in high school and college!) and many adults.

Moral, Conventional, and Personal Values Domains.   It is not uncommon for moral values to be preempted by other values, for a student to determine "this is what I *ought* to do but I'm going to do something else instead." Research suggests that students conceptualize values as falling into three domains: *moral, conventional,* and *personal* (Nucci, 2001). The moral domain concerns issues of fairness, justice, and the rights and welfare of others (e.g., "You shouldn't tease others because it hurts their feelings"). In school, the conventional domain concerns behavior governed by established rules and procedures that are not grounded in moral prescriptions. That is, if the rule governing the social convention is removed, there is little reason to continue to follow the rule—the violation is not likely to harm anyone else (e.g., "homework must be completed on time," "be in class on time," "no wearing hats in school"). The personal domain concerns behaviors pertaining to the student's own health, safety, or comfort and are based on personal preference and choice, as opposed to matters of fairness, justice, the rights and welfare of others, or established rules. Examples of behaviors falling in the personal domain are one's choice of clothing, friends, music, and smoking.

In general, students of all ages believe that adults have every right to regulate behavior in the moral domain (Nucci, 2001). However, many students, but especially adolescents, frequently question rules that govern behaviors that fall in either the social conventional or personal domains. This is particularly true when such rules are viewed as being determined by others in an arbitrary manner and to be of little social or moral importance. These would include rules against talking in class, turning in homework, coming to class on time, smoking, styles of clothing, choice of music, and sexual conduct (Nucci, 2001; Smetana, 1995). *Because it is developmentally normal for adolescents to question rules that are viewed as either arbitrary or infringing on their personal rights, it should come as no surprise that these are the types of rules that students most commonly object to and disobey.*

Unfortunately, not all students distinguish behaviors based on social conventions and personal preferences from those based on moral principles. The most disruptive and aggressive youth often fail to make this distinction. This is reflected in Eric's statement that "it's a stupid rule to say you can't protect yourself. That's my own business." Antisocial students tend to view many moral and social conventional behaviors as falling in the personal domain (Blair, Monson, & Frederickson, 2001; Guerra, Nucci, & Huesmann, 1994). As such, instead of viewing stealing, cheating, fighting, and other moral transgressions as behaviors that impact the welfare of others, they view moral transgressions the same way they view such behaviors as not turning in homework or listening to music with explicit lyrics—as behaviors that have no moral basis, that are matters of personal preference, and that adults have no business regulating.

Both moral reasoning and whether or not a student perceives a behavior as falling in the moral, social conventional, or personal domains often are reflected in a student's goals in a particular situation. Instead of thinking of the welfare of others, aggressive and noncompliant students tend to think of their own desired goals, such as getting what they want or retaliating against those who block their personal goals. It is important to note that antisocial students are not the only ones who tend to look out for themselves. Although to a lesser extent than aggressive and noncompliant students, nearly all students (and adults) have a self-serving bias (Nisan, 1991). But this bias is most evident and prevalent among aggressive and noncompliant students. Not only do they hold such a bias, but they also believe that their antisocial behavior is socially acceptable, justified, and results in positive outcomes (Burks et al., 1999; Erdley & Asher, 1998). They further believe that although the goal of social acceptance may be important, it is not so important as having to forgo their aggression and noncompliance. Many of them learn to achieve both goals, however, by associating with others who share their noncompliance and aggression (Farmer, 2000).

Component 4. Doing What One Decides to Do

Far too often students are well aware how they *should* act and they decide that they will act accordingly but still fail to do so. As noted earlier, in a given situation self-serving goals often override more prosocial ones. This may occur when a student is deciding on alternative courses of action or after an alternative has already been chosen. For example, a student may decide to return money she found on the bus, but upon walking past a store decide to spend it instead. In addition to a self-serving bias, two social cognitive phenomena play a critical role in linking both moral reasoning and decisional choices to actual behavior: *perceptions of self-efficacy* (e.g., "I'm confident that I can do it") (Bandura, 1997) and *attributions, or judgments, of responsibility* ("If I don't do it, there's no one to blame except myself") (Weiner, 2001).

Perceptions of Self-Efficacy.   Perceived self-efficacy is the judgment or belief that one has the ability to achieve what one desires to achieve (Bandura, 1997). In general, self-perceptions of self-efficacy are positively related to accepting, persisting at, and successfully completing challenging tasks. These tasks can be moral or immoral. For example, research shows that moral exemplars hold strong beliefs that they can act successfully to improve the welfare of others (Colby & Damon, 1999). Research also shows, however, that aggressive students tend to have positive feelings of self-efficacy, believing that aggression is easier for them than more prosocial alternatives (Erdley & Asher, 1998). They believe that their aggressive behavior will be more effective than prosocial alternatives in achieving the self-serving outcomes they desire (Quiggle, Garber, Panak, & Dodge, 1992).

Feelings of low self-efficacy concerning prosocial behavior are understandable among many antisocial students (Goldstein, Harootunian, & Conoley, 1994; Kauffman, 2001). That is, research shows that it is not uncommon that chronically aggressive and noncompliant students fail to learn prosocial behavior beginning at an early age. In everyday social exchanges between family members, they are directly taught noncompliant and aggressive patterns of behavior through modeling of overly harsh, coercive, and inconsistent discipline and the actual reinforcement of noncompliant and aggressive behavior (Dishion, French, & Patterson, 1995; Patterson, Capaldi, & Bank, 1991). This begins long before these students enter school and often continues throughout their school years.

Attributions of Responsibility.   In many social situations there is another important social cognitive variable that influences the consistency between decision making and actual behavior (including consistency between Components 2 and 3 mentioned previously): attributions that students make regarding what has happened, or is currently happening, and who is responsible (Weiner, 2001). Students ask themselves such questions as "Why is this happening?" "Did I do something that caused it?" and "Am I responsible for the situation?" They are less likely to act on their decisional choices if they believe that the social problem is caused by factors beyond their control or the control of others (e.g., "I would hit him but I guess he can't help being such a klutz," or "I know I should help and I thought I would, but I'm not responsible for his problem").

Related to responsibility, most teachers have witnessed another reason why many students fail to act consistently with their reasoning and intentions: They simply *deny* responsibility for actions for which they are truly responsible (Gibbs, Potter, & Goldstein, 1995). They attribute blame to others or otherwise disengage themselves from the consequences of their behavior. Students do this in various ways, such as by outright blaming others ("I didn't throw it, Maurice did"), attributing their behavior to factors beyond their control ("I couldn't help it, I'm hyperactive") or to other factors viewed as justifying the action ("I hit him but, he started it"), and favorably comparing their behavior to the behavior of others or to their own previous behavior ("I wasn't anywhere as bad as the others," "but I only did it a little this time"). These processes, or *cognitive distortions,* may come into play either before or after a decisional choice is made regarding intended actions. Often they follow rather than precede actual behavior. Regardless of when they occur, they serve to protect the self from feelings of failure that often result when students fail to act in a manner that is consistent with their convictions. However, the distortions also serve as excuses that often allow students to avoid blame, negative perceptions from others, and punishment.

S T O P   A N D   R E F L E C T
Why Do Kids Think That Way?

Research shows that the following deficits and deficiencies in social and moral problem solving are related to aggression and other types of behavior problems:

- Failure to read social cues correctly.
- Hostile attributional bias.
- Memory and retrieval deficits.
- Cognitive scripts reflecting personal beliefs, attitudes, and values that support antisocial behavior.
- Insensitivity to social and moral cues.
- Alternative solutions limited in number or of poor quality.
- Failure to consider multiple consequences of misbehavior.
- Moral reasoning that is self-centered, based on rewards and punishment as opposed to the needs and perspectives of others.
- Impulsive and nonreflective thinking.
- Viewing "moral" transgressions as issues of personal choice.
- Believing that antisocial behavior is acceptable, justified, and results in positive, self-serving outcomes.
- Lack of self-efficacy, or self-confidence, in performing appropriate behavior in a given situation.
- Failure to accept responsibility for one's actions.

Think of specific instances of aggressive, noncompliant, and antisocial behavior that you have witnessed. Which of the foregoing factors might account for such behavior?

Strategies and Techniques for Developing Social and Moral Problem Solving

Given that research shows that social and moral problem-solving skills and processes within the preceding four components mediate social and moral behavior, it makes sense that educators target them for instruction and development if an aim of education is self-discipline. The four research-based components to social and moral problem solving presented previously translate directly into four basic goals that educators should embrace in developing student self-discipline.

Goal 1:   Develop sensitivity to social and moral problems.

Goal 2:   Develop social perspective taking and moral reasoning.

Goal 3:   Develop decision making that is responsive to mature moral reasoning and prosocial goals rather than to peer pressure and self-serving interests.

Goal 4:   Develop the self-confidence and social skills necessary to do what one intends, and ought, to do.

Within the context of achieving these four goals, students should be taught the following social cognitive skills and processes, which are commonly taught in most character education and social and emotional learning programs. It should be noted that, although some of these skills and processes are more specific to one of these four goals than another, many apply across goals.

1. *Read social and emotional cues accurately.* This entails both the encoding and interpretation of cues. Students should learn that cues might be experienced within themselves (e.g., feelings or thoughts of anger and frustration), observed in the thoughts, feelings, and behaviors of others, or observed in other aspects of a situation (e.g., a weapon is seen, it's late at night and the area is unsafe, a known bully is approaching). They also need to learn to identify cues accurately and not make the mistake of assuming that the intentions of others are necessarily hostile.

2. *Envision the consequences of one's decisional choices and actions.* As recommended by Elias and Tobias (1996), students should be taught to "envision," rather than "think about," positive and negative consequences that are likely to result from their choices and actions. As these researchers discovered while working in the schools, "Students think about short- and long-term consequences, consequences for themselves and others, and alternative consequences more easily if we ask them to picture, imagine, describe, walk us through, make a visual video of, put on the mental monitor what might happen" (p. 8).

3. *Evaluate the moral consequences of decisional choices and behavior.* Simply envisioning what might happen is not sufficient for effective moral problem solving. Students also need to learn to *evaluate* the alternatives and consequences that they envision. This entails moral reasoning, envisioning consequences of their choices and actions on others, and envisioning choices that are responsive to the perspectives, rights, and needs of others. Students need to be discouraged from envisioning consequences that are self-centered and hedonistic.

4. *Generate multiple alternative solutions.* Students who can think of several potential solutions to a social problem are more likely to find a satisfactory solution than students who think of a limited number of ideas. Thus, students should be taught that situations often call for the generation of more than one or two good solutions.

5. *Focus more on the quality than the quantity of alternative solutions.* The ability to offer a few reasonable solutions is more strongly related to social adjustment than proposing many unreasonable ones. Therefore, students should not be taught to use brainstorming solutions indiscriminately. Little is gained by eliciting a large number of alternative solutions that are of poor quality.

6. *Reflect on the causes of social and moral problems, especially the social perspective of others.* Students should be encouraged to infer how current events in a given situation are determined by prior events. This helps them better understand the situation and, thus, generate better solutions. The process of assuming the social perspective of others is the most important ability underlying causal thinking.

7. *Reflect on and evaluate one's personal goals.* When presented with a given situation, students should be taught to reflect on and evaluate their personal goals(s) by asking themselves such guiding questions as "What would I like to happen in this situation?" "What exactly do I hope to achieve by . . . ?" and then to reflect on whether or not their decisional choice will help them achieve their goal(s). Students also should be encouraged to compare their immediate goal(s) with their more long-term goal(s), while reflecting on inconsistencies that might exist between the two goals. For example, if a student responds that the immediate goal is to retaliate, the teacher should ask if that goal conflicts with other personal life goals such as maintaining friendships, succeeding in school, and being viewed favorably by important others.

8. *Assume responsibility for one's decisional choices and actions.* If students desire to be autonomous and independent, they must accept responsibility for their decisions and the consequences. Thus, students should be taught to ask themselves such questions as "If my goal results in harm to others, will I accept responsibility for my choice?" "Is that a consequence that I'm willing to be responsible for?" When excuses and blaming are seen, they should be confronted tactfully. A good way for a teacher to do this is by assuming the position of devil's advocate, playing the role of someone negatively impacted by the student's behavior and advocating that person's perspective. Another good way is by having the student assume the role of the other person.

9. *Develop a plan, when needed, for achieving one's goal and following through on one's decisional choice.* Whereas some problems can be resolved in a simple manner, more complex ones require a well-thought-out plan. The plan should include the logistics for its implementation (i.e., when, where, and how it is to be implemented). It also should include the recognition that obstacles, or roadblocks, are likely to be encountered while executing a problem-solving plan and, thus, need to be addressed. Students should be prepared to accept the fact that they might not be able to overcome anticipated obstacles, which is likely to result in a failed plan and the need for a new one. Techniques for helping students develop problem-solving plans are presented throughout this chapter.

10. *Learn and practice the necessary social skills to act on one's decision.* Unless a teacher has seen the student exhibit the social skills necessary for implementing a plan, it should not be assumed that the social skill is in the student's repertoire. Thus, some students need to be directly taught not only the social cognitive skills and processes to help them decide *what* to do, and *why,* but also the social skills to actually do what they have decided on. Such social skills would include assertion, negotiation, cooperation, listening, resisting peer pressure, and self-regulation skills.

11. *Experience the motivation, assumption of responsibility, and self-confidence to act on one's decision.* Too often students possess adequate social cognitive skills and social skills, but lack the motivation and self-confidence to act on their decisions. To help bolster motivation and a sense of self-efficacy, teachers should provide encouragement and coaching when needed.

The remainder of this chapter presents three basic strategies for achieving the four goals presented earlier and for developing the related eleven skills and processes just presented. Within each strategy, more specific, practical, and research-based techniques are offered. It should be emphasized that although the strategies and techniques presented here are primarily for the long-term development of self-discipline, certainly they also should be used to help achieve the aims of *preventing and correcting misbehavior.*

Strategy 1: Provide Multiple Models of Social and Moral Problem Solving and Reinforce Students When They Demonstrate Effective Problem-Solving Skills

The effects of modeling are seen every day in the classroom. Students often act similarly to their peers, dress the same as others they admire, and strive to excel in academics or sports because they want to be like others who are successful. They also tend to think and reason similarly to peers and adults whom they desire to emulate or please. In support of the idea that people should "practice what they preach," research also shows that *how* adults act has a stronger impact on students' behavior and thinking than *what* they say (Bandura, 1986). Indeed, modeling is widely recognized as the most powerful way to teach new thinking and behavioral skills and to motivate students to use skills already in their repertoires. Modeling is particularly effective when students are reinforced for correctly exhibiting the behaviors modeled (Bandura, 1986). Modeling influences behavior in four important ways:

- It informs students of appropriate ways of thinking and acting.
- It motivates students to engage in the behavior observed.
- It helps develop values and standards that underlie the actions observed.
- It triggers emotional reactions observed in others (i.e., empathy).

Recommendations for Using Modeling

1. *Present different types of modeling.* For example:
   - Model thoughts and behavior yourself, either "live" or in "real time" or by simply describing your thoughts and behavior verbally or in writing.
   - When students misbehave, ask them to model the appropriate behavior (while thinking aloud).
   - Highlight models in the media, as well as in literature, history, and so on.
2. *Use modeling as a deliberate instructional technique to teach a new skill as follows:*
   - Identify the skill to be modeled and discuss its importance.
   - Model the skill and associate positive outcomes with its correct use.

- Have the student rehearse the skill.
- Provide feedback on the student's performance (praise correct usage and suggest ways to improve).
- Discuss where, when, and how the skill might be used in similar situations.

3. *Use several models rather than one.* Make sure that the models are consistent in their modeling. For example, after modeling the skill, have several peers do the same or show a videotape of others using the skill. Or, if models are presented in curriculum materials, highlight them across different lessons.

4. *Use models that approximate the following characteristics.*
- They are viewed by students as being competent in the skill modeled.
- They possess qualities, or control rewards, desired by the students.
- They are closely similar to the students (e.g., same sex, race, age, and social status).
- They are friendly and helpful. Generally, peers offer the best models, especially peers of high social status in the school.

5. *Model multiple behaviors in multiple settings.* Instead of showing students only one way to appropriately respond to a given situation, provide models who demonstrate a wide range of appropriate responses to similar problems in similar situations. When modeling or role-playing problem-solving skills, the situations should be as similar as possible to the situations students actually face in real life. If you use modeling of inappropriate behavior (e.g., videotaping a student's misbehavior on a bus, in the classroom, or in the cafeteria), be sure to also model the appropriate behavior.

6. *Make sure the model is reinforced for correctly applying the skill.* During role-playing situations, praise the student for doing a good job. Moreover, emphasize *why* the modeled skill is important. When role models are presented in the curriculum, highlight the positive consequences of the model's behavior.

7. *Provide guided and independent practice and reinforcement in a variety of situations.* Repeated practice is critical in order for skills learned in the context of curriculum lessons to transfer to natural situations. When modeling is used to teach a skill, be sure to follow the lesson with opportunities for the student to practice the skill and also be sure that the skill is reinforced.

STOP AND REFLECT

Although research shows that models of aggression and violence on television and in movies and videos foster aggression (Hughes & Hasbrouck, 1996), many students (including the Japanese students noted earlier) observe aggression in media, play violent computer games, and listen to violent music. However, their classroom behavior is no different from students who rarely view models of aggression. What do you think best explains this?

Strategy 2: Implement Curriculum Activities That Directly Teach Social and Moral Problem-Solving Skills

For teachers with extensive training in social and moral problem solving, the informal use of modeling over the course of everyday teaching and instruction may be sufficient for developing social and moral problem-solving skills. Many teachers, however, benefit from the more structured, systematic approach to implementing an organized curriculum that delineates skills to be taught and the techniques for teaching them. Two common approaches to implementing a curriculum are (1) adopt an existing, or packaged, curriculum, and (2) infuse or integrate the teaching of social and moral problem-solving skills into the general curriculum. (A third approach is to develop one's own social and moral problem-solving curriculum, but this approach is less common due to the time, effort, and resources required.) Regardless of the approach one uses, a best practice would be to ensure that the program is based on research in social cognition, as reviewed previously, and employs techniques presented throughout this chapter, including the extensive use of modeling.

Packaged Programs for Teaching Social and Moral Problem-Solving Skills.   Many schools implement a variety of curricular programs, both published and unpublished, designed specifically to teach students social and moral problem-solving skills. These include character education and social and emotional learning programs. Such programs tend to focus on teasing, bullying, school violence, substance abuse, and getting along with others. Unfortunately, some of these programs are not supported by research as to their effectiveness in developing self-discipline and reducing behavior problems in the areas targeted. Two exceptions (and favorites of the author) are *Second Step: A Violence Prevention Curriculum* (Committee for Children, 2003) and *Quest Skills Series* (Quest International, 1998). (See CASEL.com, the website for the Collaborative for Academic, Social, and Emotional Learning, for many more model programs.) These highly recommended programs consist of structured classroom lessons that are taught from one to three times a week. *Second Step* covers grades K–9 and *Quest* extends to grade 12. In each of these programs students are taught specific problem-solving skills (including skills of impulse control, anger management, perspective taking, empathy, and sensitivity to individual and cultural differences) and how to apply them when solving the hypothetical social problems presented in the lessons, as well as problems in real life. Problems of teasing, bullying, and peer pressure are presented in multiple formats, such as videos, photographs, vignettes, and stories. *Quest* also covers alcohol and drug abuse prevention and citizenship education and includes a service-learning component in which students participate in school–community partnership projects. Both *Second Step* and *Quest* have been widely used and shown to be effective with children and adolescents of socially and culturally diverse backgrounds, including African Americans, Latinos, and Caucasians.

Typically, students are taught to apply their social and moral problem-solving skills in a stepwise fashion, such as by following the steps in the *Second Step* program:

Step 1:   What is the problem?

Step 2:   What are some solutions?

Step 3:   For each solution, ask:
           Is it safe?
           How might people feel?
           Is it fair?
           Will it work?

Step 4:   Choose a solution and use it.

Step 5:   Is it working? If not, what can I do now?

Steps such as these are highlighted on the board, charts, cue cards, or in workbooks. Students discuss the importance of each step and the skills required and engage in role-plays in which they model and practice using the steps in solving interpersonal problems. This is followed by feedback from the teacher and peers on how well they did, reinforcement of the skills modeled correctly, and discussion about when and how they might use the skills in the future. Each of the preceding programs offers in-service training to teachers on how to teach lessons and implement the program. Regardless of whether teachers adopt a purchased program or use other strategies for teaching social and moral problem solving, a program's effectiveness is likely to be enhanced if adequate in-service training and ongoing supervision are provided, and if parents are routinely encouraged (via newsletters, meetings, parent training sessions, etc.) to reinforce at home the same skills that are taught at school. Note that many programs, including *Second Step* and *Quest,* include a parent component in which parents are informed of the social problem-solving skills taught in the lessons and how they can promote their use at home.

Infusion of Social and Moral Problem Solving into the General Curriculum.   An alternative to choosing among existing curriculum programs is infusing social and moral problem solving into the general curriculum. Better yet, a teacher may decide to do both—to teach lessons from an established curriculum together with lessons that are integrated into the general curriculum. At all grade levels the general curriculum provides a rich source of topics and issues for teaching social and moral problem-solving skills. In addressing the topics and issues in the general curriculum, teachers can use the same instructional techniques presented in most packaged programs, including the use of verbal instruction, discussion, modeling, role-playing, and reinforcement.

The infusion method has several major advantages over the packaged curriculum method. First, nothing is necessarily *added* to the curriculum. That is, many educators are concerned, and rightfully so, when asked to add something new to the curriculum (typically without getting to take anything away). Packaged programs are add-ons. The infusion method does not add more to the curriculum but simply redirects the teacher's focus to social and moral issues. Second, the infusion method is less expensive because nothing has to be purchased. Third, lessons often are more realistic, consisting of real-life problems and issues. It is for these reasons that infusion is the choice method among most character educators (Lickona, 2004).

Social studies, health, and language arts are three particular areas of the general curriculum that contain rich content for teaching social and moral problem-solving skills, as well as more general values (note, however, that other areas of the curriculum, including music and art, include excellent content). Topics and issues range from the general importance of constitutional rights, checks and balances in government, rules, laws, and communities to specific social problems and moral dilemmas, such as the Holocaust, the Vietnam War, slavery, the treatment of American Indians, the Revolutionary War, woman's suffrage, and the imprisonment of Japanese Americans during World War II. Likewise, current social issues addressed in the newspapers, on television, and in the movies provide excellent material to use to promote social and moral awareness of the rights and social perspectives of others, as well as overall moral reasoning. Such topics include local crimes, environmental issues, international relations, poverty, and so forth. Topics in health also are ripe for fostering social and moral decision making and problem solving, including the topics of self-concept, drug and alcohol use, smoking, sex, AIDS, and peer pressure.

Finally, perhaps more so than social studies and health, language arts content provides a bounty of topics for developing social and moral problem-solving skills. Multiple resources (see Recommended Resources at end of this chapter) exist to help teachers select from literally thousands of classic and modern books for storytelling and for students to read and discuss a full range of social or moral topics [e.g., *Huckleberry Finn, Tom Sawyer's Cabin,* and *Lord of the Flies* for older students and the *Berenstain Bears* (Berenstain & Berenstain, 1986) and the *Serendipity* series (Cosgrove, 1983) for younger students]. In the context of the language arts curriculum, teachers can use creative writing assignments, essays, journal writing, and poetry to help develop social and moral problem-solving skills. Additional techniques that teachers can use to integrate social and moral problem solving into the general curriculum include the use of art, drama, music, computer simulation games, debate, film production (e.g., students create a video on how to resolve conflicts peacefully), and research surveys and interviews.

Strategy 3: Provide Ample Opportunities for Students to Apply Social and Moral Problem-Solving Skills to Real-Life Problems in the Classroom and School

The ultimate aim of providing models of and teaching curriculum on social and moral problem solving is for students to develop self-discipline and to use these skills when solving social and moral problems they face in real life. What follows are three contexts in which social and moral problem-solving skills can be developed and practiced: individual problem solving and disciplinary encounters, peer mediation and conflict resolution programs, and class meetings.

Individual Problem Solving and Disciplinary Encounters. During the course of the day, nearly all students encounter problem-solving situations, some of which entail the correction of misbehavior. These situations and disciplinary encounters offer excellent opportunities for teachers to provide guidance in the application of skills previously taught and for students to practice such skills. Just as students need guidance and practice when solving problems in math, science, and other academic subjects, so too do they need guidance and practice when faced with everyday social and moral problems such as teasing, peer rejection, stealing, and fighting.

A good metaphor for viewing the amount of support and guidance needed for a student to successfully achieve a given task is that of *scaffolding,* which is a support system used when constructing a building (Brown & Palincsar, 1989; Stone, 1998). Following this metaphor, some buildings require more scaffolding than others. When construction is completed, scaffolding is removed and the building stands on its own. As when constructing buildings, just enough scaffolding as is necessary should be used when teaching students to solve social and moral problems on their own. As such, the amount of scaffolding should be systematically reduced and ultimately removed as students improve their social and moral problem-solving skills and assume greater responsibility for applying these skills. Because the aim is to develop self-discipline, it is important to note that what is being scaffolded is not solving the specific problem but instead the student's social problem-solving skills.

Scaffolding allows students, especially younger students and those with social cognitive deficits, to achieve tasks that they would not ordinarily achieve on their own. Whereas students with undeveloped or poor problem-solving skills require a lot of scaffolding (e.g., direct instruction and modeling), more skilled students require much less (e.g., reminders, Socratic questioning). A practical technique for applying the metaphor of scaffolding to the teaching of social and moral problem solving is *dialoguing* (Shure, 1992). As noted by Shure (2001), "Punishing, threatening, suggesting, and even explaining to children what they should and should not do are monologues. The adult is doing all the talking for the child" (p. 278). In contrast to monologues, dialogues require students to share in the talking and to apply the social problem-solving skills that they have been previously taught in curriculum lessons. In dialoguing, teachers pose guiding questions designed to help students apply and practice their social problem-solving skills.

STOP AND REFLECT

Case Study on the Use of Dialoguing

When time allows, Mrs. Dougherty uses dialoguing in her fourth-grade class to help resolve interpersonal conflicts and develop social and moral problem-solving skills. Here's an example of using dialoguing in helping two student resolve a conflict over sharing the use of a computer.

> **MRS. DOUGHERTY:** Juanita and Michael, what's the problem? (promoting problem identification)
>
> **JUANITA (AGE 10):** Michael won't let me use the computer and he's been on for the whole period when he's supposed to share.
>
> **MRS. DOUGHERTY:** Juanita, did you tell Michael how you felt? (promoting expression of feelings, or "I" messages, instead of threats)
>
> **JUANITA:** No, I told him to get off.
>
> **MRS. DOUGHERTY:** What might you have said instead? (promoting "I" messages and alternative solutions)
>
> **JUANITA:** I could have told him that I was getting angry and that it's not fair.
>
> **MRS. DOUGHERTY:** Michael, would you feel the same if Juanita didn't let you use the computer? (promoting social perspective taking and empathy)
>
> **MICHAEL:** I guess I would be mad, but yesterday she did the same thing.
>
> **MRS. DOUGHERTY:** Let's not discuss yesterday. Instead, let's talk about how you two can resolve this problem on your own, without me having to intervene. What do *you* think you should do, and why? (promoting alternative thinking and moral decision making)

JUANITA: I should ask him to share. First politely, and then tell him why it's unfair.

MICHAEL: Maybe we should keep time, and I shouldn't hog the computer.

MRS. DOUGHERTY: Very good thinking. Did you try that? (reinforcing problem solving)

JUANITA: No, I told him to get off because it was my turn.

MRS. DOUGHERTY: What do you think might happen if you tried those solutions? (promoting consequential thinking)

JUANITA: He probably would say no, or yes. I don't know.

MRS. DOUGHERTY: If he says no, what else might you try? (promoting alternative thinking)

JUANITA: I could yell "You're hogging the computer. Get off of it now."

MRS. DOUGHERTY: You could say that, but what might happen if you did? Why might that be a *poor* solution? (promoting consequential thinking and evaluation)

JUANITA: He might get mad and push me away or ignore me.

MRS. DOUGHERTY: Okay, then what else might you do that wouldn't cause Michael to get angry and for me not to feel upset? (promoting alternative thinking and social perspective taking)

JUANITA: I could ask politely "How many more minutes do you need on the computer before I can use it?" Or we could do what he suggested and time each other.

MRS. DOUGHERTY: That's a good idea that should work. Can I count on you trying those solutions next time? (reinforcing thinking skills and encouraging responsibility)

The Implementation Tip presents questions that teachers of all grade levels can use in dialoguing to help achieve the four social and moral problem-solving goals presented previously. Students should be encouraged to ask themselves such questions to help guide their thinking. These guiding questions also should be used within the context of teaching curriculum lessons, conducting class meetings, and preventing and correcting misbehavior.

IMPLEMENTATION TIP

Types of Questions Students Should Be Encouraged to Ask Themselves When Solving Social and Moral Problems

Goal 1: Develop student sensitivity to social and moral problems.

What's happening in this situation?

Is there a problem? If so, what is it?

What makes this situation a problem?

Is someone likely to be hurt?

What are the perspectives, feelings, goals, and intentions of others?

What happened before this? What might happen next?

How am I feeling?

Am I listening to what others are saying?

Am I communicating clearly?

(continued)

I M P L E M E N T A T I O N   T I P *(continued)*

What happened last time there was a situation like this?

What did I do last time there was a problem like this one? Should I do the same thing or do I need to think more about this situation?

Goal 2: Develop social perspective taking and moral reasoning.

What should I do? What is the right thing to do?

How do I determine what is the right thing to do?

What might my personal beliefs and values guide me to do?

How might my decisional choice hold up to the following nine ethical tests (as proposed in *Character Matters* by Lickona (2004):

1. The Golden Rule (reversibility) test: Would I want people to do this to me?

2. The fairness test: Is this fair to everybody who might be affected by what I say or do? Who might be affected, and how?

3. The what-if-everybody-did-this test: Would I like it if everyone else did this? Would I want to live in that kind of world?

4. The truth test: Does this action represent the whole truth and nothing but the truth?

5. The parents test: How would my parents feel if they found out I did this? What advice would they give me if I asked them if I should do it?

6. The religion test: Does this go against my religion?

7. The conscience test: Does this go against my conscience? Will I feel guilty afterward?

8. The consequence test: Might this have bad consequences, such as damage to relationships or loss of self-respect, now or in the future? Might I come to regret doing this?

9. The front-page test: How would I feel if my action were reported on the front page of my hometown paper? (Lickona, 2004, p. 47)

Several additional ethical tests that might be used:

10. The safety and respect test: Will my action harm anyone? Does it respect the rights of others? Will it harm anyone physically, or emotionally?

11. The classroom- and school-rule test: Will my action violate a school rule? If so, what is the purpose of that rule?

Goal 3: Develop decision making that is responsive to mature moral reasoning and prosocial goals rather than to peer pressure or self-serving interests.

What would I like to happen? What is my goal? Is my goal the same as what I ought to do? If not, which is more important?

What action would be most caring or prosocial?

How might I focus more on what I ought to do than what others want me to do?

Is my goal consistent with my values, or what I "ought" to do?

Is my goal realistic?

What alternative should I try first? If my first choice doesn't work, what other alternatives do I have? Are they good ones? Are they what one *should* do? That is, are they fair, safe, and the right thing to do?

Goal 4: Develop motivation, self-confidence, and the social skills necessary to do what one intends, and ought, to do.

Do I need a plan to do what I decided to do?

Do I have the self-confidence and skills to do what I decided to do?

Can I do it?

If my first choice doesn't work, what will I try next?

How might I resist negative peer pressure?

Do I need to regulate my feelings?

How do I know if my choice "works?"

Will I feel better?

Will others feel better?

Will there still be a problem?

What obstacles might keep me from achieving my goal? How might I overcome them?

Do I need assistance? If so, whom should I ask?

Peer Mediation and Conflict Resolution Programs.   In peer mediation and conflict resolution programs students are trained in a broad range of social and moral problem-solving skills and are taught to apply them in resolving interpersonal conflicts on the playground, in the classroom, in the hallways, or anywhere else on school grounds. The primary difference between these programs and most other curriculum programs that teach social and moral problem-solving skills is that the focus is not on teaching students to solve their own problems (although students learn to do so) but on helping their peers solve interpersonal conflicts or disputes. Peer mediators receive extensive training in communication, negotiation, mediation, and consensus decision making, in addition to such basic social and moral problem-solving skills as social perspective taking, brainstorming alternative solutions, evaluating solutions, and implementing a plan. Peer mediation and conflict resolution programs are typically implemented schoolwide, with either a small cadre of students trained or every student in the school trained to serve as peer mediators.

One of the more popular peer mediation programs, and the most researched, is the *Teaching Students to Be Peacemakers Program* (Johnson & Johnson, 1995, 1996). (Although the focus of less research, another highly recommended peer mediation and conflict resolution program and practical resource is *Peer Mediation: Conflict Resolution in Schools* [Schrumpt, Crawford, & Bodine, 1997].) In the *Teaching Students to Be Peacemakers Program,* peer mediators are taught negotiation and mediation skills, which are similar to the basic social and moral problem-solving skills presented earlier. The lessons are thirty minutes long and are taught over thirty days. The program has been implemented successfully in elementary schools, middle schools, and high schools. Drawing from the pool of trained peer mediators, two students are appointed by their teachers each day to assume the role of "Peacemaker" in the school. Wearing "Peacemaker" t-shirts, their primary goal is to facilitate a joint problem-solving process between disputants that will result in solutions that are acceptable and fair to all parties involved.

The *Teaching Students to Be Peacemakers Program* has been found to be effective in teaching students to use negotiation and mediation skills to resolve conflicts successfully. The program is viewed favorably by students, school personnel, and parents and is associated with an improved school climate (Johnson & Johnson, 1996). There is less empirical evidence, however, that this program, as well as peer mediation and conflict resolution programs, is effective in preventing or reducing disciplinary problems.

Peer mediation programs provide students with excellent opportunities to apply and practice social and moral problem-solving skills and to develop self-discipline. They should not be viewed as substitutes, however, for the need for adult intervention in most matters of classroom discipline. Many interpersonal conflicts (e.g., fighting, stealing, cheating) are not appropriate for peer mediation and conflict resolution and, thus, need to be handled by teachers. Even when peer mediation and conflict resolution are appropriate, teachers need to be actively involved in the peer mediation process. This is necessary to help ensure that the mediation process does not result in simplistic and ineffective solutions (e.g., "we will stay away from each other") or that peer mediators come to be viewed negatively by their peers.

Cooperative Learning. Cooperative learning is a popular form of instruction in which students work together in small groups for mutual benefits. To achieve a common goal (e.g., solve a particular problem or learn the assigned material), students in the group need to assume responsibility for their own work as well as the work of others in their group. They also must demonstrate interpersonal social skills commonly associated with cooperation. The focus is on interdependence and cooperation, not independence and competition. A wealth of research shows that cooperative learning results in positive academic, social, and emotional outcomes for students across subject areas, grade levels, and racial and ethnic groups (Slavin, 1994).

Although cooperative learning is most often used to promote academic achievement, it also is effective in promoting social and emotional learning. Among the positive social and emotional outcomes are improved self-esteem, social perspective-taking skills and enhanced peer relations, social support, concern for others, and class cohesion (including acceptance of minority students and students with disabilities) (Johnson & Johnson, 1999; Nastasi & Clements, 1991). However, there are many forms of cooperative learning, and results do vary depending on the form used, as well as the manner by which a program is implemented. In general, cooperative learning activities tend to be successful when teachers practice the following (Johnson & Johnson, 1999; Nastasi & Clements, 1991):

1. Present clear and attainable learning goals (and directions, as needed, on how to best achieve them).
2. Emphasize the importance of social support within the group (model examples, as needed).
3. Teach specific communication skills (e.g., active listening), conflict resolution skills (e.g., negotiating), and skills of coping with disappointment or failure (see Chapter 9 for suggestions on coping).
4. Ensure heterogeneity with respect to race, ethnicity, gender, achievement levels, motivation, and so on. Provide models of motivated and competent students within each group (e.g., don't place all of the best problem solvers in the same group).
5. Closely monitor group behavior, providing students with informational feedback and social reinforcement of their appropriate behavior.

**"Everyone in my biology class voted against dissecting a frog.
But we almost had enough votes to dissect the teacher!"**

Copyright 2001 Randy Glasbergen. www.glasbergen.com

6. Reward students for achieving both short-term and long-term goals.
7. Encourage students to solicit, challenge, and respect the viewpoints of others.

The last technique mentioned is particularly relevant to the promotion of social and moral decision making. That is, students find groups motivating when they engage in disagreement or controversy by challenging the perspectives of others prior to reaching (or attempting to reach) group agreement (Mitchell, Johnson, & Johnson, 2002). Cognitive development, including moral reasoning, is best promoted during cooperative learning activities that induce cognitive conflict—when students are challenged to consider and resolve opposing viewpoints (particularly viewpoints held by their peers).

Class Meetings for Social and Moral Problem Solving. As reviewed in Chapters 5 and 6, both the Dreikurs and Glasser models of classroom discipline strongly endorse the use of problem-solving class meetings to teach students social problem-solving skills and to remind them of their individual and group responsibilities. Today, class meetings are important components of many other models and programs of classroom discipline, including the research-supported and highly recommended *Responsive Classroom* (Charney, 2002) and *Child Development Project* (Developmental Studies Center, 2000) programs. Although these two programs focus on grades K–8, class meetings can be used in all grades. Indeed, class meetings have been found to be a very effective method of fostering moral reasoning and democratic decision making among high school students (Power, Kohlberg, & Higgins, 1989). Class meetings are designed to serve multiple purposes, one of which is for students to develop and practice social and moral problem-solving skills. Depending on the preference of the teacher, class meetings are held daily (more common in elementary grades), several times a week, or only as warranted (more likely to be the case after elementary school).

When used to develop and practice social and moral problem solving, class meetings can focus on the full range of social and moral problems and topics, drawn primarily from the life of the classroom, school, and community. For privacy reasons, however, family-related problems that students face at home should be avoided or handled with extreme care. Although the teacher chooses problems and issues for discussion, suggestions always should be solicited from students. Different methods can be used to solicit problems and topics for class discussions. In addition to offering ideas to the teacher verbally (with or without discussion of the problem before a class meeting), teachers should be allowed to submit topics confidentially, such as in writing (e.g., writing down the topic and inserting it in a "Problem-Solving" shoebox that is always available for confidential submissions).

STOP AND REFLECT

What "problems" might you anticipate students in elementary, middle school, and high school would submit for class discussion? Which ones do you think might not be best to discuss in a class meeting? How might you handle these problems?

Although there is no standard format for conducting class meetings, most authorities would agree to the following points and general guidelines:

1. Class meetings are appropriate for all grade levels. However, care must be taken to ensure that the topics and discussion techniques are developmentally appropriate.
2. Class meetings should be held in a nonthreatening classroom atmosphere characterized by mutual respect and trust where students feel free to voice their opinions and not be intimidated when others challenge their comments.
3. The classroom should be arranged so that all students can see one another. Ideally, students should be seated in a circle.
4. Whereas it is quite appropriate to discuss classwide disciplinary issues during class meetings, extreme care must be taken in discussing the misbehavior of individual students. Individual cases of misbehavior should only be discussed when:
   - There is a well-established climate of trust and mutual respect.
   - There is little or no risk of students experiencing negative emotions (e.g., feeling upset, embarrassed, shameful, angry) or negative reactions from peers (e.g., ostracism, rejection, retaliation).
   - All individuals involved in a problem situation agree to a class discussion.
   - The meeting focuses on solutions and how to prevent reoccurrences of the behavior, as opposed to blaming and proposing punitive consequences for the misbehavior.
5. A class meeting should not be used as a "kangaroo court" to determine the consequences of misbehavior exhibited by individual students (Developmental Studies Center, 2000). It is appropriate, however, to use class meetings to discuss the appropriate consequences, in general, of misbehavior.
6. The primary role of the teacher is that of facilitator. Students, especially adolescents, are much more responsive to the perspectives and criticisms of their peers than of adults. Thus, regardless of the grade level, the class meeting should not be used as a

forum in which the teacher lectures students about "good" behavior, *telling* them what they should do. This would be inconsistent with the goal of developing self-discipline. The goal is to develop thinking skills. In the role of facilitator, teachers should:

- Model good listening skills, such as attending and paraphrasing.
- Avoid the tendency to respond immediately to students' comments with their own opinions (but they should not necessarily avoid voicing their own opinions when appropriate). The role of the teacher is facilitator, not lecturer.
- Ensure that the participation (and reasoning) of all students is included in the discussion and that a few outspoken students do not control the discussion.
- Keep the discussion going by praising students for good reasoning, ideas, and comments, encouraging the consideration of different perspectives and solutions, and using guiding questions (such as in the Implementation Tip on p. 160).
- Maximize opportunities for small-group discussion. Where feasible, arrange students in small heterogeneous groups of four to eight students.

Although the role of facilitator should be followed, teachers should consider a more active, judgmental, and often confrontative role in class meetings in which students fail to challenge the moral reasoning, blaming, biases, distortions, excuses, irresponsible behavior, and poor solutions of their peers. By all means, students should be strongly encouraged to do so. As noted previously, disagreement often fosters learning. When confrontation and disagreement fail to occur among peers, and poor "solutions" go unchallenged, the role of the teacher should shift from facilitator to *moral advocate*—someone who advocates for moral principles of fairness, justice, caring, and the rights and welfare of others (Gibbs, Potter, & Goldstein, 1995; Power, Higgins, & Kohlberg, 1989). This is best done by assuming a Socratic questioning approach or the approach of devil's advocate, who for the sake of argument challenges students to hear the perspectives of others and challenges their decisions and reasoning. But instead of advocating for a bad cause (i.e., the devil's cause), the teacher advocates for the viewpoint of others who are negatively influenced by faulty thinking. More specific recommended procedures for conducting class meetings that focus on social and moral problem solving are presented in Appendix A. When used together with other strategies and techniques presented in this chapter and in the next chapter on emotion, class meetings provide a powerful means of helping to develop self-discipline.

SUMMARY AND KEY POINTS

- In developing self-discipline, it is not sufficient that students learn *what* to think; they also need to learn *how* to think.
- Research in social cognition demonstrates that many differences exist between the thinking and reasoning of students who are frequently aggressive and noncompliant and those who are not. These differences lie within four general components of social and moral problem solving: (1) perceiving that a social or moral problem exists,

(2) determining what one *ought* to do, (3) deciding what one will do after weighing values, goals, and alternatives, and (4) actually doing it.

- In teaching social and moral problem-solving skills, educators should target the thinking skills and processes within the foregoing four components that researchers have shown to mediate behavior. These skills and processes include reading social and emotional cues accurately; thinking of causes, alternatives, and consequences; considering goals, moral reasoning, and assuming responsibility; and acting in a manner that is consistent with one's moral reasoning and values.

■ Modeling has a powerful effect on behavior. There are four ways or functions by which modeling influences behavior: informative, motivational, valuation, and emotive.

■ Many curriculum programs exist from which teachers can choose in implementing lessons in a structured and systematic fashion. However, educators are strongly advised to select from the relatively few programs that have been empirically shown to be effective in improving both thinking and behavior.

■ A viable alternative to adopting an existing curriculum program is to infuse curriculum lessons into the general curriculum, particularly into language arts, social studies, and health.

■ Students need to be provided ample opportunities to apply social and moral problem-solving skills to real-life problems. Three excellent contexts for providing these opportunities are individual problem-solving and disciplinary encounters, peer mediation and conflict resolution programs, and class meetings.

KEY TERMS AND CONCEPTS

Attributions of responsibility
Class meetings
Cognitive distortions
Cognitive scripts
Curriculum infusion
Dialoguing

Hostile attributional bias
Modeling
Moral reasoning and values
Peer mediation and conflict
   resolution

Personal values
Scaffolding
Self-efficacy
Social conventional values
Social problem-solving steps

RECOMMENDED READINGS AND RESOURCES

Recommended Books on Developing
Social and Moral Problem Solving

Bodine, R. J., & Crawford, D. K. (1999). *Developing emotional intelligence: A guide to behavior management and conflict resolution in schools.* Champaign, IL: Research Press.

Charney, R. S. (2002). *Teaching children to care: Classroom management for ethical and academic growth, K–8* (Rev. ed.). Greenfield, MA: Northeast Foundation for Children.

Coles, R. (1997). *The moral intelligence of children.* New York: Random House.

Damon, W. (1988). *The moral child.* New York: Free Press.

Developmental Studies Center (2000). *Ways we want our class to be: Class meetings that build commitment to kindness and learning.* Oakland, CA: Author.

DeVries, R., & Zan, B. (1994). *Moral classrooms, moral children: Creating a constructivist atmosphere in early education.* New York: Teachers College Press.

Elias, M. J., & Tobias, S. E. (1996). *Social problem solving: Interventions in the schools.* New York: Guilford.

Elias, M. J., Zins, J. E., Weissberg, R. P., Frey, K. S., Greenberg, M. T., Haynes, N. M., Kessler, R., Schwab-Stone, M. E., & Shriver, T. P. (1997). *Promoting social and emotional learning: Guidelines for educators.* Alexandria, VA: Association for Supervision and Curriculum Development.

Watson, M. (2003). *Learning to trust: Transforming difficult elementary classrooms through developmental discipline.* San Francisco, CA: Jossey-Bass.

Zins, J. E., Weisberg, R. P., Wang, M. C., & Walberg, H. J. (2004). *Building academic success on social and emotional learning: What does the research say?* New York: Teachers College Press.

For information on social and emotional learning, including social and moral problem solving, and reviews of evidence-based programs (including *Second Step* and *Quest*) see the website for the Collaborative for Academic, Social, and Emotional Learning (CASEL) at www.casel.org.

Although more specific to the programs sponsored by these two nonprofit organizations, two other useful websites on social and emotional learning, which also include much information on class meetings, are the website for the Responsive Classroom and the website for the Developmental Studies Center, the Child Development Project, and the Caring School Community. These websites are dedicated to fostering children's academic, ethical, and social development. These sites provide research-supported information, resources, and curriculum materials on child development and education, with an emphasis on promoting self-discipline.

www.devstu.org
www.responsiveclassroom.org

Information on Second Step and Quest Programs

www.cfchildren.org (Committee for Children website)
www.lions-quest.org (Lions-Quest website, of the Lions Clubs International)

Information to Assist in Selecting Storybooks and Literature That Address Social and Moral Problem Solving

www.scholastic.com (Scholastic Publishing)
www.NancyKeane.com (Nancy Keane's Booktalks)

Research-Based Computer Simulation Games for Teaching Social and Moral Problem Solving

www.tomsynder.com

Commercially-Produced Materials for Teaching Social and Moral Problem Solving, Social Skills, and Peer Mediation

www.researchpress.com (Research Press)
www.scholastic.com (Scholastic Inc.)
www.sopriswest.com (SOPRIS West Educational Services)
www.cfchildren.org (Committee for Children)
www.goodcharacter.com (Live Wire Media)

For articles, research, video clips, and other resources related to social and emotional learning, visit the website of the George Lucas Educational Foundation at www.glef.org.

For practical tips for class meetings, as well recommendations on a variety of other topics on classroom discipline and classroom management, visit www.proteacher.com.

REFERENCES

Bandura, A. (1986). *Social foundations of thought and action: A social cognitive theory.* Upper Saddle River, NJ: Prentice-Hall.

Bandura, A. (1989). Self-regulation of motivation and action through internal standards and goal systems. In L. A. Pervin (Ed.), *Goal concepts in personality and social psychology* (pp. 19–85). Hillsdale, NJ: Erlbaum.

Bandura, A. (1997). *Self-efficacy: The exercise of control.* New York: W. H. Freeman.

Barriga, A. Q., Landau, J. R., Stinson, B. L., Liau, A. K., & Gibbs, J. C. (2000). Cognitive distortion and problem behaviors in adolescents. *Criminal Justice and Behavior, 27,* 36–56.

Bear, G. G. (1989). Sociomoral reasoning and antisocial behaviors among normal sixth graders. *Merrill-Palmer Quarterly, 35,* 181–196.

Bear, G. G., Manning, M., Shiomi, K., & Kurtz, K. (2004, July). *Emotions and moral reasoning among children in Japan and the United States.* Paper presented at the International Association of School Psychologists. Exeter, England.

Bear, G. G., Manning, M. A., & Izard, C. (2002). Responsible behavior: The importance of social cognition and emotion. *School Psychology Quarterly, 18,* 140–157.

Bear, G. G., Richards, H. C., & Gibbs, J. (1997). Sociomoral reasoning and behavior. In G. G. Bear, K. M. Minke, and A. Thomas (Eds.), *Children's needs II: Development, problems, and alternatives* (pp. 13–25). Bethesda, MD: National Association of School Psychologists.

Bear, G. G., & Rys, G. S. (1994). Moral reasoning, classroom behavior, and sociometric status among elementary school children. *Developmental Psychology, 30,* 633–638.

Berenstain, S., & Berenstain, J. (1986). *Berenstain Bears series.* New York: Random House.

Blair, R. J. R., Monson, J., & Frederickson, N. (2001). Moral reasoning and conduct problems in children with emotional and behavioural difficulties. *Personality and Individual Differences, 31,* 799–811.

Boldizar, J. P., Perry, D. G., & Perry, L. C. (1989). Outcome values and aggression. *Child Development, 60,* 571–579.

Brown, A. L., & Palincsar, A. (1989). Guided cooperative learning and individual knowledge acquisition. In L. Resnick (Ed.), *Knowing, learning, and procedure* (pp. 393–452). Hillsdale, NJ: Erlbaum.

Burks, V. S., Laird, R. D., Dodge, K. A., Pettit, G. S., & Bates, J. E. (1999). Knowledge structures, social information processing, and children's aggressive behavior. *Social Development, 8,* 220–236.

Charney, R. S. (2002). *Teaching children to care: Classroom management for ethical and academic growth, K–8* (Rev. ed.). Greenfield, MA: Northeast Foundation for Children.

Coie, J. D., & Dodge, K. A. (1998). Aggression and antisocial behavior. In W. Damon (Series Ed.), &

N. Eisenberg (Vol. Ed.), *Handbook of child psychology, Vol. 3. Social, emotional, and personality development* (5th ed., pp. 779–862). New York: Wiley.

Colby, A., & Damon, W. (1999). The development of extraordinary moral commitment. In M. Killen & D. Hart (Eds.), *Morality in everyday life: Developmental perspectives* (pp. 342–370). New York: Cambridge University Press.

Colby, A., & Kohlberg, L. (1987). *The measurement of moral judgment: Vol. 1. Theoretical foundations and research validation.* New York: Cambridge University Press.

Committee for Children. (2003). *Second Step: A violence prevention curriculum.* Seattle, WA: Author.

Cornell, D. G., & Loper, A. B. (1998). Assessment of violence and other high-risk behaviors with a school survey. *School Psychology Review, 27,* 317–330.

Cosgrove, S. (1983). *Serendipity Books.* New York: Price Stern Sloan.

Crick, N. R., & Dodge, K. A. (1994). A review and reformulation of social information-processing mechanisms in children's social adjustment. *Psychological Bulletin, 115,* 74–101.

Crick, N. R., & Ladd, G. W. (1990). Children's perceptions of the outcomes of social strategies: Do the ends justify being mean? *Developmental Psychology, 26,* 612–620.

Developmental Studies Center (2000). *Ways we want our class to be: Class meetings that build commitment to kindness and learning. Ideas from the Child Development Project.* Oakland, CA: Author.

Dewey, J. (1916/1944). *Democracy and education.* New York: The Free Press.

Dishion, T. J., French, D. C., & Patterson, G. R. (1995). The development and ecology of antisocial behavior. In D. Cicchetti & D. J. Cohen (Eds.), *Developmental psychopathology, Vol. 2: Risk, disorder, and adaptation* (pp. 421–471). New York: John Wiley.

Disney, W. (Producer). (1940). *Pinocchio* [Film]. Buena Vista, FL: Walt Disney Productions.

Dodge, K. A., & Tomlin, A. M. (1987). Utilization of self-schemas as a mechanism of interpretational bias in aggressive children. *Social Cognition, 5,* 280–300.

Dunn, J., Cutting, A. L., & Demetriou, H. (2000). Moral sensibility, understanding others, and children's friendship interactions in the preschool period. *British Journal of Developmental Psychology, 18,* 159–177.

Dunn, J., & Herrera, C. (1997). Conflict resolution with friends, siblings, and mothers: A developmental perspective. *Aggressive Behavior, 23,* 343–357.

Eisenberg, N. (2000). Emotion, regulation, and moral development. *Annual Review of Psychology, 51,* 665–697.

Eisenberg, N., & Fabes, R. A. (1998). Prosocial development. In W. Damon (Series Ed.) & N. Eisenberg (Vol. Ed.), *Handbook of child psychology: Vol. 3. Social, emotional, and personality development* (5th ed., pp. 701–778). New York: Wiley.

Elias, M. J., & Tobias, S. E. (1996). *Social problem solving: Interventions in the schools.* New York: Guilford Press.

Elias, M. J., Zins, J. E., Weissberg, R. P., Frey, K. S., Greenberg, M. T., Haynes, N. M., Kessler, R., Schwab-Stone, M. E., & Shriver, T. P. (1997). *Promoting social and emotional learning: Guidelines for educators.* Alexandria, VA: Association for Supervision and Curriculum Development.

Erdley, C. A., & Asher, S. R. (1998). Linkages between children's beliefs about the legitimacy of aggression and their behavior. *Social Development, 7,* 321–339.

Farmer, T. W. (2000). Misconceptions of peer rejection and problem behavior. *Remedial and Special Education, 21,* 194–208.

Giancola, S. P., & Bear, G. G. (2003). Face validity: Perspectives from a local evaluator. *Psychology in the Schools.* (Special issue: *Safe Schools/Healthy Students: National Projects), 40,* 515–529.

Gibbs, J. C., Potter, G. B., & Goldstein, A. P. (1995). *The EQUIP program: Teaching youth to think and act responsibly through a peer-helping approach.* Champaign, IL: Research Press.

Goldstein, A. P., Harootunian, B., & Conoley, J. C. (1994). *Student aggression: Prevention, management, and replacement training.* New York: Guilford.

Guerra, N. G., Nucci, L., & Huesmann, L. R. (1994). Moral cognition and childhood aggression. In L. R. Huesmann (Ed.), *Aggressive behavior: Current perspectives* (pp. 13–33). New York: Plenum.

Hoffman, M. L. (2000). *Empathy and moral development: Implications for caring and justice.* New York: Cambridge Press.

Hubbard, J. A., Dodge, K. A., Cillessen, A. H. N., Coie, J. D., & Schwartz, D. (2001). The dyadic nature of social information processing in boys' reactive and proactive aggression. *Journal of Personality and Social Psychology, 80,* 268–280.

Hubbs-Tait, L., & Garmon, L. C. (1995). The relationship of moral reasoning and AIDS knowledge to risky sexual behavior. *Adolescence, 30,* 549–564.

Huesmann, L. R. (1988). An information processing model for the development of aggression. *Aggressive Behavior, 14,* 13–24.

Hughes, J. N., & Hasbrouck, J. E. (1996). Television violence: Implications for violence prevention. *School Psychology Review, 25,* 134–151.

Johnson, D. W., & Johnson, R. T. (1995). *Teaching students to be peacemakers* (3rd ed.). Edina, MN: Interaction Books.

Johnson, D. W., & Johnson, R. T. (1996). Conflict resolution and peer mediation programs in elementary and secondary schools: A review of research. *Review of Educational Research, 66,* 459–506.

Johnson, D. W., & Johnson, R. T. (1999). Making cooperative learning work. *Theory into Practice, 38,* 67–73.

Kauffman, J. M. (2001). *Characteristics of emotional and behavioral disorders of children and youth* (7th ed.). Columbus, OH: Prentice-Hall.

Kohlberg, L. (1984). *Essays on moral development: Vol. II. The psychology of moral development.* New York: Harper & Row.

Kuther, T. L. (2000). Moral reasoning, perceived competence, and adolescent engagement in risky activity. *Journal of Adolescence, 23,* 599–604.

Lickona, T. (2004). *Character matters: How to help our children develop good judgement, integrity, and other essential virtues.* New York: Touchstone.

Manning, M., & Bear, G. G. (2002). Are children's concerns about punishment related to their behavior? Examining the link between moral reasoning and aggression. *Journal of School Psychology, 40,* 523–604.

Miller, P. A., Eisenberg, N., Fabes, R. A., & Shell, R. (1996). Relations of moral reasoning and vicarious emotion to young children's prosocial behavior toward peers and adults. *Developmental Psychology, 32,* 210–219.

Mitchell, J. M., Johnson, D. W., & Johnson, R. T. (2002). Are all types of cooperation equal? Impact of academic controversy versus concurrence-seeking on health education. *Social Psychology of Education, 5,* 329–344.

Natasi, B. K., & Clements, D. H. (1991). Research on cooperative learning: Implications for practice. *School Psychology Review, 20,* 110–137.

Nisan, M. (1991). The moral balance model: Theory and research extending our understanding In W. M. Kurtines & J. L. Gewirtz (Eds.), *Handbook of moral behavior and development, Vol. 3. Application* (pp. 213–249). Hillsdale, NJ: Erlbaum.

Nucci, L. P. (2001). *Education in the moral domain.* New York: Cambridge University Press.

Palmer, E. J., & Hollin, C. R. (2001). Sociomoral reasoning, perceptions of parenting, and self-reported delinquency in adolescents. *Applied Cognitive Psychology, 15,* 85–100.

Patterson, G. R., Capaldi, D., & Bank, L. (1991). An early starter model for predicting delinquency. In D. J. Pepler & K. H. Rubin (Eds.), *The development and treatment of childhood aggression* (pp. 139–168). Hillsdale, NJ: Lawrence Erlbaum.

Power, F. C., Higgins, A., & Kohlberg, L. (1989). *Lawence Kohlberg's approach to moral education.* New York: Columbia University Press.

Quest International (1998). *Lions Quest life skills programs* (K–5, 6–8, 9–12). Oak Brook, IL: Lions-Quest Lions Clubs International Foundation.

Quiggle, N. L., Garber, J., Panak, W. F., & Dodge, K. A. (1992). Social information processing in aggressive and depressed children. *Child Development, 63,* 1305–1320.

Rubin, K. H., Briem, L. A., & Rose-Krasnor, L. (1991). Social problem solving and aggression in childhood. In D. J. Pepler & K. H. Rubin (Eds.), *The development and treatment of childhood aggression* (pp. 219–248). Hillsdale, NJ: Erlbaum.

Schrumpt, F., Crawford, D. K., & Bodine, R. J. (1997). *Peer mediation: Conflict resolution in the schools.* Champaign, IL: Research Press.

Shure, M. B. (1992). *I can problem solve: An interpersonal cognitive problem-solving program: Intermediate elementary grades.* Champaign, IL: Research Press.

Shure, M. B. (2001). How to think, not what to think: A problem-solving approach to prevention of early high-risk behaviors. In A. C. Bohart and D. J. Stipek (Eds.), *Constructive and destructive behavior: Implications for family, school, and society* (pp. 271–290). Washington, DC: American Psychological Association.

Slaby, R. G., & Guerra, N. G. (1988). Cognitive mediators of aggression in adolescent offenders: I. Assessment. *Developmental Psychology, 24,* 580–588.

Slavin, R. E. (1994). *Cooperative learning: Theory, research, and practice.* Boston, MA: Allyn & Bacon.

Smetana, J. G. (1995). Parenting styles and conceptions of parental authority during adolescence. *Child Development, 66,* 299–316.

Spivak, G., Platt, J. J., Jr., & Shure, M. (1976). *The problem solving approach to adjustment.* San Francisco: Jossey Bass.

Spivak, G., & Shure, M. B. (1982). The cognition of social adjustment: Interpersonal cognitive problem-solving thinking. In B. B. Lahey & A. E. Kazdin (Eds.), *Advances in clinical child psychology, Vol. 5* (pp. 323–369). New York: Plenum.

Stone, C. A. (1998). The metaphor of scaffolding: Its utility for the field of learning disabilities. *Journal of Learning Disabilities, 31,* 344–364.

Taylor, J. H., & Walker, L. J. (1997). Moral climate and the development of moral reasoning: The effects of dyadic discussions between young offenders. *Journal of Moral Education, 26,* 21–43.

Tsuchida, I., & Lewis, C. C. (1996). Responsibility and learning: Some preliminary hypotheses about Japanese elementary classrooms. In T. P. Rohlen & G. K. LeTendre (Eds.), *Teaching and learning in Japan* (pp. 190–212). New York: Cambridge University Press.

Turiel, E. (1998). The development of morality. In W. Damon (Ser. Ed.) & N. Eisenberg (Vol. Ed.), *Handbook of child psychology: Vol. 3. Social, emotional, and personality development* (5th ed., pp. 863–932). New York: Wiley.

Weiner, B. (2001). Responsibility for social transgressions: An attributional analysis. In B. F. Malle, L. J. Moses, & D. A. Baldwin (Eds.), *Intentions and intentionality: Foundations of social cognition* (pp. 331–344). Cambridge, MA: MIT Press.

Zahn-Waxler, C., Friedman, R. J., Cole, P. M., Mizuta, I, & Hiruma, N. (1996). Japanese and United States preschool children's responses to conflict and distress. *Child Development, 67,* 2462–2477.

Zelli, A., Dodge, K. A., Lochman, J. E., & Laird, R. D. (1999). The distinction between beliefs legitimizing aggression and deviant processing of social cues: Testing measurement validity and the hypothesis that biased processing mediates the effects of beliefs on aggression. *Journal of Personality and Social Psychology, 77,* 150–166.

CHAPTER

9 Developing Emotional Competencies and Self-Discipline

CO-AUTHOR MAUREEN A. MANNING

GUIDING QUESTIONS

- Which emotions are related to self-discipline, prosocial behavior, and antisocial behavior? *How* are they related to behavior?
- How is one's self-concept related to self-discipline and behavior?
- What are the primary determinants of self-worth? How do teachers and schools influence the self-worth of students?

173

- What roles do teacher–student relationships and classroom climate play in the development of emotions and self-discipline?
- Should teachers refrain from inducing feelings of guilt and shame in students?
- How might both overregulation and underregulation of emotions contribute to mental health and behavioral problems?
- What techniques can teachers use to promote "positive" emotions of happiness, pride, and empathy and help translate these into prosocial behaviors?
- What techniques can teachers use to foster empathy, caring, and prosocial behavior and to help students inhibit frustration and aggression?

> The educational task, then, is to educate the passions, especially the moral sentiments. Faced with evil, we must feel revulsion. Faced with another's pain, we must feel the desire to remove or alleviate it. Faced with our own inclinations to cause harm, we must be both shocked and willing to face the reality. Then we can invite reason to serve our corrected passions. (Noddings, 2002, p. 8)

> The major "take home" message from our book is that, over the years, guilt has received a bad rap. In a rush to free ourselves from a repressive, "old-fashioned" morality, we may have dismissed too quickly the adaptive function of guilt. In the course of day-to-day life, people do occasionally transgress, offend, or otherwise cause harm to others. It may be uncomfortable but still adaptive (for ourselves and others) to experience guilt in connection with such specific behavioral transgressions. The tension, remorse, and regret of guilt causes us to stop and re-think—and it offers a way out, pressing us to confess, apologize, and make amends. We become better people, and the world becomes a better place. (Tangney & Dearing, 2002, p. 180)

Emotions provide insight as to *why* many behaviors occur and direction to educators as to *how* to best develop self-discipline and prevent and correct misbehavior. Typically, emotions are closely linked to social and moral problem solving: How we think influences how we feel, and vice versa. With respect to behavior, emotions often provide the spark that translates thought into action, either prosocial or antisocial. As is true with social and moral problem solving, an emphasis on emotion is not new to classroom discipline. Recall that emotions were the focus of Rousseau's philosophy and of the Enlightenment period, which had a major influence on moral education. Likewise, consistent with their psychoanalytic backgrounds, both Dreikurs and Glasser emphasized the importance of various emotions. For example, they argued that educators must meet children's psychological needs, especially the need for positive self-worth and for social belonging (or relatedness), and warned educators to avoid inducing anger and fear. Glasser in particular highlighted the role of guilt in responsible behavior by emphasizing choice and responsibility.

Self-discipline is closely linked to emotional competence, or to what in recent years has come to be called *emotional intelligence*. Emotional intelligence refers to skills such as recognizing emotions in oneself and others, regulating emotions, motivating oneself, and handling relationships (Salovey & Mayer, 1990). Emotional intelligence is highly integrated with social and moral competence (Hoffman, 2000; Saarni, 1999); thus it is difficult to separate the social, emotional, and moral elements in responsible behavior, self-control, sympathy, fairness, caring, and so forth. Emotion is central to each of these aspects of character, and social and emotional learning. The recent emphasis on emotion in classroom discipline is consistent with the arguments of a growing number of researchers that emotion plays an equal, if not greater, role than social cognition in motivating students' behavior (e.g., Goleman, 1995; Hoffman, 2000; Kochanska, 1994; Saarni, 1999).

Emotions are commonly grouped into two categories: *positive* and *negative.* Positive emotions are those that educators desire to develop among students: happiness, pride, joy, excitement, and interest. Research links positive emotions to prosocial behavior, motivation, popularity among peers, high self-esteem, and greater tolerance for frustration (Eisenberg, 2000; Harter, 1999). In contrast to positive emotions, negative emotions are those that educators tend to discourage in students, or try not to induce: anger, fear, jealousy, contempt, and disgust. Among the negative emotions, it is anger and fear that are most relevant to classroom behavior. Whereas anger often leads to aggression, fear frequently stifles motivation and self-discipline.

Some emotions are difficult to classify as either "good" or "bad" (or "positive" or "negative"). This is particularly true with guilt, shame, and sorrow—emotions that educators often are reluctant to target for development but that are perhaps most critical to self-discipline. Indeed, many theorists and researchers view guilt, shame, and empathy (which is closely related to sorrow, as explained below) as the *moral emotions* because they have been most directly linked to the display of prosocial behavior and the inhibition of antisocial behavior (Eisenberg, 2000).

It should be noted that although the preceding emotions are often viewed as positive, negative, or moral, no emotion is necessarily good, bad, moral, or immoral. Rather, each emotion serves an important adaptive, biological function (Izard, 1991). For example, whereas anger often triggers horrendous acts of violence, it also triggers us to take action, both aggressive and peaceful, against acts of injustice. Likewise, whereas moderate levels of anxiety, guilt, fear, joy, and excitement are generally adaptive, extremely low or high levels of these and other emotions may contribute to multiple negative outcomes, including impaired academic and social functioning.

Most behavior problems in school that are rooted in emotion can be prevented. This is done when educators address classroom and school factors that influence whether students feel angry, fearful, happy, proud, or responsible for their behavior. For example, effective teachers help prevent negative emotions by avoiding public humiliation, harsh and unfair punishment, and frustrating assignments. Because many factors outside the classroom also influence students' emotions, there are limits to the extent to which teachers can help cultivate positive emotions and curtail negative emotions. For example, low self-esteem, poor motivation, anger, and fear are influenced by many factors beyond the control of the classroom teacher, such as families and peers. Nevertheless, it is clear that teachers and schools have both a short-term and long-term impact on the emotions of every child.

Goals, strategies, and techniques for developing students' emotions, especially those more directly related to self-discipline, are the focus of this chapter. Consistent with the three categories of emotion presented previously, three educational goals for teachers are presented: (1) develop positive emotions, especially those related to positive self-worth; (2) develop moral emotions, especially those associated with caring and responsibility; and (3) develop self-regulation and coping skills. The importance of each of these goals in the development of self-discipline is discussed, followed by practical, research-based strategies and techniques for achieving them.

STOP AND REFLECT
Three Emotions-Focused Case Studies

Eric

"Eric's a kid who can't control his anger. When he gets mad, it's hard to predict how he's going to vent his frustration. He doesn't seem to think before he acts, about the consequences for himself or for others. But even when he does, he doesn't seem to care. He shows neither empathy nor any remorse when he hurts someone. I don't think he *understands* how others feel. No one likes him, which is understandable given his uncaring attitude and behavior. But I'm not sure if this even bothers him. I understand that he also was like this in elementary and middle school."

Chris

"Chris is really a good kid, but he's a puzzle. He's a B student, happy, and one of the most popular kids in our high school. He always accepts responsibility for his actions and is quick to make amends whenever he behaves in an irresponsible manner. I think this is because he feels a bit guilty after doing something he knows he shouldn't. He's also concerned about how others feel about his behavior, especially those whom he likes, respects, and believes care about him. If he doesn't like and respect you, look out because you're in for a challenge. His worst behavior is in health and gym where he's constantly rebelling against what he perceives as the teacher's noncaring and authoritarian attitude.

Chris can be the most kind, polite, and caring kid I know, but he often does stupid things that get him into trouble. Most are minor, and sometimes humorous, like making silly noises in class, locking the gym teacher in a closet, and rearranging the Christmas lawn ornaments throughout his neighborhood late one night (for which the police removed him from school and reprimanded him). He was suspended two other times this year. In both of these cases he thought he did the right thing, and perhaps he did. The first time he was suspended he came to the defense of a girl in my class who was being slapped by her ex-boyfriend. It was during homeroom period and I had stepped out into the hallway. When I returned, Chris punched the girl's boyfriend. The second time he was suspended it was for a fight during gym. A classmate was teasing a student with a physical disability, and Chris told him several times to stop. I guess when Chris said, 'don't do it again,' he meant it. In both cases, when the principal asked Chris why he did what he did, Chris said that it makes him angry to see kids who can't protect themselves being bullied. Chris emphasized, '*Someone* has to do something about it. I would feel awful if I just stood there and didn't help.' I honestly don't think Chris would ever harm anyone unless it was either to defend himself or to help someone else. It's a shame that his record shows two suspensions."

Natasha

"I was shocked to hear that Natasha attempted suicide over the weekend. I was less surprised to hear that she had low self-esteem and viewed herself negatively. She often said that no one cares about her. I noticed a drop in her grades this marking period: She didn't turn in several homework assignments and skipped several classes. She seemed to be 'tuned out' during class and had an 'attitude problem.' I thought she was a bit passive aggressive, and I knew she didn't have many friends. In addition, her boyfriend broke up with her last month and her parents were having marital problems. I guess she just couldn't handle all the stress in her life."

The preceding cases are real-life stories of "discipline problems" that were brought to the attention of the authors. Note that in each case the teacher consistently refers to *emotions* when describing the student, implying that emotions play a central role in each student's behavior. Identify the emotions in each case and the behaviors to which the emotions were linked. In what ways might, or should, an emphasis on understanding each student's emotions impact how you correct his or her misbehavior?

Emotion-Related Goals for Developing Self-Discipline

Develop Positive Emotions, Especially Those Related to Positive Self-Worth

Feelings of happiness and pride characterize, if not define, positive self-worth and emotional well-being. Positive self-worth, or self-esteem, tends to be associated with high achievement motivation (Dweck, 2002) and overall life satisfaction (Gilman & Huebner, 2003). Conversely, low self-worth tends to be associated with poor achievement motivation and mental health problems, particularly depression (Harter, 1999). Of practical value to classroom teachers concerned about understanding and developing emotions linked to self-discipline, it is important to note that happiness and pride and, thus, positive self-worth and emotional well-being tend to develop among students who (1) perceive their behavioral conduct favorably and (2) perceive others as valuable sources of social support (Harter, 1999).

Self-Perceptions of Behavioral Conduct.   Students with positive global self-worth tend to perceive their behavior, in general, to be consistent with their personal standards and the standards of others they desire to emulate. Behavioral conduct is one of five domains of competency or adequacy that researchers have consistently found to be related to feelings of global self-worth or self-esteem (Harter, 1999). The other four domains are academic competence, athletic competence, social acceptance, and physical appearance. The extent to which students perceive themselves as competent in these general domains (as well as in more specific areas, such as math, soccer, and music) largely determines their feelings of global self-worth. The relationship between global self-worth and self-perceptions of competence is not always simple and direct, however. Rather, it is influenced by (1) the importance that students attach to each domain and (2) the attributions they make about their competency, or lack thereof, in domains that are important to them.

With respect to perceived importance, a student's self-perception of incompetence in a specific domain is unlikely to have a negative impact on self-worth if that domain is viewed as unimportant. For example, low self-perceptions of athletics are unlikely to impair overall self-worth among students who do not value athletics. Whereas the same logic also applies to behavioral conduct, it should be noted that very few students actually dismiss the importance of the behavioral domain (Clever, Bear, & Juvonen, 1992; Harter, 1999). This may be true because no other domain, with the exception of academics, receives as much attention and is valued as highly by others in school, at home, and in society. Most students view their behavioral conduct as central to their sense of self and, thus, strive to act in accord with personal and social standards (Damon & Hart, 1988; Harter, 1999). Among the few students who believe that moral behavior is unimportant, a relationship between their behavior and self-esteem should not be expected. Indeed, research shows that many aggressive children and adolescents view themselves as favorably as, or sometimes even more favorably than, their nonaggressive peers (David & Kistner, 2000; Hughes, Cavell, & Grossman, 1997; Zakriski & Coie, 1996). Thus, contrary to popular perception, many aggressive children and adolescents, *including bullies,* do not experience low self-esteem. To these students, their attitude is "Nothing's wrong with stealing, lying, or fighting, so why should I feel bad about doing it?" Indeed, many leaders of violent gangs feel very proud of their "leadership skills." The lack of self-esteem is certainly not among their many problems. Thus, it would be foolish to try to change the behaviors of these students by encouraging them to feel more highly about themselves.

The second major factor that determines the extent to which self-perceptions of behavioral conduct influence self-worth relates to whether students attribute their conduct to their *own* efforts or to forces beyond their control (e.g., luck, genetics). Attributing responsible behavior to one's own efforts fosters feelings of pride and autonomy, which are key ingredients of positive self-worth (Harter, 1999), and motivates further responsible behavior. In contrast, attributing behavior to external events is less likely to have the same effect. For example, it may be difficult for students, particularly older students, to feel good about themselves for sharing and helping others when they did so solely because "the teacher told me to" or because "the teacher said she would put a marble in the reward jar."

STOP AND REFLECT

To avoid both internal negative consequences (i.e., feelings of guilt, shame, or lower self-esteem) and external negative consequences (i.e., punishment), many students deny that good behavior or not getting into trouble is important or that they are responsible for their actions. Make a list of common comments students use to avoid responsibility and to protect their self-worth. Beside each comment write how you can verbally respond in a manner that might tactfully challenge the self-protecting comment while doing the least harm to the positive teacher–student relationship. (For this exercise do not think about what consequences should follow the behaviors.)
For example:

Student's Response	Teacher's Response
"I don't care if I get into trouble."	"I think you do care, and I certainly care about you, your behavior, and how your behavior affects others."
"I didn't do it" (when you know he did).	"I'm sorry that you did do it, and I'm disappointed that you're not accepting responsibility. Now, what can you do to 'fix' the problem? I'm confident you know how."
"But Natasha started it!"	"Kellie, I saw what happened and I'm less concerned about how this started than I am about how you chose to respond. I've seen you respond better in similar situations."

Social Support.   Another important contributor to self-worth, as well as to motivation and overall emotional well-being, is self-perceptions of social support, that is, perceptions among students that others *care* about them (Harter, 1999). It was social support that both Dreikurs (Dreikurs & Cassel, 1972) and Glasser (1969) were referring to when they emphasized the psychological need of social belonging. They argued that students who fail to experience a sense of social belonging are likely to harbor feelings of inferiority or low self-worth and, consequently, exhibit maladaptive and disruptive behavior. Research in psychology supports these arguments.

Research shows that students who feel rejected by their teachers and peers are at great risk for a variety of negative outcomes, including low self-worth, depression, anxiety, poor academic achievement, dislike and avoidance of school (including truancy and dropping out), and a wide range of conduct problems (Hawker & Boulton, 2000; Pianta, 1999). The harsher the social rejection, the greater is the risk. Risk is particularly great when feelings of social rejection are associated with the chronic victimization that characterizes bullying by peers (Egan, Monson, & Perry, 1998) or the use of corporal punishment and emotional maltreatment by parents and teachers (Hyman & Snook, 1999). Unfortunately, failure to experience a sense of belonging or attachment to others begins early for many students. Developing positive, trusting relationships with these students is a particular challenge for teachers. Given their history of insecure relationships, they are unlikely to trust others and are likely to view themselves as undeserving of caring. However, as found in a study of teachers of students living in poverty (Haberman, 1995), effective teachers accept this challenge and recognize that their relationship with individual students, together with motivating instruction, are critical to their success.

In contrast to the negative outcomes associated with social rejection, positive outcomes are associated with caring and supportive relationships (Pianta, 1999). Not only do such relationships promote positive self-worth (Harter, 1999) but, as correctly noted by Dreikurs and Glasser, they also are the key to developing self-discipline and preventing behavior problems. For example, substantial research indicates that *students tend to internalize the values and standards of those with whom they share warm relationships and, thus, are more likely to listen to and comply with their requests than with the requests of those whom they perceive as harsh or uncaring* (Grusec & Goodnow, 1994; Hoffman, 2000).

Positive emotions define not only healthy individuals but also healthy schools. In schools viewed most favorably by researchers, educators, parents, and students, the students and staff alike experience a positive climate characterized by a sense of caring, belonging, and *community* (Noddings, 1992; Solomon, Battistich, Watson, Schaps, & Lewis, 2000; Solomon, Watson, Battistich, Schaps, & Delucchi, 1996). Students who feel connected to the school community recognize that their own behavior contributes to the welfare of the community and tend to act in ways that strengthen their attachment to the community and to avoid behaviors that weaken it. As a result, they often exhibit greater empathy for others, better conflict resolution skills (Solomon et al., 1996, 2000), reduced drug use and delinquency (Battistich & Hom, 1997; Battistich, Schaps, Watson, Solomon, & Lewis, 2000), decreased absenteeism and suspension (Haynes, Emmon, & Ben-Avie, 1997; Welsh, 2000), and higher academic effort and achievement (Haynes, Emmons, & Woodruff, 1998; Solomon et al., 1996, 2000) than students who do not feel connected to the school community. The positive effects of a caring school community are evident across socioeconomic groups but are strongest among students in high-poverty schools (Battistich, Solomon, Kim, Watson, & Schaps, 1995). Interestingly, experiencing a sense of caring and belonging at school has been shown to be a greater predictor than either race or social class of one's behavior in school (Jenkins, 1997).

Not only does a positive and caring environment help develop self-discipline and prevent behavior problems, but it also is of great importance in the correction and remediation of behavior problems. Research indicates that aggression actually decreases after students are placed among teachers with whom they develop positive relationships (Hughes, Cavell, & Jackson, 1999). Similarly, many teachers can attest that during disciplinary encounters students are less prone to resist and argue when they perceive the person administering the discipline as caring and fair.

Teacher support and encouragement promote positive self-esteem and achievement motivation not only directly but also indirectly through more favorable perceptions from peers. Students show greater social acceptance toward classmates who receive frequent praise and social support from their teachers (Hughes, Cavell, & Willson, 2000). That is, although students tend to reject classmates who exhibit frequent disruptive and aggressive behavior (e.g., Arnold, Homrok, Ortiz, & Stowe, 1999), social acceptance, particularly in the lower grades, appears more highly influenced by the teacher's response to student behavior, including the *public display* of social support or the lack thereof (Hughes et al., 2000; Ladd, Birch, & Buhs, 1999), than by the student's actual behavior.

IMPLEMENTATION TIP

Fostering Self-Esteem

Unfortunately many educators purchase a wealth of materials that espouse the popular and misleading belief that simply telling kids that they are wonderful, terrific, nice, and so on builds self-esteem. Seldom do any of these materials work (Bear, Minke, Griffin, & Deemer, 1997). Recent theory and research show that self-esteem is much more complex. As reviewed previously, such theory and research recognize the critical importance of students' self-perceptions in multiple domains of competence, their valuing of these domains, their assumptions of autonomy or responsibility, and their self-perceptions of social support. Consistent with such theory and research, it behooves teachers not to waste their money and time on self-esteem–building materials but to devote greater attention to everyday classroom techniques that enhance self-esteem such as the following:

- Demonstrate social support by showing personal interest in every individual student. For example:
  - Discover each student's strengths, interests, favorite sports, hobbies, television shows, books, family background, and so on and refer to this information during daily discourse with the individual student and the class. Such information can be gathered by distributing a simple survey (e.g., What are your favorite hobbies? What do you enjoy doing the most?), by asking students to write about what they are most proud of or what they do best, by personally interviewing each student, or by having students interview one another and report their results to the class. Students also can be asked to develop an autobiography in which they profile their backgrounds, achievements, hobbies, and future goals.
  - Demonstrate sincere concern and strong support for students during times of need and hardship. Encourage students to do the same with their peers. One way to discover when students need emotional support is by requiring a journal in which students may (but are not required to) express emotional needs.

- ■ Consistently demonstrate respect, acceptance, and care toward all students, regardless of their backgrounds and past or present behavior.

  - ▪ When addressing misbehavior, the message should be that although the student's misbehavior is unacceptable, the student is always acceptable and worthwhile. Avoid attacks on the student's character and instead focus your remarks on the student's behavior (e.g., instead of "you're irresponsible," say "what you did was irresponsible").
  - ▪ Draw a distinction between students' feelings and their behaviors. Teach students that "all feelings are okay but all behaviors are not okay." For example, emphasize that it is "okay" for them to feel angry, but that it is "not okay" for them to express their anger in a way that could hurt themselves or others. One way that students can often express their feelings without hurting anyone is simply by telling someone how they feel.
  - ▪ Display a positive and optimistic attitude. Even when working with students with the most challenging behavior problems, demonstrate confidence that their behavior will improve. Research shows that effective classroom managers view every day "as a new day" and do not hold the past behaviors of students against them (Brophy, 1996).
  - ▪ View mistakes of behavior as learning experiences, not failures. Use these mistakes as opportunities to teach students more responsible behavior.
  - ▪ Exhibit random acts of kindness and encourage students to do the same.

- ■ Avoid social comparisons (e.g., posting of grades). Encourage students to compare their performance (including in behavior) not to that of their peers but to personal goals or previous performance (e.g., instead of saying "Why don't you act like others in the class?" you should say "Your behavior is much better than last week when you show that you can ignore others when they bother you").

- ■ Avoid public humiliation. When possible, handle discipline problems privately, not publicly.

- ■ Garner social support from others, especially parents and peers, to help bolster positive emotions and behavior. A two-minute phone call home, informing parents that their child could use some emotional support after experiencing an unexpected failure, is likely to be time well spent.

- ■ To help protect feelings of autonomy and, thus, self-esteem, apply only as much external regulation as necessary to bring about compliance. Referred to as the *principle of minimal sufficiency* (Lepper, 1983), educators should use "just enough" external pressure to bring about compliance without making students feel that they are being coerced. When external pressure is not obvious, students tend to believe that they perform a requisite behavior for reasons that are intrinsically motivated and, thus, are more likely to engage in that behavior in the future (Hoffman, 2000).

Develop Moral Emotions, Especially Those Associated with Caring and Responsibility

The focus of the preceding section was on the importance of positive feelings about oneself, including feelings of happiness, pride, social belonging, and self-worth. Of equal if not greater interest to educators is fostering emotions among students that promote the happiness and welfare of *others*—emotions that motivate caring and responsible behavior. At the core of caring and responsible behavior are *empathy* and *guilt*.

Empathy.   Empathy is the ability to feel or experience the same or similar emotion as another person. Empathy is evident when one feels sad, angry, or afraid of seeing another person hurt, upset, or being bullied. The experience of empathy requires cognitive as well as affective abilities, including the ability to recognize emotional cues in others, the ability to assume the perspective of others, and the ability to share in the emotions of others (Hoffman, 2000). Although students who are high in empathy often help and share more than their peers, the relationship between empathy and prosocial behavior is not particularly strong (Miller, Eisenberg, Fabes, & Shell, 1996). Because many other factors account for prosocial behavior (e.g., peer influences), some students who are high in empathy fail to act any more prosocially than those who are low in empathy. One important consideration is whether empathy results in feelings of *sympathy,* which are feelings of sincere concern about the other person, or in self-centered feelings of *personal distress,* such as anxiety or fear for one's own safety or comfort (Eisenberg, 2000). Whereas sympathy motivates students to help *others,* personal distress motivates students to help *themselves* by avoiding, withdrawing, or otherwise reducing their negative feelings. A practical implication of this distinction is that teachers should encourage students to focus on the feelings of others.

In contrast to its sometimes weak and inconsistent relationship with prosocial behavior, empathy is related more strongly and consistently to aggressive behavior. In general, empathic students tend to exhibit less aggression and aggressive students tend to exhibit less empathy than their peers (although the exact findings depend on the measure used to assess empathy; Miller & Eisenberg, 1988). Among aggressive students, deficits in the cognitive aspects of empathy often preclude the capacity for an affective response. For example, as noted in the previous chapter, aggressive students tend to have difficulty recognizing emotional cues in others and taking the perspective of others (Blair & Coles, 2000; Cohen & Strayer, 1996); as a result, they may be less likely to anticipate, let alone experience, empathy.

Guilt.   Guilt is the uncomfortable feeling, often stimulated by empathy, that an individual experiences after violating a personal moral standard and attributing responsibility for the violation to oneself. Guilt typically occurs when students cause emotional or physical harm to someone else or believe that they could have (and *should* have) done something to prevent such harm (Eisenberg, 2000; Tangney & Dearing, 2002). However, guilt is experienced not only when one's behavior (or the lack thereof) impacts others but also when one fails to live up to one's own personal standards, irrespective of the impact of the behavior on others. For example, guilt may be experienced when a student fails or cheats on a test (Bybee, Merisca, & Velasco, 1998; DePalma, Madey, & Bornschein, 1995).

It is the *anticipation* of guilt, rather than the presence or absence of external rewards and punishment, that prevents many moral transgressions and promotes much prosocial behavior. Students often refrain from hurting others, or decide to help others, because they would not like how they would feel if their behavior was discrepant with their personal standards (e.g., "If I don't help now I know I'll feel awful later if she suffers" or "I don't think I could live with myself if I hurt him"; Bandura, 1986; Hoffman, 2000). As such, guilt functions as a "self-administered sanction" (Williams, 1998, p. 234) that is experienced whether or not a student's misbehavior is detected by adults.

Guilt not only prevents most students from committing moral transgressions but also motivates students to act responsibly after they have harmed others or have otherwise violated personal or social standards (Bandura, 1986; Hoffman, 2000). That is, it is guilt that often motivates students to "fess up," apologize, or repair any harm that they caused. They do so to reduce or eliminate their feelings of remorse, and to feel better about themselves. Guilt is the emotional basis of social and moral responsibility, and social and moral responsibility largely defines self-discipline.

Students who are more prone to guilt than their peers tend to be less impulsive, coercive, aggressive, and disruptive (Loper, Hoffschmidt, & Ash, 2001; Williams, 1998) and more likely to help others (Chapman, Zahn-Waxler, Cooperman, & Iannotti, 1987). Such students also are frequently viewed by their teachers and peers as caring, considerate, honest, and trustworthy (Williams, 1998). Research showing that increases in guilt are related to decreases in antisocial behavior (Born, Chevalier, & Humblet, 1997) suggests that teachers might reduce misbehavior among students by inducing feelings of guilt by emphasizing social and moral responsibility. They should be cautious in any efforts to do so, however, as noted below.

As is true with all emotions, intense feelings of guilt can be maladaptive. Thus, educators must be cautious in using techniques, especially over time, that induce strong feelings of guilt. More importantly, educators should be cautious in inducing *shame*—an emotion closely related to guilt. Although it is sometimes difficult to differentiate the two emotions, guilt and shame differ in very important ways (Tangney & Dearing, 2002). Shame occurs when students believe that their behavior fails to meet standards set by themselves or by others, *and* such failure is perceived to reflect a serious deficiency in the self that causes others to view them negatively. *In contrast to guilt, it is the overall self, and not simply the misbehavior, that is devalued.* Consequently, in experiencing shame students feel that there is little, if anything, that they can do about their behavior. For example, they do not believe "what I did was wrong and I need to fix it," which is common with feelings of guilt, but instead that "others think I'm an awful person, and I agree" (i.e., "I can't do anything about it.").

Like all other emotions, shame *can* serve an adaptive function (Harter, 1999; Izard, 1991). As with guilt, the anticipation of shame can be a powerful deterrent against moral transgressions. Many students refrain from the most reprehensible acts because they know that they would experience shame if they were to engage in such behavior. In this manner, shame, like guilt, serves as an invaluable internalized sanction against moral transgressions and socially irresponsible behavior (Izard, 2001).

Despite its adaptive functions, shame often has deleterious effects and, thus, should be minimized in the classroom. Unlike guilt, which motivates students to make retribution or "fix" the misbehavior, shame motivates students to escape, hide, or avoid those who "shamed" them. Among many students, shame, but not guilt, tends to be associated with high rates of anger and aggression (Eisenberg, 2000; Tangney & Dearing, 2002). If intense or repeated often, feelings of shame also may lead to poor motivation, sadness, hopelessness, and depression (Harter, 1999). When infrequent and mild (e.g., "You should feel ashamed of yourself for intentionally hurting someone"), shame is unlikely to have significant negative effects on a student and may very well serve to help the student internalize moral standards. It is likely to be harmful, however, when it communicates the message that a student consistently fails to meet important standards, that such failure is the student's responsibility, that the failure reflects a "bad" or unworthy person, and that there is nothing the student can do to correct the behavior. Thus, such statements as "I don't understand why you're so bad" and "You're the worst kid in the class" are likely to induce shame. These comments are particularly damning when made in the context of yelling and other forms of public humiliation. Matters are even worse when teachers fail to alleviate lasting feelings of shame by providing little, if any, support and guidance on how to improve the behavior, by overlooking positive behaviors, and by using punishment as the primary, if not exclusive, means of correction.

STOP AND REFLECT

Reflect upon the preceding distinctions between guilt and shame and educational practices that might induce these two emotions. What role did guilt and shame play in your social and emotional development? Who helped develop it? How? Was it adaptive or maladaptive? What are some examples of "shaming" that educators use today (and should be avoided)?

Develop Self-Regulation and Coping Skills

Stress and Coping. When we think of major life stressors faced by many students, we tend to think of divorce, poverty, abuse, and violence. Although these are significant sources of stress, students report feeling more distress over their *relationships* with parents, siblings, and friends (Spirito, Stark, Grace, & Stamoulis, 1991). Inability to cope with these conflicts renders students just as prone to social, emotional, and academic problems as students who are exposed to the more serious risk factors mentioned previously. In fact, the ability to cope with "minor" day-to-day stressors (e.g., being teased by siblings, threatened by a bully, rejected by classmates, or humiliated by the teacher) is just as important to mental health, if not more so, than the ability to cope with a major, even life-threatening, stressful event (e.g., experiencing a serious illness or accident; losing a parent or sibling to death; Rowlison & Felner, 1988). For example, students who experience frequent bullying are at increased risk for anxiety, depression, low self-esteem, loneliness, dislike and avoidance of school, peer rejection, conduct problems, and poor attention to academics (Egan & Perry, 1998; Elias & Zins, 2004).

Irrespective of the source or severity of the stress, it is a student's ability to *cope* with stress that is the strongest determinant of negative outcomes. *Coping* entails the use of strategies that alleviate stress by addressing either the source of the stress (problem-focused coping) or one's reaction to it (emotion-focused coping; Eisenberg & Fabes, 1998; Lazarus & Folkman, 1984). Problem-focused strategies are typically enacted when students believe that they can modify a situation by changing some aspect of the environment. For example, a student may decide to take an alternate route if frequently harassed by a peer on the way home from school. Because many events are beyond a student's control, however, direct problem solving is not always feasible. In such situations students may need to redirect their focus from control of external events to control of internal events, that is, control over their thoughts and feelings. For example, students who are frequently teased by peers may learn strategies for coping with their hurt feelings (e.g., cognitive restructuring or distraction, as explained later).

Regulation of one's cognitions and emotions is a critical component of coping and has been identified as a "key to success in life" (Baumeister, Leith, Muraven, & Bratslavsky, 1998). Effective self-regulation is characteristic of students who are resilient and "bounce back" from stressful, if not traumatic, situations (Wolin & Wolin, 1993). Because no single coping strategy is effective across all situations, there is no simple recipe for resilience. Instead, students who are resilient have developed a wide repertoire of protective strategies by which they persevere when faced with challenges and express their emotions in ways that do not harm themselves or others. In an interesting study of African American students who succeeded in high school despite living in poverty and facing great adversity, Floyd (1997) found that the major keys to their resilience were "a supportive, nurturing family and home environment; the youths' interactions with and the involvement of committed, concerned educators and other adults in their lives; and the development of two key personality traits—perseverance and optimism" (p. 184). Other students who lack resiliency, however, adopt nonconstructive coping strategies by acting out (e.g., yelling, fighting, blaming others) or turning inward (e.g., withdrawing from others, blaming themselves; Blechman, Prinz, & Dumas, 1995). As discussed next, these coping strategies are associated with the underregulation and overregulation of emotions.

Underregulation. Discipline problems typically are equated with the *under*regulation (or undercontrol) of emotions, especially anger. Students with difficulty regulating anger become angry quickly and often respond to frustration and stress in an antisocial manner, directing hostility and aggression toward others. Among aggressive students, anger is commonly associated with cognitive distortions and deficiencies, particularly in social and moral problem solving. For example, it often arises from the misperception that someone, or something, is blocking the attainment of personal goals ("I had it first") or threatening one's dignity or self-esteem ("No one pushes me around"). Anger may not only *result* from errors in encoding and interpreting social cues but may also *cause* such errors. When students are angry, they are likely to both receive and process information incorrectly, especially when cues are ambiguous (Zelli, Dodge, Lochman, & Laird, 1999). A good example is when an angry student fails to hear anything favorable or constructive when being corrected for misbehavior.

To understand the role of anger in aggression, it is important to recognize that intense feelings of anger are experienced physiologically. The physiological experience of anger occurs at two levels (Goleman, 1995), consisting of (1) a sudden rush of energy that lasts for several minutes (which is triggered by the release of catecholamines from the limbic system) and (2) an underlying state of readiness for action (which is triggered by the amygdala and affects the nervous system). Changes at the second level may occur before or after changes at the first level and last for hours or days. Each level of anger builds on the other.

Examples of anger being experienced at two physiological levels are common in many classrooms: Eric comes to school "stewing" over something that happened at school or at home the previous day. Physiologically, the second level of aggression exists, rendering him irritable and prone to aggression. The slightest comment made by a teacher or peer may be misinterpreted, supported by Eric's attributions of hostile intent and externalization of blame; in turn, these cognitions "set him off," triggering the limbic surge which is characteristic of level 1. At both physiological levels, emotional arousal interferes with effective processing of social information, causing social cues to be misread and misinterpreted. It also decreases the likelihood that a student will retrieve from memory and reflect on socially appropriate alternatives to aggression. When angry, a student's initial response is not reflective but impulsive, with anger flooding the processing of information and activating existing schema and beliefs that support aggression (e.g., "people should not push me around" or "I can't control myself").

Overregulation.   Although discipline problems are more often associated with the under-regulation of emotion, they also can arise from the *over*regulation, or overcontrol, of emotion. Internalized anger, fear, anxiety, shyness, guilt, and shame can cause poor concentration, attention, and achievement motivation. Outcomes can be more serious when strong emotions continue to be suppressed or avoided, debilitating a student's coping and social problem-solving skills. For example, the primary source of a student's poor attention and motivation in the classroom may be feelings of sadness, anger, and/or guilt due to the divorce of his or her parents or the loss of a close friend. Other than the student's declining grades, few external indicators may be evident. That is, the student may be quite skilled at regulating the external expression of emotion, especially in school, but regulating the internal emotional experience may be more difficult. It is not unusual for "bottled up" emotions among students to eventually reveal themselves in clear external emotional displays, such as eating disorders, suicide attempts, or acts of serious violence.

STOP AND REFLECT

Think of students (or adults) who exhibit under- and overregulation of their emotions. How is this seen in their behavior? What behavior problems are better explained by under- and overregulation? How might such emotion-based problems be avoided?

Strategies and Techniques for Emotional Competence (and for Effective Classroom Discipline)

What follows are strategies and techniques for (1) developing positive emotions, especially those related to positive self-worth, (2) developing moral emotions, especially those related to caring and responsible behavior, and (3) developing self-regulation and coping skills. The primary purpose of presenting these strategies and techniques is to help teachers *develop* self-discipline and *prevent* misbehavior, not correct or remediate it. Nevertheless, it should become clear that these strategies and techniques can and should be used in combination with other strategies and techniques when correcting and remediating behavior problems.

The strategies and techniques apply to all three of the foregoing goals and to the development of emotional competencies in general. Although each of these strategies and techniques has shown moderate degrees of effectiveness when used alone, more substantial results are likely to occur when they are used in combination. Furthermore, it should be noted that many of the strategies and techniques presented in the previous chapter for developing social and moral problem solving also are valuable in developing emotional competence. For example, by helping students learn to resolve conflicts peacefully, teachers also help promote self-confidence, self-esteem, empathy, and emotion regulation. Conversely, many of the strategies and techniques for promoting emotional competence also help promote social and moral problem solving. For example, social and moral problem solving is enhanced when students feel good about themselves, experience empathy, and regulate their emotions effectively. In sum, the skills associated with social and moral problem solving and emotional competence both affect and are affected by each other.

Together, these strategies and techniques help create a *sense of community* in which students "care" and are "cared for" (Noddings, 1992, p. xi) and where "troublesome behavior is a problem to be solved together" (Kohn, 1996, p. 71) rather than solely by the teacher. In such a climate, students are motivated to behave appropriately out of respect for their teachers and peers rather than out of a fear of punishment. As noted by Lewis, Schaps, and Watson (1995), "The idea of a caring community may seem like motherhood and apple pie—something so good that everyone would support it" (p. 551). However, some popular practices (e.g., a zero tolerance approach) undermine this sense of community at school. For example, instead of creating a community where all students feel welcome, educators often communicate that only certain students (e.g., those who are compliant) are welcome at school and that the others do not belong. As a result, they tend to promote feelings of "unbelonging" (Brendtro & Brokenleg, 1996, p. 97) in students and may thereby contribute to the exacerbation of misbehavior.

Strategy 1: Provide Multiple Models of Positive Emotions, Responsibility, and Self-Regulation

Teaching by example, or modeling, is the most powerful technique that educators can employ to develop emotional competence (Elias et al., 1997). Recommendations on the use of modeling for teaching social and moral problem-solving skills were presented in the preceding chapter. In general, these same recommendations apply to the teaching of positive emotions, moral emotions, and self-regulation. Additional recommendations and techniques for modeling include the following:

- Convey those qualities that Dreikurs (Dreikurs & Cassel, 1972) noted are associated with democratic teachers and warm and supportive teacher–student relationships. Dreikurs found that democratic teachers are friendly, cooperative, supportive, impartial, and self-confident in both their teaching and their discipline. They also have a sense of humor, show a sincere interest in each student, demonstrate empathy and respect toward all students, and involve the entire class in democratic decision making and classroom activities. Displaying these qualities not only fosters warm and supportive relationships but also helps teach students to display the same qualities.
- Provide a variety of models of positive emotions, moral emotions, and emotion regulation. For example:
  - When you engage in prosocial behavior, especially behavior grounded in empathy, express your empathy and positive feelings to the class (e.g., "I feel really good about myself when I help others").
  - When you make a mistake that impacts a student unfavorably, publicly express responsibility and sorrow and undo the harm caused (e.g., "I incorrectly punished Jill for something she did not do and I made a mistake. Jill, I'm sorry").
  - When you feel upset or frustrated, demonstrate how you can calm yourself down by talking yourself (aloud) through the situation (e.g., "I'm feeling a little angry right now so I'm going to take three deep breaths").
  - Use expression of your own negative emotions to facilitate students' understanding of emotions but not necessarily to change their behavior. Expression of negative

emotions by adults may produce more positive outcomes when it leads to discussions of feelings rather than only an attempt to modify behavior (Eisenberg, Cumberland, & Spinrad, 1998).

- Whenever students exhibit emotional competencies, bring this to the attention of the class (e.g., "Eric seems to feel really good about having helped Jonathan," "Great going Keisha, I saw that you and other members of the Band Club volunteered this weekend at the Senior Citizens Center. I'm sure that meant a lot to the seniors").

- Highlight examples of positive emotions, moral emotions, and emotion regulation in the general curriculum, such as in language arts and social studies. Noddings (1992) recommends reorganizing the curriculum around themes of care—"caring for self, for intimate others, for strangers and global others, for the natural world and its nonhuman creatures, for the human-made world, and for ideas" (p. 675).

- When providing models, be sure to emphasize how optimal levels of certain emotions (e.g., empathy, pride, feelings of responsibility) lead to positive outcomes but poor regulation of emotions leads to negative outcomes.

Strategy 2: Praise and Reward Students When They Show Positive Emotions, Responsibility, and Self-Regulation

An important source of information that students use when judging their social and emotional competence is feedback from important others. In the school setting, the classroom teacher is the most important source of such feedback (although parents, peers, and close friends also are critical sources of feedback, both inside and outside of school). General recommendations for the use of praise and other forms of positive reinforcement are presented in Chapters 10 and 11 but also apply here. With respect to developing emotions, the following suggestions and techniques are particularly important:

- Encourage internal attributions for success by focusing on pride and effort when praising and rewarding appropriate display of emotions or self-regulation. When praising students for prosocial behavior, attribute the behavior to internal motives (e.g., "You must really enjoy helping others," "You should feel much better since you decided to apologize for what you said to Geraldine," "You should feel proud that you were able to control your anger when he pushed you") rather than simply labeling the act as positive (e.g., "That was so nice of you to help," or "That's good you're not angry any more"). Such statements not only reinforce empathy, responsibility, emotion regulation, and prosocial behavior but also link these outcomes to positive self-worth.

- When rewarding prosocial behavior, focus on the emotions experienced by the teacher and all students involved (e.g., "Ed, I'm proud of you for helping Cynthia. I'm sure that you feel good about yourself, and I expect that Cynthia also feels good about what you did").

Strategy 3: Actively Teach and Encourage Positive Emotions, Responsibility, and Emotion Regulation

Encourage all students to value and experience positive self-worth, caring, responsibility, and emotion regulation. It is through the encouragement of emotional competence that prosocial behavior and self-discipline become both classwide and schoolwide norms rather than exceptions to the norm (Noddings, 2002). Whereas modeling and reinforcement certainly encourage emotional competence, so too can the following techniques:

- Use multiple means to communicate to all students and their parents that it is expected (and valued) that students will experience positive self-worth, will practice (and receive) caring and responsible behavior, and will regulate their emotions. This message should be communicated in school policies, letters to parents, newsletters, posters, parent meetings, and so forth.
- Implement research-supported curriculum activities that foster empathy, responsibility, and emotion regulation. In combination with techniques for infusing the teaching of emotional competence throughout the regular curriculum, teach more structured lessons from a "packaged" curriculum program that has been shown to be effective. The two model prevention programs for developing social and moral problem solving that were mentioned in the previous chapter also are designed to develop empathy, responsibility, and emotion regulation. They are *Second Step: A Violence Prevention Curriculum* (Committee for Children, 2003; Grossman et al., 1997) and the *Quests Skills* series (Quest International, 1998). Each of these programs contains curriculum lessons that use class discussions of social problems and moral issues, role plays, modeling, and direct instruction to develop specific social and emotional competencies.
- Implement a schoolwide campaign that reinforces caring behaviors and establishes norms of caring, respect, and responsibility. In one exemplary middle school the author visited recently, the walls of the hallway were covered with positive quotes and sayings, including "Practice random acts of kindness." The principal set the example by making sure that each day he "caught more students behaving than misbehaving." Students who demonstrated the greatest improvements in behavior (but not necessarily the best behaved) were often honored as "students of the week," and their parents were readily notified of their behaviors. Assemblies were held several times a year to highlight and reinforce prosocial values and behavior.

Strategy 4: Provide Opportunities for Students to Experience Positive Self-Concept and to Practice Empathy, Responsible Behavior, and Emotion Regulation

- Strive to foster positive emotions, moral emotions, and emotion regulation by providing ample opportunities for students to *experience* and *practice* emotional competence. For example:
  - Encourage active participation in class meetings, student government, peer tutoring, and peer mediation.
  - Outside of school, encourage caring behavior through volunteer activities and community services.
  - Make frequent use of cooperative learning and friendship-building activities while emphasizing the importance of mutual respect, responsibility, and caring about others.

■ When opportunities arise throughout the day, prompt or remind students to practice various behaviors related to positive emotions, feelings of responsibility, and emotion regulation. For example, prompt students to think about how others might feel and remind them to self-regulate their feelings of anger or frustration. As noted by Elias et al. (1997), a common mistake made by educators is to assume that emotional instruction is so "obvious" that students learn the skills once they are presented. Prompting is critical because students may learn *how* to use a particular skill but may not always recognize *when* to use it.

■ Encourage students to verbalize how they feel using the word *I* along with an emotion vocabulary word. Research indicates that people respond more negatively to messages that begin with *you* (such as "You make me so mad!") than to messages that begin with *I* (such as "I feel mad when you do that") (Kubany, Richard, Bauer, & Muraoka, 1992). Thus, messages may not only facilitate students' expression of their feelings but also may in fact lead to an avoidance of conflict.

   ▪ Similarly, as recommended by Dreikurs (Dreikurs & Cassel, 1972), use "I" messages to communicate your own feelings about students' prosocial or antisocial behavior. Instead of saying "you make me angry," say "I feel angry when I see you hurt others."

■ Use class meetings as opportunities for students to share their feelings with each other, to become more aware of the feelings of others, and to gain an understanding of the causes and consequences of emotions. These discussions may be structured around a particular emotion (e.g., asking all students to recall a time when they felt sad) or incident (e.g., discussing what "triggered" an emotional or behavioral problem). Identification of these "triggers" may help students predict how they will feel when the particular situation occurs again and thereby better prepare themselves for how they will respond. Not only should students predict how they will feel in a particular situation, but they also should predict how others will feel.

■ Provide opportunities and strongly encourage involvement in service learning. Help arrange for students to assist others throughout the community. Many private and public high schools now require that students participate in service learning.

■ Provide ample opportunities for students to experience enjoyment and fun in school!

STOP AND REFLECT

Should Teachers Hug Students?

Most preschool and primary children need and seek physical displays of our affection. They frequently want to lean against us, hug us, or hold our hand. We need to accept and return these gentle expressions of need and affection; to pull away would convey rejection. (Watson & Ecken, 2003, p. 46)

In demonstrating care toward students, when is it appropriate for teachers to hug students? In what other ways would it be appropriate to convey caring or affection to older students? Should you pull away when a student tries to hug you?

Strategy 5: During Disciplinary Encounters, Promote Feelings of Responsibility for One's Own Behavior

■ Use *induction.* Induction is a disciplinary technique in which empathy and adaptive guilt—key elements of responsibility—are brought to the forefront during disciplinary encounters. Although punitive consequences for one's misbehavior are not necessarily overlooked, emphasis is placed on promoting empathy and attributions of responsibility. By focusing on the impact of the behavior on others and on class norms, the teacher redirects the student's attention from a fear of punishment to a concern about others. The use of induction by parents has been shown to foster empathy among children (Krevans & Gibbs, 1996; Lopez, Bonenberger, & Schneider, 2001) and the internalization of values, especially when used in combination with strategies that teach social problem solving and democratic decision making (Eisenberg & Fabes, 1998). Unfortunately, research has not yet examined the use of induction by teachers, but similar results should be expected. Following are some examples of how teachers might use induction:

  ▪ Instead of saying "Don't tease Lauren or you'll lose 10 minutes of recess," say: "I don't like it when you tease Lauren because when you tease others it makes them feel bad. If you were Lauren, how would you feel?" Or (and in combination with a punitive technique such as when the behavior continues to occur) say: "Because you have continued to tease Lauren and make her feel bad, you have a choice: You can either lose 10 minutes of recess, or you can apologize and say five nice things to her before recess. I think it's very important that students in this class do not hurt the feelings of others."

  ▪ Instead of saying: "Because you lied to me about your homework, I'm going to call your parents," say: "Although I'm concerned about your homework, I'm more concerned about your lying. The reason we don't like lying in this class is because you can't trust someone who tells lies. The person you lied to can no longer believe what you say."

■ When students (or others, including characters in literature or history) engage in behaviors that result in harm to others, be sure to highlight the discrepancy between the students' behavior and what you believe are (or at least *should* be) their personal standards and self-perceptions.

■ Express optimism that students will attempt to act more consistently with personal and social standards in the future. For example, when cheating is suspected, initiate a discussion of what it means to be trustworthy and honorable and convey that these are qualities that you and others highly value. However, as recommended by Glasser (1965), don't argue with those students who deny the importance of such values but simply remind them of the necessary consequences of the respective misbehavior.

■ Consistent with Glasser's (1965) approach to classroom discipline, emphasize that students *choose* to behave or misbehave. Although teachers and classmates share some responsibility, it is the individual student who decides to behave correctly or not and, thus, must assume primary responsibility for his or her behavior.

Strategy 6: Help Students Cope with Stress and Situations in Which They Have Little Control

For situations that are within students' control (e.g., a minor conflict with a peer), the social and moral problem-solving techniques in Chapter 8 are most appropriate. That is, students should be taught and encouraged to take active steps to solve the problem by brainstorming, evaluating, and implementing alternative solutions. For example, students may be able to solve the conflict with the peer by telling the peer how they feel (using an "I" message), by negotiating a compromise, or by seeking problem solving or emotional support from a parent, teacher, or peer. For situations over which students have little or no control (e.g., being consistently rejected by a peer), such techniques often are ineffective and require specific coping skills. Depending on the degree of stress experienced by the student, these skills may best be taught by school counselors or school psychologists. However, there are two coping techniques that teachers can use to help many students cope with everyday stressors by learning that they can change how they feel about a situation by changing how they think about the situation. Both techniques are relatively simple to teach. They are *cognitive restructuring* and *distraction*.

Cognitive restructuring refers to the reevaluation of a situation in a more positive way by minimizing its unpleasant aspects or by attempting to find some meaning in it. Problems are reframed as challenges, learning opportunities, or other worthwhile experiences. For example, teasing can be reframed as a way for students to become more aware of the behaviors considered inappropriate by their peers (Hoover, Oliver, & Thomson, 1993). Another example would be to encourage students to perceive failure as a temporary, normal setback rather than a permanent life sentence. The basic goal of teachers when using cognitive restructuring is to challenge students to find something positive in their problem situation.

Distraction refers to an active, intentional effort to take one's mind off a problem by diverting attention, either physically or cognitively, to something else. Distraction serves an important regulatory function because it reduces arousal and any accompanying feelings of anger, distress, and frustration, thereby providing a calming effect (Sandler, Wolchik, MacKinnon, Ayers, & Roosa, 1997). One way students can employ distraction is by removing themselves from a stressful situation in order to engage in an alternate, more pleasurable activity. For example, if students are being teased on the playground or in the gym, they may walk away from one group of peers and find another group.

At other times, however, physical escape from a situation may not be possible. For example, if students are being teased on the school bus, they cannot simply get up from their seats and walk away. In these cases, it may be beneficial for students to try a form of cognitive distraction in which they "turn off" everything that's going on around them and use their mind to think of other, more pleasant things. For example, students can be encouraged to distract themselves from the teasing by thinking about what they are going to do when they get home (e.g., play their favorite game, watch their favorite television show, or read their favorite book). They also can be encouraged to distract themselves from overwhelming feelings of academic or social failure by focusing attention on their strengths rather than their weaknesses. A final method of distraction is the use of specific relaxation techniques, similar to those used for anger control, such as taking a deep breath, counting to ten, or making self-calming statements (e.g., "stay calm and think this through").

IMPLEMENTATION TIP

A particularly effective anger management technique for younger students is "turtling" (Robin, Schneider, & Dolnick, 1976). In using this technique, students are told how turtles often outlive and outsmart more ferocious animals by staying calm during times of stress. They pull themselves within their shells, where they can think about how to solve their problem, instead of fighting or arguing. Students are then encouraged "to turtle" when angry by placing their heads on their desk.

For both younger and older students, it often helps to remind them to take a few deep breaths or to follow one of Thomas Jefferson's top ten words of wisdom: "When angry, count to 10. When really angry, count to 100" (which also is good advice to teachers when they are frustrated or angry). Other suggestions for helping students manage anger are to remove themselves from the situation, talk to others, reframe the problem, or use relaxation techniques.

SUMMARY AND KEY POINTS

■ Attention to students' emotions provides valuable insight into why many behaviors, both positive and negative, occur and thereby assists with the development of self-discipline.

■ Teachers can promote the development of emotional intelligence, or emotional competence, in students by encouraging positive emotions, fostering moral emotions, and promoting effective regulation of emotions.

■ Positive emotions such as happiness and pride tend to develop among students who (1) perceive their behavioral conduct favorably and (2) perceive others as valuable sources of social support (Harter, 1999). Attention to these factors will likely produce more favorable effects on students' self-esteem than implementing packaged "self-esteem enhancement" programs.

■ Although educators are often reluctant to promote feelings of sorrow and guilt among students, these emotions are critical to the development of self-discipline. Guilt in particular serves as a powerful internalized sanction against wrongdoing. Teachers should strive to promote healthy feelings of empathy (similar to sorrow) and guilt in students but generally avoid promoting shame.

■ Many discipline problems occur because students underregulate their emotions; however, overregulation of emotions can also be problematic. Optimal regulation of emotions is characteristic of students who successfully cope with, or "bounce back," from stressful situations. Such students have developed a repertoire of prosocial coping strategies that allows them to cope with stress in ways that do not harm themselves or others.

KEY TERMS AND CONCEPTS

Anger
Coping
Empathy
Guilt

Induction
Overregulation
Resiliency
Self-worth or self-esteem

Shame
Social support
Sympathy
Underregulation

RECOMMENDED READINGS AND RESOURCES

Recommended Books on Developing Social and Emotional Learning at Home and in School

Bodine, R. J., & Crawford, D. K. (1999). *Developing emotional intelligence: A guide to behavior management and conflict resolution in schools.* Champaign, IL: Research Press.

Elias, M. J., Arnold, H., & Hussey, C. S. (2003). *EQ + IQ: Best leadership practices for caring and successful schools.* Thousand Oaks, CA: Corwin.

Elias, M. J., Zins, J. E., Weissberg, R. P., Frey, K. S., Greenberg, M. T., Haynes, N. M., Kessler, R., Schwab-Stone, M. E., & Shriver, T. P. (1997). *Promoting social and emotional learning: Guidelines for educators.* Alexandria, VA: Association for Supervision and Curriculum Development.

Goleman, D. (1995). *Emotional intelligence.* New York: Bantam.

Gottman, J. (1997). *Raising an emotionally intelligent child: The heart of parenting.* New York: Simon & Schuster.

Novick, B., Kress, J. S., & Elias, M. J. (2002). *Building learning communities with character: How to integrate academic, social, and emotional learning.* Alexandria, VA: Association for Supervision and Curriculum Development.

Tobias, S. E., Friedlander, B. S., & Elias, M. J. (2000). *Emotionally intelligent parenting: How to raise a self-disciplined, responsible, socially skilled child.* New York: Three Rivers Press.

For information on social and emotional learning, including social and moral problem solving, and reviews of evidence-based programs, see the website for the Collaborative for Academic, Social, and Emotional Learning (CASEL): www.casel.org.

For articles, research, video clips, and other resources related to social and emotional learning, visit the website of the George Lucas Educational Foundation at www.glef.org.

For More Information on the Second Step and Quest Programs

www.cfchildren.org (Committee for Children Website)
www.lions-quest.org (Lions-Quest Website, of the Lions Clubs International)

For Information to Assist in Selecting Storybooks and Literature That Address Social and Moral Problem Solving

www.scholastic.com (Scholastic Publishing)
www.NancyKeane.com (Nancy Keane's Booktalks)

REFERENCES

Arnold, D. H., Homrok, S., Ortiz, C., & Stowe, R. M. (1999). Direct observation of peer rejection acts and their temporal relation with aggressive acts. *Early Childhood Research Quarterly, 14,* 183–196.

Bandura, A. (1986). *Social foundations of thought and action: A social cognitive theory.* Englewood Cliffs, NJ: Prentice-Hall.

Battistich, V., & Hom, A. (1997). The relationship between students' sense of their school as a community and their involvement in problem behaviors. *American Journal of Public Health, 87,* 1997–2001.

Battistich, V., Schaps, E., Watson, M., Solomon, D., & Lewis, C. (2000). Effects of the Child Development Project on students' drug use and other problem behaviors. *Journal of Primary Prevention, 21,* 75–99.

Battistich, V., Solomon, D., Kim, D., Watson, M., & Schaps, E. (1995). Schools as communities, poverty levels of student populations, and students' attitudes, motives, and performance: A multilevel analysis. *American Educational Research Journal, 32,* 627–658.

Baumeister, R. F., Leith, K. P., Muraven, M., & Bratslavsky, E. (1998). Self-regulation as a key to success in life. In D. Pushkar, W. M. Bukowski, A. E. Schwartzman, D. M. Stack, & D. R. White (Eds.), *Improving competence across the lifespan: Building interventions based on theory and research* (pp. 117–132). New York: Plenum.

Bear, G. G., Minke, K. M., Griffin, S. M., & Deemer, S. A. (1997). Self-concept. In G. G. Bear, K. M. Minke,

and A. Thomas (Eds.), *Children needs II: Development, problems, and alternatives* (pp. 257–269). Bethesda, MD: National Association of School Psychologists.

Blair, R. J. R., & Coles, M. (2000). Expression recognition and behavioural problems in early adolescence. *Cognitive Development, 15,* 421–434.

Blechman, E. A., Prinz, R. J., & Dumas, J. E. (1995). Coping, competence, and aggression prevention: Part 1. Developmental model. *Applied and Preventive Psychology, 4,* 211–232.

Born, M., Chevalier, V., & Humblet, I. (1997). Resilience, desistance and delinquent career of adolescent offenders. *Journal of Adolescence, 20,* 679–694.

Brendtro, L. K., & Brokenleg, M. (1996). Beyond the curriculum of control. In N. J. Long & W. C. Morse (Eds.), *Conflict in the classroom: The education of at-risk and troubled students* (5th ed., pp. 65–147). Austin, TX: ProEd.

Brophy, J. E. (1996). *Teaching problem students.* New York: Guilford Press.

Bybee, J., Merisca, R., & Velasco, R. (1998). The development of reactions to guilt-producing events. In J. Bybee (Ed.), *Guilt and children* (pp. 185–213). San Diego: Academic Press.

Chapman, M., Zahn-Waxler, C., Cooperman, G., & Iannotti, R. (1987). Empathy and responsibility in the motivation of children's helping. *Developmental Psychology, 23,* 140–145.

Clever, A., Bear, G. G., & Juvonen, J. (1992). Discrepancies between competence and importance in self-perceptions of children in integrated classrooms. *Journal of Special Education, 26,* 125–138.

Cohen, D., & Strayer, J. (1996). Empathy in conduct-disordered and comparison youth. *Developmental Psychology, 32,* 988–998.

Committee for Children. (2003). *Second Step: A violence prevention curriculum.* Seattle, WA: Author.

Damon, W., & Hart, D. (1988). *Self-understanding in childhood and adolescence.* New York: Cambridge University Press.

David, C. F., & Kistner, J. A. (2000). Do positive self-perceptions have a "dark side"? Examination of the link between perceptual bias and aggression. *Journal of Abnormal Child Psychology, 28,* 327–337.

DePalma, M. T., Madey, S. F., & Bornschein, S. (1995). Individual differences and cheating behavior: Guilt and cheating in competitive situations. *Personality and Individual Differences, 18,* 761–769.

Dreikurs, R., & Cassel, P. (1972). *Discipline without tears: What to do with children who misbehave.* New York: Hawthorn Books.

Dweck, C. S. (2002). The development of ability conceptions. In A. Wigfield & J. S. Eccles (Eds.), *Development of achievement motivation* (pp. 57–88). San Diego: Academic Press.

Egan, S. K., Monson, T. C., & Perry, D. G. (1998). Social-cognitive influences on change in aggression over time. *Developmental Psychology, 34,* 996–1006.

Eisenberg, N. (2000). Emotion, regulation, and moral development. *Annual Review of Psychology, 51,* 665–697.

Eisenberg, N., Cumberland, A., & Spinrad, T. L. (1998). Parental socialization of emotion. *Psychological Inquiry, 9,* 241–273.

Eisenberg, N., & Fabes, R. A. (1998). Prosocial development. In W. Damon (Series Ed.) & N. Eisenberg (Vol. Ed.), *Handbook of child psychology: Vol. 3. Social, emotional, and personality development* (5th ed., pp. 701–778). New York: Wiley.

Elias, M. J., & Zins, J. E. (2004). *Bullying, peer harassment, and victimization in the schools.* Binghamton, NY: Haworth Press.

Elias, M. J., Zins, J. E., Weissberg, R. P., Frey, K. S., Greenberg, M. T., Haynes, N. M., Kessler, R., Schwab-Stone, M. E., & Shriver, T. P. (1997). *Promoting social and emotional learning: Guidelines for educators.* Alexandria, VA: Association for Supervision and Curriculum Development.

Floyd, C. (1997). Achieving despite the odds: A study of resilience among a group of African American high school seniors. *Journal of Negro Education, 65,* 181–189.

Frey, K., & Rivara, F. P. (1997). Effectiveness of a violence prevention curriculum among children in elementary school. *Journal of the American Medical Association, 277,* 1605–1611.

Gilman, R., & Huebner, E. S. (2003). A review of life satisfaction research with children and adolescents. *School Psychology Quarterly, 18,* 192–205.

Glasser, W. (1969). *Schools without failure.* New York: Harper & Row.

Goleman, D. (1995). *Emotional intelligence.* New York: Bantam.

Gottman, J. (1997). *Raising an emotionally intelligent child: The heart of parenting.* New York: Simon & Schuster.

Grossman, D. C., Neckerman, H. J., Koepsell, T. D., Liu, P., Asher, K. N., Beland, K., Frey, K., & Rivara, F. P. (1997). Effectiveness of a violence prevention curriculum among children in elementary school. *Journal of the American Medical Association, 277,* 1605–1611.

Grusec, J. E., & Goodnow, J. J. (1994). Impact of parental discipline methods on the child's internalization of values: A reconceptualization of current points of view. *Developmental Psychology, 30,* 4–19.

Haberman, M. (1995). *Star teachers of children in poverty.* West Lafayette, IN: Kappa Delta Pi.

Hawker, D. S. J., & Boulton, M. J. (2000). Twenty years' research on peer victimization and psychosocial maladjustment: A meta-analytic review of cross-sectional studies. *Journal of Child Psychology and Psychiatry, 41,* 441–455.

Harter, S. (1999). *The construction of the self: A developmental perspective.* New York: Guilford.

Haynes, N. M., Emmons, C., & Ben-Avie, M. (1997). School climate as a factor in student adjustment and achievement. *Journal of Educational & Psychological Consultation, 8,* 321–332.

Haynes, N. M., Emmons, C. L., & Woodruff, D. W. (1998). School Development Program effects: Linking implementation to outcomes. *Journal of Education for Students Placed at Risk. Special Issue: Changing schools for changing times: The Comer School Development Program, 3,* 71–85.

Hoffman, M. L. (2000). *Empathy and moral development: Implications for caring and justice.* Cambridge, UK: Cambridge University Press.

Hoover, J. H., Oliver, R. L., & Thomson, K. A. (1993). Perceived victimization by school bullies: New research and future directions. *Journal of Humanistic Education and Development, 32,* 76–83.

Hughes, J. N., Cavell, T. A., & Grossman, P. A. (1997). A positive view of self: Risk or protection for aggressive children? *Development and Psychopathology, 9,* 75–94.

Hughes, J. N., Cavell, T. A., & Jackson, T. (1999). Influence of teacher–student relationships on aggressive children's development: A prospective study. *Journal of Clinical Child Psychology, 28,* 173–184.

Hughes, J. N., Cavell, T. A., & Willson, V. (2001). Further support for the developmental significance of the quality of the teacher–student relationship. *Journal of School Psychology, 39,* 289–301.

Hyman, I. A., & Snook, P. A. (1999). *Dangerous schools.* San Francisco: Jossey-Bass.

Izard, C. E. (1991). *The psychology of emotions.* New York: Plenum.

Izard, C. E. (2001). Emotional intelligence or adaptive emotions? *Emotion, 1,* 249–257.

Jenkins, P. H. (1997). School delinquency and the school social bond. *Journal of Research in Crime & Delinquency, 34,* 337–367.

Kochanska, G. (1994). Beyond cognition: Expanding the search for the early roots of internalization and conscience. *Developmental Psychology, 30,* 20–22.

Kohn, A. (1996). *Beyond discipline: From compliance to community.* Alexandria, VA: Association for Supervision and Curriculum.

Krevans, J., & Gibbs, J. C. (1996). Parents' use of inductive discipline: Relations to children's empathy and prosocial behavior. *Child Development, 67,* 3263–3277.

Kubany, E. S., Richard, D. C., Bauer, G. B., & Muraoka, M. Y. (1992). Impact of assertive and accusatory communication of distress and anger: A verbal component analysis. *Aggressive Behavior, 18,* 377–347.

Ladd, G. W., Birch, S. H., & Buhs, E. S. (1999). Children's social and scholastic lives in kindergarten: Related spheres of influence? *Child Development, 70,* 1373–1400.

Lazarus, R. S., & Folkman, S. (1984). *Stress appraisal and coping.* New York: Springer.

Lepper, M. (1983). Social-control processes and the internalization of social values: An attributional perspective. In E. T. Higgins, D. Ruble, & W. Hartup (Eds.), *Social cognition and social development: A socio-cultural perspective* (pp. 294–330). New York: Cambridge University Press.

Lewis, C., Schaps, E., & Watson, M. (1995). Beyond the pendulum: Creating challenging and caring schools. *Phi Delta Kappan,* 547–554.

Loper, A. B., Hoffschmidt, S. J., & Ash, E. (2001). Personality features and characteristics of violent events committed by juvenile offenders. *Behavioral Sciences & the Law. Special Issue: Youth Violence, 19,* 81–96.

Lopez, N. L, Bonenberger, J. L., & Schneider, H. G. (2001). Parental disciplinary history, current levels of empathy, and moral reasoning in young adults. *North American Journal of Psychology, 3,* 193–204.

Miller, P. A., & Eisenberg, N. (1988). The relation of empathy to aggressive and externalizing/antisocial behavior. *Psychological Bulletin, 103,* 324–344.

Miller, P. A., Eisenberg, N., Fabes, R. A., & Shell, R. (1996). Relations of moral reasoning and vicarious emotion to young children's prosocial behavior toward peers and adults. *Developmental Psychology, 32,* 210–219.

Noddings, N. (1992). *The challenge to care in schools: An alternative approach to education.* New York: Teachers College Press.

Noddings, N. (2002). *Educating moral people: A caring alternative to character education.* New York: Teachers College Press.

Pianta, R. C. (1999). *Enhancing relationships between children and teachers.* Washington, DC: American Psychological Association.

Quest International (1998). *Lions Quest life skills programs* (K–5, 6–8, 9–12). Oak Brook, IL: Lions-Quest Lions Clubs International Foundation.

Robin, A. L., Schneider, M., & Dolnick, M. (1976). The Turtle Technique: An extended case study of self-control in the classroom. *Psychology in the Schools, 13,* 449–453.

Rowlison, R. T., & Felner, R. D. (1988). Major life events, hassles, and adaptation in adolescence: Confounding in the conceptualization and measurement of life stress and adjustment revisited. *Journal of Personality & Social Psychology, 55,* 432–444.

Saarni, C. (1999). *The development of emotional competence.* New York: Guilford.

Salovey, P., & Mayer, J. D. (1989–1990). Emotional intelligence. *Imagination, Cognition & Personality, 9,* 185–211.

Sandler, I. N., Wolchik, S. A., MacKinnon, D., Ayers, T. S., & Roosa, M. W. (1997). Developing linkages between theory and intervention in stress and coping processes. In S. A. Wolchik & I. N. Sandler (Eds.), *Handbook of children's coping: Linking theory and intervention* (pp. 3–40). New York: Plenum.

Solomon, D., Battistich, V., Watson, M., Schaps, E., & Lewis, C. (2000). A six-district study of educational change: Direct and mediated effects of the Child Development Project. *Social Psychology of Education, 4,* 3–51.

Solomon, D., Watson, M., Battistich, V., Schaps, E., & Delucchi, K. (1996). Creating classrooms that students experience as communities. *American Journal of Community Psychology, 24,* 719–748.

Spirito, A., Stark, L. J., Grace, N., & Stamoulis, D. (1991). Common problems and coping strategies reported in childhood and early adolescence. *Journal of Youth and Adolescence, 20,* 531–544.

Tangney, J. P. (2002). Constructive and destructive aspects of shame and guilt. In A. C. Bohart & D. J.

Stipek (Eds.), *Constructive & destructive behavior: Implications for family, school, & society* (pp. 127–145). Washington, DC: American Psychological Association.

Tangney, J. P., & Dearing, R. L. (2002). *Shame and guilt.* New York: Guilford.

Watson, M., & Ecken, L. (2003). *Learning to trust: Transforming difficult elementary classrooms through developmental discipline.* San Francisco: Jossey-Bass.

Welsh, W. N. (2000). The effects of school climate on school disorder. *The Annals of the American Academy of Political and Social Science, 567,* 88–108.

Williams, C. (1998). Guilt in the classroom. In J. Bybee (Ed.), *Guilt and children* (pp. 233–243). San Diego: Academic Press.

Wolin, S. & Wolin, S. (1993). *The resilient self: How survivors of troubled families rise above adversity.* New York: Random House.

Zakriski, A. L., & Coie, J. D. (1996). A comparison of aggressive-rejected and nonaggressive-rejected children's interpretations of self-directed and other-directed rejection. *Child Development, 67,* 1048–1070.

Zelli, A., Dodge, K. A., Lochman, J. E., & Laird, R. D. (1999). The distinction between beliefs legitimizing aggression and deviant processing of social cues: Testing measurement validity and the hypothesis that biased processing mediates the effects of beliefs on aggression. *Journal of Personality and Social Psychology, 77,* 150–166.

10 Preventing Misbehavior with Effective Classroom Management

GUIDING QUESTIONS

- How is classroom management related to developing self-discipline, correcting misbehavior, and teaching academics?
- What are the primary characteristics of teachers who are effective classroom managers?
- How is an authoritative approach to classroom management more effective than an authoritarian or permissive approach?

- How might working with parents and families enhance the effectiveness of classroom management? What strategies and techniques should teachers use when working with parents and families in preventing misbehavior?

- How is student motivation related to academic achievement, behavior problems, and classroom management? What strategies and techniques can teachers use to enhance student motivation?

- What is the basis of one of the most heated current debates concerning classroom discipline and classroom management: The use of rewards in the classroom? Do rewards cause more harm than good? How might praise and rewards best be used in the classroom?

- What important issues should teachers consider when developing and implementing classroom rules?

When integrated throughout instructional practices, school policies, and curricula, the strategies and techniques presented in the previous two chapters for fostering social and moral problem solving and for promoting emotional competence help develop self-discipline. They are key elements of character education and social and emotional learning. They also help achieve another critical and often more immediate aim in the classroom—the *prevention* of misbehavior. There is ample evidence that time spent implementing preventive strategies and techniques is time well spent. It is estimated that, when implemented correctly, preventive strategies and techniques are effective in preventing behavior problems among 75% to 85% of students (Reid, 1993). By preventing misbehavior, teachers enhance their own instructional effectiveness, foster the academic achievement and self-discipline of their students, and help establish a positive and safe classroom and school climate.

The idea that most behavior problems are preventable is not new to educators. In the early 1900s character educators and educational psychologists wrote extensively about preventing behavior problems through the development of character and the creation of positive and well-managed classrooms and schools. An emphasis on prevention also is apparent in the classic models of Dreikurs and Glasser. Both emphasize that few discipline problems exist in classrooms characterized by effective classroom management, consisting of positive teacher–student relations, clear rules and fair consequences, developmentally appropriate and motivating instruction, favorable physical arrangements, and the frequent use of encouragement, modeling, and classroom meetings. These and other characteristics of effective *classroom management* are the focus of the present chapter.

Note that although the two are closely related, classroom management and classroom discipline are not one and the same. The distinction is an important one, especially with respect to developing self-discipline. *Classroom management* refers to "actions taken to create and maintain a learning environment conducive to successful instruction (arranging the physical environment of the classroom, establishing rules and procedures, maintaining attention to lessons and engagement in academic activities)" (Brophy, 1996, p. 43). According to Brophy, classroom management is one of the four major functions of teaching, with the other three being academic instruction, disciplinary intervention (i.e., correction), and student socialization (i.e., the development of self-discipline).

Classroom management and student socialization share the aim of preventing academic and behavior problems. They differ, however, in that the aim of classroom management tends to be more immediate and less long term: The aim of classroom management is to establish and maintain a classroom climate that is orderly, safe, and conducive to teaching and learning. Such a climate is necessary for teachers to achieve the more long-term aim of developing self-discipline. Although necessary, it certainly is not sufficient. That is, a teacher may be very effective in establishing and maintaining order and safety, preventing behavior problems (in the short term), and promoting academic achievement but still fail to foster student socialization or self-discipline. Thus, it is important to keep in mind that if the primary aim of classroom discipline is the development of self-discipline, the strategies and techniques of classroom management, including those in this chapter, always should be used in combination with strategies and techniques for developing self-discipline. Indeed, as seen throughout this chapter, the most effective classroom managers—"authoritative" classroom managers—ensure that this occurs.

Guiding Research for Effective Classroom Management

Research on Characteristics of Effective Classroom Managers

Jacob Kounin (Kounin, 1970; Kounin & Gump, 1974) was one of the first educational psychologists to demonstrate the critical importance of classroom management in teaching and classroom discipline. Initially, Kounin was interested in studying how teachers correct discipline problems. Upon observing the videotapes of teachers and classrooms, however, he quickly discovered that effective and ineffective teachers differ little in the strategies and techniques they use to correct discipline problems. Instead, they differ greatly in the strategies and techniques they use to manage group behavior and instruction. Kounin identified certain classroom management skills that the most effective teachers exhibit, including those listed next. Note that although these are not all of the skills identified by Kounin, they are the ones that have been consistently supported by research.

> *Withitness*—closely monitoring each student's behavior and responding to misbehavior promptly before it escalates into a behavior problem that interferes with learning and instruction. For example, in displaying withitness, a teacher scans the classroom and notices that a student is about to leave his or her seat. The teacher then makes eye contact with the student and moves in that direction. As a result of these preemptive actions, the student returns to work.

> *Overlapping*—dealing with multiple events or demands at the same time. For example, at the same time that the teacher is moving toward the student who is about to leave his or her seat, the teacher continues teaching the lesson, praises other students for working quietly, and nods to a student who asks to be excused.

> *Momentum*—starting and presenting lessons at a brisk pace, while allowing for only brief and efficient transitions. For example, when the social studies period begins, the teacher immediately starts teaching a quickly paced, motivating lesson that entails a combination of lecture, group discussion, and cooperative learning.

> *Smoothness*—presenting lessons at an even flow, free from interruptions. For example, while presenting the social studies lesson, the teacher ignores a question that has nothing to do with the topic and continues to emphasize the key concepts.

Group alerting—establishing and maintaining everyone's attention. For example, the teacher asks the class to give a "thumbs up" signal to demonstrate that they are listening and then proceeds with a "popcorn" group activity that requires every student to "pop" and thereby contribute to the group discussion.

Building on Kounin's work, more recent researchers have studied literally thousands of teachers and classrooms in search of factors that best differentiate the least and most effective teachers. (For reviews, see Emmer, Evertson, & Worsham, 2003; Evertson, Emmer, & Worsham, 2003; Good & Brophy, 2000; Marzano, 2003.) With respect to classroom management and classroom discipline, and consistent with Kounin's findings, these researchers have shown that the greatest difference between effective and ineffective teachers is that effective teachers focus primarily on the *antecedents* of misbehavior rather than the consequences. Antecedents refer to the causes of, or contributors to, misbehavior. By focusing on antecedents, effective classroom managers are able to devote more time to instruction and less time to the correction of misbehavior. Antecedent-focused techniques can be grouped according to four functions that they tend to serve in classroom management and in the prevention of misbehavior: *establishing rules, procedures, and an organized environment; maintaining motivation; enhancing relationships; and providing early intervention.* A general description of these categories is presented next while more specific techniques within each category are presented later.

Establishing Rules, Procedures, and an Organized Environment. Effective teachers are well aware that certain activities and physical arrangements tend to invite misbehavior, such as transitional periods, recess, lunch, long student presentations, poorly organized lessons, and activities in which students frequently move about in close proximity to others. Therefore, effective teachers make sure that expectations, routines, procedures, and rules pertaining to these situations are clear, that their classrooms and lessons are well organized, and that the physical environment is conducive to learning.

Maintaining Motivation. Effective classroom managers understand that the best way to curtail misbehavior is to keep students actively involved in developmentally appropriate and motivating academic activities. For example, they are well aware that one of the primary causes of misbehavior is requiring a student to work on a task that is too difficult or of little interest. Thus, they employ instructional and curricular methods and activities that enhance student interest and desire to learn. This includes using a variety of stimulating instructional methods and materials that are adapted to the needs and developmental levels of all students. It also includes Kounin's concepts of momentum, smoothness, and group alerting.

Enhancing Relationships. Relational techniques focus on enhancing relations between teachers and students, between teachers and parents, and among students. Such techniques seek to promote communication, mutual respect, shared responsibility, collaborative problem solving, positive emotions, and a positive classroom climate.

Intervening Early. With respect to classroom management, intervening early refers to catching misbehavior in its very early stages before the misbehavior escalates or becomes "contagious" (spreading among others in the class) and evolves into a problem that requires systematic and planned corrective techniques. It means being preemptive rather than reactionary. This entails providing close monitoring and supervision, or what Kounin referred to as withitness and overlapping. Many of the techniques presented in the next chapter for correcting minor behavior problems after they already have occurred are the same techniques that teachers might use when responding to the early signs of a behavior that has the potential of evolving into a significant disciplinary problem. For example, teachers might redirect students by calling their names when they observe them exhibiting a minor rule violation, such as talking to classmates when they shouldn't be, and teachers might use the same technique when they observe students about to start a fight by teasing a peer who is easily angered.

Research on the Authoritative Approach to Childrearing and Teaching

Whereas the preceding research has focused primarily on specific practices and techniques that best differentiate effective and ineffective teachers, another body of research has focused more on the general approach or style that characterizes the most effective parents and teachers, especially with respect to discipline. Recall that Dreikurs (1968; Dreikurs & Cassel, 1972) emphasized what he referred to as a *democratic style* of teaching and leadership. He argued that a democratic style is related to effective instruction, socialization, discipline, and classroom management. Dreikurs described democratic teachers as those who demonstrate warmth and friendliness, a sincere interest in and respect toward each student, a sense of humor, self-confidence, organizational skills, frequent use of encouragement, and a commitment to democratic decision making. At the time of Dreikurs's writings, his democratic approach to classroom discipline was based on little empirical research. Since then, however, much research has accumulated in support of the preceding characteristics of democratic teaching (with the exception of a commitment to democratic decision making). As one might guess, students prefer teachers who display warmth, friendliness, humor, and other attractive personality characteristics (Good & Brophy, 2000). There is little evidence, however, that students prefer teachers who practice true democracy in the classroom or that such teachers are any more effective than other teachers in managing their classrooms and preventing misbehavior. Indeed, it is questionable whether many teachers are truly committed to and able to practice democratic governance. Few, if any, public schools allow students to determine curriculum, rules, or consequences by majority rule (Brophy, 1996). And perhaps for good reasons. For sure, many teachers do and should provide ample opportunities for students to participate in democratic decision making, but this is not the same as democratic governance.

Because true democracy is unrealistic in school settings, Brophy (1996) recommends that teachers be *authoritative* rather than *democratic* in their style of teaching and leadership. In describing the authoritative teacher, Brophy draws primarily from theory and research in developmental psychology on effective childrearing, particularly the work of Dianna Baumrind (1971, 1978, 1996). Because this research has clear and direct implications for all aspects of classroom management, as well as for the development of self-discipline and the correction of misbehavior, all educators should be familiar with it, as reviewed here.

Authoritative Childrearing.   Over the past forty years, Baumind (1971, 1978, 1996) and many other researchers (e.g., Kurdek & Fine, 1994; Lamborn, Mounts, Steinberg, & Dornbusch, 1991; Steinberg, 1996; Steinberg, Elmen, & Mounts, 1989) have amassed ample evidence showing that an authoritative approach to childrearing is effective in bringing about both compliance in the short term and the development of self-discipline over the long term. Their research indicates that compared to children and adolescents reared by parents who are overly authoritarian or permissive, those reared by authoritative parents exhibit higher self-esteem, moral maturity, social competence, and academic achievement and fewer behavior problems. Two key dimensions to childrearing that are responsible for these positive outcomes are responsiveness and demandingness.

Responsiveness refers to the extent to which an adult responds to a child's social, emotional, physical, and cognitive needs; demonstrates warmth, acceptance, support, love, and caring; and communicates openly and clearly using persuasion and moral reasoning rather than one's position of authority. Adults high in responsiveness are successful in fostering autonomy and individuality in children and adolescents. *Demandingness* refers to the extent to which an adult provides close monitoring and supervision; presents clear and consistent guidelines, expectations, and responsibilities; and uses discipline in a firm, fair, and consistent manner. Adults high in demandingness are successful in eliciting compliance.

The authoritative approach balances high responsiveness with high demandingness. In so doing, it promotes *both* autonomy and compliance. As argued by Baumrind (1996), the authoritative approach views autonomy and compliance "not as mutually exclusive but rather as interdependent objectives: Children are encouraged to respond habitually in prosocial ways and to reason autonomously about moral problems, and to respect adult authorities and learn how to think independently" (p. 405). Hence, the authoritative approach is responsive to both sides of classroom discipline: developing self-discipline and using discipline to manage and correct misbehavior. This balanced and moderate approach is in sharp contrast to the permissive and authoritarian approaches to childrearing (and teaching), which are unbalanced and ineffective in developing self-discipline. Whereas overly permissive adults are high in responsiveness and low in demandingness, overly authoritarian adults are low in responsiveness and high in demandingness.

Authoritative Classroom Management.   Unfortunately, very little research has examined an authoritative approach to classroom management. One exception, however, was a study conducted by Brophy and McCaslin (1992; Brophy, 1996). Upon observing and interviewing ninety-eight experienced teachers, these researchers found that Baumrind's

Relationship between Authoritative Discipline and Student Behavior

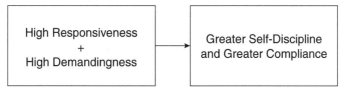

(1996) authoritative style of childrearing characterizes classroom teachers who are most effective in preventing, managing, and correcting behavior problems. These teachers are high in both responsiveness and demandingness. With respect to responsiveness, they display warmth, care, support, and respect toward *all* students. They listen to and guide students rather than direct and control them. In guiding students, they rely on induction to foster empathy and perspective taking and on dialoguing to foster social and moral problem solving and social decision making. They model prosocial behavior, positive emotions, and social and moral problem-solving and decision-making skills and frequently reinforce both compliant and autonomous behavior.

With respect to demandingness, authoritative teachers set high academic and behavioral expectations, present clear rules and procedures, and frequently monitor classroom behavior. Their style is *informative* rather than *assertive.* Instead of focusing on why it is important *to teachers* that students behave appropriately, authoritative teachers focus on why it is important *to students:* not simply so they can avoid negative consequences or earn immediate rewards but for them to reap more important and long-lasting academic, social, and emotional outcomes. Students also are informed *why* a particular rule or procedure is important. Authoritative teachers do not justify rules or procedures by simply stating "because I said so" or "because that's the rule." Instead, they present clear and coherent rationales that help students develop an understanding of and appreciation for the rules. When rules are violated, authoritative teachers do not hesitate to use discipline, including punishment, but they always do so in a fair, reasonable, consistent, and firm manner. Although they expect and demand appropriate behavior in the classroom, they strive to develop individuals who function autonomously rather than simply in response to rewards, punishment, or adult demands.

Authoritative classroom managers not only combine responsiveness and demandingness when preventing misbehavior (and promoting self-discipline), but they also do so when correcting misbehavior after it has occurred. They view disciplinary encounters not merely as situations that require correction but also as opportunities to discuss and teach appropriate behavior and for students to learn and develop social problem solving, moral reasoning, and decision-making skills. Again, the authoritative style is more informative than assertive. Accordingly, disciplinary encounters include the use of inductions that focus on the reasons why a given behavior is inappropriate and a more appropriate behavior should be valued. They also include guidance as to how a student can avoid repeating the misbehavior in the future. In teaching students to respect the authority of teachers and other adults, authoritative teachers make sure that their authority is fair and morally justified. As such, reasoning and issues of fairness and justice, rather than authority per se, are emphasized during disciplinary encounters.

Brophy (1996) recommends two additional techniques that teachers should use to inform students, particularly when discipline problems are expected or encountered, that students should focus less on avoiding negative consequences and more on obtaining positive outcomes. First, teachers should always emphasize the value of the desired behavior rather than the undesired behavior. This includes an emphasis on the behavioral, cognitive, and emotional skills that reduce the likelihood of a misbehavior occurring, or recurring, such as the application of specific social skills (e.g., ignoring a peer), social and moral problem-solving skills (e.g., thinking of alternative solutions), and moral reasoning and emotional skills (e.g., self-regulation of anger). As noted by Brophy (1996), when feasible, teachers should "phrase corrections as friendly reminders rather than as power assertive commands, and encourage students to see themselves as regulating their own behavior rather than as being controlled externally ('You only have a few more minutes to finish your assignment' is better than 'If you don't finish that assignment before the bell, you'll have to stay in during recess')" (p. 17).

Second, when a student fails to respond to positive techniques for preventing and correcting a misbehavior and a punitive technique is necessary, teachers should deliver the punitive technique in a tone of voice that conveys their disappointment about the student's behavior and the need for teachers to do something that they don't enjoy doing, which is using punishment (Brophy, 1996). Teachers should convey that the "punishment is not an arbitrary display of your authority; rather, it is an unfortunate but necessary consequence of the student's repeated misbehavior, and one that the student can avoid in the future if he or she chooses to do so" (p. 18). Finally, teachers should convey, to both the offending student and the rest of the class, the message that instead of using punishment, they would rather help students develop and practice self-discipline.

Additional research shows that students *prefer* teachers who are high in both responsiveness and demandingness. For example, research by T. Wubbels and colleagues (Wubbels, Brekelmans, van Tartwijk, & Admiral, 1999) found that teachers whom students like best are moderate to high in qualities of *both* cooperation and dominance (similar to Baumrind's constructs of responsiveness and demandingness). That is, students prefer teachers who value student responsibility and exhibit concern about the needs, interests, and opinions of all students but who also demonstrate strong guidance and management of student behavior. They do *not* like teachers who are extremely cooperative or dominating.

STOP AND REFLECT

While creatively teaching a language arts lesson in poetry, Mrs. Moxley reminds you of an air traffic controller, a comedian, and a motivational speaker. Wearing a tie-dyed t-shirt, beads, and dangling earrings, with classroom lights dimmed and each student sipping from his or her cup of "coffee" (i.e., fruit juice), she dramatically reads a few of her favorite poems. They include a humorous poem she wrote about the class and poems written by students of diverse abilities and backgrounds in her fifth-grade inclusive classroom of students with and without disabilities. After each poem, students gently snap their fingers in unison. Most students are mesmerized, except for Geraldine and Jill on the opposite side of the room. Without missing a beat, she makes eye contact with the two students, moves in their direction, and gently places a hand on Jill's shoulder. As she stands next to them she finishes the poem, calling on Geraldine to comment on what her favorite part of the poem is and asking Jill if she agrees. Upon reading several poems, she directs the class to return to working on their own poems, while praising the class for their courteous listening throughout the poetry reading and enthusiastically assuring them that she expects great readings and courteous behavior when they read their own poems at the "1960s Coffee House" next week.

What are the skills that Mrs. Moxley uses to make her an effective classroom manager? How do these skills help prevent misbehavior?

Strategies and Techniques for Effective Classroom Management

Drawing from the preceding research in educational and developmental psychology, nine general strategies are presented next to help teachers with classroom management. Although the first two strategies were emphasized in previous chapters within the context of developing self-discipline, they also apply to the prevention of behavior problems through effective classroom management. The third strategy highlights the need to establish positive relationships with parents or caregivers, and the fourth and fifth strategies address the role of motivation in classroom management. Because the use of praise and rewards has been the focus of considerable controversy and debate in recent years, this issue is discussed in depth before presenting specific techniques for the strategic and effective use of praise and rewards. Techniques related to organization, rules, and procedures are presented in Strategies 6, 7, and 8. Given the salience and importance of classroom rules in classroom management, Strategy 7 receives the most attention. The final strategy for effective classroom management addresses a preventive function that overlaps substantially with the correction of discipline problems: early intervention. As noted previously, effective teachers employ many of the same techniques when preventing behavior problems as they do when correcting minor acts of misbehavior and when responding to the early signs of potentially serious behavior problems.

Strategy 1: Demonstrate Warmth, Support, and Caring

As emphasized in the previous chapter on emotions, the qualities of warmth, support, and caring are critical to emotional development and the promotion of self-discipline. They also are critical to effective classroom management. Both common sense and research suggest that students prefer teachers who are warm, supportive, and caring (i.e., high in responsiveness) and that students are less likely to misbehave among teachers who demonstrate these qualities, particularly when they are combined with demandingness. Thus, by following techniques recommended in the previous chapter, teachers not only help promote the emotional development and self-discipline of students but also help prevent misbehavior from occurring and help create a positive climate that is conducive to teaching and learning. These techniques include showing a sincere interest in the lives of *all* students, encouraging open communication and mutual respect, and displaying interpersonal qualities such as humor, friendliness, self-confidence, empathy, understanding, respect, honesty, and trust.

Strategy 2: Foster Social and Moral Problem-Solving and Decision-Making Skills

It is much easier to manage classrooms when students are skilled in social and moral problem solving, when they value these skills, and when they apply them in the classroom. As such, techniques for developing social and moral problem solving, as presented in Chapter 8, should be used not only for developing self-discipline but also for managing classrooms. These techniques include the direct teaching and modeling of specific social problem-solving steps, fostering moral reasoning through moral discussions, and confronting unacceptable excuses and irrational and self-centered thinking. They also include providing students with plenty of opportunities to voice class- and school-related concerns and to address them through active participation in social and moral problem-solving activities.

Strategy 3: Establish and Maintain Close Communication with Each Student's Parents and Work Hard to Garner Their Support

It is well documented that parents, or caregivers, are critically important in all aspects of their children's development, including academic, social, and emotional development (Minke, 2000; Steinberg, 1996). Parents and families profoundly influence students' motivation, values, attitudes, goals, and behavior. This influence is seen both inside and outside of school. As such, they greatly influence not only whether students complete homework or study for a test but also whether they perceive teachers as being fair or unfair, kind or mean, caring or cold, and so forth. Whether parents perceive teachers or schools positively or negatively often is reflected in their child's thoughts and behaviors. Thus, a few minutes each week spent developing positive relationships with parents is time well invested, often preventing teachers from having to spend hours in the future addressing problems of motivation and discipline.

Establishing and maintaining close communications is not only a wise strategy to adopt from the perspective of enhancing instruction, classroom management, the development of self-discipline, and the correction of discipline problems, but it also simply is the right strategy to adopt for ethical and legal reasons. That is, parents are legally responsible for their children. As such, they have a moral right to be kept informed of their children's behavior or misbehavior (Jone & Jones, 2002). This right pertains not only to parents being informed of their children's serious violations of school rules that lead to suspension or expulsion, as typically required by law, but also to being informed of their children's positive behaviors, achievements, and successes.

Some techniques for helping to establish and maintain close communication and positive working relations with parents follow:

1. *Beginning the first week of school, communicate with parents by meeting with them.* Or send a letter home in which you describe your expectations, your desire to work together, and the best way to contact you whenever they have concerns about their children's behavior or academic progress. Invite them to participate in classroom and school activities and give them suggestions about how to do so. For example, invite parents to observe your classroom, contact you about their concerns, to volunteer to help in the classroom or on field trips, or to join and participate in the school's parent–teacher organization.

2. *Continue to communicate with parents on a regular basis.* This can be done using a variety of means, such as phone calls, group letters, notes and cards to individual students and parents, newsletters, e-mail, conferences, and group meetings. Be sure to emphasize students' positive achievements, behaviors, and progress instead of waiting until there is a problem to contact a parent. A short, positive phone call or e-mail to parents can go a long way, especially for students with some of the most significant behavior problems. One good system for fostering communication is a homework notebook that parents sign daily or at least weekly.

3. *Recognize that the majority of parents are friendly, supportive, and cooperative.* However, also realize that it is unrealistic to expect all parents (and teachers) to act that way all of the time. As is true with teachers, principals, and other professionals, parents include all types of individuals, ranging from the most pleasant and supportive to the cruelest and most socially maladjusted. Regardless of how positive you are, some parents will be difficult to work with. Take comfort, however, in knowing that difficult parents are the minority. Don't let a few negative experiences with parents dissuade you from working to establish positive relations with other parents.

4. *When encountering parents who seem resistant to your efforts to help their children, consider the following techniques.* These techniques will help overcome resistance and make meetings more productive.

- Focus on their child's needs and your joint sincere desire to address them. Be specific as to what behaviors are problematic and emphasize the positive behaviors that should replace them. Describe the student's behavior in specific, nonjudgmental terms (e.g., "Jacob has not turned in six of the last ten assignments," instead of "Jacob is lazy and doesn't care about school"). When feasible, reframe problems in more positive terms (e.g., "This might be an excellent opportunity for us to help Angela develop greater responsibility for her homework").

- Emphasize a sincere desire and the necessity of the school, home, and student to work together as a team. Don't overlook the value of including students in meetings concerning their behavior. If you seek to change students' behavior, it only makes sense to have them present and involved in generating a plan for change.

- Demonstrate basic interpersonal skills that you would like to see exhibited if you were in the parents' position (e.g., empathy, listening, interest, caring, trust, sincerity, calmness, cooperation, self-confidence, and an optimistic "can do" attitude). In other words, treat parents as you would like to be treated.

- Try to understand the nature of parents' resistance. Examine the situation from their point of view and recognize that they are often doing the best they can under the circumstances. Always acknowledge their point of view, even when you disagree. If parents resist your recommendations or dismiss your concerns during the meeting, it might be helpful to act puzzled or confused and ask them to help you understand their perspective. Another useful technique is to repeat and emphasize what both of you agree about before continuing to address disagreements.

- Discuss factors that might contribute to the student's problem behavior. However, avoid blaming parents for the problem. Assigning blame is often a guarantee to fostering greater resistance and harming a cooperative relationship.

- Focus on exploring solutions rather than simply rehashing problems. Solicit solutions from parents and students.

- Solicit and respect the parents' concerns, ideas, and recommendations. Be open to constructive criticism and reflect on the accuracy and potential usefulness of the criticism.

- Avoid discussing the situation when anyone (e.g., you, a parent, or the student) is angry. Likewise, where feasible, try to avoid confrontation unless the relationship with the parents is positive.

- At the end of the meeting, as well as throughout the meeting as needed, check to make sure that the parents correctly understand your concerns and recommendations.
- Write a summary of any action plan that you jointly develop and to which all parties agree. Give a copy to the parents and student to document the progress that was made during the meeting.

Strategy 4: Provide Academic Instruction and Activities That Motivate Learning

Effective classroom managers focus more attention on academic learning than on misbehavior, knowing that students learn more and misbehave less when they are actively engaged in academic activities. As such, they use instructional methods, curricula, and materials that are designed to motivate students to exert their best effort (Morrone & Pintrich, 1997; Stipek, 2002). Some recommended techniques for fostering motivation follow:

1. *Demonstrate momentum and smoothness.* These two characteristics of effective classroom managers described by Kounin are most directly related to student motivation.

2. *Use a variety of methods that are developmentally appropriate, sufficiently challenging, and interesting.* Avoid tasks that are too easy or too difficult. Offer activities that are novel and that spark curiosity. Strive to make tasks meaningful and relevant to the lives and interests of all students. Devote much more time to problem solving, discussion, exploration, and other activities that require active intellectual challenge and higher-order thinking skills than to tasks that simply require memorization and repetition.

3. *Demonstrate your own interest and enthusiasm toward a given activity and explain how the behaviors you are attempting to motivate are consistent with important values.* For example, explain why completing homework was important to you when you were a student and point out how you continue to make every effort to complete your "homework" (e.g., grading tests, planning lessons).

4. *Be sure that your expectations, standards, and requirements are clear, reasonable, and attainable.* Model the behaviors you desire and give concrete examples of what you expect from students. Convey high (yet realistic) expectations for all students, along with optimism that they can meet these expectations. Never hold low expectations of students because of their education, family, or cultural background.

5. *Hold students accountable for their academic achievement and classroom behavior.* Encourage students to set reasonable goals and to assess their own performance. Such assessment should complement, not replace, assessment by the teacher.

6. *Ensure high rates of success, especially when new concepts are first introduced.* Initial failure on a task is a sure way to diminish motivation.

7. *Provide feedback for both effort and achievement.* Always provide more positive than negative feedback, but don't hesitate to use constructive criticism when your expectations are not met or when effort and achievement are lacking. Feedback, including grades, should be informational rather than controlling or punitive. (Further guidance on the effective use of praise is presented later.)

8. *Encourage activities that allow students to work together.* Research demonstrates that students prefer cooperative learning activities to didactic instruction and that such activities are effective in motivating academic achievement and prosocial behavior (Johnson & Johnson, 1999). Cooperative learning results in positive outcomes, however, only if group members are friendly and respectful toward each other.

9. *Offer opportunities for students to participate in instructional decisions.* For example, allow students to choose a topic to study and the means by which they can demonstrate mastery. This might entail giving students a choice of books on which to complete a book report and allowing them to supplement a written book report with a video, interview, or creative presentation (e.g., wearing a costume, using a role-play or drama).

10. *When students experience failure, attribute such failure to a lack of sufficient effort or to the use of ineffective strategies, and not the lack of ability.* This technique is important in helping to protect students' self-esteem and intrinsic motivation.

11. *Modify instruction, curriculum, and academic materials to meet the needs, goals, interests, abilities, and cultural differences among individual students.* This includes enriching and extending the curriculum to meet the needs of gifted and talented students and to be responsive to cultural diversity. It also includes adapting instruction, curriculum, and materials to meet the needs of students with learning difficulties—students particularly at risk for behavior problems. The following adaptive techniques have been shown to be particularly effective for children with learning difficulties (Waldron, 1997). Note, however, that most of these techniques (especially the first nine) are often appropriate not simply for students with learning difficulties but also for all students.

- Preview what is to be taught and preteach critical vocabulary.
- Highlight and repeat key concepts.
- Present information in multiple formats (e.g., written, oral, video, computer, games).
- Present clear samples of work products that demonstrate exactly what is expected from students.
- Where feasible, match materials to the individual interests of the students.
- Allow students to demonstrate mastery in different ways.
- Employ cooperative learning activities, especially peer tutoring.
- Closely align instruction and curriculum with evaluation measures and with the individual needs of students.
- Avoid material that is too difficult or too easy.
- Provide extra time for students to learn material and to complete projects and tests.
- Break instruction into smaller units and shorter assignments.
- Emphasize repeated practice of new skills, including practice at home.
- Provide modified tests and grading.
- Emphasize the teaching of functional skills, including vocational and daily living skills.

12. *Avoid "wasting" time.* Students are more likely to misbehave when they are not engaged in academic learning. Obviously, students are not engaged when they have nothing to do, such as when they have finished a class assignment before others, or are otherwise "waiting" (e.g., for lunch, the bell, etc.). Time spent waiting should be minimized by ensuring that students always have something constructive to do. This might include the use of learning

"Do I get partial credit for simply having the courage
to get out of bed and face the world again today?"

centers, providing extra credit activities and enrichment activities, allowing students to complete their homework in class, and offering various other free-time activities.

Strategy 5: When Using Praise and Rewards, Do So Strategically Such That You Maximize Their Effectiveness in Improving Behavior while Minimizing the Risk of Diminishing Intrinsic Motivation

Over the centuries nearly all teachers have used praise and other external incentives as rewards for good behavior. At the same time, however, some educators have voiced strong opposition against the use of rewards. In recent years the greatest controversy over the use of rewards, and to a lesser extent praise, has been over their impact on students' motivation. Whereas some authorities argue rewards and praise enhance motivation, others warn that under certain conditions, including those that are common in most classrooms, external rewards actually undermine intrinsic motivation. Because this controversy has been the focus of considerable attention in recent years, it is reviewed here before recommendations on the use of praise and rewards are presented.

Do Praise and Rewards Undermine Intrinsic Motivation? Before discussing the current debate over this question, it is important to emphasize several points to avoid misinterpretation of the research findings that are presented. First, the debate does not center on the effectiveness of rewards in bringing about obedience and short-term improvements in behavior. There is little disagreement that rewards *are* effective in achieving this goal (when teachers need to achieve it). Second, the debate does not concern whether rewards are appropriate for helping motivate students who lack intrinsic motivation, such as students with serious behavioral or academic problems or students who demonstrate lack of interest in an activity or refusal to follow rules and procedures. Few authorities disagree that under these circumstances students benefit, at least in the short term, from the use of external rewards, and that such use typically does more good than harm. Finally, the debate concerns older students more so than younger students. Whereas students of all ages tend to value positive feedback from their teachers, younger children tend to be more responsive to praise than adolescents (Bear, Minke, Griffin, & Deemer, 1998; Stipek, 2002).

The issue of greatest controversy centers on teachers rewarding students for doing something that they already enjoy doing—praising or giving them tangible rewards when they do not lack intrinsic motivation. Examples of this happening in the classroom include rewarding students who love to complete puzzles with a certificate after they successfully complete a puzzle, rewarding students who always help others with "citizen of the week" awards after they exhibit sharing and other helping behaviors, and rewarding well-behaving students with free time or a pizza party contingent upon their continuation of good behavior. The crux of the argument against such uses of rewards is that they diminish intrinsic motivation and perceptions of autonomy or self-determination (Deci, Koestner, & Ryan, 1999; 2001; Ryan & Deci, 2000). As a consequence of being rewarded for what they already enjoy doing, students become less interested in the given activity and, thus, are less likely to desire or freely choose to engage in that activity in the future. It is argued that these negative outcomes are most likely to occur when students believe that rewards are being used to manipulate or control their behavior.

In explaining this phenomenon, Deci et al. (1999, 2001) posit that there are two aspects to rewards (including praise, which they refer to as a verbal reward): *informational* and *controlling*. Whereas the informational aspect "conveys self-determined competence and thus enhances intrinsic motivation," the controlling aspect "prompts an external perceived locus of causality (i.e., low perceived self-determination) and thus undermines intrinsic motivation" (Deci et al., 2001, p. 3). Whether a student experiences a reward as informational or controlling is determined primarily by the *interpersonal context* in which the reward is used. If the interpersonal context is one in which a teacher intends to make students be obedient and "think, feel, or behave in particular ways" (Deci et al., 2001, p. 4), rewards are likely to be viewed as controlling. In general, tangible rewards (e.g., prizes, points) are more likely than verbal rewards to be controlling because they tend to be used deliberately to get students to do something they would not ordinarily do. That is, the rewards are administered contingent upon students exhibiting a specific behavior, such as engaging in a given activity (e.g., "You have to pay attention and work on your assignment to earn your recess"), completing the activity (e.g., "You have to finish the assignment first"), or completing the activity and meeting or exceeding a given criteria (e.g., "You have to get 80% of the items correct"). Typically, verbal rewards are not as controlling as tangible rewards, but they can be. For example, teachers might only praise students when they do exactly what teachers demand.

Rewards are not always used in a controlling interpersonal context, however, and thus they do not always have a negative effect on students' intrinsic motivation (Deci et al., 2001). According to Deci et al. (1999, 2001), rewards are not likely to be perceived as controlling when (1) they are administered unexpectedly (e.g., students are rewarded with a "no homework pass" after everyone turns in their homework, but the students are not told beforehand that the reward might be given) and (2) they are more informational than controlling, such as when they clearly communicate that a student performed well on a task compared to the norm or compared to other standards valued by the student. Such information serves to affirm the student's self-evaluation of competence on the task required.

On the basis of reviewing over a hundred studies, Deci et al. (1999, 2001) concluded that research supports each of the preceding tenets of their cognitive control theory. That is, they concluded that under interpersonal contexts that are controlling, verbal rewards do not enhance children's intrinsic motivation (*nor do they harm it*). However, tangible rewards significantly *decrease* intrinsic motivation. This negative effect is greatest when children receive smaller rewards than those received by other students because their performance is considered "second rate." Different results emerge when rewards are used in interpersonal contexts that are informational rather than controlling. When the context is informational, verbal rewards actually *enhance* intrinsic motivation. In fact, this is one of the strongest effects of verbal rewards. Tangible rewards also seem to *enhance* intrinsic motivation when used in an informational context; however, Deci et al. discovered only one study (Ryan, Mims, & Koestner, 1983) that examined this condition. Finally, as also concluded by Deci et al., rewards tend to have no effect (either positive or negative effect) when administered in an unexpected rather than contingent or controlling fashion.

Of the foregoing findings, the one that has been the center of the greatest controversy is that intrinsic motivation is not enhanced, but rather often diminished, when rewards are administered in a controlling fashion—as is common in many classrooms. Many researchers (e.g., Baumrind, 1996; Cameron, 2001; Cameron & Pierce, 1994) disagree with the conclusion of Deci et al. (2001) for several reasons. First, they argue that nearly all of the studies reviewed by Deci et al. (1999) were conducted in experimental laboratories and, thus, are unlikely to reflect the complex classroom conditions under which rewards are actually used (Baumrind, 1996; Cameron, 2001; Everston et al., 2003). More importantly, they point out that other reviews of the literature have concluded that rewards are very effective in increasing desired behaviors and decreasing undesired behaviors (e.g., Stage & Quiroz, 1997) and that only rarely do they decrease intrinsic motivation (Cameron, 2001; Cameron & Pierce, 1994). For example, in their reviews of the literature Cameron and Pierce (1994; Cameron, 2001) found that both verbal and tangible rewards have positive effects on intrinsic motivation when students are rewarded for tasks that are of little interest to them and have mostly positive effects when students are rewarded for tasks that are of high interest to them. As found by Deci et al., Cameron and Pierce found a small negative effect when tangible rewards are offered for the completion of high-interest tasks *and* the rewards are given without any informational feedback or with only a loosely specified level of performance (e.g., giving students rewards for completing assignments regardless of their accuracy). However, in contrast to the findings of Deci et al., Cameron and Pierce found that tangible rewards have *positive* effects on intrinsic motivation when linked to explicit and clear standards of performance. Their findings held true for both high-interest and low-interest tasks, leading Cameron and Pierce to conclude that teachers have little reason to worry about using rewards in the classroom.

In sum, researchers agree that rewards are most effective in improving behavior when students view them as signifying their competence or self-efficacy. When rewards are perceived as informational rather than controlling, several important positive outcomes occur: (1) Perceptions of competence and self-efficacy are enhanced, (2) intrinsic motivation and feelings of autonomy are enhanced, and (3) improvements in behavior tend to endure over time (instead of being temporary, as is true when rewards are perceived as controlling). Researchers disagree, however, about the effectiveness of using rewards under interpersonal contexts that are controlling. Whereas researchers agree that such use is likely to bring about short-term improvements in behavior, some argue (e.g., Deci et al., 2001) that the short-term gain is not worth the potential negative impact on intrinsic motivation, especially when rewards are given for behaviors that children readily exhibit. Others (e.g., Baumrind, 1996; Cameron, 2001; Evertson et al., 2003), however, argue that although a controlling interpersonal context may not be the best context for administering rewards, few teachers need be overly concerned about the routine use of praise and rewards in the classroom. They also note that it is wiser for teachers to offer rewards to motivate success than to lower their expectations and standards or to use threats and punishment (Evertson et al., 2003).

Overall, research indicates that how *often* students are praised and rewarded is much less important than the *manner* in which this occurs. That is, both the interpersonal context (Deci et al., 2001) and the quality of rewards (Bandura, 1986; Brophy, 1981) are more important than the frequency of rewards.

Recommendations on the Use of Praise and Rewards. Drawing largely from research, especially the research and recommendations by Bandura (1997), Brophy (1981), Cameron (2001), Deci, Koestner, and Ryan (1999, 2001; Ryan & Deci, 2000), Henderlong & Lepper (2002), and Stipek (2002), the following recommendations are offered when using rewards and praise to prevent misbehavior, as well as to correct misbehavior (see Chapter 11).

1. *Use tangible rewards only occasionally, if at all, when rewarding behavior that is intrinsically motivated.* For example, if students already demonstrate appropriate behavior, do not begin rewarding them in a contingent and regular fashion for the same behavior (e.g., "If you work real hard each week you'll earn a 'no homework pass' "). Not only is such use of rewards unnecessary, but it may be perceived by students, especially older ones, as controlling.

2. *When rewards are used, adopt the following strategies to help reduce the likelihood that they will be perceived as controlling.*

- Emphasize the informational aspect of the reward and the importance of intrinsic motivation (e.g., "You earned the reward yourselves by showing that you understand the importance of responsible behavior. I'm proud of the class for achieving a goal that you set").
- Highlight the value or usefulness of the behavior that is rewarded (e.g., "That's terrific that you were able to control your anger when teased by Jerome. That's an important skill that will help you keep friends and avoid being sent to the office").
- Highlight the student's specific achievement or the skills and effort demonstrated toward the achievement. For example, instead of saying "Nice job," say "Nice job ignoring Andy after he teased you" or "I was very pleased to see that you tried your best to get away from Andy on the playground and play with someone else."
- Allow the student to play an active role in determining the reward (e.g., giving the student choices) and what must be done to earn it. Emphasize that the students (and not you) determine whether they earn the reward.
- Administer the reward in an unexpected or surprise fashion (e.g., "You have worked so hard during the past two weeks that I decided to bring in popcorn and drinks for everyone!").
- Do not promise rewards that you don't plan to or can't deliver.

3. *Use praise and tangible rewards in a sincere, credible, and timely manner.* Insincere or faint praise can be quite damning (e.g., "You finally got that right"). Likewise, rewards can harm motivation and the teacher–student relationship when you indicate a lack of support or enthusiasm (e.g., "Ok, here's your reward"). Both praise and rewards also can be ineffective if given a long time after the behavior occurred.

4. *Recognize that students' interpretation of praise depends on not only the actual words said but also on the manner by which they are communicated.* For example, tone of voice, facial expression, and timing can determine whether praise is perceived as sincere, faint, or sarcastic. Praise should not be presented in a soft monotone or in an overly enthusiastic and exaggerated manner. To enhance its credibility, praise should be administered in a straightforward and spontaneous manner, in a variety of ways, and with a smile (Brophy, 1981).

5. *Make praise and rewards contingent on success or effort.* Do not praise or reward students for poor performance or effort. Although that recommendation may sound obvious, it should be noted that teachers often praise students, particularly low-achieving students, for *poor* performance and lack of effort, perhaps because they fear damaging the students' self-esteem. Such praise conveys low expectations and often results eventually in lower self-esteem.

6. *Be careful when praising and rewarding students for behavior that they believe is not worthy of receiving praise or rewards.* For example, this would *include* praising students for success on easy tasks or for performing well but "not good enough." Although such use of praise or rewards may be intended to protect students' self-esteem and reinforce continued effort, it is likely to have little positive effect on self-esteem and may actually backfire. That is, students may interpret such praise or rewards as conveying that you think less of them than others, that they are not capable of doing well, or that praise and rewards are given indiscriminately and, thus, are not meaningful.

7. *Rely less on public praise and more on private praise, especially with adolescents.* Public praise is more likely to be perceived as controlling, and embarrassing in front of peers, especially by older students.

8. *Do not hesitate to use tangible rewards to motivate behavior that is not intrinsically motivated.* When using tangible rewards to manage or correct misbehavior, follow recommendations given in the next chapter, such as making sure that the reward is actually reinforcing, linking the reward to specific criteria that must be met, and fading use of the reward so that the behavior is likely to be maintained by praise and other natural reinforcers (including intrinsic motivation) after the reward is removed.

Strategy 6: Create a Physical Environment That Is Conducive to Teaching and Learning

Both teachers and students appreciate working in an environment that is physically attractive and comfortable. Obviously, it is difficult to concentrate in a room that is hot, crowded, and otherwise physically unattractive. Not only do individuals fail to look forward to returning to these conditions, but they also are more prone to violence when crowded and uncomfortable (Berkowitz, 1989a, b). Unfortunately, teachers often are limited in the improvements they can make to their classroom environment due to factors beyond their control, such as the size and construction of the classroom, the number of students, and the availability of resources, equipment, and materials (e.g., computers, furniture, air conditioning, colorful walls). Nevertheless, there are many ways to enhance the physical environment of classrooms and, thus, enhance teaching and learning, such as those that follow:

1. *Enhance the physical attractiveness of the room.* For example, use colorful posters, bulletin boards, interesting educational materials, plants, sofas, and so forth. Provide students with opportunities to contribute to decisions about the arrangement and décor of the classroom.

2. *Arrange furniture, materials, and supplies in an organized and efficient manner.* Arrange materials and supplies that students might need, such as markers, staplers, paper clips, and reference books, in a well-organized fashion and in locations where they can be obtained easily without disrupting the class. Arrange chairs, desks, and tables to reduce congestion and to facilitate quiet and easy movement around the classroom.

3. *Arrange seating such that all students can clearly see the board and other instructional visual displays and can attend to instruction.* Arrange student desks or tables in the manner that is most conducive to the instructional method being used at the time. The same seating arrangements for attending to teacher-led lessons may not be suitable for group discussions and cooperative learning activities.

4. *Arrange your desk in a position that allows for easy scanning of all students and for quick movement toward each student when necessary.* Your desk may be placed in the front or the back of the room, as long as you are facing all of the students. Recognize, however, it is more effective to monitor behavior while moving about the room than while sitting at your desk.

5. *Allow students to sit where they like, but inform them that this is a privilege that must be earned and can be taken away.* Do not allow students to continue to sit where they like if they exhibit behaviors that interfere with their own learning or the learning of others. Students who frequently misbehave while at their seats lose this privilege and should be seated where you can monitor them closely. Be careful, however, not to punish a student's misbehavior by seating the student next to you, especially for an extended period of time (days or weeks). This is likely to contribute to peer rejection while doing little to teach the student appropriate behavior. Instead, seat this student in a position where he or she can observe positive role models while simultaneously be closely monitored by you.

Strategy 7: Establish Fair Rules and Consequences

Among the high behavioral expectations set by effective classroom managers is that all students are expected to act responsibly and respectfully. Rules communicate these expectations and they set standards for acceptable behavior. Nearly all researchers and theorists (e.g., Canter & Canter, 2001; Curwin & Mendler, 1999; Dreikurs, 1968; Duke, 2002; Emmer, Evertson, & Worsham, 2003; Jones & Jones, 2002; Weinstein, 1996) agree to the following recommendations for classroom rules:

1. *Make rules clear and understandable.* Present rules in writing, using language that is appropriate for students' developmental levels. Post the rules in the classroom and send home a copy to parents asking them to review and discuss the rules with their children (when feasible, include a copy of the school rules as well). Most rules should be written in positive language, stating the behavior that should be exhibited rather than the behavior that is prohibited (e.g.,"Raise your hand to speak" instead of "Don't call out"). Do not establish rules that you cannot or do not intend to enforce. Discuss each rule and present clear examples of behaviors that conform and do not conform to the rule.

2. *Make sure rules are fair and reasonable.* As an authoritative classroom manager, you are the final judge of what is fair and reasonable. It is important, however, that you always consider what the students themselves are likely to view as *fair* and *reasonable* and that you recognize that students are likely to resist rules that they perceive to be overly harsh, trivial, or otherwise unreasonable. In helping to determine what is a "fair" rule, several authors suggest that rules be grounded in, or referenced to, the rights that are granted in the United States Constitution (Duke, 2002; Gathercoal, 2001). Gathercoal (2001) gives four examples of rules grounded in the Constitution: (1) Act in a safe and healthy way, (2) treat all property with respect, (3) respect the rights and needs of others, and (4) take responsibility for learning (pp. 36–37). From a legal perspective, Gathercoal (2001) advises teachers not to make any rule that violates the U.S. Constitution, state or federal laws, or policies and regulations set by the state department of education, a collective bargaining agreement, school board, superintendent, or principal. In addition to being fair, rules should be reasonable. Rules that are not necessary are not reasonable. A rule is reasonable if there is a compelling reason for it and it makes the classroom more pleasant, increases opportunities to learn, can be explained rationally to students, and does not interfere with institutional goals and learning (Weinstein, 1996).

3. *Develop no more than five or six general classroom rules.* It is better to have a few general rules than a large number of specific ones. A long list of rules is difficult for students to remember and for teachers to manage. Moreover, a long list is not consistent with the goal of developing a positive classroom climate. Instead, it conveys distrust and an authoritarian approach to discipline and fosters student resistance (Duke, 2002).

Jones and Jones (2004, p. 261) suggest six classroom rules for all grade levels:

1. Treat each other politely and kindly.
2. Treat school and personal property respectfully.
3. Follow teacher requests.
4. Be prepared for class.
5. Make a good effort at your work and request help if you need it.
6. Solve conflicts nonviolently.

Focusing more on secondary students, Evertson et al. (2003, p. 23) offer these:

1. Be polite and helpful.
2. Respect other people's property.
3. Listen quietly while others are speaking.
4. Respect and be polite to all people.
5. Obey all school rules.

Note that both lists contain a small number of rules that cover a large number of specific behaviors.

4. *Discuss classroom rules during the first days of school and review them periodically thereafter.* Nearly all researchers and authorities in the area of classroom management agree that during the first days of school the development and review of rules should be among the first orders of business. There is little agreement, however, and little guiding research regarding what role students should play in this process (Duke, 2002). Whereas some argue that rules should be developed either by students themselves or as a collaborative effort between teachers and students (e.g., Charney, 2002; Curwin & Mendler, 1999; Jones & Jones, 2004), others argue that this is not necessary (e.g., Duke, 2002; Evertson et al., 2003).

Evertson et al. (2003) question the appropriateness of actively involving students in the development of classroom rules, noting that such involvement is not recommended for three good reasons: "First, the domain in which student participation is acceptable is limited. Schoolwide rules must be accepted as they are. Second, policies essential to managing instruction cannot be left to student discretion. Third, elementary age students may require considerable prompting to produce a comprehensive list of general rules" (p. 24). Accordingly, Everston et al. recommend that teachers develop and present classroom rules, while ensuring that students are involved in the discussion of the rules and are given a clear rationale for each one.

Duke (2002) suggests several formats that can be used to present or discuss classroom rules: (a) presenting rules in orientation sessions during the first days of school or over the summer; (b) discussing rules within the context of subject-area lessons (e.g., the importance of rules in civics and social studies); (c) covering rules in lessons on character education or social problem solving; (d) reviewing rules and social skills in small-group classes for students who frequently violate rules; and (e) demonstrating rules and related behaviors through modeling.

5. *Support rules with fair, reasonable, and judicious consequences.* Rules are of little value in managing classroom behavior if they are not supported by consequences. Consequences should be fair and implemented in a consistent and judicious manner to be effective in helping to bring about what Brophy (1996) describes as "willful" as opposed to "grudging" compliance (with the latter promoting resentment, revenge, disliking of the teacher, and only short-term effectiveness). Fair consequences are those that "fit" or are commensurate with the misbehavior. That is, the harshness or severity of the consequence matches the seriousness of the offense. It is unfair (and possibly illegal) to suspend students for minor disruptive behaviors. Likewise, it is perhaps unfair *not* to suspend students (or move them to alternative settings) as the consequence of serious violent acts.

6. *Be consistent but fair. Consistency* often is viewed as an important dimension of fairness (e.g., "It's unfair not to be consistent. If you expelled Ed for fighting, you also should expel Jorge"). Although both consistency and fairness are important with respect to rules and classroom management, teachers should be careful not to fuse these two concepts. Consistency can be either fair or unfair. It is fair and highly recommended that teachers respond to violations of rules in a consistent manner *when* they entail the same circumstances. For example, if a teacher warns Ed after he got out of his seat without permission, it is only fair that the teacher does the same when Jorge exhibits the same behavior (assuming similar circumstances). However, it would be unfair to expel both students for fighting if the circumstances differ markedly, despite the behavior being the same. For example, assume that Ed clearly started the fight, as he had done several times before, and caused serious and intentional harm to the victim. But Jorge, with no record of disciplinary problems, responded in self-defense. For the sake of consistency, should both be expelled?

To be sure, *proceeding carefully and wisely before invoking serious consequences* requires much more time and effort than simply responding in an automatic and consistent, yet unfair, authoritarian manner. Careful, fair, unbiased, and sound judgment, which includes consideration of mitigating circumstances, is the cornerstone of the judicial system in a democratic society. Lack of time and an unwavering need for consistency (without fairness) are poor excuses for educators not to follow the same basic judicial principles, especially before invoking harsh consequences.

Strategy 8: Establish Predictable Procedures and Routines

Procedures are similar to rules in that both communicate expectations for behavior. Procedures differ from rules, however, in that their primary purpose is not to regulate behavior per se but to define the appropriate course of action for carrying out a particular activity or function (Weinstein, 1996). Unlike rules, procedures are seldom written. A procedure becomes a *routine* when it is repeated over and over in an unvarying or habitual manner, requiring minimal teacher supervision. Procedures and routines are as important as rules in the management of classrooms. They guide student behavior, facilitate order, and help prevent misbehavior. As is the case with rules, procedures should be discussed, modeled, and practiced.

Evertson et al. (2003) recommend that teachers establish the following six types of procedures for effective classroom management:

1. Procedures for room use (e.g., correct usage of storage and supply areas and of the items and materials located in those areas; procedures for using the sink, drinking fountain, pencil sharpener, and bathroom).
2. Procedures during individual work and teacher-led activities (e.g., procedures for attending and participating, talking to others, obtaining assistance, turning in homework, and finishing assignments early).
3. Procedures for transitions into and out of the room (e.g., procedures for beginning and ending the school day or class period and for leaving and returning to the room).
4. Procedures during small-group instruction (e.g., procedures that prepare the class for the activity, facilitate the movement of students into and out of the group, and define the expected behavior of students who participate and do not participate in the activity).
5. Procedures during cooperative group activities (e.g., talk and movement, working together, individual accountability).
6. General procedures (e.g., procedures for distributing materials, dealing with interruptions or delays, using bathrooms located outside of the classroom, leaving the room to go the library, resource room, or school office; procedures that stipulate behavior in the cafeteria, on the playground, and during fire and disaster drills).

Strategy 9: Frequently Monitor Student Behavior and Respond Quickly to Signs of Misbehavior

Misbehavior is most likely to occur when students are aware that their behavior is not being monitored or supervised. This is especially true among students who lack self-discipline.

Acts of misbehavior are most frequent in hallways, on the playground, during unstructured activities and transitions, or in other situations in which monitoring and supervision tend to be absent or lacking. Effective classroom managers recognize that these situations foster misbehavior and they respond accordingly by providing close monitoring and supervision, where feasible. Effective classroom managers also anticipate when misbehavior is likely to occur and are particularly vigilant at these times. They anticipate misbehavior not only in the preceding situations but also when individual student characteristics are present that tend to contribute to misbehavior. For example, recognizing that Julio is in an angry mood, or that Tasha has threatened to "get Julio back" for a previous insult, teachers would monitor these students closely. By anticipating the occurrence of misbehavior and responding with increased monitoring and supervision, teachers can prevent many acts of misbehavior.

When signs of misbehavior are first seen, teachers should respond immediately, at the earliest point possible in the progression of the misbehavior. This helps prevent the misbehavior from escalating and, thus, requiring harsher techniques of correction that are likely to harm the teacher–student relationship and disrupt the classroom. For example, when Julio first rises to get out of his seat, the teacher should immediately establish eye contact, move close to him, and redirect him or remind him to apply his social problem-solving skills. Such a reaction is much wiser than waiting until the behavior escalates and then implementing more systematic and intrusive techniques of correction.

STOP AND REFLECT

A Case Study

As soon as the bell rang, Mr. Thomas, sitting at his desk, reminded his English class of the school rules as he threatened to write in-school suspension slips for two students who were late for class: "You know that the school's code of conduct doesn't allow for tardiness. This is the third time both of you have been late. Next time, you're going to the office." Mr. Thomas then spent five minutes collecting homework assignments and another five minutes preparing and organizing for the day's lesson. During this time most students chatted, while others did nothing.

Mr. Thomas handed out a class assignment in which students were to work cooperatively in groups of five to answer and discuss ten questions about the story they had been studying. He read the directions for the assignment and returned to his desk to grade papers. Of the five groups in the class, three began the assignment immediately and worked quietly, at least for a while. Members of the fourth group were confused about the questions and, after making a feeble attempt to discuss the first question, decided to talk about the upcoming football game. Because they talked quietly, Mr. Thomas didn't notice that they weren't working on the assignment. However, several others in the first three groups did notice and also began talking about the game and anything but the assignment. The fifth group also seemed confused about the assignment and, when one student in the group mispronounced several words in the first question, Andrew responded, "Great, I have to work with two dummies who can't read." In reaction, Julio stood up and shouted, "Did you call me a dummy, asshole?" Although Mr. Thomas had not responded to the off-task behavior of others, Julio certainly gained his attention.

What characteristics of effective teachers did Mr. Thomas fail to exhibit? What might he have done to prevent the misbehavior in his class?

SUMMARY AND KEY POINTS

- *Classroom management* refers to strategies and techniques used to create and maintain a positive learning environment that facilitates teaching, learning, organization, and safety. Effective classroom management promotes self-discipline, but it is not sufficient for achieving this aim.

- Techniques for effective classroom management can be grouped into four general categories: organization, rules, and procedures; motivational techniques; relational techniques; and early intervention techniques.

- A wealth of research in developmental psychology attests to the effectiveness of an *authoritative* approach to childrearing. Authoritative parents balance high responsiveness with high demandingness. Recent research in education shows that an authoritative approach also characterizes the most effective classroom managers.

- Effective classroom managers recognize that classroom management is easier when they adopt the strategies and techniques for promoting social and moral problem solving and for fostering emotional competence.

- Effective classroom managers work closely with the home of each student, recognizing and respecting the right of parents to ongoing communication and the importance of supportive teacher–parent relations in preventing misbehavior, as well as in fostering self-discipline and academic achievement.

- Effective classroom managers understand the critical importance of academic engagement and motivation in classroom behavior. Thus, effective teachers use a variety of instructional techniques and curricular activities designed to enhance student interest, motivation, and task engagement.

- One of the biggest debates pertaining to classroom discipline and classroom management concerns the appropriate use of verbal rewards (including praise) and tangible rewards. Despite differences of opinion, most researchers agree that the limitations of rewards can be avoided and that the effectiveness of rewards can be enhanced by using them strategically.

- Effective classroom managers are well aware that physical features of the classroom influence learning and behavior and act accordingly.

- Effective classroom managers are well aware that rules and their consequences must be fair and reasonable and be enforced in a fair, judicious, and consistent manner. Likewise, they are aware of the critical importance of clear procedures. In developing and implementing rules and procedures, they follow sound, research-based guidelines for enhancing their effectiveness.

- Effective classroom managers understand that, when not caught early, minor acts of misbehavior often evolve into serious disciplinary problems. Thus, they avoid many disciplinary problems by responding to the first signs of their occurrence.

KEY TERMS AND CONCEPTS

Authoritative classroom
  management
Classroom management
Demandingness
Group alerting

Interpersonal context
Intrinsic motivation and rewards
Momentum
Overlapping
Praise

Responsiveness
Rules and procedures
Smoothness
Withitness

RECOMMENDED READINGS AND RESOURCES

***Books on Evidence-Based Techniques
for Preventing Misbehavior with
Effective Classroom Management***

Brophy, J. E. (1996). *Teaching problem students*. New York: Guilford Press.

Cangelosi, J. S. (2004). *Classroom management strategies: Gaining and maintaining students' cooperation*. New York: Wiley.

Emmer, E. T., Evertson, C. M., & Worsham, M. E. (2003). *Classroom management for secondary teachers* (6th ed.). Boston: Allyn and Bacon.

Evertson, C. M., Emmer, E. T., & Worsham, M. E. (2003). *Classroom management for elementary teachers* (6th ed.). Boston: Allyn and Bacon.

Good, T. L., & Brophy, J. E. (2003). *Looking in classrooms* (9th ed.). Boston: Allyn and Bacon.

Jones, V. F., & Jones, L. S. (2004). *Comprehensive classroom management: Creating communities of support and solving problems* (7th ed.). Boston: Allyn and Bacon.

Levin, J., & Nolan, J. F. (2000). *Principles of classroom management: A professional decision-making model.* Boston: Allyn and Bacon.

Marzano, R. J. (2003). *Classroom management that works: Research-based teachers.* Portland, ME: Stenhouse Publishers.

Wormeli, R. (2003). *Day one & beyond: Practical matters for new middle-level teachers.* Portland, ME: Stenhouse Publishers.

Websites for Information on Classroom Management and on the Correction of Misbehavior

www.behavioraladvisor.com
Contains thousands of tips for classroom management and correction. Includes basic information on behavior management, recommendations for behavior problems, a self-assessment survey of your behavior management skills, resources, links to other sites, and a bulletin board on which individuals can post their behavior problems and receive advice from others.

www.drwilliampmartin.tripod.com/classm.html
Site for the "really big list of classroom management resources." Developed by graduate students at Monmouth University, this site has links to over 500 other sites that address issues of classroom management.

www.education-world.com/preservice/learning
Good source of information on general education, including classroom management.

www.thegateway.org
The Gateway to Educational Materials provides an excellent place to start in a search for information and resources on any topic in education, including classroom management.

www.proteacher.com
Excellent source of information on classroom management (including specific information on conducting class meetings), teaching, and child development.

www.teachervision.com
Contains general information on classroom management, as well as more specific techniques for correcting misbehavior.

www.interventioncentral.org
Provides teachers and parents with techniques and resources for preventing and addressing a variety of behavior and academic problems.

For additional resources on prevention, see resources in Chapter 8 for developing social and moral problem solving and in Chapter 9 for developing emotional competencies.

REFERENCES

Bandura, A. (1986). *Social foundations of thought and action: A social cognitive theory.* Englewood Cliffs, NJ: Prentice-Hall.

Bandura, A. (1997). *Self-efficacy: The exercise of control.* New York: W. H. Freeman.

Battistich, V., Solomon, D., & Delucchi, K. (1993). Interaction processes and student outcomes in cooperative learning groups. *Elementary School Journal, 94,* 19–32.

Baumrind, D. (1971). Current patterns of parental authority. *Developmental Psychology Monographs, 4,* 1–103.

Baumrind, D. (1978). Parental disciplinary patterns and social competence in children. *Youth and Society, 9,* 239–276.

Baumrind, D. (1996). The discipline controversy revisited. *Family Relations, 45,* 405–414.

Bear, G. G., Minke, K. M., Griffin, S. M., & Deemer, S. A. (1997). Self-concept. In G. G. Bear, K. M. Minke, and A. Thomas (Eds.), *Children needs II: Development, problems, and alternatives* (pp. 257–269). Bethesda, MD: National Association of School Psychologists.

Bear, G. G., Minke, K. M., Griffin, S. M., & Deemer, S. A. (1998). Achievement-related perceptions of children with learning disabilities and normal achievement: Group and developmental differences. *Journal of Learning Disabilities, 31,* 91–104.

Berkowitz, L. (1989a). Situational influences on aggression. In J. Groebel & R. A. Hinde (Eds.), *Aggression and war: Their biological and social bases* (pp. 91–100). Thousand Oaks, CA: Sage.

Berkowitz, L. (1989b). Frustration-aggression hypothesis: Examination and reformulation. *Psychology Bulletin, 106,* 1, 59–73.

Brophy, J. (1981). On praising effectively. *Elementary School Journal, 81*(5), 269–278.

Brophy, J. E. (1996). *Teaching problem students.* New York: Guilford Press.

Brophy, J. E., & McCaslin, M. (1992). Teachers' reports of how they perceive and cope with problem students. *Elementary School Journal, 93,* 3–68.

Cameron, J. (2001). Negative effects of reward on intrinsic motivation—A limited phenomenon: Comment on Deci, Loestner, and Ryan (2001). *Review of Educational Research, 71,* 29–42.

Cameron, J., & Pierce, W. D. (1994). Reinforcement, reward, and intrinsic motivation: A meta-analysis. *Review of Educational Research, 64,* 363–423.

Canter, L., & Canter, M. (2001). *Assertive discipline: Positive behavior management for today's classroom.* Santa Monica, CA: Canter & Associates.

Charney, R. S. (2002). *Teaching children to care: Classroom management for ethical and academic growth, K–8* (Rev. ed.). Greenfield, MA: Northeast Foundation for Children.

Curwin, R. L., & Mendler, A. N. (1999). *Discipline with dignity.* Alexandria, VA: Association and Curriculum.

Deci, E. L., Koestner, R., & Ryan, R. M. (1999). A meta-analytic review of experiments examining the effects of extrinsic rewards on intrinsic motivation. *Psychological Bulletin, 125,* 627–668.

Deci, E. L., Koestner, R., & Ryan, R. M. (2001). Extrinsic rewards and intrinsic motivation in education: Reconsidered once again. *Review of Educational Research, 71,* 1–27.

Developmental Studies Center (2000). *Ways we want our class to be: Class meetings that build commitment to kindness and learning. Ideas from the Child Development Project.* Oakland, CA: Author.

Dreikurs, R. (1968). *Psychology in the classroom: A manual for teachers.* New York: Harper & Row.

Dreikurs, R., & Cassel, P. (1972). *Discipline without tears: What to do with children who misbehave.* New York: Hawthorn Books.

Duke, D. L. (2002). *Creating safe schools for all children.* Boston: Allyn and Bacon.

Emmer, E. T., Evertson, C. M., & Worsham, M. E. (2003). *Classroom management for secondary teachers* (6th ed.). Boston: Allyn and Bacon.

Evertson, C. M., Emmer, E. T., & Worsham, M. E. (2003). *Classroom management for elementary teachers* (6th ed.). Boston: Allyn and Bacon.

Gathercoal, F. (2001). *Judicious discipline* (5th ed.). San Francisco: Caddo Gap Press.

Good, T. L., & Brophy, J. E. (2000). *Looking in classrooms* (8th ed.). New York: Addison-Wesley Educational Publications.

Henderlong, J., & Lepper, M. R. (2002). The effects of praise on children's intrinsic motivation: A review and synthesis. *Psychological Bulletin, 128,* 774–795.

Johnson, D. W., & Johnson, F. P. (1999). *Looking together and learning alone: Cooperative, cooperative, and individualistic learning* (5th ed.). Boston: Allyn and Bacon.

Jones, V. F., & Jones, L. S. (2004). *Comprehensive classroom management: Creating communities of support and solving problems* (7th ed.). Boston: Allyn and Bacon.

Kounin, J. (1970). *Discipline and group management in classrooms.* New York: Holt, Rinehart and Winston.

Kounin, J. S., & Gump, P. (1974). Signal systems of lesson settings and the task-related behavior of preschool children. *Journal of Educational Psychology, 66,* 554–562.

Kurdek, L. A., & Fine, M. A. (1994). Family acceptance and family control as predictors of adjustment in young adolescents: Linear, curvilinear, or interactive effects? *Child Development, 65,* 1137–1146.

Lamborn, S. D., Mounts, N. S., Steinberg, & Dornbush, S. M. (1991). Patterns of competence and adjustment among adolescents from authoritative, authoritarian, indulgent, and neglectful families. *Child Development, 62,* 1049–1065.

Marzano, R. J. (2003). *Classroom management that works: Research-based strategies for every teacher.* Alexandria, VA: Association for Supervision and Curriculum Development.

Minke, K. M. (2000). Preventing school problems and promoting school success through family-school-community collaboration. In K. M. Minke and G. G. Bear (Eds.), *Preventing school problems—Promoting school success: Strategies and programs that work* (pp. 377–420). Bethesda, MD: National Association of School Psychologists.

Morrone, A. S., & Pintrich, P. R. (1997). Achievement motivation. In G. G. Bear, K. M. Minke, and A. Thomas (Eds.), *Children needs II: Development, problems, and alternatives* (pp. 387–395). Bethesda, MD: National Association of School Psychologists.

Morrone, A. S., & Schultz, P. A. (2000). Preventing academic failure. In K. M. Minke and G. G. Bear (Eds.), *Preventing school problems—Promoting school success: Strategies and programs that work* (pp. 171–210). Bethesda, MD: National Association of School Psychologists.

Pianta, R. C. (1999). *Enhancing relationships between children and teachers.* Washington, DC: American Psychological Association.

Reid, J. (1993). Prevention of conduct disorder before and after school entry: Relating interventions to developmental findings. *Development and Psychopathology, 5,* 243–262.

Ryan, R. M., & Deci, E. L. (2000). Self-determination theory and the facilitation of intrinsic motivation, social development, and well-being. *American Psychologist, 55,* 68–78.

Ryan, R. M., Mims, V., & Koestner, R. (1983). Relation of reward contingency and interpersonal context to intrinsic motivation: A review and test using cognitive evaluation theory. *Journal of Personality and Social Psychology, 45,* 736–750.

Stage, S. A., & Quiroz, D. R. (1997). A meta-analysis of interventions to decrease disruptive classroom behavior in public education settings. *School Psychology Review, 26,* 333–368.

Steinberg, L. (1996). *Beyond the classroom: Why school reform has failed and what parents need to do.* New York: Simon & Schuster.

Steinberg, L., Elmen, J. D., & Mounts, N. S. (1989). Authoritative parenting, psychosocial maturity, and academic success among adolescents. *Child Development, 60,* 1424–1436.

Stipek, D. (2002). *Motivation to learn: Integrating theory and practice* (4th ed.). Boston: Allyn and Bacon.

Waldron, N. L. (1997). Inclusion. In G. Bear, K. M. Minke, and A. Thomas (Eds.), *Children needs II: Development, problems, and alternatives* (pp. 501–510). Bethesda, MD: National Association of School Psychologists.

Waldron, N. L., & McLeskey, J. (2000). Preventing academic failure. In K. M. Minke and G. G. Bear (Eds.), *Preventing school problems—Promoting school success: Strategies and programs that work* (pp. 171–209). Bethesda, MD: National Association of School Psychologists.

Weinstein, C. S. (1996). *Secondary classroom management: Lessons from research and practice.* New York: McGraw-Hill.

Wubbels, T., Brekelmans, M., van Tartwijk, J., & Admiral, W. (1999). Interpersonal relationships between teachers and students in the classroom. In H. C. Waxman & H. J. Walberg (Eds.), *New directions for teaching, practice, and research* (pp. 151–170). Berkeley, CA: McCutchan.

11 Behavior Replacement Techniques for Correcting Misbehavior

ALBERT R. CAVALIER & GEORGE G. BEAR

GUIDING QUESTIONS

- What behavioral techniques are recommended for replacing inappropriate behaviors with appropriate behaviors?
- What are the underlying premises on which behavior replacement techniques are based and what are their implications for a teacher's approach to discipline?
- What role does positive reinforcement play in correcting misbehavior and what are recommended ways to most effectively use positive reinforcement?

- What are the major categories of positive reinforcers and why should reinforcers be "scheduled"?

- How is negative reinforcement often a compromising factor in achieving a positive learning environment and in developing self-discipline?

- How might teachers directly instruct students to self-manage their own behavior in order to help develop self-discipline and reduce the need for external supervision?

> Although it may be fashionable or lucrative to criticize behavioral interventions, anyone who has spent years teaching knows that some students desperately need the assistance provided by behavioral interventions thoughtfully applied within the context of a caring classroom community . . . the goal of the effective use of behavioral principles is to increase, not decrease, options available to students . . . These methods also increase students' freedom and positive sense of self. (Jones & Jones, 2004, p. 375)

At one time or another nearly all students display minor acts of misbehavior in the classroom, such as talking or getting out of one's seat without permission, not completing homework or other assignments, and teasing others. These behaviors occur even in classrooms managed by the best of teachers, including those who routinely use the strategies and techniques presented in the previous chapters for the development of self-discipline and the prevention of misbehavior. To be sure, such techniques greatly reduce the frequency and severity of misbehavior in their classrooms. There are times, however, when even the best of teachers find it necessary to *correct* misbehavior when or after it occurs.

The present chapter and the following chapter focus on techniques for the correction of misbehavior. Correction helps develop self-discipline, particularly when combined with techniques presented in previous chapters. The primary goal of correction, however, is to reduce the likelihood that a given misbehavior will recur in the future and increase the likelihood that a behavior appropriate to the situation will occur in its place. For sure, many techniques for developing social and emotional competencies are useful in achieving this goal, and often these techniques alone are sufficient for correcting misbehavior, especially acts of minor misbehavior. For example, common misbehaviors often require only teacher–student discussion and social problem solving (including the use of induction when the offense impacts others). To be effective, however, teachers frequently must combine techniques for developing self-discipline and preventing misbehavior with more deliberate and systematic techniques for the correction of misbehavior.

Corrective techniques can be grouped into two general categories: techniques that focus on *replacing* undesired behaviors with desired behaviors and techniques that focus on *reducing* undesired behaviors. These two categories will be referred to as *behavior replacement techniques* and *behavior reduction techniques,* respectively. The explicit purpose of behavior replacement techniques is to decrease undesired behavior indirectly—by focusing on the desired behavior and increasing its occurrence. These techniques are explained in the present chapter. Behavior replacement techniques are not always sufficient, however, for correcting misbehavior. Under those circumstances, it is appropriate also to employ behavior reduction techniques, as presented in Chapter 12, that directly target the undesired behavior. Together, behavior replacement and behavior reduction techniques comprise a critical component of comprehensive school discipline—the correction of misbehavior.

Authoritative Discipline in the Correction of Misbehavior

As noted in the previous chapter, research documents that teachers who are most effective in classroom management and discipline—authoritative teachers—emphasize the use of techniques for developing self-discipline *and* preventing misbehavior. It is important to note that they do so even when correcting misbehavior (Brophy, 1996). That is, instead of viewing encounters over misbehavior as occasions when "discipline" (i.e., punishment) is to be used, they view them as "teachable moments"—opportunities for teachers to help students develop self-discipline. Effective teachers also view these occasions as opportunities to reflect on how they might change their own practices to help prevent repetition of the misbehavior by the same student or by others. During these encounters, emphasis is placed on providing guidance and support to help bring about more lasting improvements in behavior. When appropriate, this emphasis includes the use of social and moral problem solving and emotion-focused techniques (as presented in Chapters 8 and 9). But often it also includes corrective techniques targeted more specifically at increasing appropriate behavior and decreasing inappropriate behavior.

To be sure, authoritative teachers expect and demand appropriate behavior. Indeed, research shows that in classrooms of effective teachers a misbehaving student may very well receive a firm but not emotionally intense "lecture" that explains the social inappropriateness of the behavior and describes better, alternative choices (Brophy, 1996). Moreover, fair and logical consequences are likely to be invoked. This balanced moderate approach to correction is in contrast to that used by *authoritarian* teachers. Authoritarian teachers tend to rely on the frequent use of threats, scolding, contacting other authorities, and the use of similar punitive techniques for the purpose of asserting their power and controlling behavior. Unlike authoritarian teachers who ask, "What techniques can I use to stop the misbehavior?" authoritative teachers ask, *"What techniques can I use to stop the misbehavior now that will also serve to help prevent the misbehavior from recurring in the future?"* In answering this important question, authoritative teachers apply many of the basic guidelines and techniques presented in previous chapters for developing self-discipline and preventing misbehavior. These guidelines and techniques are summarized in the accompanying "Implementation Tip." In addition to following these tips, however, they also equip themselves with techniques more specific to correcting misbehavior. These would include the use of corrective techniques presented throughout previous chapters and behavior replacement and behavior reduction techniques described in this chapter and the next chapter.

IMPLEMENTATION TIP

Basic Tips for Correcting Misbehavior

- Recognize that minor misbehavior is developmentally normal for children and adolescents. Hold high behavior expectations but understand that such expectations will not always be met. Don't expect perfect behavior.
- Be patient. Understand that rarely do behaviors improve immediately and that the development of self-discipline takes a long time.

(continued)

I M P L E M E N T A T I O N T I P *(continued)*

- Recognize that thoughts, emotions, and behaviors are interrelated. When correcting misbehavior, consider how thoughts and emotions influence and are influenced by one's behavior.
- Closely examine environmental factors that might have contributed to the misbehavior. Reflect on how the curriculum, your teaching, and other classroom (and school) factors might be adapted to improve the student's behavior.
- Be sensitive to cultural and racial differences. Respect the feelings, thoughts, and dignity of *all* students.
- Do not argue: speak calmly, firmly, and respectfully.
- Focus on how the behavior is to improve.
- Use the occasion as an opportunity to develop social and moral problem-solving skills and emotional competencies (e.g., ask the student to identify the problem, its consequences, and personal goals; consider feelings and thoughts of others; think of alternatives; try a plan and evaluate it).
- Reinforce effort and achievement, not obedience.
- Include the student in developing intervention plans. Allow for student input and negotiation when appropriate.
- Recognize the multiple limitations to the use of punishment (see Chapter 2) and the student's right to due process when certain types of punishment are used (e.g., suspension).
- Before correcting misbehavior, make sure that the student is actually responsible for the misbehavior, especially when correction entails the use of punitive techniques. Students are entitled to the right to due process.
- Make sure that students understand what they did wrong, why it was wrong, and what they should have done differently.
- Intervene early, before the misbehavior escalates.
- Do not model aggression, either verbally or nonverbally. If you're very angry or upset, wait until you calm down. Or have someone else deal with the misbehavior.
- Be fair. Consequences should be consistent with the severity of the misbehavior.
- Be consistent. The same consequences should be used when the same behavior is exhibited under the same circumstances.
- Be aware of and responsive to all laws and school regulations and policies that govern school discipline.
- Make sure your expectations and standards for improvement are clear, reasonable, and realistic.
- Convey a sense of optimism and trust that the student's behavior will improve and meet your expectations.
- Use the least amount of external control necessary to bring about a change in behavior.
- Work to establish and maintain a positive teacher–student relationship. If the relationship is harmed due to the use of correction, work to restore it by demonstrating warmth, caring, and support.
- Support a positive self-concept:
  - Focus on the behavior, not the person.
  - Respect the student's need to feel a sense of belonging. Thus, avoid public humiliation. If the misbehavior requires more than a mild verbal correction, then make every attempt to handle the correction privately.
  - Respect the student's need for autonomy. Give choices when appropriate.
  - Emphasize that you are trying to *help* the student.
  - When feasible, point out the student's strengths and progress.
  - View the correction of misbehavior as similar to the correction of an academic problem: The problem presents an opportunity for the student to learn and practice important skills.

- Use induction. Your message should:
  - Arouse empathy and perspective taking but not anger.
  - Focus on the impact of the behavior on others.
  - Emphasize the values and moral reasoning that underlie the inhibition of inappropriate behavior and the exhibition of prosocial behavior.
  - Emphasize responsibility for one's own actions.
  - Involve parents, especially when correction needs to be repeated. Establish a support system to help the student improve his behavior.
  - Don't hesitate to seek assistance and support from others, including fellow teachers, administrators, school psychologists, and counselors.
  - In general, be authoritative, not authoritarian!

Applied Behavior Analysis

The techniques presented in this chapter and the following chapter are derived largely from *applied behavior analysis*—a field of psychology based on the experimental analysis of behavior and dedicated to the systematic application of techniques for changing behavior. Applied behavior analysis has its historical roots in the philosophy of John Locke and the learning theories of John Watson, Edward Thorndike, and B. F. Skinner. Referred to in the past as *behavior modification,* these techniques began to be widely used in schools in the 1970s and 1980s. As noted in Chapter 7, the 1976 model of *assertive discipline* (Canter, 1976) claimed to represent the best of behavior modification (a claim that many behavior analysts would deny primarily because of its emphasis on the use of punishment rather than reinforcement). Now more refined and researched, techniques of applied behavior analysis continue to be popular among educators. And for good reason: There is ample research demonstrating their effectiveness when implemented properly (Stage & Quiroz, 1997).

It is important to note that, whereas applied behavior analysis provides educators with a wide range of effective techniques for increasing and decreasing behaviors, it is the responsibility of the teacher to decide *which* behaviors are to be addressed and *why* such behaviors are important. That is, as with all clinical and educational techniques, techniques of applied behavior analysis can be used wisely or unwisely, skillfully or incompetently. When used wisely and skillfully, behavior analytic techniques are invaluable to teachers for correcting misbehavior and for helping students develop "habits" of appropriate behavior.

Underlying Premises of Applied Behavior Analysis

The research that refined the techniques explained in this chapter and the next chapter is founded on some basic beliefs or premises that underlie applied behavior analysis. These premises also have value in orienting teachers when they are analyzing a behavior problem situation and designing a responsive intervention. The premises serve here as a foundation for understanding the behavior replacement techniques explained in this chapter and the behavior reduction techniques in the next chapter.

Premise 1: Appropriate and Inappropriate Behaviors Are Learned.   The same principles of behavior that are responsible for the learning and performance of appropriate behaviors are responsible for the learning and performance of inappropriate behaviors. Therefore, a teacher should look for the causes of a specific behavior in the operation of these principles in a student's life. And when intervening to teach, eliminate, increase, or decrease a student's behavior, behavior analysts hold that teachers should use the techniques derived from these principles. Following the behavior analytic approach, the primary task of the educator is to identify and change variables in the social and physical environment that influence a student's behavior. This includes relevant variables that precede a specific behavior (i.e., the *antecedents*) and stimuli that immediately follow a specific behavior (i.e., the *consequences*).

Premise 2: Problem Behaviors Are Related to the Context in Which They Occur.   Misbehavior does not occur in a vacuum. It takes place within a myriad of social, cognitive, emotional, physical, and historical events (i.e., stimuli), any one or combination of which is related to the behavior. In other words, a student's behavior does not occur indiscriminately—despite what a casual observer might think. It is influenced by some of the stimuli that are operating before or at the time of its occurrence. These stimuli include both nonschool factors, such as negative family influences, deficient coping skills, and low self-perceptions, and factors in the immediate school situation, such as teacher demands and peer provocation. Therefore, a major part of the key to understanding and changing a problem situation lies in identifying those relevant antecedent contextual stimuli. This can be accomplished by conducting a "functional behavioral assessment" (Sugai, Lewis-Palmer, & Hagan-Burke, 1999–2000).

In conducting a functional behavioral assessment (FBA), a teacher acquires information about the antecedents in a situation and generates reasonable hypotheses about which ones actually predispose a student to misbehave. Often an FBA reveals that factors that cause students to feel frustrated, bored, overstimulated, or provoked trigger a given misbehavior (McConnell, Hilvitz, & Cox, 1998).

Premise 3: Problem Behaviors Serve Some Function for Students.   Often students misbehave because their misbehavior is successful either in getting them something they like (such as attention) or in getting them away from something they do not like (such as a difficult academic task). These consequences make the misbehavior reasonable and logical from the perspective of the student. Thus, in a behavior analytic conception, antecedent stimuli (broadly defined) trigger misbehavior and its consequences serve to reinforce it. An FBA also should provide information about the possible functions of the misbehavior and thereby enable a teacher to generate reasonable hypotheses about which ones actually serve to maintain it. Functional behavioral assessments have revealed that the most common functions of misbehavior are to get attention or other reinforcers, avoid or escape from situations that are aversive to the student, and increase stimulation or excitement (Day, Horner, & O'Neill, 1994). To be sure, there are other factors that cause or contribute to misbehavior, but these functions are commonly observed in the classroom.

Premise 4: Effective Interventions Are Based on a Thorough Understanding of the Student, Including the Student's Strengths, Weaknesses, Preferences, the Social and Physical Context of the Misbehavior, and the Function of the Misbehavior.   Techniques that a teacher employs to correct a student's misbehavior will be more successful to the degree that information about the student and the student's problem situation guides a teacher's choices. This information should be available from an FBA. The resultant corrective techniques typically will involve both modifying the context in which the student exhibits the misbehavior (e.g., adapting the assignment, removing distractions) and directly teaching appropriate replacement skills that serve the same function for the student as the misbehavior but which are more efficient and effective. When teachers confront persistent behavior problems, interventions should be based on an FBA rather than intuition alone.

Premise 5: Effective Interventions Expand a Student's Behavioral Repertoire and Competence. The success of any intervention should be defined not only by decreases in the student's misbehavior but also and more importantly by increases in the targeted replacement skills and improvements in the student's overall quality of life. An intervention should not result in a student simply being able to do *less* than she could before the intervention was implemented. And from a broader perspective, the net effect of the behavioral changes must be that the student derives greater enjoyment from her participation in the classroom and a more positive self-perception about her behavior; that is, the teacher's efforts must make a substantive difference in the student's day-to-day functioning.

Fundamentals of Reinforcement

Positive reinforcement is the *cornerstone* of effective approaches to correcting misbehavior. It is also, however, the source of much confusion and many problems in addressing misbehavior. It is easy to use positive reinforcers ineffectively. This factor has rendered many well-intentioned "positive" behavior intervention plans to be not so positive (from the student's perspective) and, as a result, not so successful (from the teacher's perspective). A successful teacher must have a firm and accurate grasp of the concept and also of the research-validated techniques for using it to advance a student's development of self-discipline. The sections that follow contain important explanations and some basic rules for using positive reinforcers effectively, that is, for using positive reinforcers in ways that are indeed reinforcing.

The simple (but important) definition of a positive reinforcer is something that *increases* the strength of a behavior when it is *delivered* to the student *after* the behavior occurs. If any of the three attributes that are emphasized in this definition is not present, a teacher is *not* using a positive reinforcer, no matter what he or she calls it (e.g., a "reward"). In practical terms, if a student is not willing to work for that "something" (i.e., expend some effort), then it is *not* a positive reinforcer, at least not at that point in time.

Categories of Positive Reinforcers. Because reinforcement is so important to correcting misbehavior and to teaching in general, it is important for teachers to have convenient ways to conceptualize the different types of reinforcers that are available for use with students. The concepts of *primary reinforcers* versus *secondary reinforcers* distinguish between items that have biological impact (e.g., foods, liquids, and sex) and those that have social or psychological impact. Secondary reinforcers can be subdivided further into five subcategories: tangible reinforcers, privilege reinforcers, activity reinforcers, social reinforcers, and token reinforcers.

Tangible Reinforcers. Common tangible or material reinforcers used in classrooms are edibles (e.g., candy, pizza), stickers, toys, certificates, ribbons, and trophies. Edibles are used much less frequently today as a reinforcer because of health concerns and practical reasons (e.g., cost, the mess they create). Another limitation of edibles is *satiation* (i.e., the loss of effectiveness when the student has "had enough" of an item).

Privilege Reinforcers. The status held by certain roles in a school or classroom often is a reinforcer for students (e.g., being team captain, line leader, hall monitor). Skillful teachers can impart high status even to some of the most mundane classroom tasks by treating them with high regard. A teacher should be careful that such privilege reinforcers are equally accessible to all students in the classroom.

Activity Reinforcers. Activity reinforcement is probably most easily thought of in terms of the *Premack principle* (Premack, 1959), which is more commonly called *Grandma's rule* (e.g., "You may help me bake cookies as soon as you put away your toys"). This principle states that the opportunity to engage in highly preferred (i.e., high-frequency) behaviors can serve to reinforce less preferred (i.e., low-frequency) behaviors. This principle explains why students will readily complete their homework or clean their rooms when it is followed by time to watch television. Other examples include reinforcing desirable classroom behavior with recess, free time, a class party, watching a video, playing a game, and reading a book. Research has shown that the opportunity to engage in *any* activity will become a reinforcer if the student is deprived of performing that activity as often as he or she would perform it under conditions of unrestricted access (Timberlake & Farmer-Dougan, 1991). The Premack principle is a valuable tool for teachers in motivating students in positive and more natural ways. It also typically opens teachers up to a pool of reinforcers of nearly limitless supply. If preferred activities can function as reinforcers, then teachers need only to observe what a student does frequently when given a choice to determine what they can use as a positive reinforcer with him or her.

Social Reinforcers. Social reinforcers are delivered orally (e.g., praise), in writing (e.g., a positive note to students or to parents), physically (e.g., a pat on the shoulder, a hug), or gesturally (e.g., a smile, a "thumbs-up"). Social approval is the most common means of reinforcing appropriate behavior and is very important to the socialization process. Teachers, peers, parents, and siblings routinely socially reinforce appropriate behavior. Unfortunately, others, but especially peers, socially reinforce inappropriate behavior, such as by laughing when a student clowns around in class or otherwise misbehaves. Although typically unintentionally, *teachers* also reinforce inappropriate behavior, such as when a teacher recognizes a student who always calls out answers in class or allows a noncompliant student to sit wherever he or she desires (after telling the student that he or she was to sit in an assigned seat). Social reinforcement of undesirable behavior also occurs when negative attention (e.g., a reprimand) is the only attention teachers give to students who frequently act out.

Token Reinforcers. Token reinforcement is the awarding of "symbolic" reinforcers, such as points, check marks, or poker chips, when a desired behavior occurs. The tokens are later exchanged for a tangible or activity reinforcer. The tokens per se should have no absolute reinforcement value. Their value should reside in their association with the tangible items or activities for which they are exchanged. A *token economy* is an individual or classroom-wide program in which tokens and their back-up reinforcers are systematically used to manage classroom behavior. In implementing a token economy, teachers instruct the class about the specific behaviors that will earn tokens, the number of tokens that each targeted behavior will earn, the specific back-up reinforcers that are available for exchange, the number of tokens that each back-up reinforcer will "cost," and the way in which tokens can be exchanged for the back-up reinforcers. For examples of successful classroom token economies and detailed guidelines for their design and implementation, see Lyon and Lagarde (1997) and Myles, Moran, Ormsbee, and Downing (1992).

Schedules of Reinforcement. A *schedule of reinforcement* refers to a planned prescription of when or how often a reinforcer should be delivered to a student for a specific behavior. Different schedules produce different effects on the behavior. The ultimate objective of a schedule of reinforcement is to have appropriate behavior continue to occur even when there is no obvious reinforcement available. If a teacher chooses the wrong reinforcement schedule, achieving this objective can be hindered. There are two major categories of schedules: continuous reinforcement schedules and intermittent reinforcement schedules.

Continuous Reinforcement Schedules. In using a continuous schedule of reinforcement, a target behavior is reinforced each and every time it occurs. Continuous reinforcement is ideal for *shaping* or first establishing a behavior. New behaviors are learned more quickly when every correct instance is reinforced. In addition to shaping a new behavior, continuous reinforcement of behavior is ideal when trying to increase the frequency of a behavior that is already in a student's repertoire but at a very low strength. For example, continuous reinforcement would be appropriate when first trying to encourage a student to raise his or her hand in class.

Intermittent Reinforcement Schedules. With an intermittent schedule of reinforcement, the target behavior is not reinforced every time it occurs but only periodically. There are essentially three different types of intermittent reinforcement schedules used in classrooms, with delivery of the reinforcer based on different determinations: (1) ratio schedules, (2) interval schedules, and (3) response-duration schedules.

In *ratio schedules of reinforcement,* delivery of the reinforcer is based on the number of times the student performs the target behavior (e.g., reinforcing the student after four correct oral answers). The number of times can be either fixed (e.g., after exactly four) or variable (e.g., after *approximately* four—maybe three this time, maybe five next time, etc.). A teacher should progress to a variable ratio schedule as soon as the behavior stabilizes. Because it is more difficult for a student to predict which occurrence of the target behavior will be reinforced on variable ratio schedules, these schedules produce behaviors that continue for a long time after reinforcement is no longer forthcoming. This, of course, is a highly desirable outcome for students on the path to self-discipline.

In *interval schedules of reinforcement,* delivery of the reinforcer is based on the occurrence of the target behavior *after* an interval of time has elapsed since the last occurrence that was reinforced (responses that are made before this interval has elapsed are simply ignored). An example is reinforcing a student by acknowledging his or her raised hand no sooner than seven minutes after the last time that he or she was acknowledged. The amount of time can be either fixed or variable. A *variable interval schedule* produces a steady rate of responding. In advancing students toward self-discipline, a teacher should be

vigilant to gradually and systematically move them from fixed to variable interval schedules of reinforcement.

In *response-duration schedules of reinforcement,* delivery of the reinforcer is based
on the duration of time that the student continues to perform a target behavior (e.g., reinforcing the student after he or she has remained seated continuously at his or her desk for five
minutes). The duration of time can be either fixed or variable (Alberto & Troutman, 2003).

Any schedule in which the student is receiving a lot of reinforcers for his or her efforts
is considered a *dense* schedule of reinforcement; a schedule in which the student is performing for very little reinforcement is considered a *thin* schedule. In advancing students toward self-discipline, a teacher should be vigilant to gradually and systematically move them
from dense to thinner and thinner variable schedules of reinforcement. The net benefits of a
teacher's skill in thinning a student's schedule of reinforcement are (a) higher rates of student responding, (b) steadier rates of responding, (c) decreased expectation of reinforcement
for responding, (d) increased persistence in responding when there is no reinforcement, and
(e) removal of the teacher as the necessary monitor of the student's behavior (Schloss &
Smith, 1998). For more information on using schedules of reinforcement effectively in education, see Lattal and Neef (1996) and Lee and Balfiore (1997).

From Contrived to Natural Reinforcers.   Another categorical scheme that has important practical value for classroom teachers involves the "naturalness" of the reinforcers used
to strengthen appropriate behaviors and motivate students toward increasing self-discipline.
The categories of *extrinsic reinforcers* and *intrinsic reinforcers* distinguish, respectively, between reinforcers that are not a natural part of (and, some would say, are not related to) the
behavior in question (e.g., giving a student "points" for completing a writing assignment)
and those that the student naturally experiences as a result of the behavior (e.g., feeling pride
in accomplishing a well-written essay). A closely related and probably more useful distinction for teachers is between *contrived reinforcers* and *natural reinforcers* (Baer, 1999). Contrived reinforcers are items that are not usually present in the natural setting in which the
behavior occurs or are not a natural consequence of the behavior (e.g., a sticker for performing well during a lesson). Natural reinforcers are items that typically are available in
the natural environment (e.g., a good grade for good performance on a school assignment; a
paycheck for sustained performance in a job).

Teachers would be ecstatic to find that all students come into their classrooms on the
first day of school with intense intellectual curiosity and a love for learning. But they don't.
Contrived reinforcers frequently are necessary to use in classroom situations because they
sometimes (a) are the only items that motivate a student at that particular point in his or her
development (i.e., the student might not be aware of or desire the natural reinforcers); (b) are
easier to control and administer than the natural reinforcers (i.e., the natural reinforcers
might not occur at the optimal time for student learning and, if they did occur, they might disrupt the lesson), and (c) are quicker in their effects on the behavior (i.e., the natural reinforcers often take a long a time to produce any noticeable outcomes) (Baer, 1999).

Because the natural reinforcers in a situation often are characterized by the liabilities
mentioned previously, they typically are not the best choice for *new* learning of skills. Once
the target skills have been learned, however, it is essential for a student's generalization of
those skills to the real world that the teacher transfers the skills to natural reinforcers. "Transfer" in this case means strategically introducing the student to natural communities of rein-

forcers (i.e., teaching the student that natural reinforcers *are* reinforcers). Natural reinforcers are the best choice for *maintenance* of learned skills. Providing for transfer and maintenance is a critical step on the path to self-discipline for students with behavior problems.

Techniques for transfer consist of (a) pairing the delivery of a contrived reinforcer, such as a toy or a "no homework pass," with that of a natural reinforcer, such as praise (sometimes the natural reinforcer initially is embellished so that it is more noticeable), and then (b) gradually fading out the contrived reinforcer on a reasonable time schedule. A teacher should begin the fading aspect of this process after the student has demonstrated a stable and acceptable level of the skill. It is important not to terminate the contrived reinforcer abruptly; otherwise the student might not continue to perform the behavior. For example, when reinforcing Ringo, a chronically disruptive student, with tokens for quietly reading the whole in-class assignment, the teacher could add, "Ringo, I could tell that you worked very hard to read all of the passages because you added interesting commentary to our class discussion. You must be very proud of yourself for those accomplishments!" As should be apparent from this discussion, contrived reinforcers are very useful in teaching a student that the natural consequences of a completed behavior *are* reinforcers (Kohler & Greenwood, 1986).

STOP AND REFLECT

Some teachers do not "believe" in positive reinforcement and contend that students should "be good for good's sake." In other words, they should be good because that's what's expected of them. How do you think they would deal with students who find peer attention to their classroom antics to be more reinforcing than the teacher's lesson? With students who haven't yet learned to sustain attention to a classroom task? What might you recommend to such teachers about the progression to natural reinforcers?

Negative Reinforcement. The main focus of this chapter has been on positive reinforcement. Another process of reinforcement, however, exists. *Negative reinforcement* is the process by which the frequency of a behavior is *increased* when the behavior's occurrence results in the *removal or avoidance* of an aversive stimulus. Thus, behaviors also can be strengthened when they result in something being taken away from the student—something an observer typically would deem to be aversive to the student. In other words, behaviors "work" for students when they get students something they desire *or* get them away from something they do not want. Behaviors that "work" are reinforced by those consequences. *Reinforcement* in the labels of both positive reinforcement and negative reinforcement means that in both situations a behavior is *strengthened,* not weakened—one through the presentation of a "positive" and the other through the removal of a "negative."

It is important to be aware that negative reinforcement is associated with three difficulties in classroom management. First, negative reinforcement is often confused with punishment (discussed in more detail in the next chapter). Whereas punishment decreases a behavior, negative reinforcement increases it. The confusion appears to be based on the mistaken belief that any situation involving an aversive stimulus must be punishment

(Gunter & Coutinbo, 1997). This fails to recognize that negative reinforcement always involves the *threat* of punishment but not its actual use. If the desired behavior occurs, then the aversive stimulus is escaped or avoided. This is *negative reinforcement of the desired behavior.* But if the undesired behavior continues (and the desired behavior does not occur), the aversive stimulus is delivered. This is *punishment of the undesired behavior.*

Second, teachers very often fail to recognize negative reinforcement when it is operating to maintain *inappropriate* behaviors in their classrooms. This frequently leads teachers to make incorrect analyses of classroom problems and design inappropriate intervention techniques (Cipani, 1995). A common example is when a student who cannot or does not want to complete a classroom assignment misbehaves, gets sent to the principal's office, and thereby escapes the aversive situation presented by the assignment. Another involves a student who is afraid of being embarrassed when called on to read aloud in class, as a result throws a tantrum shortly before reading time, is sent to the back of the classroom, and thereby avoids the stressful activity. In these situations, the problem behaviors have been reinforced by the teacher's action and will continue to occur.

Third, some teachers employ negative reinforcement rather than positive reinforcement as their primary means of managing a classroom. From a teaching standpoint, the critical difference between the two processes is that negative reinforcement always is linked to an aversive stimulus in some way. Thus, teachers who rely on negative reinforcement to strengthen good behaviors in their students communicate, either implicitly or explicitly, the threat: "Be good or else!" These teachers are partnering with fear to control their students. But it takes no more effort (and sometimes less!) to give students positive reasons (i.e., reinforcers) for behaving appropriately—with the added benefit that the students are less fearful and enjoy the classroom experience more (Cipani & Spooner, 1997).

Negative reinforcement is a complicating and compromising factor in effective classroom management. As described throughout this chapter, teachers have many more positive and better ways to motivate and strengthen their students' appropriate behaviors.

Behavior Replacement Techniques

The rich knowledge base in applied behavior analysis that researchers have compiled over the past thirty years offers classroom teachers extensive guidance on the design and implementation of effective techniques for both teaching and strengthening behaviors that are appropriate replacements for a student's misbehavior. Of course, these same techniques and the recommendations for their effective use are also very valuable in teaching students prosocial behavior from the outset. Six highly recommended techniques, and specific steps for their implementation are (1) skillbuilding through positive reinforcement, (2) behavior report cards, (3) behavioral momentum, (4) contingency contracts, (5) group contingencies, and (6) self-management techniques.

Skill Building through Positive Reinforcement

The following six sets of recommendations apply broadly to the use of positive reinforcement in educational situations. They are important recommendations not only for correcting misbehavior but also for fostering self-discipline.

1. *Don't assume that rewards are reinforcing.* Even though something (e.g., an object, comment, or activity) looks attractive to you or it has reinforced the behavior of another student, there is no assurance that it will be reinforcing for the particular student with whom you are now concerned. Some of the factors that influence the reinforcement value of any particular object, comment, or activity for a student are (a) the student's learning history with the item (e.g., has the student discovered that it is desirable?), (b) the balance between how much of the item the student desires and how much of it the student has received recently (e.g., has the student had his or her "fill" of it for awhile?), (c) its perceived value by the student (e.g., is it worth the effort?), (d) its consistency of delivery to the student (e.g., has it been delivered more or less reliably in the past?), and (e) its age appropriateness (e.g., does the student perceive it as too "babyish" for him or her?). It is important to begin with the expectation that reinforcers must be individualized when correcting misbehavior.

Before investing a considerable amount of time, materials, and energy in developing and implementing a behavior intervention plan, teachers should be certain that they have identified some real reinforcers. This is not a trivial issue. It is not uncommon to hear teachers lament "Nothing motivates her!" Fortunately, a variety of practical techniques exist to assist teachers in identifying a student's reinforcers, as listed here:

- Directly ask students about their preferred objects, privileges, and activities. This often yields the most accurate information.
- Offer a reinforcement rating menu in which lists of different items are presented and students rate them in terms of their personal preferences.
- Offer a forced-choice reinforcement menu in which students are presented a series of pairs of items and asked to select the one item from each pair that they prefer the most.
- Offer *free* access to potential reinforcers; referred to as reinforcer sampling, this is useful especially for items that students have never experienced before.
- Carefully observe students during unstructured time, which might reveal the different objects and activities that they prefer.

2. *When first establishing or correcting a behavior, reinforce the appropriate behavior immediately, contingently, consistently, and continuously. Gradually shift to an intermittent reinforcement schedule once the behavior is established.* In teaching a student new tasks or skills, present the reinforcer while or immediately after the target behavior occurs rather than permitting a delay between the behavior and the reinforcement. The behavior that is strengthened is the one that occurs right before the reinforcer is presented. Therefore, delays in reinforcement increase the chances that some behavior other than the intended one will "slip in" and be strengthened. Delays also make it more difficult for students to learn the relationship between what they did and the teacher's positive reaction. This is an important association for the student to learn. Immediate reinforcement is particularly important with students who exhibit a high rate of inappropriate behavior or an extremely low rate of the targeted desirable behavior (e.g., the withdrawn or immature child). Students who are more cognitively advanced, however, can tolerate longer delays if the teacher takes advantage of their verbal mediation abilities by telling them explicitly the reason for the reward (at the later time that the teacher delivers it). Especially when first establishing a new target behavior, it is critical that reinforcer delivery is consistent. Reinforcing a behavior on one occasion, while punishing the same behavior on another occasion, characterizes the parenting of many aggressive and maladjusted children (Strassberg, Dodge, Pettit, & Bates, 1994).

In the early phases of teaching a new behavior, reinforce every correct response exhibited by the student (i.e., use continuous schedules). Once the behavior is established, reinforce the same behaviors only occasionally (i.e., use intermittent schedules). As long as the behavior persists, use thinner and thinner variable intermittent schedules of reinforcement, with the goal that the behavior will be maintained by natural reinforcers such as social approval and self-reinforcement. This should not be done haphazardly but rather following a systematic plan for advancing students along this progression.

3. *Use a variety of reinforcers and advance the student toward social and self-reinforcers.* When the same reinforcer is repeatedly used, such as constantly saying the same praise (e.g., "good job") or using the same tangible reward (e.g., stickers), its strength diminishes. The use of different reinforcers, both within and across categories of reinforcers, increases the effectiveness of reinforcement. Thus, plan ahead and vary the reinforcers that you use, preferably from among those personally selected by the students. For most students, teachers should rely mainly on natural reinforcers, particularly social and self-reinforcers, whenever possible. Social reinforcement should come from a variety of sources, including peers, parents, teachers, and others (principal, siblings, etc.) in multiple settings. Furthermore, social reinforcement should be used to encourage and reinforce self-reinforcement—the ultimate type of reinforcement. The goal is for students to reinforce themselves for appropriate conduct rather than rely on others for reinforcement. When natural reinforcers are ineffective in strengthening behavior, contrived reinforcers should be considered.

4. *Don't implement an intervention employing external and contrived reinforcers if natural reinforcers already maintain appropriate levels of desirable behavior.* As emphasized in the previous chapter when discussing the use of praise and rewards, if a student's self-reinforcement already maintains the desired behavior at an appropriate level, behavior intervention should not be implemented. In fact, such an intervention, if it relies on external reinforcers, may weaken the desired behavior. Likewise, if other effective natural reinforcers, such as social reinforcers, increase and maintain the desired behavior, the use of more contrived rewards may have a similar weakening effect. The objective is to use reinforcers that are the least coercive and still effective. This recommendation is consistent with what Lepper (1983) refers to as the *principle of minimal sufficiency,* which states that by using *just enough* external pressure to bring about compliance without making students feel that they are being coerced, an adult is more likely to foster intrinsic motivation of behavior change among students. This principle is discussed in more detail in the next chapter. Because responsibility and autonomy are not taught through coercion, and coercion is detrimental to a positive learning environment, coercive techniques should be used only when absolutely necessary. For the majority of students in the regular classroom, naturally occurring social and self-reinforcers typically are sufficient for developing and maintaining desired behavior.

5. *Reinforce improvement.* Students show wide individual differences in their abilities and their previously learned skills. Holding everyone to the same standard for reinforcement will ensure that those students who already can do the most and the best will receive the most reinforcers. Conversely, the students who know less to begin with will be reinforced less for trying—and, therefore, are likely to learn less, get frustrated most, and be most vulnerable to misbehavior. It is important not to insist on perfect performance on a student's first attempt. You should reinforce behavioral steps in the right direction, that is, progress toward the desired target behavior. In sum, it is important that reinforcement is made contingent on doing better. Standards for doing better should be clear, realistic, and based on the individual student's abilities.

6. *Don't reinforce behaviors that can be performed by a dead person!* Unfortunately, teachers sometimes reinforce behaviors that create quiet and stillness in the classroom—behaviors that can be performed by a dead person (Winett & Winkler, 1972). The absence of student activity and requests might serve to reinforce a teacher's continued use of such tactics. This teaches students only compliance (for the sake of reward), while failing to teach appropriate social skills. More importantly, it fails to teach or encourage self-discipline. It is important for teachers to resist the seductiveness of the subtle negative reinforcement that these situations entail.

Behavior Report Cards

Collaboration between school staff and a student's family greatly enhances the prospects that an intervention will be effective. A simple strategy for forging such partnerships, facilitating teacher–parent communication, and improving student behavior involves the use of daily or weekly "behavior report cards" (BRCs). In the education literature, these are frequently labeled "school–home contingency notes" (Kelley & McCain, 1995). The basic components involve a teacher sending home a brief written report on a student's behavior in class that day and a parent reviewing the report, delivering the prescribed consequences to the child, signing the report, and sending it back to the teacher. The driving force in this technique is the administration of the consequences by persons who often possess the most potent reinforcers for a child—the parents (such as a parent's personal pride, the keys to the car, etc.). The behaviors occur in the classroom; the contingent reinforcers are delivered at home. The link between school and home is direct and unmistakable. Behavior report cards have been described as "one of the most effective techniques for improving a student's motivation and classroom behavior. It also is one of the most mismanaged and underutilized techniques" (Jenson & Reavis, 1996a, p. 29).

How to Implement Behavior Report Cards

1. Design a simple BRC. Include space for the student's name, teacher's name, date, time of day that the report covers, and a brief description of the activities that occurred during that time.

2. Meet with the student and the student's parents to explain "the BRC system" and enlist their cooperation and collaboration. If the parents cannot meet, collaborate with them by phone, e-mail, or in writing. With the parents and the student, identify (a) the behaviors to be targeted for the intervention, (b) the manner in which they will be reported, (c) the positive reinforcers that the parents will administer at home for reports of good student performance, (d) the behavior reduction technique (see Chapter 12), if any, that the parents will administer at home for poor student performance and for failing to bring the BRC home, and (e) how frequently BRCs will be used each week.

3. Explain that the parents' responsibilities are to (a) read the BRC each day, (b) check to see that it is initialed by the teacher, (c) administer the positive or reductive consequences, and (d) sign it to confirm that they have read the note and administered the appropriate consequences.

4. Drawing from the Implementation Tip on page 227, review with the parents basic recommendations for correcting misbehavior.

5. Initiate the BRC system. When handing the BRC to the student, describe in specific terms its content (i.e., explain the behaviors that the student performed well and those that need improvement).

6. Contact the parents periodically to find out how well the system is working at home, to problem-solve with them on any difficulties, and to support their efforts. It is not uncommon for teachers to discover at this time that parents might require a little basic training in "behavior analytic" skills.

7. Meet again with the student and parents after the BRC system has been operating for some stretch of time (e.g., four weeks) to review the "smoothness" of the system and the student's performance. Make any necessary changes to the system.

8. Be progressive. It is customary to begin a BRC system by sending a BRC home every day. As the student's behavior improves, gradually increase the number of days that intervene between report cards until they are sent home only on Fridays. The objective is to fade out BRCs completely.

Behavioral Momentum

When asked by a teacher to perform a task or complete an assignment that they do not like, some students refuse, either passively or actively. Interventions that strengthen student compliance with teacher requests usually also result in reduced classroom disruption. To enhance a student's compliance with teacher requests that are not preferred, a strategic teacher first can issue a series of requests with which the teacher knows the student is likely to comply. Such requests might be for activities that are reinforcing to the student in and of themselves (i.e., students "enjoy" doing them). Or, based on previous experience, the teacher may know that the student's compliant responses to those requests have been reinforced in the past and, therefore, are strong. Through this series of compliant responding, the student builds up a "momentum" of compliance such that, when the heretofore noncomplied with request is made, it has a much higher probability of triggering the student's compliance (Mace et al., 1988). Of course, as soon as the student complies with this target request, the student should be rewarded. This represents another good "rule of thumb": A teacher should start a school day or class period with a few requests for high-probability (i.e., easy or preferred) tasks/ activities before moving on to requests for low-probability (i.e., difficult or undesired) tasks/activities. Behavioral momentum techniques reduce a student's task refusal, strengthen compliance, and facilitate academic learning by increasing time on-task.

How to Implement Behavioral Momentum

1. Identify at least three behaviors that a student typically performs when asked by the teacher. A good rule of thumb is that the student complies with at least 70% of the teacher's requests for these behaviors (Mace et al., 1988).

2. Select a behavior reduction technique (see Chapter 12) to implement if the student fails to comply with the forthcoming low-probability request.

3. Ask the student to do each of the three high-probability behaviors. Deliver these requests individually. That is, request one behavior and then wait for the student to comply; then request the next behavior.

4. To increase compliance, use "precision requests" whenever asking for high- and low-probability behaviors: (a) use the student's name and look directly in the student's eyes, (b) describe the requested behavior in specific terms, (c) politely and unemotionally issue the request in a soft but firm voice, and (d) wait at least 5 seconds for the student's response (Jenson & Reavis, 1996b).

5. If the student successfully completes the three high-probability requests, then request the low-probability behavior. If the student does not successfully complete one of the high-probability requests, repeat that request.

6. As soon as the student successfully completes the low-probability behavior, reinforce the student's behavior. Be explicit in stating why the student has earned a reinforcer.

7. If the student fails to comply with the low-probability request, issue a second request. Second precision requests for low-probability behaviors should use words such as "need" and "now" to signal the student that noncompliance at this point will result in the reductive consequence that the teacher has selected. For example, "Ralph, you need to take your math disc to the computer and solve problem 4 now."

8. If the student fails to comply with the second low-probability request, implement the preselected behavior reduction technique for noncompliance. Be consistent: Implement it for every such instance of noncompliance. Then repeat the request for the low-probability behavior. If the student complies, be sure to reinforce the student. It is important that the teacher continues to request the low-probability behavior; that is, the student should not learn that he or she can escape the request by refusing to comply.

9. Keep track of the percentage of low-probability and high-probability requests with which the student complies. If the weekly percentages are not satisfactory, modify the technique to increase its effectiveness. Consider (a) requesting different high-probability behaviors, (b) requesting a larger number of high-probability behaviors before requesting the low-probability behavior, (c) changing the type or amount of the positive reinforcer for complying, and (d) strengthening the reductive technique for noncomplying.

10. Be progressive. When the student's compliance with low-probability requests approaches 70%, gradually decrease the ratio of high-probability requests to low-probability requests. The objective is to achieve the ratio that is typical for other students in the classroom.

Contingency Contracts

A contingency contract is a written document that states the responsibilities of student and teacher (and sometimes others) in implementing contingencies for a student's advancement. Most importantly, it represents a *process of negotiation* between student and teacher. If negotiated correctly, it typically increases ownership of the plan and thereby cooperation by the student (Lassman, Jolivette, & Wehby, 1999). The contract also provides a written record that can be referred to at a later time if questions arise. A contingency contract can be a very effective behavior replacement technique.

Teachers sometimes experience a great temptation to *impose* a contingency contract on a student without any input from the student. This is certain to make the contract an aversive event and to invite rejection of it by the student. The driving force behind a successful contract is that (a) the student is meaningfully involved in developing it, (b) it binds the behaviors of *both* parties (this is an important realization by the student), and (c) it is attractive to *both* parties (Carns & Carns, 1994). A teacher should be certain that any contracts he or she negotiates are characterized by these three attributes.

How to Implement a Contingency Contract

1. Develop a contingency contract through mutual negotiation between you and the student. Consider the student's interests, preferences, and expectations and your objectives for the student.

2. State the positive reinforcement contingencies that will apply when the student fulfills his or her responsibilities noted in the contract. Be specific about the antecedent conditions, target behaviors, consequences, and any other relevant items.

3. State the behavior reduction contingencies (see Chapter 12), if any, that will apply when the student does not fulfill his or her responsibilities noted in the contract. Avoid the temptation to spontaneously punish minor misbehaviors that are not specified in the contract.

4. Specify your responsibilities in the contract, along with those of any other adults. Be sure to include mention of the ways you will facilitate the student's success in the contract. Conclude the contract with a section for your signature and the student's signature, and the dates of signing.

5. Be progressive. Include maintenance objectives in the contract to ensure that the student sustains his or her progress once the initial objectives have been achieved. These should represent progressively thinner schedules of reinforcement and fewer antecedent supports (such as prompts) from you.

6. Emphasize to the student the benefits associated with meeting the terms of the contract over the liabilities associated with failing to meet them.

7. Keep the contract simple enough to be meaningful to the student and to be administered easily by you. The exact wording of the contract should depend on the comprehension skills of the student.

8. Any participant in the contract can request a renegotiation of the terms of the contract at any time. Schedule regular review sessions with the student to review the data and discuss the student's performance under the contract.

Group Contingencies

It is important for teachers to recognize that contingencies of reinforcement (and punishment) can be applied to groups of students as well as individual students. There are three major categories of group contingencies: dependent, independent, and interdependent. In a *dependent group contingency,* consequences administered to the whole group depend on the behavior of a particular individual or subgroup. The entire class would receive a reward, or punishment, if one particular student or a subgroup in the class exhibits the targeted behavior. Examples are a teacher rewarding the class with five extra minutes of recess because Jerome turns in his homework or a bus driver stopping the bus because Alicia refuses to stay in her seat. Teachers must be cautious when deciding to use a dependent group contingency because of the possibility of peers exerting negative pressure on the selected students. Also, if a punishment contingency is used, issues of fairness (and effectiveness) arise when an entire class is punished because of the behavior of one or more students.

In an *independent group contingency,* the consequences that each student experiences are based on only that student's behavior. That is, whether or not a particular student receives a consequence is independent of the behavior of others in the class. For example, extra recess is given to each student who demonstrates a target behavior. The only "group" aspect of this contingency is that the same contingency is in effect for each member of the group (Brantley & Webster, 1993).

In an *interdependent group contingency,* consequences administered to the whole group are a function, in some way, of the group's performance as a whole. The group can be the entire class or a subgroup of students within the class. One popular variation of the interdependent group contingency system is the *Good Behavior Game* (Barrish, Saunders, & Wolf, 1969). In the Good Behavior Game, reinforcers are contingent on the behavior of subgroups, or teams, of students who are selected by the teacher. In a game-like atmosphere, each team of students earns points, which are recorded on the board or chart, and later exchanged for tangible or activity reinforcers. The awarding of points to each team is contingent on the behavior of each team. Teams "compete" against each other, although all teams can "win" by earning a predetermined number of points for following the rules of the "game." The rules focus on those behaviors that the teacher desires to change (e.g., students will raise their hand before talking, students will respect the property of others). How, and how many, points are earned varies with different versions of the game, as well as the preferences of the individual teacher (Kosiec, Czernicki, & McLaughlin, 1986).

Researchers attribute the success of interdependent group contingency systems to the reinforcement available, the group cohesiveness and positive peer pressure that can result, and the gamelike atmosphere. Although peer pressure and competition can be advantageous, they also have their shortcomings (Skinner, Cashwell, & Dunn, 1996). In particular, peers may threaten and harass team members who were responsible for their team losing or failing to earn points. In such cases, a teacher should target collaboration skills or use different contingencies.

How to Implement the Good Behavior Game

1. Divide the class into two or more teams, depending on class size. Let the students name their teams. To the degree possible, comprise the teams so that they are reasonably balanced in terms of the members' behavioral and academic characteristics. (When the game is being played, if one student continues to cost a team points, consider making that student a separate "team.")

2. Remind the class of and discuss the importance of classroom rules and review the rules that apply during the Good Behavior Game (e.g., respect the viewpoints of others, do not talk while others are speaking). Emphasize cooperation, not competition, and that all teams can win.

3. Decide on a reasonable and fair class reinforcer for good behavior. Solicit recommendations from students following the guidelines presented earlier. Commonly reported reinforcers are extra recess, a popcorn party, free time, and homework passes. You might want to offer a bonus for exceptionally good behavior. Decide on the time of day (or the day of the week) that an earned reinforcer will be provided.

4. Divide the class period into a set number of intervals, such as five- or ten-minute intervals. The interval length should depend on the severity of the behavior problems: Use shorter intervals for more frequent behavior problems. (Note: you can always change the interval length.)

5. Decide on the number of intervals, out of the total for the period, that the students must behave appropriately in order to earn the predetermined reinforcer. For example, a team must behave during at least 70% or fourteen of the twenty-five-minute intervals in order to receive the reinforcer. If a bonus is possible, establish the criterion (e.g., if you receive at least fourteen points, you get a popcorn party. If you receive twenty points, you also get extra recess.). Be sure the criterion for reinforcement is reasonable for the skill level of your students. It is important to remember that you can make the criterion "loftier" as students' behavior improves.

6. At the end of each interval in which a team exhibits the targeted appropriate behaviors, record the points earned on the board or a chart so that the entire class sees them. Total the points across intervals at the end of each period. Compute each team's standing at the end of each day (and week if the game is played for the week) until the game ends.

7. Encourage student involvement in as many "administrative" activities of the game as possible, such as defining and setting the overall goals of the game, specifying the rules of the game, monitoring and recording the target behaviors, and awarding and totaling points. This step can increase student interest in and ownership of the game and also transfer some of the management from you to them.

STOP AND REFLECT

A Case Study of the Good Behavior Game

As a substitute teacher at Middletown High School, Mrs. Cottrell did not look forward to teaching the ninth-grade science classes. She always felt that she spent far too much time correcting misbehavior. Verbal warnings, reprimands, the "evil eye," physical proximity, and other techniques of correction had to be used throughout the entire class, and they didn't seem to work. Sending four students to the office had only a short-term effect on the class and made the four suspended more uncooperative when they returned the following day. She decided to try the Good Behavior Game.

Upon beginning class, Mrs. Cottrell cheerfully announced: "We're going to do something different during the next three days that I am substituting. We're going to play a game, what I call the Good Behavior Game. Here's how it goes: The class is going to be divided into five teams of five to six students each. Each team has the opportunity to earn a 'no homework pass' at the end of the three days. I'll inform your teacher which teams win, and she'll give out the passes. The game is easy to play. First, let's divide the class into five sections, without anyone having to move. You five are on the first team, you (moving about and pointing to five to six others) are on the second team. . . . Now, every ten minutes each team can earn one to five points, based on my judgment of the extent to which your team exhibits the following behaviors, which I'm going to write on the side of the board: (1) talking only when you have permission to do so; (2) listening to me and others during the lesson and discussion, and demonstrating respect for others; and (3) arriving to class on time and being in your seat ready for the lesson when the bell rings. Your team will get five points if you show each of these behaviors for ten minutes (note, however, that rule 3 applies only to the first ten minutes of the fifty-minute class period). Easy, huh? I'll give your team four points if there's only one to two minor exceptions (e.g., someone forgets to raise his or her hand and interrupts me while I'm speaking), and I'll give you two to three points if there are a few more violations of the rules, and so on. Roughly at the end of each ten-minute period, I'm going to walk over to the side of the board and record how many points I believe your team earned. I am *not* going to stop teaching and explain my scores or argue with you about them" (however, throughout the lesson, Mrs. Cottrell *should* clearly draw attention to teams that are "winning," praising the teams, and highlighting why they are earning points).

"At the end of the period, we'll add up the points for each team. What is the maximum number of points your team can earn in one day? (There are five ten-minute periods, so 5×5 maximum points = 25.) If your team receives 90% of the points possible, which is an average of twenty-two points each of the three days and sixty-six points total for the three days, everyone on your team gets a 'no homework pass.' And if you do better than that and earn over 95%, I'll throw in a surprise bonus (e.g., ten minutes of free time in class). Any questions? Okay, let's begin by naming each team. Each team has five minutes to come up with an agreed-upon name—keep it clean!" (After each team comes up with a name, Mrs. Cottrell lists each name above five columns she has written on the side of the board. Each column has five rows for recording points during each ten minute interval.) "Okay, let's play." (Mrs. Cottrell teaches for about ten minutes and at the end of the first period reviews how each team performed, highlighting the positive behaviors.)

At the end of three days, all five teams won—they all achieved at least 90% of the points and all students earned a no homework pass (plus ten minutes of free time to talk and play computer games in the classroom).

- What is likely to be the difference in classroom climate for the students before and after Mrs. Cottrell implemented the Good Behavior Game group contingency?
- How do you think Mrs. Cottrell might coach members of a team who started to "put down" a teammate who was responsible for the team earning only one point during a ten-minute period?
- As the students' behavior improved, how might Mrs. Cottrell alter the criteria to motivate even better performance?

Self-Management Techniques

In many respects, techniques to directly teach and strengthen students' self-management of their own behaviors and skills represent the pinnacle of behavior analytic corrective approaches. Interestingly, they also share more methodological details with social cognitive approaches to developing self-discipline than any other behavioral technique, though the differences in terminology between these approaches are often pronounced. The objectives of self-management techniques are typically for students to *self-observe* their own behavior either periodically or continuously; *self-record* the occurrences of the target behavior; *self-evaluate* the behavior with respect to some standard for appropriate behavior; if the behavior is deemed to be inappropriate, then cease it and replace it with an appropriate alternative; if the behavior is deemed to be appropriate, then maintain it and administer self-feedback and/or, at the proper time, *self-reinforcement* (Johnson & Johnson, 1999). Self-observation and self-recording together are frequently referred to as *self-monitoring.* Self-monitoring permits students to become aware of the magnitude of their behavior problems and provides a basis for their objective evaluation of their progress (McConnell, 1999). Because each of these components of self-management represents a new skill, they must be taught to students if they are to be used successfully. The overall goal of self-management is for students to increasingly assume adultlike responsibility for their own proper demeanor by fluidly and seamlessly performing these steps as the situation warrants, thereby eliminating the need for external supervision of their behavior (Carter, 1993; Cavalier, Ferretti, & Hodges, 1997).

How to Implement Self-Management

1. First, bring the target behavior under control using externally managed (i.e., teacher-administered) intervention techniques, when necessary.

2. Select a system of data recording that is appropriate to the target behavior and to the abilities of the student. Acquire or construct the necessary materials (e.g., recording sheets, clipboards, timers, wrist counters).

3. Let the student determine, with your guidance, the performance criterion that must be achieved to earn a reinforcer. This criterion should be specific and challenging but also achievable. In the early stages, it should be possible to attain it immediately rather than distantly. Let the student determine, with your guidance, the amount and type of reinforcer to be administered.

4. Instruct the student how to use the data recording system. Consider modeling its use, simulations, and role-playing. Conduct and supervise some practice data-recording sessions in the environment in which the student's actual recordings will occur. Reinforce the student when the student's recordings match yours. Retrain the student if the student's recordings are too inaccurate.

5. Begin the actual student self-management sessions and unobtrusively monitor the student's performance. Reinforce the student (with a bonus) when the student's self-evaluation of his or her performance (against the criterion) matches your evaluation. Permit the student to self-reinforce for achieving the performance criterion.

6. Be progressive. Gradually fade the matching requirement and permit the student to self-record and self-evaluate independently. Gradually increase the performance criterion for reinforcement. Conduct periodic unannounced checks of the student's accuracy in self-recording and appropriateness in self-reinforcement.

STOP AND REFLECT

It is probably very safe to say that all teachers desire that their students will need no external supervision to behave appropriately. Why is it important for a teacher to know how to directly *teach* a student the skills involved in self-management? How is the self-reinforcement that behavior analytic researchers refer to related to the intrinsic motivation that other researchers refer to? How is it related to self-discipline?

SUMMARY AND KEY POINTS

- Teachers who adopt an authoritative approach to classroom management emphasize the development of self-discipline and prevention even when correcting misbehavior.
- Behavior replacement techniques are drawn largely from the extensive knowledge base on effective behavioral interventions derived from research within the applied behavior analytic tradition.
- The basic premises of applied behavior analysis are (a) appropriate and inappropriate behaviors are learned, (b) problem behaviors are related to the context in which they occur, (c) problem behaviors serve some function for the student, (d) effective interventions are based on a thorough understanding of the student, and (e) effective interventions expand a student's behavioral repertoire.
- A positive reinforcer increases the strength of a behavior when it is delivered to the student after the behavior occurs. Reinforcers can be classified as primary (e.g., food) and secondary (which includes tangible reinforcers, privilege reinforcers, activity reinforcers, token reinforcers, and social reinforcers). They also can be classified as extrinsic or intrinsic, and as contrived and natural.
- Different schedules of reinforcement produce different effects on the behavior. The two major categories of schedules are continuous reinforcement schedules and intermittent reinforcement schedules. The main subcategories of intermittent schedules are ratio, interval, and response-duration schedules.
- Negative reinforcement increases the strength of a behavior when the behavior's occurrence results in the removal or avoidance of an aversive stimulus.

Negative reinforcement is often a complicating and compromising factor in effective classroom management. It often functions to maintain and strengthen inappropriate behaviors that students exhibit.

- In using positive reinforcement in their classrooms, teachers should observe the following guidelines: (a) Don't assume that rewards are reinforcing. (b) When first establishing or correcting a behavior, reinforce the appropriate behavior immediately, contingently, consistently, and continuously. Gradually shift to an intermittent reinforcement schedule once the behavior is established. (c) Use a variety of reinforcers and move the student toward social and self-reinforcers. (d) Don't implement an intervention employing external and contrived reinforcers if natural reinforcers already maintain appropriate levels of desirable behavior. (e) Reinforce improvement. (f) Don't reinforce behaviors that can be performed by a dead person!
- Behavior report cards can provide a strong link between teachers and parents and open up a range of potent reinforcers for use in intervention plans. Behavioral momentum techniques can unobtrusively circumvent a student's task refusal and replace it with compliant behavior and increased learning. Contingency contracts can facilitate a sense of ownership and commitment to an intervention plan. Group contingencies can involve multiple students, even whole classes, in an intervention technique, some of which are "packaged" in motivational gamelike formats. Self-management techniques offer teachers powerful tools for directly teaching students to regulate their own behavior without external supervision.

KEY TERMS AND CONCEPTS

Antecedents	Contrived reinforcer	Natural reinforcer
Behavioral momentum	Functional behavioral assessment	Negative reinforcement
Behavior replacement techniques	Good Behavior Game	Operational definition
Behavior report card	Grandma's rule	Precision request
Consequences	Group contingencies	Schedules of reinforcement
Contingency contract	Positive reinforcement	Self-management

RECOMMENDED READINGS AND RESOURCES

Recommended Books with an Emphasis on Applied Behavior Analysis for Working with Children with Behavior Problems

Alberto, P. A., & Troutman, A. C. (2003). *Applied behavior analysis for teachers* (6th ed.). Upper Saddle River, NJ: Merrill Prentice-Hall.

Kerr, M. M., & Nelson, C. M. (2002). *Strategies for addressing behavior problems in the classroom* (4th ed.). Upper Saddle River, NJ: Merrill Prentice-Hall.

Martella, R. C., Nelson, J. R., & Marchand-Martella, N. E. (2003). *Managing disruptive behaviors in the schools*. Boston: Allyn and Bacon.

Websites for Information on Correcting Misbehavior and Classroom Management

www.behavioradvisor.com
Contains thousands of tips for classroom management and correction. Includes basic information on behavior management, recommendations for specific behavior problems, a self-assessment survey of behavior management skills, resources, links to other sites, and a bulletin board on which individuals can post behavior problems and receive advice from others.

www.drwilliampmartin.tripod.com/classm.html
Site of the "really big list of classroom management resources." Developed by graduate students at Monmouth University, this site has links to over 500 other sites that address issues of classroom management.

www.education-world.com/preservice/learning
Good source of information on general education, including classroom management.

www.pbis.org
Website for the government's Office of Special Education Programs technical support center on Positive Behavioral Interventions and Supports. Information, including research reviews, fact sheets, and resources, focuses on the application of applied behavior analysis to prevention, correction, and schoolwide programs.

www.proteacher.com
Excellent source of information on classroom management (including specific information on conducting class meetings), teaching, and child development.

www.teachervision.com
In addition to general information on classroom management, this site includes information links related to special education. Excellent site for links to recording forms and resources for applied behavior analysis.

www.interventionCentral.org
Provides teachers and parents with techniques and resources for addressing a variety of behavior and academic problems.

Note that a wealth of information and resources on specific intervention techniques, including free forms and manuals, can easily be obtained by using most Internet search engines and entering a keyword for the technique, such as: "Good Behavior Game," "reinforcer menu," "reinforcer checklist," "token economy," and so on.

REFERENCES

Alberto, P. A., & Troutman, A. C. (2003). *Applied behavior analysis for teachers* (6th ed.). Upper Saddle River, NJ: Merrill Prentice-Hall.

Baer, D. M. (1999). *How to plan for generalization* (2nd ed.). Austin, TX: Pro-ed. Inc.

Barrish, H. H., Saunders, M., & Wolf, M. M. (1969). Good Behavior Game: Effects of individual contingencies for group consequences on disruptive behavior in a classroom. *Journal of Applied Behavior Analysis, 2,* 119–124

Brantley, D. C., & Webster, R. E. (1993). Use of an independent group contingency management system in a regular classroom. *Psychology in the Schools, 30*(1), 60–66.

Brophy, J. E. (1996). *Teaching problem students.* New York: Guilford.

Canter, L. (1976). *Assertive discipline: A take charge approach for today's educator.* Santa Monica, CA: Lee Canter and Associates.

Carns, A. W., & Carns, M. R. (1994). Making behavioral contracts successful. *The School Counselor, 42,* 155–160.

Carter, J. F. (1993). Self-management: Education's ultimate goal. *Teaching Exceptional Children, 25,* 28–32.

Cavalier, A. R., Ferretti, R. P., & Hodges, A. E. (1997). Self-management within a classroom token economy for students with learning disabilities. *Research in Developmental Disabilities, 18,* 167–178.

Cipani, E. C. (1995). Be aware of negative reinforcement. *Teaching Exceptional Children, 27,* 36–40.

Cipani, E., & Spooner, F. (1997). Treating problem behaviors maintained by negative reinforcement. *Research in Developmental Disabilities, 18,* 329–342.

Day, H. M., Horner, R. H., & O'Neill, R. E. (1994). Multiple functions of problem behaviors: Assessment and intervention. *Journal of Applied Behavior Analysis, 27,* 279–289.

Gunter, P. L., & Coutinbo, M. J. (1997). Negative reinforcement in classrooms: What we're beginning to learn. *Teacher Education and Special Education, 20,* 249–264.

Jenson, W. R., & Reavis, H. K. (1996a). Homenotes to improve motivation. In H. K. Reavis, S. J. Kukic, W. R. Jenson, D. P. Morgan, D. J. Andrews, & S. Fister (Eds.), *Best practices: Behavioral and educational strategies for teachers* (pp. 29–39). Longmont, CO: Sopris West.

Jenson, W. R., & Reavis, H. K. (1996b). Reprimands and precision requests. In H. K. Reavis, S. J. Kukic, W. R. Jenson, D. P. Morgan, D. J. Andrews, & S. L. Fister (Eds.), *Best practices: Behavioral and educational strategies for teachers* (pp. 49–57). Longmont, CO: Sopris West.

Johnson, L. R., & Johnson, C. E. (1999). Teaching students to regulate their own behavior. *Teaching Exceptional Children, 31,* 6–10.

Jones, V. F., & Jones, L. S. (2004). *Comprehensive classroom management: Creating communities of support and solving problems* (7th ed.). Boston: Allyn and Bacon.

Kelley, M. L., & McCain, A. P. (1995). Promoting academic performance in inattentive children: The relative efficacy of school-home notes with and without response cost. *Behavior Modification, 19*(3), 357–375.

Kerr, M. M., & Nelson, C. M. (2002). *Strategies for managing behavior problems in the classroom* (4th ed.). Upper Saddle River, NJ: Pearson Education.

Kohler, F. W., & Greenwood, C. R. (1986). Toward a technology of generalization: The identification of natural contingencies of reinforcement. *The Behavior Analyst, 9,* 19–26.

Kosiec, L. E., Czernicki, M. R., & McLaughlin, T. F. (1986). The Good Behavior Game: A replication with consumer satisfaction in two regular elementary school classrooms. *Techniques, 2,* 15–23.

Lassman, K. A., Jolivette, K., & Wehby, J. H. (1999). Using collaborative behavioral contracting. *Teaching Exceptional Children, 31,* 12–18.

Lattal, K., & Neef, N. (1996). Recent reinforcement-schedule research and applied behavior analysis. *Journal of Applied Behavior Analysis, 29,* 213–230.

Lee, D., & Balfiore, P. (1997). Enhancing classroom performance: A review of reinforcement schedules. *Journal of Behavioral education, 7,* 205–217.

Lepper, M. (1983). Social-control processes and the internalization of social values: An attributional perspective. In E. T. Higgins, D. Ruble, & W. Hartup (Eds.), *Social cognition and social development: A socio-cultural perspective* (pp. 294–330). New York: Cambridge University Press.

Lyon, C. S., & Lagarde, R. (1997). Tokens for success: Using the graduated reinforcement system. *Teaching Exceptional Children, 29,* 52–57.

Mace, F. C., Hock, M. L., Lalli, J. S., West, B. J., Belfiore, P., Pinter, E., & Brown, D. K. (1988). Behavioral momentum in the treatment of noncompliance. *Journal of Applied Behavior Analysis, 21,* 123–141.

McConnell, M. E. (1999). Self-monitoring, cueing, recording, and managing: Teaching students to manage their own behavior. *Teaching Exceptional Children, 32,* 14–21.

McConnell, M. E., Hilvitz, P. B., & Cox, C. J. (1998). Functional assessment: A systematic process for assessment and intervention in general and special education classrooms. *Intervention in School and Clinic, 34,* 10–20.

Myles, B. S., Moran, M. R., Ormsbee, C. K., & Downing, J. A. (1992). Guidelines for establishing and maintaining token economies. *Intervention in School and Clinic, 27,* 164–169.

Premack, D. (1959). Toward empirical behavior laws: I. Positive reinforcement. *Psychological Review, 66,* 219–233.

Schloss, P. J., & Smith, M. A. (1998). *Applied behavior analysis in the classroom* (2nd ed.). Boston: Allyn and Bacon.

Skinner, C. H., Cashwell, C. S., & Dunn, M. (1996). Independent and interdependent group contingencies: Smoothing the rough waters. *Special Services in the Schools, 12*(1–2), 61–78.

Stage, S. A., & Quiroz, D. R. (1997). A meta-analysis of interventions to decrease disruptive classroom behavior in public education settings. *School Psychology Review, 26,* 333–368.

Strassberg, Z., Dodge, K. A., Pettit, G. S., & Bates, J. E. (1994). Spanking in the home and children's subsequent aggression toward kindergarten peers. *Development and Psychopathology, 6,* 445–461.

Sugai, G., Lewis-Palmer, T., & Hagan-Burke, S. (1999–2000). Overview of the functional behavioral assessment process. *Exceptionality, 8,* 149–160.

Timberlake, W., & Farmer-Dougan, V. A. (1991). Reinforcement in applied settings: Figuring out ahead of time what will work. *Psychological Bulletin, 110*(3), 379–391.

12 Behavior Reduction Techniques for Correcting Misbehavior

ALBERT R. CAVALIER

GUIDING QUESTIONS

- Under what conditions is it appropriate to consider using a reductive technique for correcting a student's misbehavior?
- When a reductive technique is selected and used, what guiding principles should apply?

- Reductive techniques can be ranked according to the degree to which they restrict a student's personal freedom, intrude upon his or her personal space, and are easy to implement. How would knowing a technique's relative ranking facilitate better decision making?

- In what ways can a teacher influence a reductive technique's relative ranking?

- How might a problem behavior be *reduced* via positive reinforcement?

- Why should most techniques that reduce a student's behavior never be used alone?

- Under what conditions, if any, is the use of a reductive technique that causes physical pain to a student justified?

> I have come to a frightening conclusion that I am the decisive element in the classroom. It's my personal approach that creates the climate. It's my daily mood that makes the weather. As a teacher, I possess a tremendous power to make a child's life miserable or joyous. I can be a tool of torture or an instrument of inspiration. I can humiliate or humor, hurt or heal. In all situations, it is my response that decides whether a crisis will be escalated or de-escalated and a child humanized or de-humanized. (Ginott, 1972, p. 57)

From the perspective of most teachers, in an ideal classroom students would exhibit self-discipline and there would be few, if any, occasions when the use of discipline is necessary. Moreover, when discipline is used to correct misbehavior, the replacement techniques presented in the previous chapters would be sufficient. That is, induction, social problem solving, natural reinforcers, self-management, and so on would eliminate future misbehavior. Unfortunately, such an ideal exists in few classrooms. In situations in which an all-positive approach to correcting misbehavior is insufficient, it is necessary for teachers to combine techniques presented previously with techniques that are designed more specifically to *reduce* misbehavior. Some, but not all, of these reductive techniques are forms of punishment. As discussed extensively in Chapter 2, under the right conditions there are several good reasons why punitive techniques are used in schools. But, as also discussed, there are many limitations to the use of punishment. These limitations are particularly serious when teachers use punishment as the primary or sole disciplinary technique and when punishment is harsh or used often. Contemporary classroom-based research vividly demonstrates that there is a broad range of effective reductive techniques that vary in their degree of "harshness" or "punitiveness." As one might expect, the greater the punitiveness, the greater the negative side effects. It makes sense, then, to use the least punitive techniques that are necessary.

Thus, it is important for the responsible teacher to be both knowledgeable and skilled in a wide range of reductive techniques—particularly those that do not result in physical or emotional harm—and to be able to select the most appropriate ones to correct misbehavior. In choosing among the reductive techniques, it is very important for teachers to make the best selection on a *principled* basis. Because this is so important, a set of six guiding principles is presented first in this chapter before a wide range of reductive techniques is reviewed.

Guiding Principles for Selecting Reductive Techniques

Principle 1. Minimal Sufficiency: First Try the Least Coercive Techniques That Are Likely to Be Effective

When a choice of techniques to reduce or eliminate a student's behavior is available, the least coercive technique with documented effectiveness should be chosen and implemented first. As emphasized by Lepper (1983), by using just enough external pressure to bring about compliance without making students feel that they are being coerced, a teacher is more likely to foster intrinsic motivation of behavior change, which is a critical component of self-discipline. The principle of minimal sufficiency is similar to what others refer to as the *least restrictive alternative* (i.e., interventions that limit or restrict the student's freedom the least and yet still achieve the desired objective) (Barton, Brulle, & Repp, 1983). If a teacher's goal is to develop self-discipline and create positive learning environments, adherence to principle 1 only makes sense.

Principle 2. The Least Intrusive Alternative: Implement the Least Intrusive Techniques That Are Likely to Be Effective

Related to but different from minimal sufficiency, intrusiveness refers to the degree to which a technique encroaches or intrudes on a student's body, personal rights, or educational curriculum. Intrusiveness involves physical pain, psychological discomfort, or social stigma (Kerr & Nelson, 2002). Implement the least intrusive technique that is effective before considering more intrusive techniques. When the options are a less intrusive but ineffective technique and a more intrusive but effective procedure, choose the effective technique (Gast & Wolery, 1987).

Principle 3. Data-Based Changes: Before Changing Techniques, Document That the Current Technique Is Not Working

Before deciding that the reductive technique that currently is being implemented to correct a student's misbehavior is ineffective and then switching to a technique that is more restrictive, a teacher should record data documenting the ineffectiveness of the current technique (Kerr & Nelson, 2002). This also is referred to as the principle of hierarchical application. This principle helps to objectify teacher decision making and safeguard students from impulsive or biased judgments. Implicit in this principle is the assumption that the less restrictive and intrusive technique has been implemented competently and systematically.

Principle 4. Social Validation: Choose Techniques That Other Persons Support

The technique selected for implementation should be viewed as appropriate, fair, reasonable, and necessary by teachers, parents, significant others concerned with the student's well-being and educational progress, and, whenever possible, the student. In other words, the intervention technique, as well as the intervention objectives and outcomes, should have *social validity*

(Wolf, 1978). This is important for at least three reasons: (a) More acceptable techniques typically are used more enthusiastically and consistently by teachers (an especially relevant consideration at this time because reductive techniques increasingly are being recommended to regular education teachers who have students with disabilities in inclusive classrooms); (b) less acceptable techniques often are viewed as violating a student's rights; and (c) social validity improves the accountability of the reductive technique decision-making process. Research has revealed that acceptability typically depends on the amount of teacher time and effort that the technique requires, the degree of risk to the student, and the negative effects on other students (Witt, Elliott, & Martens, 1984). More restrictive and intrusive techniques often are considered more acceptable when students display highly disruptive and injurious behaviors. Of course, teachers also must follow school, district, and state policies and codes that govern the use of reductive (typically the most restrictive) techniques.

Principle 5. Parsimony: Choose the Simplest Technique That Is Likely to Be Effective

If two different techniques with demonstrated effectiveness and equal acceptability can be implemented to correct a student's misbehavior, the simplest technique should be used first (Wolery, Bailey, & Sugai, 1988). The simplest reductive technique often equates with the one that involves the least amount of effort for the teacher and the student and is the speediest to implement.

Principle 6. The Functional Alternative: Not Only Reduce but Also Expand the Student's Repertoire of Behaviors

This principle summarizes much of the focus of the previous chapter. That is, when a technique has been selected to reduce or eliminate a student's misbehavior, an appropriate alternative behavior simultaneously should be strengthened to take its place. This replacement behavior should achieve the same function as the misbehavior achieved, or an even more desirable function, for the student in an appropriate or prosocial way and it should obtain at least the same amount of reinforcement with no more effort for the student than the misbehavior. Are there always functional alternatives? In the majority of cases there are. The principle of the functional alternative affirms a commitment to *teaching* (i.e., to expanding a student's behavioral repertoire and developing self-discipline).

These six principles should guide a teacher's decisions regarding which reductive techniques to incorporate in a student's behavior intervention plan. Three of the principles involve dimensions that also can be used to *rank* the reductive techniques in a hierarchy and thereby provide teachers a valuable tool for use in the decision-making process.

The Hierarchy of Restrictiveness

Based on estimates of each technique's general degree of *restrictiveness, intrusiveness,* and *parsimony,* Table 12.1 presents a preliminary hierarchical listing of reductive techniques. Not only does this hierarchy emphasize important differences among the various techniques, but also it serves as a helpful organizational structure and memory prompt for the range of

TABLE 12.1   The Hierarchy of Restrictiveness of Reductive Techniques

Level One	Praising Around the Misbehavior
	Differential Reinforcement of Incompatible Behavior
	Differential Reinforcement of Lower Rates of Behavior
	Differential Reinforcement of the Omission of Behavior
Level Two	Extinction
	Redirection
	Proximity Control
	Verbal and Symbolic Aversives
Level Three	Response Cost
	Inclusionary Time-Out
	Exclusionary Time-Out
	Seclusionary Time-Out
	In-School Suspension
Level Four	Unconditioned Aversives
	Overcorrection

techniques available for consideration when facing a problem situation. (Note: For convenience, the term *restrictiveness* is used hereafter to refer to the dimensions of restrictiveness, intrusiveness, and parsimony.)

In choosing among the various reductive techniques, teachers should strive for the optimal balance between maximal effectiveness and parsimony, on the one hand, and minimal restrictiveness and intrusiveness, on the other hand; between correcting the problem behavior effectively and expeditiously and protecting a student's rights and well-being. Sometimes achieving such a balance is a difficult proposition. In many cases, restrictiveness is a matter of judgment. Using a restrictive technique is unacceptable unless there is evidence that it is necessary to produce significant behavior change; using a nonrestrictive technique is also unacceptable if there is evidence to indicate that other techniques would be more effective and efficient, particularly if a slower, weaker intervention increases the student's risk (Van Houten et al., 1988).

In all cases, the actual restrictiveness of a technique—as well as its effectiveness—is a function of many specific choices that a teacher makes in implementing the technique. Parameters such as the quality and type of punishers and reinforcers, the amount and intensity of the punishers and reinforcers, the timing of the punishers and reinforcers, the type of instructions or cues, the nature of the setting, the type of task or activity, the rapport with and respect for the teacher, and the unique learning history of the particular student all serve to influence the speed, safety, restrictiveness, intrusiveness, parsimony, impact, and acceptability of a technique (Axelrod & Apsche, 1983). Each case and context is different. Thus, restrictiveness, intrusiveness, parsimony, and effectiveness always are relative. Consequently, it is important to remember that the position of any reductive technique in the hierarchy of restrictiveness can be lowered or raised depending on the specific choices that a teacher makes in implementing it. That is why it is labeled a *preliminary hierarchical listing.* The reductive techniques in this hierarchy are listed from less to more restrictive *in general.* They are explained later, along with specific recommendations and limitations on their implementation.

Although variations of many of the reductive techniques explained later can be found under different labels throughout the history of school discipline, they were elaborated, refined, and systematically researched within the contemporary field of applied behavior analysis, which was described in the previous chapter. Before "how to" recommendations for each of the specific reductive techniques are explained, it is important to recognize that there are some fundamental steps that should be a part of the implementation of *any* reductive technique. These include (a) operationally defining the student's misbehavior and an educationally relevant and appropriate replacement behavior; (b) observing and recording the preintervention baseline levels of those behaviors; (c) engaging the student in a problem-solving and goal-setting discussion prior to implementing the intervention plan; (d) deciding on the reinforcing items, activities, or privileges and the aversive items or activities that the teacher will use in his or her intervention techniques; (e) removing, if possible, the naturally occurring reinforcers that have maintained the problem behavior thus far; and (f) periodically recording the levels of the misbehavior and the replacement behavior and evaluating the effectiveness of the intervention plan. These steps are explained more fully by Scott and Nelson (1999).

Whereas the reductive techniques in the hierarchy are sequenced along an approximate continuum from the least to the most restrictive, the hierarchy also is subdivided into four levels. Each level represents a substantial increase in restrictiveness over the preceding level, with Level Four comprised of the most restrictive techniques.

Level One: Positive Reductive Techniques

Techniques at Level One are unique in that their primary behavior-changing force is positive reinforcement. The use of positive reinforcement to *reduce* problem behaviors can seem like a paradox to some professionals. As a result, many teachers do not readily consider these techniques when facing a problem situation. Because they typically involve no social, psychological, or physical pain, stress, or discomfort, however, they are the least restrictive and least intrusive techniques available to teachers to reduce behaviors. Some of them even simultaneously strengthen prosocial behavior. As a result, a teacher should consider them first before moving farther down the hierarchy of restrictiveness. While studying these techniques, remember that the feature that distinguishes them from the techniques discussed in the previous chapter is that the initiating event for the teacher—and the teacher's primary motivation—is a problem behavior that needs to be reduced.

Praising Around the Misbehavior

A simple and popular way to reduce a student's misbehavior is to praise another student for exhibiting the desired replacement behavior, which is referred to as "praising around the misbehavior" (Paine, Radicchi, Rosellini, Deutchman, & Darch, 1983). Typically, the student ceases the misbehavior and initiates the behavior that the student observes his or her peer doing. Although reinforcement is not directly administered to the student (at least not at the outset), research has shown that the student receives indirect "vicarious" reinforcement for the appropriate behavior when the student sees it being reinforced in one of his or her peers (Kazdin, 1979). This technique has a long successful history in the field of classroom management and has been referred to sometimes as "proximity praise" and the resultant change in the student's behavior as "the ripple effect" and "the spillover effect" (Gunter, Shores, Jack, Rasmussen, & Flowers, 1995). This technique incorporates extinction (i.e., ignoring) of the inappropriate behavior, peer modeling, and vicarious reinforcement of the appropriate behavior.

Praising around the misbehavior has a number of advantages that serve to recommend its consideration as a first resort. Unlike many of the reductive techniques to follow, this one integrally involves a skill-building component: The student is presented numerous visual and verbal cues to learn which behaviors are appropriate under which conditions. The technique also provides opportunities for social comparison by the student of his or her typical behaviors and their likely consequences with the behaviors of peers who receive positive consequences. To the degree that the teacher rewards multiple peer models for the appropriate behavior under multiple circumstances, the student also is provided numerous "training exemplars" that facilitate the student's transfer of the replacement behavior to other appropriate situations. Another advantage is that the technique is an efficient way of promoting successful behavior in a large number of students through the ripple effect.

How to Implement Praising Around the Misbehavior

1. Be sure that the replacement behaviors that you select for reinforcement are already in the target student's behavioral repertoire and that they are frequently exhibited by the potential peer models.

2. Prior to initiating the technique, select peers to be reinforced as the models when they perform the replacement behavior(s). Ideally, to provide numerous opportunities for the student to make social comparisons with peers, select more than one peer model to reinforce.

3. Once you initiate the technique, ignore any new occurrences of the misbehavior by the student. In other words, begin the process of extinction (see later) by not delivering any new reinforcers (such as attention).

4. Praise a peer model when he or she is engaged in one of the replacement behaviors. For optimal effect, whenever possible do this in close proximity to the target student at the time that you observe him or her engaging in the misbehavior.

5. Once the target student engages in one of the replacement behaviors, deliver praise in an effective way directly to the student. Since this behavior is weak in the student's behavioral repertoire, initially don't miss any opportunities to "catch the student being good." Thereafter, when the misbehavior is reducing and the replacement behaviors are increasing, reinforce on an intermittent basis.

Limitations.   Praising around the misbehavior will be effective only to the degree that praise from the teacher is a reinforcer for the student. If this is not the case, efforts first should be directed to establishing the reinforcing power of teacher praise. The student also must be able to identify the appropriate behavior for which his or her peer is being reinforced. Otherwise, the student will perform other behaviors in his or her attempts to follow the model's lead and some of them might be inappropriate in the classroom (Wolery, Bailey, & Sugai, 1988).

Differential Reinforcement of an Incompatible Behavior (DRI)

At its core, DRI consists of reinforcing a student whenever the student performs a particular educationally appropriate behavior that is *physically incompatible* with the problem behavior. The problem behavior and the replacement behavior are mutually exclusive (i.e., the student cannot do both of them at the same time); thus, as the replacement behavior increases in strength, the problem behavior must weaken (Webber & Scheuermann, 1991). It is important to recognize the simple elegance in this reductive technique: It accomplishes its objective of reducing a problem behavior by simultaneously building the student's prosocial behavioral repertoire. Because the behavior-changing force that drives the reduction of the problem behavior is positive reinforcement and because a prosocial replacement skill is simultaneously established in the student's behavioral repertoire, DRI and praising around the misbehavior enjoy special advantages among the array of reductive techniques available to teachers.

How to Implement DRI

1. Identify a desirable behavior that the student has ample opportunity to perform, is at less than optimal strength in the student's repertoire, *and* is physically incompatible with the misbehavior. If a physically incompatible replacement behavior cannot be identified, then an alternative appropriate behavior that serves the same function as the misbehavior should be selected. In this latter case, however, it becomes especially important to identify and eliminate the reinforcement that has been maintaining the inappropriate behavior.

2. Focus attention on occurrences of the incompatible (or alternative) behavior and ignore occurrences of the misbehavior.

3. Administer a reinforcer whenever the incompatible (or alternative) behavior occurs.

4. As the incompatible (or alternative) behavior gains strength, gradually and systematically reduce the frequency of its reinforcement so that the more natural reinforcers in the environment can take over.

Limitations.   The primary limitation in the use of DRI is in identifying a suitable replacement behavior—one that is both educationally relevant and physically incompatible. In many educational situations, such choices are not always available.

Differential Reinforcement of Lower Rates of Behavior (DRL)

The DRL technique consists of administering a reinforcer to the student whenever the number of times that the student performs the misbehavior *is less than or equal to* a specified limit (the performance criterion). There are two versions of the technique: (a) full-session DRL, in which the teacher evaluates the student's performance against the criterion at the end of the whole intervention session (the whole class period, whole morning, whole afternoon, or whole day), and (b) interval DRL, in which the intervention session is divided into intervals (e.g., five minutes, ten minutes), and the teacher evaluates the student's performance against the criterion at the end of each interval. A primary advantage of this reductive technique is that it teaches self-control of the problem behavior in progressive, reasonable increments, rather than requiring it in a drastic single step (Vollmer & Iwata, 1992).

How to Implement DRL

1. Decide on full-session DRL versus interval DRL. This choice should be based on the student's current level of functioning and degree of self-control. If the student needs more frequent feedback on his or her performance, then interval DRL provides more opportunities. Choose the initial length of the intervals based on information obtained during the baseline recordings. As the student's self-control increases, systematically lengthen the intervals until the student can perform successfully with a full-session DRL (Alberto & Troutman, 2003).

2. Decide on the initial performance criterion that the student must meet to earn the reinforcer. Again, the best source of information to guide this decision is the baseline level of the misbehavior that was recorded before initiating the technique. To increase the student's motivation and bolster his or her confidence, this initial criterion should be easily attainable by the student.

3. Decide on whether or not to provide feedback to the student within a session (or interval) on the number of behavior occurrences that the student has accumulated thus far.

4. When the student meets the initial criterion on three (or more) consecutive days, set a lower criterion level. Choose a *reasonable* level (e.g., the lowest number of occurrences of the misbehavior on the previous days, or the average number of misbehaviors across the previous days). It is important that the student succeeds and improves.

5. Keep repeating Step 4 until the student's misbehavior reduces to an acceptable level (e.g., the goal that you and the student established together at the outset).

Limitations. Differential reinforcement of lower rates of behavior achieves *gradual* behavior reduction; therefore, the teacher (and the rest of the class) must be able to tolerate the misbehavior while the technique is in effect. This typically influences the choice of problem behavior to which it is applied. Also, interval DRL, while being tailored to a student's need for frequent feedback, can be disruptive to the flow of an instructional session, especially at the beginning when the length of the intervals is short.

Differential Reinforcement of Omission of Behavior (DRO)

DRO consists of administering a reinforcer to the student whenever the student does *not* exhibit the target behavior for a period of time; in other words, reinforce its absence. As with DRL, there are two versions of the procedure: full-session DRO and interval DRO (Deitz & Repp, 1983). Interval DRO provides more opportunities for a teacher to provide feedback to a student who needs it.

How to Implement DRO

1. Decide on full-session DRO versus interval DRO, weighing considerations similar to those described under DRL.

2. Decide on an initial criterion interval of time during which the student must refrain from performing the misbehavior to earn the reinforcer. To guide you in setting this criterion, be sure to measure the typical amount of time that occurs between instances of the misbehavior (called the "interresponse time") when you record its baseline level. Although this initial criterion should represent an increase over the student's baseline level, it also should be small enough to be easily attainable by the student and thereby permit the student to earn more reinforcers for not behaving than the student could for performing the misbehavior. (Note: This step is already completed if you are implementing a full-session DRO procedure.)

3. Decide what to do when the problem behavior occurs—either start the next DRO interval at that instant or wait until the current interval times out before starting the next one.

4. When the student successfully refrains from performing the misbehavior during most of the intervals on three (or more) consecutive days, increase the duration of the criterion interval. Choose a *reasonable* increase (e.g., the longest duration between two occurrences of the misbehavior on the previous days or the average duration across the previous days).

5. Keep repeating Step 4 until the student does not perform the misbehavior for an acceptable length of time (e.g., the goal that you and the student established together at the outset).

Limitations.   The primary limitation in the use of interval DRO concerns the requirement to frequently deliver reinforcement to the student (when he or she is successful) in the early stages of the technique.

IMPLEMENTATION TIP

If a student has refrained successfully from performing the problem behavior for the required length of time, do *not* deliver the reinforcer if the student happens to be engaged in some other inappropriate behavior at that time. Although the student technically has met the conditions for reinforcement specified in the technique, practicality dictates that a teacher should override this "success" and encourage the student to do better next time.

Various differential reinforcement reductive techniques are sometimes confusing to teachers, due primarily to their similarities. They are distinguished by important procedural differences: DRI strengthens an *appropriate* behavior to weaken (indirectly) an inappropriate one; DRL rewards *less and less* of the misbehavior; and DRO rewards *not* misbehaving. It can be helpful to focus specifically on what the student must *do* to earn the reinforcer; this performance criterion is the key difference among the techniques and the "flashpoint" for a teacher's reinforcing action.

Level Two: Mildly Restrictive Techniques

The reductive techniques at Level Two in the hierarchy of restrictiveness do not employ positive reinforcement as their driving force in correcting misbehavior. Rather, each one strives in some way to make the performance of the problem behavior less attractive—without going as far as punishing the student with strong aversives for performing it. They also frequently are combined with other procedures in the hierarchy in a multicomponent behavior intervention plan.

Extinction

At its fundamental level, extinction consists of not delivering a reinforcer to the student after a problem behavior occurs. To exert any reductive force on the behavior, this failure to deliver a reinforcer makes sense only in the context of a problem behavior that, until the time of the intervention initiation, *was* being reinforced. The implicit assumption underlying extinction is that if a problem behavior regularly occurs it is because the behavior is serving some useful function for the student. And, therefore, if that function is no longer served, the behavior will weaken in strength until the student no longer performs it (Benoit & Mayer, 1974). In school applications, the most frequent use of extinction is in those situations in which a teacher's attention to a student's misbehavior has positively reinforced the misbehavior; the teacher reduces or eliminates the misbehavior by "turning off" the attention (i.e., by ignoring the behavior).

How to Implement Extinction

1. During the baseline observation sessions, identify all sources of reinforcement, positive or negative, that are serving to maintain the misbehavior.

2. For any new occurrences of the problem behavior, cease delivery of any positive reinforcers to the student or do not permit the student to escape from any negative reinforcers.

3. Be vigilant for a "response burst" of the misbehavior shortly after implementing the procedure and resist the temptation to react to it (see later).

4. Also be vigilant for "spontaneous recovery" of the misbehavior after it seems to have been completely extinguished (see later).

Limitations. Whereas extinction is frequently advocated as a simple and low-effort approach to reducing an annoying behavior, it is fraught with many difficulties when trying to use it successfully in classroom situations. The wise teacher is well aware of these difficulties before deciding to use this reductive technique in any particular situation.

- *Slow behavior change.* The behavior-weakening effects of extinction are gradual, so choose this technique only when the problem behavior can be tolerated in your classroom for some time to come. It is not appropriate for behaviors that are disruptive or aggressive.

- *A response burst.* Typically, after the extinction technique begins, the problem behavior will show an initial increase in strength (i.e., frequency, duration, or intensity) prior to its eventual decline. It is as if the behavior is "determined" to leverage the reinforcer with increased vigor. Thus, don't be alarmed if the problem appears to get worse before it gets better.

- *Temptation to attend.* Because the misbehavior is, by definition, a problem in the classroom, it is easy for a teacher to direct attention to its occurrence. Teacher vulnerability to attend is exacerbated when the behavior occurs with even greater vigor or frequency, as in a response burst. Of course, attending to the problem behavior at the height of a response burst is the worst possible time to deliver a reinforcer. Expect the burst and be committed to ignoring it.

- *Imitation by others.* While the extinction technique is in effect, the problem behavior is still occurring at some level in your classroom and you appear to the other students to be doing nothing about it. Some students can view this as a "green light" to engage in the same problem behavior.

- *Reinforcement by others.* In many situations, the teacher is not the only one who possesses the reinforcers (attention) to which the student's behavior responds (e.g., laughter from peers when the student "cuts up" in class). Of course, if the teacher does not control the reinforcers, then it is impossible for the teacher to actually implement extinction. Sometimes teachers may gain control over these "peer-administered" reinforcers by enlisting the support of peers and providing them strong incentives to ignore the student's problem behavior.

- *Induced aggressive behavior.* Sometimes the use of extinction with certain students will trigger the occurrence of other problem behaviors. These behaviors typically express frustration or aggression. Often it is as if the student has come to expect the reinforcer that was previously being delivered and now reacts emotionally to its absence.

- *Forced compliance.* By definition, escape extinction means that a student's attempt to escape a task that he or she does not prefer must fail. The implication is that the teacher must *force* the student to comply with the task demands. These circumstances obviously increase the likelihood of more intense and potentially aversive interactions with the student.

- *Spontaneous recovery.* A typical finding is that, after a problem behavior has been extinguished (i.e., been reduced to 0 occurrences), some day some time when you least expect it, the behavior returns. Thus, even after what appears to be a successful implementation of extinction, a potential threat still exists. It is important that a teacher does not accidentally reinforce these spontaneously recurring misbehaviors. Such accidents usually result in the flare-up of a much more resistant problem situation.

- *Limited generalizability.* And finally, even if a teacher successfully achieves complete and durable extinction of a problem behavior in his or her classroom, the suppressive effects on the behavior typically do not transfer automatically to other classrooms or situations.

Implications.   From the preceding discussion, it is apparent that this "simple" reductive technique actually can be quite complex in many educational situations (Lerman & Iwata, 1996). Thus, there is no mystery to why it frequently achieves less than satisfactory results. Teachers should consider using an extinction technique to reduce a student's problem behavior only (a) after having tried less restrictive methods and found them to be ineffective, (b) after having reflected on the difficulties mentioned earlier and being prepared to meet their demands and/or tolerate their effects, and (c) when they are able to simultaneously praise around the student's misbehavior. Extinction has an increased likelihood of being effective when the student observes peers earning reinforcers for their appropriate behavior, while the student earns nothing for his or her inappropriate behavior (Schloss & Smith, 1998).

Redirection

At its core, redirection involves orienting a student who is engaged in an inappropriate behavior to a more appropriate behavior. The principles underlying redirection are (a) self-comparison by the student (of what he or she currently is doing with what he or she could be doing), (b) response interruption through some type of prompt by the teacher to begin another behavior, and (c) natural reinforcement (eventually) when the student engages in the appropriate behavior. In its simplest form, it involves distracting a student just by initiating a more attractive (to the student) activity than the one the student is currently performing. In its more elaborate forms, redirection also may include one or more of the following: (a) a statement by the teacher of the inappropriate behavior that the student is currently performing, (b) modeling by the teacher or a peer of the correct way to engage in the appropriate activity, and (c) positive reinforcement from the teacher or peer if the student engages in the appropriate activity. Thus, in an elaborated form, redirection may become a hybrid reductive procedure that combines elements at different levels in the hierarchy of restrictiveness.

Redirection is one of the more frequently used techniques to correct misbehavior in school settings. It can be used with individual students or with a group or whole class of students. In its elaborated forms, it not only reduces the problem behavior but also provides guidance about correct forms of behavior. Both forms can serve to prevent minor episodes of off-task or other inappropriate behaviors from escalating into major incidents. For example,

- For a young child who is beginning to throw toys, a teacher might pull out a favorite puzzle and begin working with it in close proximity to the student.
- To a student who is gazing blankly out the window, a teacher might quietly walk past the student's desk and gesture with his or her hand where the student should be working on the page.
- To a student who is playing with items in his desk, a teacher might say: "Robert, you are playing with items in your desk. You should be completing your math problems now. [Robert starts to work on the math assignment.] That's the way to focus, Robert! You'll soon be ready for that new job!"

How to Implement Redirection   To put into practice an elaborated form of redirection, a teacher should:

1. Identify one or more appropriate replacement behaviors or activities that will be more highly preferred by the student than the misbehavior in which he or she is currently engaged. If possible, predetermine these preferences before implementing the technique. The most important factor in the success of redirection is *choice;* appropriate alternative activities must be made available to the student. Otherwise, the likelihood is great that the student will resume the inappropriate behavior as soon as the teacher's back is literally or figuratively turned (Wilson, 2000).

2.   When a student is observed engaging in a misbehavior, immediately establish eye contact, call the student's name, and in a firm but nonthreatening tone state what the student is doing and recommend the replacement behavior in which the student should be engaged.

3.   If the misbehavior continues, explain why the behavior is inappropriate. Be sure to state this contingency in specific, age-appropriate terms for the student.

4.   Be consistent. Every episode of redirection should include the same intervention elements, and no instance of the misbehavior should be allowed to continue without redirection.

5.   When the student terminates the misbehavior and initiates the replacement behavior, administer a positive reinforcer that is appropriate for the student.

Limitations.   Unless the alternative activity to which the student is redirected provides potent natural reinforcers, the simple form of redirection typically does not include any skill-building component. The most likely factors to impede the effectiveness of elaborated forms of redirection are a teacher's inappropriate tone and style, such as judging the student's behavior or character, preaching to the student about the correct way to behave, and threatening the student if the student doesn't comply (Ray, 2000). Another potential limitation is the need for adult participation. Redirection typically requires active, hands-on involvement of the teacher in the alternative activity. This active adult involvement is the driving force behind the positive guidance that redirection can provide (Gramling, 2000). In some classroom situations, however, such involvement might not always be feasible. Finally, it is important to be aware that behavior reduction may be gradual and that teacher persistence often will be needed.

I M P L E M E N T A T I O N   T I P

A teacher should be careful that his or her use of redirection does not backfire by taking the form of reinforcing a mildly preferred activity (the inappropriate one) with access to a more preferred activity (the appropriate one). This inadvertent and undesirable use of the Premack principle will serve only to exacerbate the problem. This can occur when access to the more preferred activity is available to the student *only* after the inappropriate behavior is displayed. The solution is to be sure to structure the learning environment so that preferred and appropriate choices of behavior are always available to the students.

Proximity Control

A variety of studies of classroom dynamics have shown that the physical proximity of a teacher can act as a source of control for misbehavior that a student has initiated (Good &

Brophy, 2002). For example, when teachers remain in the front of the classroom, student disruptions are likely to occur in the back of the room, but when teachers move around the classroom, misbehavior decreases everywhere (Fifer, 1986). A teacher's physical presence can involve walking toward the student, standing near the student, gently touching the student on his or her shoulder or arm, or placing a particular student's desk in close proximity to the teacher's. Such *proximity control* enables a teacher to intervene without publicly, verbally identifying the student who is misbehaving. While being relatively simple and easy to implement, proximity control is not a regular part of many teachers' classroom management practices. Of course, as discussed previously under prevention techniques, circulating around the classroom and being in close proximity to students also improves teacher–student interactions in general (Gunter, Shores, Jack, Rasmussen, & Flowers, 1995). Proximity control also concerns the proximity of students to each other.

How to Implement Proximity Control

1. To the degree that a particular academic lesson permits and especially during independent seatwork, be "on the move." Engage in brief interactions with students as you circulate. Some teachers ask a student a personal question about classroom work as a pretense for moving closer to the student and thereby interrupting his or her misbehavior. Of course, these opportunities also should be used to praise students when appropriate.

2. Arrange students' desks far apart enough to inhibit a misbehaving student from distracting another student and to allow the teacher to move about easily, and yet close enough to permit the "spillover effect" of a teacher's reprimands to individual students (Gunter et al., 1995). Be sure to create clear lines of sight from each student to the teacher and from the teacher to each student.

3. In the event that a student does not cease the misbehavior after the teacher has come into close proximity, then initiate another reductive technique that is appropriate to the situation and student, such as a redirection technique or a soft reprimand (see later).

4. Create a way to periodically assess your movement pattern in the classroom. Some teachers have simply asked a peer teacher or supervisor to observe their movement patterns and provide feedback; some have constructed simple data collection schemes to self-record their movement patterns, such as setting their wristwatches to subtly beep every five minutes and then noting on a form their specific location in the room every time it beeps; or positioning notecards at key locations around the classroom and marking one each time he or she passes it (Fifer, 1986); and some have videotaped samples of their classroom instruction. Each of these methods permits a teacher to determine how he or she distributes her movement and attention across students and to make appropriate adjustments.

Limitations. The use of effective proximity control can be limited if a particular academic lesson requires the teacher to remain in a specific location (e.g., near the chemistry equipment or at the blackboard). Also, depending on a particular student's learning history, if praise is insufficient to strengthen appropriate replacement behaviors, then proximity control will have only temporary effects on the problem behavior.

Verbal and Symbolic Aversives

The presentation (rather than removal) of any word, object, or event to a student, as a direct response by the teacher to some misbehavior that the student has just performed, fits the technical definition of *punishment* if the net effect is a reduction in the strength of the misbehavior. Just as in the discussion of reinforcers in the previous chapter, because children have different learning histories and different likes and dislikes, it doesn't really matter what the word, object, or event looks like; the *key element is that the behavior decreases* as a result of its presentation to the student. Items that function in this way are labeled *aversive*. Thus, some students have been punished by a teacher's presentation of praise, privileges, and stickers—just as some students have been reinforced by a teacher's presentation of grimaces, frowns, and reprimands. It is important to recognize, therefore, that the reduction of some student's misbehavior demonstrates that the word, object, or event is aversive *only* for that particular student.

The presentation of verbal reprimands, verbal warnings, and symbols of teacher disappointment or disapproval such as frowns, grimaces, "the evil eye," and firm tone of voice are frequent elements of teachers' classroom management systems. They are aversive events if they function to reduce the misbehavior to which they are applied. They are considered to be qualitatively different from objects, events, or activities that cause *physical* discomfort and pain. Warnings, reprimands, and frowns *acquire* aversive properties through a student's experience with them. In a technical sense, they are *conditioned aversive consequences* (Schloss & Smith, 1998). In contrast, it typically takes no prior experience with a spanking for it to be perceived as aversive. The attributes that define the position of warnings, reprimands, and frowns in the hierarchy of restrictiveness are that they are quick and easy to implement, they require no effort from the student, and when done in "soft" ways (i.e., with a regard for the dignity and feelings of the student) they are mildly restrictive (O'Leary, Kaufman, Kass, & Drabman, 1970). Can they be done in ways that cause students extreme stress or psychological pain? Yes, and if so, they would move much farther down the hierarchy.

The most common *verbal and symbolic aversives* are verbal warnings and reprimands. Verbal warnings frequently are used as a prevention technique before the occurrence of the problem behavior. Teachers also use them to terminate a misbehavior *after* it has begun, and in those circumstances warnings function in the same way as reprimands. Indeed, reprimands are among the most frequently used of all reductive techniques by classroom teachers (Brown & Payne, 1988). When used judiciously and strategically, they can be very effective.

How to Use Reprimands

1. Establish your intervention priorities and target a limited number of behaviors to reprimand.

2. When a target behavior occurs, deliver the reprimand as soon afterward and as privately as possible. While other students might possibly benefit from it, a reprimand should not provide public humiliation to the target student.

3. Look the student in the eye, however, be sensitive to any cultural differences in students' responses to this behavior. A student may not make eye contact during a reprimand to avoid showing disrespect for the teacher.

4. Make sure your body language and tone of voice communicate a consistent message that you are displeased by the student's behavior.

5. Be specific. Address the student by name tell him or her to stop the inappropriate behavior and to begin an appropriate alternative behavior.

6. Don't ask sarcastic questions, such as "How many times have I told you to sit down?" and don't use judgmental language, such as "That's gross!" or "You're lazy."

7. Don't repeat a reprimand. Otherwise, the student will learn that you do not mean what you say (at least the first time that you say it). If the reprimand does not stop the misbehavior, then initiate the next technique in your intervention plan.

8. Be sure to balance reprimands with praise. A ratio of one reprimand to every four or five praise statements is considered to be desirable (Misra, 1991).

Limitations. One of the advantages of reprimands can turn into one of its limitations: Because they are relatively easy to administer, teachers sometimes tend to overuse them. Although causing instances of the misbehavior to temporarily cease, overuse of reprimands might weaken their effectiveness in achieving long-term suppression.

STOP AND REFLECT

Some authorities conceptualize corrective interventions within a competing behavior model. That is, an appropriate behavior is competing with an inappropriate behavior to be the one to which the student turns to satisfy his or her needs under a particular set of circumstances. How could you, as the student's teacher, "tip the scales" in favor of the appropriate behavior? Consider social and emotional factors, instructional practices, and replacement and reductive corrective techniques.

Level Three: Moderately Restrictive Techniques

The reductive techniques at Level Three in the hierarchy of restrictiveness include response cost, time-out, and in-school suspension. Usually, they represent a major increase in restrictiveness over the techniques above them in the hierarchy. This qualitative shift results in their being viewed by most authorities as punitive techniques. As such, teachers should be circumspect in using them in a student's intervention plan, and the decision to use them should be made only after careful reflection on their limitations as discussed in Chapter 2 and later. Moreover, *these techniques should never be used alone* but rather only in combination with some of the techniques explained in previous chapters for developing self-discipline and strengthening appropriate replacement behaviors. Unfortunately, instead of representing reductive alternatives when more positive techniques have proven to be ineffective, techniques at this level are often the entry point into the hierarchy of restrictiveness for teachers seeking to reduce student misbehaviors.

Response Cost

Response cost involves a teacher actively removing a *previously earned* reinforcer when the student engages in the problem behavior. In essence, response cost is a fine; the student's response "costs" the student something he or she values. In practical applications, teachers have created many versions of response cost, the most common of which are (a) removal of tangible commodities (e.g., toys, stickers, candy), (b) withdrawal of favored activities that the student has already earned (e.g., recess, a movie), (c) limiting the range of commodities or activities from which the student may choose, and (d) docking a student tokens that are used in an individual or classroom token system (e.g., points, classroom "money") (Schloss & Smith, 1998).

How to Implement Response Cost

1. While determining the baseline level of the misbehavior, also determine the length of delay that would be appropriate to impose between the student's performance of the misbehavior and your removal of the reinforcer. The delay length should be short enough to permit the student to understand the link between his or her behavior and the consequence. Of course, to the degree that the student can mediate delays, longer delays provide more flexibility to the teacher and less disruption to the classroom routine.

2. Decide before initiating the intervention which reinforcers will be removed for this particular student.

3. Be careful to ensure that there are adequate opportunities in the classroom learning environment for the students to earn whatever reinforcers have been selected for the response cost.

4. Likewise, be careful to ensure that the amount of the "fine" that is imposed after an occurrence of the misbehavior is reasonable (i.e., not excessive).

5. At the time that you remove the valued item from the student, inform the student in a nonconfrontational manner specifically which behavior is being fined. If your data indicate that more reductive power is necessary, consider pairing the fine with a soft reprimand.

Limitations.   It is important to remember that the main point of response cost is to make the student's choice of performing the problem behavior less attractive. If the fines are too excessive *or* if there are too few ways to earn the reinforcers back *or* if the appropriate behaviors do not earn a sufficient number of reinforcers, *then* the danger is that the student will simply "drop out" of the system. That, of course, is not a teacher's goal. Consequently, to motivate a student to higher levels of performance, probably the most important and challenging factor in an effective response cost procedure is an appropriate *balance* between the student's acquisition of reinforcers and his or her loss of reinforcers (Schloss & Smith, 1998). A potential complication in the use of response cost is that some students, especially those who are developmentally young, sometimes become emotional at the time of the reinforcer removal (Walker, 1983). It is fundamental that the student understand the contingency—that *this* behavior results in *this* cost. If the student does not link the fine to the problem behavior, of course, no behavior reduction will occur. Moreover, if the student does not understand that reinforcers (e.g., points, stickers) can "come and go" (i.e., that they are not permanently possessed by anyone), no behavior reduction will occur. Finally, the response cost technique in itself does not leave the student more empowered to fill the new void with successful interactions.

Time-Out

At the outset, there are two essential points for a teacher to know about time-out: First, time-out is best understood as a *principle*. If teachers understand the principle, then they can design many different time-out techniques on their own that are suited to their specific situations and will be effective both in reducing problem behaviors and in assisting students to learn self-control. The converse is also true: No matter what time-out technique a teacher designs, if it doesn't hold true to the time-out principle, then the technique will not result in behavior reduction. The principle is that if a teacher removes from the student the *opportunity* to earn or receive new reinforcers as a consequence for each occurrence of some targeted misbehavior, then over time that misbehavior will reduce in strength. Of course, they must be *real* reinforcers for that student.

The second essential point about time-out is that in many instances time-out is not used for the purpose of reducing a student's problem behavior. Removing a misbehaving student from a learning situation can occur for at least three reasons: (1) to "punish" the misbehavior, that is, to reduce its future occurrence; (2) to permit the student to reflect on the misbehavior, cool down, and get composed; and (3) to temporarily get rid of the student, that is, to evict the student from the classroom for a period of time to permit the instructional lesson to continue and to provide some peace of mind to the teacher and the other students.

The first purpose, by definition, and the second purpose under circumstances that lead to behavior reduction conform to the definition of time-out. The third purpose does not conform to time-out—it typically does not result in any behavior reduction, nor should any be expected. The most important point of this discussion is that *teachers and administrators should be very clear about the reasons for which they are using a technique that looks like time-out.* If the reason is to reduce the problem behavior and teach the student better self-control (the assumption made throughout this chapter), then they need to know how to implement time-out effectively.

Because of the different purposes for time-out techniques, there is considerable confusion in schools about why they are used and how to do them well. To effectively reduce misbehaviors, time-out is a complicated technique (Cuenin & Harris, 1986). As a result, while time-out is one of the most frequently used disciplinary techniques in today's classrooms, it frequently is one of the least successful in improving student behavior (Costenbader & Reading-Brown, 1995). The key to designing and using effective time-out is not losing sight of the full name of the principle: *time-out from positive reinforcement*—if your classroom is *not* positively reinforcing to the student, then being timed out from it will *not* produce any behavior change. To put it bluntly, it is no big loss to the student.

Time-out techniques, when implemented effectively, have four reductive "pressure points": (1) losing access to reinforcers (and possibly the whole reinforcing environment) at the time that the misbehavior occurs; (2) earning a designation (and possibly a whole new location) that is undesirable (i.e., aversive) at the time that the problem behavior occurs (this is punishment); (3) receiving no attention from the teacher when complaining, protesting, having a tantrum, and so on while in time-out (this is extinction); and (4) re-gaining access to reinforcers when the student displays calm, controlled, appropriate behavior for a period of time (this is positive reinforcement).

Categories of Time-Out.   For ease of understanding, the numerous time-out techniques that teachers and researchers have devised can be categorized by the different methods of removing the opportunity to receive new reinforcers from the student and the extent to which the student is displaced from the learning activity (Costenbader & Reading-Brown, 1995). These different methods result in three broad levels of restrictiveness.

Inclusionary time-out techniques remove a student's access to reinforcers through a temporary change in the learning situation. All of them can take place at or near the student's current location in the classroom. The advantages of these techniques are that they are easy for a teacher to implement in class, are less disruptive to an instructional lesson, and permit the student still to observe (and possibly learn from) the lesson. Examples are (a) removing a student's point card, (b) removing a student's "time-out ribbon," which is a marker of some sort that all students wear, thereby indicating that the student is not to receive any attention and cannot be called on or earn reinforcers in any way, and (c) removing a student to the out-side edge of a learning activity where the student can observe the instructional lesson *and* see peers getting reinforced for appropriate behavior but cannot participate (this is called *contingent observation time-out*).

Exclusionary time-out techniques remove a student's access to reinforcers by moving the student to the outer perimeter of the classroom (e.g., in a corner of the room facing the wall or in the hallway outside the classroom door), where the student cannot actively participate in the learning activity and cannot observe the activity. This would be the better choice if the student still receives reinforcement for his or her misbehavior by observing the instructional activity with an inclusionary time-out technique. If the student still finds it to be reinforcing simply by hearing the lesson or observing the activity in the hallway (thereby invalidating the time-out principle), then modifications to the exclusionary time-out would need to be made or seclusionary time-out should be considered.

Seclusionary time-out techniques remove a student's access to reinforcers by relocating the student from the classroom to another room. Because of the forced removal of the student from teacher, peers, and the educational activity, and the loss of instructional time, this is the most restrictive and intrusive form of time-out and, therefore, its use is heavily regulated with numerous procedural safeguards (Yell, 1994). It is also the most popular time-out technique in schools and is frequently referred to as *isolation time-out* (Cuenin & Harris, 1986).

How to Implement Time-Out Effectively

1. Assess the degree to which the student is being reinforced in the classroom for appropriate academic and social behavior. As emphasized in previous chapters, the classroom must be the place where good things happen, that is, where teaching and lessons are meaningful and engaging and there is a much greater proportion of affirmation and praise than friction and frustration.

2. Assess the degree to which the intended time-out condition makes reinforcers available to the student for misbehavior. The time-out situation must *not* be reinforcing. The key to effectiveness is a noticeable difference in available reinforcement between time-in and time-out.

3. Decide on the duration of the time-out periods for this particular student; they should not vary according to which misbehavior the student displays. Also, decide on the amount of "quiet time" (i.e., time that the student is calm and composed) to complete the time-out requirements and be returned to time-in. Don't tell the student to come out "when you are ready to behave" (Jenson & Reavis, 1996).

4. Consider issuing a warning to the student, at the early signs of the problem behavior, that a time-out episode is imminent if the student does not quickly reengage in the appropriate task at hand. A warning should be brief and unemotional. Students who receive such warnings typically experience fewer time-out episodes (Twyman, Johnson, Buie, & Nelson, 1994). Do not wait until the student is out of control.

5. When the student performs the misbehavior, initiate the time-out manipulation of the environment or displacement of the student immediately and consistently. In a calm, neutral tone, identify the misbehavior (e.g., "You are fighting; go to the time-out room"). Often this is the point at which a student will defend his or her actions, protest, or demand a reason for time-out. Again, explanations to the student should be brief and unemotional. To adhere to the principle of time-out, teacher–student interactions should be reserved for time-in (Jenson & Reavis, 1996).

6. Whenever possible, do not release the student from time-out because of any inappropriate behaviors that the student performs while in time-out. Otherwise you will have set up a situation that effectively reinforces the student for misbehaving while in time-out. Some teachers add a brief, fixed amount of time to the time-out period if the student engages in such misbehavior (Cuenin & Harris, 1986).

7. After the student has fulfilled the "quiet time" requirement at the end of the time-out period, return the student's access to reinforcers (i.e., release him or her from time-out) *without* great fanfare but look for an early opportunity to reinforce some appropriate behavior that the student performs in the learning situation (Jenson & Reavis, 1996). The teacher should accentuate that *this* is the place where good things happen and thereby increase the student's motivation to stay.

8. During seclusionary time-out when the student is calm and composed, consider discussing with him or her social problem-solving strategies for handling the situation that resulted in the time-out consequence. The use of this strategy *during* a time-out period has not yet received much research attention. Indeed, some authorities expressly reject it (e.g., Jenson & Reavis, 1996). Under some circumstances, however, it seems reasonable at least to consider this period as an advantageous time for such discussions. If these discussions, however, undermine the fundamental principle of time-out, that is, if the student engages in the misbehavior to obtain these personal discussions, then, of course, revert to the basic time-out period.

Seclusionary time-out ranks up there with corporal punishment and suspension as the reductive techniques that have generated the most controversy. It originally was developed to address the most severe and resistant forms of aggressive and disruptive behavior; yet, in many situations it has become the generic teacher response to misbehavior. For example, over the course of one year in a special education facility, 12,992 episodes of time-out were recorded for the 156 students at the school, an average of 74 episodes per day. Inappropriate "talking" and "failure to follow directions" were the two most frequently recorded reasons, accounting for 60% of all episodes; verbal and physical aggression accounted for less than 7% (Costenbader & Reading-Brown, 1995). Such large amounts of time spent in an "impoverished" environment like a seclusionary time-out room equate to significant loss of classroom instruction and call into question the reductive effectiveness of this implementation of the technique.

Because of circumstances represented by such examples, the negative side effects to students mentioned in Chapter 2 (Miller, 1986), and the court case rulings and policy regulations that govern its use (Yell, 1994), it is very important for teachers to know not only how to use time-out techniques effectively but also how to use them safely.

How to Implement Time-Out Safely

1. Resort to time-out procedures only after less restrictive reductive procedures have been implemented competently and found to be ineffective.

2. Use time-out durations that are brief; typical durations are from one to five minutes per episode, depending on the developmental age of the student. There is *no* evidence of greater effectiveness with time-out periods longer than fifteen minutes, they are more difficult to enforce, and they are more vulnerable to a student finding sources of unplanned reinforcement.

3. Ensure that the physical features and conditions of the time-out location are safe. See Nelson (1997) and Yell (1994) for specific details.

4. Monitor the student continuously while the student is in the time-out situation; and if you are using seclusionary time-out, the door cannot be locked.

5. Be aware of the seductive power of time-out. Removing a "problem" student from the classroom might significantly reduce a teacher's stress, regardless of whether or not the student's misbehavior reduces. This reinforcement of the use of time-out *by removing a negative* can function to increase a teacher's propensity to use time-out when it is not warranted. Such use under some circumstances may violate professional ethics and federal law (Yell, 1994).

Limitations.   The most obvious limitation of exclusionary and seclusionary time-out is their cessation of instruction while a student is being timed-out. This is exacerbated by their demand for a teacher to be conscious of the passage of time. It can be very easy for a busy teacher to lose track of time and leave a student in time-out for longer than is appropriate. The use of a simple timer while teaching the rest of the class can avoid this form of "deprivation punishment." Furthermore, a time-out episode entails a negative interaction between the teacher and the student, which can negatively affect a child's emotions and alter the teacher–student relationship. Finally, time-out often is implemented by a teacher too late in the chain of events, when the student already is exhibiting more extreme behaviors (i.e., is "out of control"). During these times, and even before, a student sometimes will refuse to go to the time-out location. A teacher involved in such a confrontational situation then must physically direct the student to the location. This can be especially problematic, or even impossible, if the student possesses some physical stature.

STOP AND REFLECT

Richard Lavoie, educator and national consultant, reported: "A teacher once told me, 'I timed-out this kid three times a day for a month and his behavior *still* didn't change!' Circle the Slow Learner in this picture!" What are the likely reasons for a teacher's continued use of a time-out procedure with a student even when the student's misbehavior is not decreasing? What are the most likely factors to consider when time-out is not effective? Mr. Lavoie also related: "I have used Time Out in the past . . . but only as a last resort. Whenever I *do* use this strategy I view it as a failure on my part. Basically, I say to myself 'You have no tools or methods left to use with this kid. Your only choice is to send this kid away.' " If the student, by virtue of his or her behavior, deserves such a technique, why do you think Mr. Lavoie considers "sending this kid away" a failure? When designing a time-out intervention for a student, what can you do to ensure that it includes a learning component?

In-School Suspension

In-school suspension (ISS) consists of the removal of a student from the student's regularly assigned academic environment to another classroom in the school, typically for extended periods of time and with other similarly removed students in the school. Both in-school and out-of-school suspensions, as reductive techniques, are based on the assumption that being temporarily banned from the classroom or school will deter the recurrence of the problem behavior and should be implemented only after the situation has become unmanageable (Morgan-D'Atrio, Northup, FaFleur, & Spera, 1996). The educational community continues to debate whether the proper purpose of ISS is to punish or counsel the student, with presumably both leading to a reduction in the problem behavior. In its worst implementation, it can be simply a form of extended and ineffective time-out. If implemented effectively, however, the extended time that the student spends in ISS allows a school to maintain some continuity in the student's educational program, while reducing future occurrences of the problem behavior (Rhode, 1996). The topic of suspension, including its prevalence and drawbacks, is covered in depth in Chapter 13. This chapter will provide some recommendations for teachers and schools seeking to set up or improve the effectiveness of an ISS program.

How to Implement an In-School Suspension Program

1. If possible, choose an isolated, separate classroom that has ample space to accommodate all the students who are typically sent to ISS. The idea is to separate a student from peers and activities that can reinforce misbehaviors. Students who have to wait until space is available are more likely to continue their problem behavior or initiate new ones.

2. Identify teachers to supervise students in the ISS room and formulate a schedule. Some schools rotate teachers during their planning time. Increased consistency will result if the school can assign a teacher full-time to the ISS room, although this may not always be feasible. Rather than being a stern taskmaster, the best role for this teacher is that of supportive resource person.

3. Meet with representatives of all relevant school staff to decide which problem behaviors will "earn" an ISS. Some (but not many) schools address this issue in their student discipline handbooks or codes of conduct. Avoid referring students to ISS for mild misbehaviors.

4. Decide who will have the authority to refer students to ISS. Some schools reserve that function for a school administrator after receiving a recommendation from a teacher; others assign that authority directly to the teacher.

5. Develop guidelines that specify how long students must remain in ISS; typically, longer durations are assigned for more severe problem behaviors. It is important to permit some flexibility to accommodate the individual situations of particular students. General guidelines, however, facilitate consistency in the overall implementation of the program.

6. Develop a procedure to ensure that the ISS supervisor knows the proper academic assignment and has available the appropriate academic materials for any student referred to ISS *prior to or simultaneous with* the student's arrival at the ISS room. Securing assignments and materials from different teachers using different curricula can be a major challenge (Center & McKittrick, 1987). It can be essential for success, however, because there is a high probability that students who are referred to ISS are struggling academically. As a result, it is very important that the extended time away from their regular academic classroom does not cause them to get farther behind. Some schools offer an incentive, such as time reduction in ISS, to any student who collects and brings all class assignments and materials to the ISS room.

7. Distribute and post the "rules of engagement" that are in effect when students are in an ISS period. For example: (1) Quiet at all times unless given permission to talk, (2) stay in your seat, (3) work on your school assignments, (4) raise your hand to request assistance and wait to be acknowledged, and (5) no sleeping.

8. Decide on the courses of action when students break any of the rules, such as a parent conference or additional ISS time.

9. Make arrangements for restroom and lunch breaks. These are basic student rights and cannot be made contingent on the amount of work the student has completed or the student's behavior while in ISS.

10. When a student exhibits a misbehavior that warrants ISS, identify the misbehavior to the student and give the student a real opportunity to explain what happened. Avoid lecturing or arguing with the student.

11. If possible, contact the student's parents to inform them about their child's stay in ISS, the nature of the misbehavior, and the length of the stay.

12. Before an ISS period begins, review the ISS rules and the consequences for breaking them with the student.

13. Monitor the student's academic performance and social behavior while in ISS.

Limitations. Limitations to ISS programs are comparable to those described for seclusionary time-out. In addition, neither one by itself addresses school factors that contribute to problem behaviors or any underlying nonschool factors. Because few schools have formalized systems to document ISS episodes, the actual number of students being excluded from their regular classrooms can be easily masked.

Level Four: Severely Restrictive Techniques

The techniques that are listed under Level Four are generally severely restrictive of a student's personal freedom and severely intrusive on a student's personal space, and can be physically and psychologically painful. As such, they all have in common a sizable potential to do harm. They are typically perceived to be extremely punitive by persons who receive them and those who observe them being used. Many of their complexities and disadvantages were described at length in Chapter 2. As a consequence of these factors, to be used effectively and safely they require special training on the part of the teachers who will implement them (or, in the case of out-of-school suspension and expulsion, special systems to be in place). It would be naive and misleading to assume that "how to" guidelines for such techniques printed in a chapter can impart even a minimal level of competency in their use. The goal in this section is simply to explain the nature of the techniques.

Presentation of Unconditioned Aversives

In punishment via the presentation of unconditioned aversives, a teacher directly administers an aversive thing, substance, or event to a student when the student performs a problem behavior. These consequences are noxious (i.e., they do not require previous learning to be experienced as aversive). Educators have employed a range of such consequences (e.g., a paddle applied to a student's buttocks or limbs, an electric shock applied to the skin, concentrated lemon juice or vinegar squirted into the mouth, a spray of water mist to the student's face, and a capsule containing ammonia gas snapped open under a student's nose). Such extreme measures have been used to arrest severe self-injurious or aggressive behaviors after other reductive techniques have failed (Carr & Lovaas, 1983; Cavalier & Ferretti, 1980). Should they be considered a viable intervention option under such circumstances? That issue is hotly debated.

Of course, there are many procedural safeguards governing the use of such harsh aversives (Yell, 1994).

Overcorrection

Overcorrection is best understood as two related principles from which teachers have created many different techniques. *Restitutional* overcorrection involves requiring a student to restore the environment to a far better state than its condition before the misbehavior occurred.

For example, if Ralph turns over a desk and throws objects around the classroom, he would be required to place the desk upright in its original location, place all of the items in their original locations, and then straighten all of the other desks and retrieve any other items on the floor. *Positive practice* overcorrection involves requiring the student extensively to practice correct forms of some behavior that is incompatible with or a suitable alternative for the misbehavior. For example, Ralph would be required to sit at the desk and write essays. Proponents of overcorrection argue that the consequences should be meaningfully related to the problem behavior (Foxx & Bechtel, 1983), and although this might increase its acceptability, a more important dimension is the physical effort involved in those consequences (Ferretti & Cavalier, 1983). The challenge typically arises when a student refuses to perform the restitutional or positive practice components of the intervention. To prevent negative reinforcement of such escape behavior, the student must be compelled to follow through. This can lead to some intense teacher–student encounters. Also, overcorrection should be implemented at the time the misbehavior occurs, yet it is time consuming. This can be very disruptive in a classroom. Because of these factors, teachers have sometimes abandoned the technique (MacKenzie-Keating & McDonald, 1990).

STOP AND REFLECT

"If school is not inviting, if the tasks are not clear, interesting, and at an appropriate level, how can we expect pupils to be on task? Adverse student reactions should be expected when classes are dull, teaching is uninspired, and failure is built in. Their oppositional behavior is a sign of personal health and integrity" (Morse, 1987, p. 4). Do you agree with this conclusion? Would you say its primary emphasis is more on changing adult behavior or student behavior? Under the circumstances described previously, what would be some of the most likely functions of the students' oppositional behavior? What are the implications of this statement for your selection of preventive and corrective techniques?

Developing Behavior Intervention Plans

For students with severe or chronic behavior problems, teachers who are skilled in the array of preventive and corrective techniques that are explained in this book are well positioned to determine why students engage in such behavior and then design effective behavior intervention plans (BIPs). Determining the "why" involves systematically assessing the triggers and functions of a student's problem behaviors via a functional behavioral assessment (FBA). Over the years, educational researchers have defined and refined systematic protocols for conducting FBAs and then developing BIPs to address problem behaviors in classrooms that are founded upon the behavior analytic premises explained in the previous chapter. A detailed explanation of the steps for conducting FBAs and BIPs is beyond the scope of this chapter. Several excellent resources exist, however, and the reader is encouraged to refer to one or more of the following reports: Horner, Sugai, Todd, and Lewis-Palmer (1999–2000); McConnell, Cox, Thomas, and Hilvitz (2001); Scott and Nelson (1999); and Sugai, Lewis-Palmer, and Hagan-Burke (1999–2000).

SUMMARY AND KEY POINTS

- When teachers are faced with situations in which totally "positive" approaches to a student's problem behavior are ineffective, a reductive technique should be considered. These techniques vary in their degree of restrictiveness. In choosing among the reductive techniques, teachers can be guided by a set of six principles.

- The *principle of minimal sufficiency* holds that when selecting a technique to reduce or eliminate a student's behavior, the least coercive technique with documented effectiveness should be implemented first.

- The *principle of the least intrusive alternative* means that teachers should implement the technique that is effective and that encroaches or intrudes on a student's body, personal rights, or educational curriculum the least before considering more intrusive techniques.

- The *principle of data-based changes* states that before deciding that the reductive technique that currently is being implemented is ineffective and moving deeper into the hierarchy of restrictiveness, data documenting the ineffectiveness of the current technique should be recorded.

- The *principle of social validation* stipulates that the objectives, techniques, and outcomes of an intervention should be viewed as appropriate, fair, and reasonable by teachers, parents, and significant others concerned with the student's well-being and educational progress, and, whenever possible, by the student.

- The *principle of parsimony* states that if two different techniques with demonstrated effectiveness and equal acceptability can be implemented to correct a student's misbehavior, the simpler technique should be chosen first.

- The *principle of the functional alternative* holds that when a technique has been selected to reduce or eliminate a student's misbehavior, an appropri-

ate alternative behavior simultaneously should be strengthened to take its place.

- Three of these principles involve dimensions that also can be used to rank the reductive techniques in a hierarchy: the dimensions of restrictiveness, intrusiveness, and parsimony.

- In choosing among techniques in the hierarchy, teachers should strive for the optimal balance between maximal effectiveness and parsimony, on the one hand, and minimal restrictiveness and intrusiveness, on the other hand, between correcting the problem behavior effectively and expeditiously and protecting a student's rights and well-being.

- Techniques at Level One of the hierarchy are unique in that their primary behavior-reducing force is differential positive reinforcement. These include praising around the misbehavior, DRI, DRL, and DRO. DRI strengthens an appropriate behavior to weaken (indirectly) an inappropriate one; DRL rewards less and less of the misbehavior; and DRO rewards not misbehaving.

- Level Two techniques are mildly restrictive and do not employ positive reinforcement. They include extinction, redirection, proximity control, and verbal and symbolic aversives.

- Level Three techniques are moderately restrictive and are viewed by most authorities as "punitive." Popular techniques at this level are inclusionary time-out, exclusionary time-out, seclusionary time-out, and in-school suspension.

- Level Four techniques are generally the most severely restrictive of a student's personal freedom and most severely intrusive on a student's personal space. They include the presentation of unconditioned aversives and overcorrection.

- Teachers should be able to implement reductive techniques competently. Having a range of choices, however, places greater demands on teachers to make the best selection in each particular situation.

KEY TERMS AND CONCEPTS

Data-based changes	Hierarchical application	Overcorrection
Differential reinforcement	Hierarchy of restrictiveness	Parsimony
Extinction	Least intrusive alternative	Praising around the misbehavior
Functional alternative	Minimal sufficiency	Proximity control

Redirection	Social validation	Verbal reprimands
Response cost	Time-out	Verbal warnings

RECOMMENDED READINGS AND RESOURCES

Recommended Books, with an Emphasis on Applied Behavior Analysis, for Working with Children with Behavior Problems

Alberto, P. A., & Troutman, A. C. (2003). *Applied behavior analysis for teachers* (6th ed.). Upper Saddle River, NJ: Merrill Prentice-Hall.

Kerr, M. M., & Nelson, C. M. (2002). *Strategies for addressing behavior problems in the classroom* (4th ed.). Upper Saddle River, NJ: Merrill Prentice-Hall.

Martella, R. C., Nelson, J. R., & Marchand-Martella, N. E. (2003). *Managing disruptive behaviors in the schools.* Boston: Allyn and Bacon.

Websites for Information on Correcting Misbehavior, Conducting Functional Behavioral Assessments, Developing Behavior Intervention Plans, and Achieving Effective Positive Classroom Management (Please Refer to the List of Websites at the End of Chapter 11 in Addition to Those Listed Below)

www.beachcenter.org/default.asp

The Beach Center on Disability website, which provides a massive amount of resources with special emphasis on family perspectives and legal and policy issues. These include online research reports, human interest stories, and implementation tip sheets on behavior support.

http://abi.ed.asu.edu

The Creating Positive Teaching & Learning Environments website, which provides resources on implementing and sustaining school-wide positive behavioral support systems, including an instrument and manual to evaluate the current status of a school's discipline needs and develop a comprehensive action plan, descriptions of ten model school programs, and information on research-based best practices.

http://web.utk.edu/~lre4life

The LRE for Life website, which includes (a) downloadable online documents, forms, and presentations on positive behavior support and effective classroom management; (b) a directory of interesting links for educators; and (c) a bibliographic listing of recommended readings on best and promising practices in education.

www.challengingbehavior.org

The Center for Evidence-Based Practice website on young children with challenging behavior, which is funded by the U.S. Office of Special Education Programs to increase knowledge about the implementation of positive, evidence-based practices; it provides a number of downloadable and user-friendly research syntheses and presentations on behavior-related topics.

http://csefel.uiuc.edu

The Center for Social and Emotional Foundations for Early Learning website, which provides evidence-based, user-friendly information to help early childhood educators meet the needs of young children with challenging behaviors and mental health challenges. This includes downloadable training modules and What Works Briefs, summaries of effective practices for supporting children's social-emotional development and preventing challenging behaviors.

www.state.ky.us/agencies/behave/homepage.html

The Behavior Home Page website, which provides information and resources on working with children with behavior problems and on school safety. This includes resources on functional behavioral assessments, behavior intervention plans, special education and the law, and a discussion forum.

REFERENCES

Alberto, P. A., & Troutman, A. C. (2003). *Applied behavior analysis for teachers* (6th ed.). Upper Saddle River, NJ: Merrill Prentice-Hall.

Axelrod, S., & Apsche, J. (1983). *The effects of punishment on human behavior.* New York: Plenum.

Barton, L. E., Brulle, A. R., & Repp, A. C. (1983). Aversive techniques and the doctrine of the least restrictive alternative. *Exceptional Education Quarterly, 3,* 1–8.

Benoit, R. B., & Mayer, G. R. (1974). Extinction: Guidelines for its selection and use. *The Personnel and Guidance Journal, 52,* 290–295.

Brown, W. E., & Payne, T. (1988). Policies/practices in public school discipline. *Academic Therapy, 23*(3), 297–301.

Carr, E. G., & Lovaas, O. I. (1983). Contingent electric shock as a treatment for severe behavior problems. In S. Axelrod & J. Apsche (Eds.), *The effects of punishment on human behavior* (pp. 221–246). New York: Academic Press.

Cavalier, A. R., & Ferretti, R. P. (1980). Stereotyped behavior, incompatible behavior, and collateral effects: A comparison of four intervention procedures. *The Journal of Mental Deficiency Research, 24,* 219–230.

Center, D. B., & McKittrick, S. (1987). Disciplinary removal of special education students. *Focus on Exceptional Children, 20*(2), 1–10.

Costenbader, V., & Reading-Brown, M. (1995). Isolation timeout used with students with emotional disturbance. *Exceptional Children, 61*(4), 353–363.

Cuenin, L. H., & Harris, K. R. (1986). Planning, implementing, and evaluating time out interventions with exceptional students. *Teaching Exceptional Children, 18,* 272–276.

Deitz, D. E. D., & Repp, A. C. (1983). Reducing behavior through reinforcement. *Exceptional Education Quarterly, 3,* 34–46.

Ferretti, R. P., & Cavalier, A. R. (1983). A critical assessment of overcorrection procedures with mentally retarded persons. In J. L. Matson & F. Andrasik (Eds.), *Treatment issues and innovations in mental retardation* (pp. 241–301). New York: Plenum.

Fifer, F. L. (1986). Effective classroom management. *Academic Therapy, 21,* 401–410.

Foxx, R. M., & Bechtel, D. R. (1983). Overcorrection: A review and analysis. In S. Axelrod & J. Apsche (Eds.), *The effects of punishment on human behavior* (pp. 133–220). New York: Academic Press.

Gast, D. L., & Wolery, M. (1987). Severe maladaptive behaviors. In M. E. Snell (Ed.), *Systematic instruction of persons with severe handicaps* (3rd ed., pp. 300–332). Columbus, OH: Charles E. Merrill.

Ginott, H. G. (1972). *Teacher and child.* New York: Scribner.

Gramling, M. (2000). *A four-step approach to positive guidance.* Western Kentucky University: Training and Technical Assistance Services. Retrieved from the World Wide Web on March 8, 2002 at www.wku.edu/Info/General/TTAS/lc/Guidance.htm.

Good, T. L., & Brophy, J. E. (2003). *Looking in classrooms* (9th ed.). Boston: Allyn and Bacon.

Gunter, P. L., Shores, R. E., Jack, S. L., Rasmussen, S. K., & Flowers, J. (1995). On the move: Using teacher/student proximity to improve students' behavior. *Teaching Exceptional Children, 28*(1), 12–14.

Horner, R. H., Sugai, G., Todd, A. W., & Lewis-Palmer, T. (1999–2000). Elements of behavior support plans: A technical brief. *Exceptionality, 8*(3), 205–216.

Jenson, W. R., & Reavis, H. K. (1996). Reductive procedures: Time-out and other related techniques (pp. 121–145). In H. K. Reavis, S. J. Kukic, W. R. Jenson, D. P. Morgan, D. J. Andrews, S. L. Fister, & M. Taylor (Eds.), *BEST practices: Behavioral and educational strategies for teachers.* Longmont, CO: Sopris West.

Kazdin, A. E. (1979). Vicarious reinforcement and punishment in operant programs for children. *Child Behavior Therapy, 1,* 13–26.

Kerr, M. M., & Nelson, C. M. (2002). *Strategies for managing behavior problems in the classroom* (4th ed.). Upper Saddle River, NJ: Merrill Prentice-Hall.

Lepper, M. (1983). Social-control processes and the internalization of social values: An attributional perspective. In E. T. Higgins, D. Ruble, & W. Hartup (Eds.), *Social cognition and social development: A socio-cultural perspective* (pp. 294–330). New York: Cambridge University Press.

Lerman, D. C., & Iwata, B. A. (1996). Developing a technology for the use of operant extinction in clinical settings: An examination of basic and applied research. *Journal of Applied Behavior Analysis, 29,* 345–382.

MacKenzie-Keating, S. E., & McDonald, L. (1990). Overcorrection: Reviewed, revisited and revised. *The Behavior Analyst, 13,* 39–48.

McConnell, M. E., Cox, C. J., Thomas, D. D., & Hilvitz, P. B. (2001). *Functional behavioral assessment: A systematic process for assessment and intervention in general and special education classrooms.* Denver, CO: Love Publishing Company.

Miller, D. E. (1986). The management of misbehavior by seclusion. *Residential Treatment for Children and Youth, 4,* 63–73.

Misra, A. (1991). Behavior management: The importance of communication. *LD Forum, 11,* 26–28.

Morgan-D'Atrio, C., Northup, J., FaFleur, L., & Spera, S. (1996). Toward prescriptive alternatives to suspensions: A preliminary evaluation. *Behavioral Disorders, 21,* 190–200.

Morse, W. C. (1987). Introduction to special issue on preventive discipline. *Teaching Exceptional Children, 19*(4), 4–6.

Nelson, C. M. (1997). *Effective use of time out.* Kentucky Department of Education and the University of Kentucky Department of Special Education and Rehabilitation Counseling. Retrieved from the World Wide Web on June 12, 2002 at www.state.ky.us/agencies/behave/bi/to.pdf.

O'Leary, K. D., Kaufman, K. F., Kass, R. E., & Drabman, R. S. (1970). The effects of loud and soft reprimands on the behavior of disruptive students. *Exceptional Children, 37,* 145–155.

Paine, S. C., Radicchi, J., Rosellini, L. C., Deutchman, L., & Darch, C. B. (1983). Using your attention to manage student behavior. *Structuring your classroom for academic success* (pp. 43–53). Champaign, IL: Research Press.

Ray, K. (2000). *Effective behavior techniques and strategies in the classroom.* ParentsUnitedTogether.com. Retrieved from the World Wide Web on March 8, 2003 at www.parentsunitedtogether.com/page55. html.

Rhode, G. (1996). In-school suspension program (pp. 87–97). In H. K. Reavis, W. R. Jenson, D. P. Morgan, D. J. Andrews, S. L. Fister, & M. Taylor (Eds.), *BEST practices: Behavioral and educational strategies for teachers.* Longmont, CO: Sopris West.

Schloss, P. J., & Smith, M. A. (1998). *Applied behavior analysis in the classroom* (2nd ed.). Boston: Allyn and Bacon.

Scott, T. M., & Nelson, C. M. (1999). Using functional behavioral assessment to develop effective intervention plans: Practical classroom applications. *Journal of Positive Behavior Interventions, 1*(4), 242–251.

Sugai, G., Lewis-Palmer, T., & Hagan-Burke, S. (1999–2000). Overview of the functional behavioral assessment process. *Exceptionality, 8*(3), 149–160.

Twyman, J. S., Johnson, H. Buie, J. D., & Nelson, C. M. (1994). The use of a warning procedure to signal a more intrusive timeout contingency. *Behavioral Disorders, 19,* 243–253.

Van Houten, R., Axelrod, S., Bailey, J. S., Favell, J. E., Foxx, R. M., Iwata, B. A., & Lovaas, O. I. (1988). The right to effective behavioral treatment. *Journal of Applied Behavior Analysis, 21,* 381–384.

Vollmer, T. R., & Iwata, B. A. (1992). Differential reinforcement as treatment for behavior disorders: Procedural and functional variations. *Research in Developmental Disabilities, 13,* 393–417.

Walker, H. M. (1983). Applications of response cost in school settings: Outcomes, issues and recommendations. *Exceptional Education Quarterly, 3*(4), 47–55.

Webber, J., & Scheuermann, B. (1991). Accentuate the positive . . . Eliminate the negative. *Teaching Exceptional Children, 24*(1), 13–19.

Wilson, E. (2000). *Responses to misbehavior.* Stillwater, OK: Oklahoma Cooperative Extension Service, Oklahoma State University. Retrieved from the World Wide Web on June, 16, 2003 at http:// pearl.agcomm.okstate.edu/fci/family/t-2327.pdf.

Witt, J. C., Elliott, S. N., & Martens, B. K. (1984). Acceptability of behavioral interventions used in classrooms: The influence of amount of teacher time, severity of behavior problem, and type of intervention. *Behavioral Disorders, 9*(2), 95–104.

Wolery, M., Bailey, D. B. Jr., & Sugai, G. M. (1988). *Effective teaching: Principles and procedures of applied behavior analysis with exceptional students.* Boston: Allyn and Bacon.

Wolf, M. M. (1978). Social validity: The case for subjective measurement or how applied behavior analysis is finding its heart. *Journal of Applied Behavior Analysis, 11,* 203–214.

Yell, M. L. (1994). Timeout and students with behavior disorders: A legal analysis. *Education and Treatment of Children, 17*(3), 293–301.

13 Addressing Serious and Chronic Misbehavior

Alternative and Special Education

GUIDING QUESTIONS

- Under what circumstances should students be removed from school? What are the disadvantages and advantages of suspending and expelling students?
- Given that students with disabilities are guaranteed a "free public appropriate education" in the "least restrictive setting," should they be suspended and expelled from school the same as students without disabilities?

- What common disabilities should teachers expect to find among students in regular classrooms? With respect to school discipline, what responsibilities do regular classroom teachers have in meeting the needs of these students?
- Are special provisions in the federal law that govern the use of suspension and expulsion of students with disabilities fair and reasonable?
- What are alternative schools and classrooms? How might they be more effective?
- What types and level of interventions, services, and supports are most effective for remediating serious and chronic behavior problems? Should schools be responsible for providing the types and level of interventions, services, and supports that are needed?
- How might schools and teachers best be prepared to respond to crises that threaten school safety?

> Under current federal law, any student who brings a weapon to school is subject to a 1-year expulsion. If that student is served in special education, bringing a weapon may still result in disciplinary removal, but a different, more complex set of regulations governs when and how the student may be removed. . . . This difference in the treatment of students with disabilities who are violent or disruptive has created an intense controversy that continues to swirl around the disciplinary provisions of special education law. (Skiba, 2002, p. 81)

For most students, the strategies and techniques for developing self-discipline and for preventing and correcting misbehavior presented in the previous chapters are sufficient for preventing or reducing the recurrence of misbehavior. This includes the approximately 5% to 15% of students considered to be "at risk" for problem behavior, as well as the 85% to 95% not at risk. That is, the needs of most students can be met in the regular classroom using strategies and techniques that can be reasonably expected of classroom teachers. Unfortunately, there is a relatively small percentage of students, estimated to be 1% to 7% in most schools (Walker, Horner, Sugai, Bullis, Bricker, & Kaufman, 1996), who are resistant to these strategies and techniques, even when used by the best teachers and in the best schools.

These students repeatedly challenge the authority of school officials, disobey rules, and exhibit other behaviors that seriously disrupt teaching and learning. Some, but certainly not all, of these students commit serious acts of misbehavior that threaten the safety or welfare of others, such as violent fighting or possessing weapons or drugs. Chronically disruptive students are not the only ones who commit serious acts of violence or possess weapons or drugs—although they are at risk of doing so. It is not uncommon for these behaviors to be committed by students with no prior histories or who otherwise are not deemed at risk. For example, fighting and drug experimentation, especially during adolescence, are certainly not limited to students with prior histories of serious misbehavior. Nevertheless, reflecting the seriousness of their behavior, and as a consequence thereof, these students often are suspended, expelled, or otherwise removed from their classroom or school and placed elsewhere. As noted in Chapter 2, educators often have little choice in this decision. Schools do have a choice, however, in deciding if their response to chronic and serious acts of misbehavior goes beyond mere punishment.

There are two major purposes of this chapter. The first is to examine the most frequent response to serious and chronic misbehavior, which is out-of-school suspension and expulsion. About 15% of students in regular education and 17% of students in special education are suspended from school and/or placed in alternative educational settings (U.S. General Accounting Office, 2001). The limitations of suspension and expulsion are reviewed, followed by a review of the federal regulations pertaining to the use of suspension and expulsion of students with disabilities. There is a very important reason why all teachers should be familiar with these regulations: At one time or another nearly all teachers have students with disabilities in their classrooms. As will be discussed in this chapter, federal law requires that the majority of students with disabilities be educated in regular classrooms. It also requires that regular education teachers participate in the development and implementation of behavioral intervention plans designed to prevent and correct misbehavior, both minor and serious, of students with disabilities who are in their classrooms.

The second major purpose of this chapter is to examine the types and level of interventions, services, and supports that are often needed for students, with and without disabilities, who exhibit serious and chronic behavior problems. It is important to emphasize that the same strategies and techniques presented previously *should* be used with these students in developing self-discipline, preventing misbehavior, and correcting misbehavior. Indeed, it makes much sense for schools to take deliberate actions to target students early who are at risk for serious and chronic behavior problems and to ensure that they receive the above strategies and techniques, and more so than other students. Whereas the same strategies and techniques used in regular classrooms are necessary and helpful with these students, to be effective they must be delivered in an intense and sustained fashion. This goes beyond comprehensive classroom discipline. It entails intensive, sustained, and comprehensive interventions, services, and supports provided in and outside of regular education classrooms that focus on remediation. The primary responsibility for such interventions, services, and supports should not fall on regular education teachers. However, regular education teachers often are members of schoolwide teams, which include special educators, school psychologists, and intervention specialists, who work with families and community agencies in providing remediation designed to address current behavior problems and reduce their recurrence.

Common Responses to Serious and Chronic Misbehavior: Suspension and Expulsion

Out-of-school suspension (referred to as *suspension* throughout this chapter) and *expulsion* are the two most common methods used to remove students from school as a consequence of serious and chronic misbehavior. Out-of-school suspension and expulsion differ in the length of time a student is removed, with suspension entailing a shorter period of time. A further distinction often is made between *short-term* suspension and *long-term* suspension. Generally, short-term suspension consists of removing a student for only one to ten days whereas long-term suspension consists of removal for a greater number of days (Gorn, 1999; Hartwig & Ruesch, 1994). These distinctions are arbitrary ones, however, and are not always made. For example, some schools do not distinguish between long-term suspension and expulsion, choosing to refer to both types of long-term removal as expulsion. During the suspension or expulsion, a student may or may not continue to receive educational services.

When they are provided, it is in another setting, which is the home or what is typically re-ferred to as an *alternative program* (note that some schools do not call placement in an al-ternative program expulsion, but a *transfer, displacement,* or *removal*). In over half of the states, schools are required by law to provide alternative programs for suspended and ex-pelled students (Advancement Project/Civil Rights Project, 2000).

Whether a student is suspended or expelled, and for how long, depends on the seri-ousness of the offense. Most suspensions involve misbehavior that is neither dangerous nor threatening to the safety of others (Bear, 2000; Brooks, Schiraldi, & Ziedenberg, 1999). The most common misbehavior leading to suspension is defiance, disobedience, or insubordination, although fighting also typically appears among the top three reasons for suspension (Gottfredson & Gottfredson, 2001; Mendez, Knoff, & Ferron, 2002; Skiba, 2000). Other common misbehaviors that result in suspension are smoking, using alcohol, disrupting the classroom, using obscene language, excessive tardiness, skipping class, forging parent signatures, and extortion (Costenbader & Markson, 1998; Mendez et al., 2002; Skiba, 2000). Expulsion is typically limited to the most serious forms of misbehav-ior, including fighting that is chronic or results in serious injury, the possession of weapons or drugs, and other criminal acts (Advancement Project/Civil Rights Project, 2000; Skiba, 2000).

Advantages of Suspension and Expulsion

When used in response to chronic and serious acts of misbehavior, and as a "last resort"—after all else has failed—suspension and expulsion may well serve a worthwhile purpose. Indeed, in addition to being required under most codes of conduct, removal from school is used for many of the same reasons, as reviewed in Chapter 2, as are other types of punish-ment. That is, suspension and expulsion often are effective in decreasing misbehavior. For many students, suspension and expulsion highlight the seriousness of their misbehavior. These students find being removed from school to be shameful or otherwise aversive. This is particularly true in cases of suspension when the students' parents support the school's de-cision, viewing it unfavorably yet as a constructive learning opportunity (and making sure that the student continues to complete school work while at home). For such students sus-pension may well have lasting effects. It is important to note, however, that there is little, if any, reason to believe that a lengthy removal is any more effective than a short one or that these students would not respond as well to less harsh techniques.

Another argument in favor of suspension and expulsion is that they deter other stu-dents from misbehaving and help establish an environment that is safe, orderly, and con-ducive to learning. Often suspension and expulsion send the message to all students that serious and chronic misbehavior will not be tolerated. In cases involving weapons, drugs, and threats or acts of violence, removal helps create a safer environment. Likewise, removal of chronically disruptive students can help improve the learning environment for others. Fi-nally, one might argue that when used wisely, suspension and expulsion may actually pro-mote remediation. To serve this purpose, the wise use of suspension and expulsion would entail using them only as last resorts and always in combination with other techniques for developing self-discipline and for preventing and correcting misbehavior. When used wisely, suspension and expulsion would include the provision of educational and mental health ser-vices, as needed, during the period of suspension or expulsion. As such, the student would be removed from school but placed in another *educational* setting in which remedial services are provided.

Limitations to Suspension and Expulsion

Whereas suspension and expulsion may serve several worthwhile purposes, they also share the same limitations that apply to all other forms of punishment. Similar to the general limitations to punishment that were reviewed in Chapter 2, limitations to suspension and expulsion include the following:

1. *Suspension and expulsion fail to address the multiple factors that contribute to the student's misbehavior. Consequently, the effects are short term and nonlasting for many students.* The ineffectiveness of suspension and expulsion as a long-term solution, especially for students with chronic or serious behavior problems, is reflected in the finding that about 40% of students suspended are suspended again in the same year (Costenbader & Markson, 1994). This is largely because suspension and expulsion fail to teach students anything that they don't already know ("Don't get caught!").

2. *Suspension and expulsion teach students to punish others.* When overly used, suspension and expulsion teach students that the best way to deal with problems, especially with others who bother them, is not to attempt to address factors that contribute to the problem but to remove the individuals who misbehave.

3. *For many students, suspension and expulsion are reinforcing.* This applies primarily to the 40% cited previously. Suspension and expulsion are excellent examples of negatively reinforcing students who find school unpleasant and would rather be elsewhere. Allowing these students to escape from unpleasant situations (e.g., academic frustration, teasing from peers, uncaring others) simply reinforces the very misbehaviors for which they are supposedly being "punished."

4. *Suspension and expulsion are likely to produce undesirable side effects.* These include ill feelings toward school, as well as dislike, retaliation, or revenge toward those perceived by the suspended or expelled student to have "caused" the suspension or expulsion. They also include intense feelings of shame, which may lead to depression.

5. *Suspension and expulsion create a negative classroom and school climate.* This is particularly true when they are used frequently, unfairly, not as "last resorts," and not in combination with other positive strategies and techniques.

An additional limitation that was not discussed in Chapter 2, which is more specific to suspension and expulsion, is the following:

6. *Suspension and expulsion decrease time spent in academic learning and may well increase time spent learning undesirable behavior.* Lack of instruction increases the risk of academic failure, which, in turn, contributes to, rather than prevents future problems. Removing students from school also may increase opportunities for them to be exposed to negative role models and criminal activity. This is especially true when students receive little supervision and monitoring while out of school (Walker et al., 1996). In many cases, removing students from school essentially shifts the problem from the school to homes and communities that are not equipped to provide help. This increases the likelihood that additional negative outcomes will follow, such as criminal activity, unemployment, substance abuse, dropping out, and social maladjustment (Finn, 1989; Rossi, 1994). These outcomes negatively impact not only individual students but also society in general. Thus, whereas suspension and expulsion may give immediate relief to a classroom teacher (which may be needed and perhaps justified, especially from the perspective of the teacher, school, and parents of other students), it does little to help the student, home, and community. In fact, it may well make matters worse.

In light of the preceding limitations, it is understandable why suspension and expulsion should be used infrequently—only for the most serious or chronic misbehavior, especially misbehavior that harms or threatens the safety of others, and only in combination with other strategies and techniques designed to prevent the misbehavior from recurring. Given that removal from school results in the absence of education, which is linked to multiple negative outcomes, perhaps it also is understandable why concerns often arise over the disproportionate number of minority students, especially African American males, who are suspended and expelled. Recall from Chapter 2 that African American males are suspended two to three times more often than other students (Brooks et al., 1999). These same concerns apply to students with disabilities, who also tend to be disproportionately suspended and expelled (Morrison & D'Incau, 1997; Skiba, 2002). It is largely because of these concerns, but particularly the denial of education while suspended and expelled, that federal law contains special provisions governing the use of discipline, particularly suspension and expulsion, with students with disabilities.

STOP AND REFLECT

Case Study. Expulsion: Should a Disability Make a Difference?

After arguing and threatening one another for several months, Calvin and Anthony get into a fight. In helping break up the fight the teacher discovers that both students have weapons, small pocket-knives, in their coat pockets. Both insist that the knives are for fishing and that they did not use, nor intend to use, them in the fight. The school district's zero tolerance policy toward school violence mandates suspension for fighting and expulsion for possessing a weapon. The principal decides that both students are equally to blame for the fighting and for possessing a weapon and, thus, recommends expulsion to the superintendent and school board. Consequently, Anthony is expelled for the remainder of the school year, without educational services (and little, if any, supervision at home). However, because Calvin is a student with a learning disability, he is sent to an alternative school for forty-five days, after which he is allowed to return to the regular classroom.

Is this fair? Should any of the following factors influence the decision to expel these two students?

- The age of the students.
- The student's prior history of behavior problems (e.g., was this the first problem?).
- Whether or not a student has a disability.

- The nature of Calvin's disability. For example, whether his learning disability is mild or severe and whether it affects his social and moral problem-solving skills, including understanding school rules and the consequences of his behavior and his ability to manage his emotions and control his impulses?
- Whether or not the teacher or school should have anticipated that a fight would occur. That is, should it matter if the teacher, or school, knew that Calvin had a history of fighting and threatening others but took no preventive or remedial actions?

Many educators believe that expelling one student but not the other for the same offense is unfair or indicates a double standard. Others, however, argue that all children should *not* be treated the same: Just as a 3-year-old should not be treated the same as a 10-year-old, or a 10-year-old the same as an adult, neither should a student with a disability be treated the same as a student without a disability. Following this argument, one might conclude that because Calvin is a student with a disability, he should not be removed from school. Instead, the school should provide him *more,* not less, educational and mental health services. For this reason, one might also argue, however, that it makes little sense to expel *any* student if it results in the denial of services.

What is your opinion on this matter? Should students with and without diabilities be treated the same? Should public schools be responsible for the costs of mental health and alternative educational services?

Discipline and Students with Disabilities

The Individuals with Disabilities Education Act (IDEA) mandates that all students with disabilities be provided with a "free appropriate public education" (FAPE) in the "least restricted environment" (LRE). Basically, the FAPE mandate means that schools must provide an education, at no cost to the child's parents, to any child with a disability. The LRE mandate means that schools must make every effort to educate students with disabilities in the same schools and classrooms as those attended by their same-age peers without disabilities. In accordance with these two mandates, students with disabilities are to be removed from regular education classrooms only if they cannot make satisfactory progress despite the provision of supplementary aids and services, such as adapted instruction and additional tutoring. Consistent with the LRE mandate, about 70% of students with disabilities receive at least part of their education in a regular classroom (U.S. Department of Education, 2002).

Until 1997, the FAPE and LRE provisions meant that students with disabilities who misbehaved regardless of the severity of the misbehavior, could not be removed from their current educational placement, including a regular classroom or special education classroom, and placed into another setting unless their parents agreed to the removal or unless the school obtained permission through legal recourse (i.e., a court order or a ruling from a state-appointed "hearing officer"). This is because such a removal was considered a "change in placement," and as required in IDEA, the student's parents had to approve any change in placement. If not approved, a student with a disability was to "stay put" in the current placement.

In the early 1990s it became clear that the FAPE and LRE requirements conflicted with zero tolerance policies toward school violence that many schools were adopting. This included the federal Gun-Free Schools Act (1994), which mandates the expulsion of students who possess weapons on school grounds. The explicit purpose of these policies was to protect the safety of all students (an additional purpose, albeit more implicit, was to punish the violators). However, prior to changes in IDEA, unless a school received permission from a court, a student with a disability could not be suspended, expelled, or otherwise removed from the classroom or school without parental approval. To do so would violate a student's rights. Consequently, schools often faced a dilemma when removing students, including in response to serious acts of misbehavior such as possession of weapons or drugs or the use or threat of violence. On the one hand, if schools removed students with disabilities without parental permission, they would violate the FAPE and LRE mandates and risk potential lawsuits from parents of these students. On the other hand, if they did not remove them, they risked the safety of all students (as well as potential lawsuits from parents of victims of violence).

In 1997 changes were made in federal law to help resolve the preceding dilemma. In order to balance the rights of students with disabilities to FAPE and LRE with the right of all students to safe schools, IDEA allowed schools to treat students with disabilities the same as students without disabilities *but with certain provisions.* The most critical provision is that students with disabilities must continue to receive FAPE when removed from school for more than ten consecutive school days. Another important provision is that schools are to take a proactive stance in addressing behavior problems of students with disabilities. That is, for students with disabilities who exhibit behavior problems, schools must implement strategies and techniques to *prevent* such behavior problems from recurring. IDEA also requires that schools implement strategies and techniques to correct and remediate existing social, emotional, and behavioral problems that interfere with the educational performance of a student with a disability. *Note that the majority of students with disabilities do not exhibit chronic or serious behavior problems,* but for those who do, prevention, correction, and remediation are *required,* not optional. Thus, strategies and techniques presented throughout this book should not be viewed simply as "recommended best practices" but also as best practices that are legally required for many students.

Students for Whom the Federal Regulations Apply

The federal regulations governing disciplinary procedures apply to all students with disabilities who qualify for special education services. This comprises approximately 6 million children, or about 9% of all children ages 6 to 21 (U.S. Department of Education, 2002). IDEA recognizes thirteen categories of disabilities: children with autism, deaf-blindness, developmental delay, emotional disturbance, hearing impairments (including deafness), mental retardation, multiple disabilities, orthopedic impairments, other health impairments (which include attention deficit hyperactivity disorder), specific learning disabilities, speech or language impairments, traumatic brain injury, and visual impairments. To qualify under IDEA as a student with one of the preceding disabilities, the student must *need* special education services.

As defined in IDEA, *special education* means "specially designed instruction, at no cost to the parents, to meet the unique needs of a child with a disability" (34 C.F.R. 300.26). For many students with behavior problems this would include the adaptation of instructional content as well as the use of strategies and techniques that address more directly the behaviors of concern. Students with behavior problems also often require what is referred to in

IDEA as *related services*. Related services are supportive services that are necessary to assist a child with a disability to benefit from special education. With respect to students with behavior problems, related services authorized in IDEA include psychological services (including consultation to the teacher and parents), early identification and assessment, counseling services, school health services, social work services in schools, and parent counseling and training. It is important to note that IDEA requires that schools make sure that these services are provided to all students with disabilities, as needed. As such, the law recognizes that *teachers alone are not expected to address the social and emotional needs of students with disabilities.* This requires a team effort that should include the regular education teacher, special education teachers, administrators, support staff, parents, and outside agencies.

Among the thirteen categories of disabilities recognized in IDEA, the most common disabilities are specific learning disabilities, speech and language impairments, mental retardation, and emotional disturbance. About 8% of all children and adolescents receive special education services for one of these four disabilities. It should be noted that attention deficit hyperactivity disorder (ADHD) is another common disability, but students diagnosed with ADHD do not necessarily qualify for special education services under IDEA, as explained later. With the exception of speech and language impairments, each of these disabilities has been shown to be associated with a greater incidence of social, emotional, and behavior problems than found in the general population. As such, students with specific learning disabilities, mental retardation, ADHD, and emotional disturbance are at greater risk than other students for exhibiting behaviors for which the codes of conduct in many schools require suspension or expulsion. Because students with these four disabilities are at greater risk and because regular education teachers are more likely to have them than students with other disabilities in their classrooms, a brief description of each one of these disabilities follows.

Specific Learning Disabilities.   Almost half of all children with disabilities are identified as children with specific learning disabilities (U.S. Department of Education, 2002). This consists of approximately 5% of all students. Given that the majority of these students are included in regular classrooms, odds are that a teacher will have at least one student with a specific learning disability in his or her classroom. IDEA defines a specific learning disability as "a disorder in one or more of the basic psychological processes involved in understanding or in using language, spoken or written, which may manifest itself in imperfect ability to listen, think, speak, read, write, spell, or do mathematical calculations. The term includes such conditions as perceptual disabilities, brain injury, minimal brain dysfunction, dyslexia, and developmental aphasia. Such a term does not include a learning problem that is primarily the result of visual, hearing, or motor disabilities, of mental retardation, of emotional disturbance, or of environmental, cultural, or economic disadvantage." A key characteristic of children with specific learning disabilities is that that they continue to exhibit academic difficulties despite systematic attempts to address them (e.g., curriculum adaptations, tutoring). That is, they are resistant to interventions. A learning disability often is reflected in a significant discrepancy between a student's intellectual ability and academic achievement in one or more of the areas above.

Although the behavior of the majority of students with learning disabilities is no different than that of students without learning disabilities, about one-third exhibit significantly more behavior problems than normally achieving students (Gresham & Reschly, 1986). Compared to their normally achieving classmates, students with learning disabilities are more likely to be aggressive, immature, and lacking in social problem-solving skills; suffer personality problems; and have problems attending to tasks (Swanson & Malone, 1992; Vaughn & Haager, 1994).

Attention Deficit Hyperactivity Disorder (ADHD).   Another disability that is common in regular classrooms is ADHD. Approximately 3% to 5% of all children and adolescents are diagnosed as having ADHD (American Psychiatric Association, 1994).[1] The most common criteria used to diagnose ADHD require that the student frequently exhibit symptoms identified with one, or both, of two types of problem behaviors: inattention or hyperactivity-impulsivity (American Psychiatric Association, 1994). Note that hyperactivity is not necessary for the diagnosis of ADHD—a student can have an attention deficit disorder (ADD) without hyperactivity and impulsivity (and vice versa). For example, a student with ADD may find it extremely difficult to attend to educational tasks but show no hyperactivity. Common symptoms associated with an attention deficit disorder are distractibility and difficulties with attention, listening, organization, following instructions, and remembering things. Common symptoms associated with the impulsivity-hyperactivity type are talking excessively, fidgeting, interrupting others, blurting an answer before the teacher finishes the question, having difficulty remaining in one's seat, remaining on task, and taking turns. In addition to the preceding behavioral characteristics, students with ADHD, especially those with hyperactivity and impulsivity, demonstrate poor self-regulation as seen in the failure to inhibit their behavior. Thus, many also develop other disruptive disorders, such as a conduct disorder or oppositional-defiant disorder (Barkley, 1997).

STOP AND REFLECT

About 70% to 80% of students with ADHD respond favorably to medication, showing improvements in attention and concentration, impulsivity, compliance, and decreased activity levels and behavior problems (Rapport, Denney, DuPaul, & Gardner, 1994). Improvement is generally greater when medication is combined with behavioral interventions (Barkley, 1997). (Note, however, less improvement is generally seen in academic performance than in behavior.) What are your views on the use of medication to regulate the attention, activity, and perhaps misbehavior of students with and without ADHD?

Emotional Disturbance.   Although only 1% of all students receive special education services as children with emotional disturbance (also referred to as "emotional or behavioral disorders" or "behavioral disorder" in several states), nearly all authorities in special education agree that at least twice as many should qualify for special education under this category

---

[1]Note that there is no separate category for children with ADHD in IDEA. Instead, most students with ADHD who qualify for special education services under IDEA do so under the categories of "Other Health Impaired" or "Specific Learning Disability," and only if their disability has an adverse effect on educational performance.

(Kauffman, 2001). Indeed, it is widely accepted that approximately 20% of children and adolescents experience signs of a psychiatric disorder over the course of a year and 5% experience "extreme functional impairment" (U.S. Surgeon General, 1999). Much variability exists in how states define emotional disturbance, but most states have adopted the definition of emotional disturbance in IDEA or a modification thereof. As defined in IDEA, emotional disturbance is:

> a condition exhibiting one or more of the following characteristics over a long period of time and to a marked degree that adversely affects a child's educational performance:
>
> (a) an inability to learn that cannot be explained by intellectual, sensory, or health factors;
> (b) an inability to build or maintain satisfactory interpersonal relationships with peers and teachers;
> (c) inappropriate types of behavior or feelings under normal circumstances;
> (d) a general, pervasive mood of unhappiness or depression;
> (e) a tendency to develop physical symptoms or fears associated with personal or school problems.

The criterion "long-term and to a marked degree" is meant to rule out emotions and behaviors that are developmentally appropriate, or normative, but nevertheless bother teachers or parents. It is only when behaviors deviate significantly from the norm in their duration and intensity, in spite of systematic efforts to address them, that a student should be considered as a student with an emotional disturbance.

STOP AND REFLECT

An issue of ongoing debate among educators and policy makers is whether or not students with serious and chronic conduct problems should be included under the category of emotional disturbance and, thus, receive special education services. Unfortunately, the federal definition is unclear on this controversial issue. At the center of this controversy is the following exclusionary statement at the end of the federal definition of emotional disturbance: "The term does not include children who are socially maladjusted but not emotionally disturbed." Unfortunately, the term *socially maladjusted* is not defined. In light of this exclusionary clause and in the absence of any specific reference to aggression, antisocial behavior, and other conduct problems in the definition of emotional disturbance, some authorities (e.g., Slenkovich, 1992) argue that chronically disruptive students are not entitled to special education services (but that other agencies are responsible). Others (e.g., Skiba & Grizzle, 1991, 1992) argue that the federal definition of IDEA *does* include children and adolescents who are socially maladjusted (as long as they also are emotionally disturbed) and, thus, that the definition applies to most students with serious and chronic antisocial behavior. Many school districts agree with the former position (i.e., disruptive students are not emotionally disturbed) but largely for administrative and financial reasons. That is, by not classifying these students as emotionally disturbed, schools have greater flexibility in matters of discipline and are less likely to be required to provide costly special education services. For example, if chronically disruptive students are not identified as emotionally disturbed, they can be suspended for a long period of time, or expelled, without schools having to continue to provide FAPE. On the other hand, if students are identified as emotionally disturbed and it becomes evident that the school cannot meet their educational needs, the school must provide FAPE. This could be in a private residential

(continued)

STOP AND REFLECT *(continued)*

school setting where the costs often exceed $100,000 per year. Many believe that it is largely for this reason that the number of students actually identified as emotionally disturbed is much less than the actual number of such students.

Assume the perspectives of classroom teachers, school administrators, taxpayers, the student who is "socially maladjusted," the student's parents, and other students in the classroom (and their parents). *Should* public schools be responsible for providing special education or related services to students who are "socially maladjusted?" How about those with emotional disturbance?

Mental Retardation.   In IDEA, mental retardation is defined as "significantly subaverage general intellectual functioning, existing concurrently with deficits in adaptive behavior and manifested during the developmental period, that adversely affects a child's educational performance." Although states vary somewhat in their interpretation of this definition and, thus, adopt different criteria, most agree that in order to be eligible for special education as a student with mental retardation the student must have an IQ of 75 or below (some states require 70, however) and demonstrate significant deficits in adaptive behavior (e.g., self-care, social skills, communication).

IMPLEMENTATION TIP

Referring Students for Special Education Services

IDEA requires that children suspected of disabilities be referred for a comprehensive evaluation to determine eligibility for special education services. A referral for an evaluation is warranted when it becomes clear that the student's educational and mental health needs cannot be met without special education and related services. Such referrals generally come from the student's regular classroom teacher or parents and are made to the school's principal, coordinator of special education services, or child study team. Before and after referring a student for an evaluation, the following are recommended:

- Familiarize yourself with your district's requirements and procedures pertaining to referring students for special education services.
- Be sure to review the student's school records. Check to see if others suspected a disability before, if evaluation results and recommendations are available, what interventions might have been attempted in the past, and if the student has had a behavior intervention plan.
- Before referring the student, seek assistance from others in selecting, designing, and implementing interventions. In addition to assistance and support from the student's parents, consult and collaborate with other teachers and members of the school's or district's support staff. This would include fellow regular classroom teachers, special education teachers, the school psychologist, school counselor, and school social worker. In most schools, these individuals serve on a team, often called a child study team, intervention assistance team, or a prereferral intervention team, that is devoted to providing intervention assistance to students, teachers, and parents.

- Be sure to document behaviors of concern and the interventions that you have tried. Describe the behaviors in a log including behaviors of concern reported by others and when and how frequently they occur. Document that a variety of preventive and corrective techniques have been implemented, but especially replacement techniques, to address the behaviors of concern.
- If you continue to believe that the student needs special education, refer the student for a comprehensive psychoeducational evaluation. Work closely with others throughout the referral and evaluation process. As part of the evaluation, it is likely that you will be asked to share your observations of the student, complete a checklist or rating scale of the student's behavior, and document the interventions you have tried and are currently using.
- Be sure to collaborate with the student's *parents* throughout the prereferral, referral, and evaluation processes. Their written permission is required before the student can be evaluated and before the student can receive special education or related services. Not only is their support required, but it also greatly enhances the likelihood that necessary services and interventions will be effective.

The Individualized Education Program

All students suspected of a disability are to be referred for a comprehensive evaluation. Based on the results of the evaluation, it is to be determined if the student is eligible for special education and related services. If it is determined that the student is eligible, the school must develop an *individualized education program* (IEP) for the student within thirty calendar days. Services begin after the IEP is written, but only if the parents consent to such services. The IEP specifies the services, accommodations, modifications, and supports that are to be provided.

The process of developing and implementing an IEP requires teamwork, including efforts to assess and target multiple risk and protective factors that influence a student's behavior. In most cases the student's regular education teacher must be a member of the team, referred to as the IEP team, which is responsible for developing, reviewing, and revising the IEP. As required by IDEA, if the student with a disability participates in the regular education classroom, and over 70% do so, then at least one regular education teacher for that student must be a member of the IEP team. Together with other members of the IEP team, the regular education teacher is to help decide on the student's involvement and progress in the general curriculum, participation in the regular education environment, and how best to meet the student's needs. Active participation of the student's regular classroom teacher in the IEP process makes perfect sense, because it is quite likely that the regular education teacher will be required to implement interventions, as included in the IEP, for improving the student's learning and behavior. Often it is the regular education teacher who best knows the general education curriculum and what is needed to help meet the student's academic, social, and emotional needs.

Who are the members of the IEP team? In addition to the regular classroom teacher, the IEP team consists of the student's parent (or guardian); the student's special education teacher; an individual who can interpret the results of evaluations of the student, including the implications of the results for addressing the student's academic and behavioral needs; and an individual with the authority to represent the school system and the ability to ensure that the IEP will be implemented as planned (e.g., the principal or special education coordinator). When appropriate, the student should be a member of the team. In addition to the preceding members, the IEP team may include individuals with knowledge or special expertise about the student. For example, if the student has serious social or emotional problems, the team should include a school psychologist or counselor.

The IEP and School Discipline.   IDEA requires that certain items must be included in the IEP, including what special education and related services are to be provided, the duration of the services, annual goals for the student, and other items beyond the scope of this text. With respect to school discipline, IDEA also mandates that "If a child has behavior problems that interfere with his or her learning or the learning of others, the IEP team must consider whether strategies (including positive behavioral interventions, strategies, and supports) are needed to address the behavior." IDEA does not define "positive behavioral intervention, strategies, and supports." However, most authorities interpret this provision as requiring that the IEP must include strategies and techniques designed to *increase* desirable behavior. Strategies and techniques are not to be limited to punitive or reductive ones. Positive strategies and techniques consist of those presented throughout this book—those for developing self-discipline, preventing misbehavior with effective classroom management, and for correcting misbehavior using behavioral replacement techniques.

Consistent with IDEA, most authorities in special education recommend that positive behavioral interventions be based on a *functional behavioral assessment* (FBA) (Tilly, Knoster, & Ikeda, 2000). As noted in Chapters 11 and 12, an FBA would examine multiple factors that contribute to behavior problems that interfere with learning. Although not specific to addressing behavior problems, IDEA requires that the IEP include supplementary aids and services, program modifications and supports for school personnel, as needed. These elements serve primarily to allow a student to remain in the regular classroom or school environment and to progress in the general curriculum. Requiring these elements is consistent with the basic principle of IDEA that services are to be provided in the least restricted environment. With respect to matters of school discipline, the primary intent of this requirement is to encourage schools to take a proactive approach in addressing behavior problems, thus reducing the extent to which schools use suspension and expulsion. As noted by the U.S. Department of Education Office of Special Education and Rehabilitative Services (1999), "Of course, in the case of less serious infractions, schools can address the misconduct through appropriate instructional and/or related services, including conflict management, behavior management strategies, and measures such as study carrels, time-outs, and restrictions in privileges, so long as they are not inconsistent with the child's IEP. *If a child's IEP or behavior intervention plan addresses a particular behavior, it generally would be inappropriate to utilize some other response, such as suspension, to that behavior* (italics added)."

Suspensions and Expulsion of Students with Disabilities

Although IDEA makes it clear that the IEP is to include positive strategies and techniques for preventing behavior problems, it also allows schools to remove students with disabilities from school. As noted previously, special provisions apply when the school decides to re-

move students with disabilities from their current placement and such removals (a) constitute a *change of placement* and (b) the parents object to the change of placement. It is important to emphasize that *if the students' parents agree to the consequences of the
misbehavior, including removing the student from the current placement, the disciplinary
provisions under IDEA need not apply.* In many cases, parents do agree with the school.

Common examples of changes in students' placements are removing students with
disabilities from the regular classroom and placing them in more restricted special education
classrooms and removing them from their current school and placing them in a separate special education or alternative education program. As made clear in IDEA, however, long-term
suspension and expulsion also constitute a change in placement. Except under the circumstances discussed later, a change in placement requires a change in the student's current IEP,
which requires parental consent. There are two very important caveats, however, that apply
even when the parents agree to the change in placement: (1) The student cannot be treated
differently than students without disabilities (e.g., suspended for a longer period of time for
the same behavior), and (2) the student must continue to receive a free appropriate public
education (albeit in another setting) that includes all educational services and related services provided in the previous setting, as specified in the IEP.

The special provisions in IDEA on the use of discipline with students with disabilities
are not always clear. In an attempt to help clarify them, they are discussed here in a question
and answer format that addresses the most common questions educators ask about the disciplinary provisions in IDEA.

***Can a student with a disability be suspended, or otherwise removed from their class-
room or school without the removal constituting a "change of placement" and,
thus, requiring that he or she continue to receive educational and related services
specified in the IEP?*** Yes, but only if the suspension or removal from their current
placement is short-term, not exceeding more than ten consecutive school days in the same
school year for separate incidents of misbehavior, and the student is treated the same as
other students. Most commonly, such placements consist of in-school suspension or out-
of-school suspension at home (U.S. General Accounting Office, 2003). IDEA does allow
for additional removals, but it is not exactly clear under what circumstances. The regulations state that "Additional removals may occur as long as they are not for more than ten
consecutive school days or they do not constitute a pattern because they cumulate to more
than ten school days in a school year, and because of factors such as the length of each removal, the total amount of time the child is removed, and the proximity of removals to one
another" (IDEA Regulations 34 C.F.R. 300.520–300.529). This means that under certain
circumstances, a student with a disability may be suspended for separate incidents of misbehavior over the course of the school year for a total of more than ten school days, without the suspensions constituting a change in placement.

For example, let's say that a student is suspended for a total of eight school days in the
fall for several incidents of fighting. Much later in the school year, the same student gets into
another fight, for which the school's code of conduct calls for an automatic suspension of
three days. The school can suspend the student without violating the law, as long as it continues to provide educational services. Although the total number of days exceeds ten, there
is no change of placement because the suspensions are for separate incidents and are far
apart. However, if the same student had been suspended eight or nine days at a time during

the school year, such a pattern would constitute a change in placement, and thus would be a violation of the regulations (Hartwig & Ruesch, 2000). Because the circumstances under which a school may remove a student for more than ten days are unclear, schools should be extremely cautious in removing students with disabilities for more than ten school days in a given school year.

When must the school provide special education and related services to a student with a disability who is removed from the classroom or school?   Schools are not required to provide special education and related services if a student is suspended or otherwise removed for disciplinary reasons provided that the number of days does not exceed ten school days in the same school year. When this number is exceeded, however, the school must provide educational and related services to enable the student to continue to appropriately progress in the general curriculum and appropriately advance toward the goals in the IEP. In most cases, on the eleventh school day the student would return to the original placement, unless the placement (and, thus, the IEP) is changed with parental approval. As seen later, however, under certain circumstances the student may be suspended for more than ten days, or be placed elsewhere—in an *interim alternative educational setting*—if the parent refuses to approve the change in placement.

May a student with a disability be removed for more than ten days without changing the IEP (i.e., without the removal constituting a change in placement)?   Yes, in disciplinary cases involving weapons, drugs, or the threat of injury a student may be placed in an interim alternative educational setting. *School personnel* may remove a student with a disability and place the student in an interim alternative educational setting if the student carries or possesses a weapon or knowingly possesses or uses illegal drugs or sells or solicits the sale of a controlled substance. These two behaviors must occur while the student is at school or on school premises or is going to or at a school function. A student with a disability also can be placed in an interim alternative educational setting if it is determined that there is "substantial evidence" that the student is likely to injure others or himself or herself. In this case, however, a hearing officer, who is appointed by the state, must make the determination of removal.

However, a hearing officer can refuse to remove a student with a disability who is perceived by the school to be a threat to others, if the hearing officer determines that (a) the student's current placement remains appropriate despite the student's behavior, (b) the proposed interim alternative educational setting is inappropriate, or (c) the school failed to take reasonable actions to prevent the behavior from occurring (e.g., the teacher failed to use common classroom management techniques that have been shown to be effective with most students, or the student had a history of similar behavior problems and the school failed to provide the student and teacher with supportive services).

What is an appropriate interim alternative educational setting?   IDEA does not define an interim alternative educational setting. Most authorities, however, agree that an interim alternative educational setting (IAES) can be a setting within or separate from the classroom or school building in which the student is currently placed. IDEA does stipulate, however, that the setting must enable the student to continue to receive services, including those described in the student's current IEP, that will allow the student to progress in the general curriculum. This also includes services and modifications that address the behavior that led to removal and that are designed to prevent the behavior from recurring.

Thus, the setting must be an *educational* setting in which preventive and remedial services are provided that help prevent the behavior from recurring (Bear, Quinn, & Burkholder, 2001). As also denoted in the terms *interim* and *alternative,* the educational setting is to be for a brief period of time (during which more long-term solutions are addressed) and that it is an alternative to the student's current placement and to the denial of continued educational services.

For how long may a student with a disability be placed in an interim alternative educational setting? The placement cannot exceed forty-five calendar days or the amount of time a student without a disability would be placed for the same infraction. However, placement in an interim alternative educational setting can be extended beyond forty-five days if:

1. The student's parents agree with the school to change the student's IEP to allow for a longer placement in the interim alternative educational setting for disciplinary reasons.
2. A judge orders that the student be placed in the interim alternative educational setting for more days.
3. A hearing officer determines that the student is still at risk for injuring others or himself or herself and, thus, places the student in the interim alternative educational setting for another forty-five days.
4. It is determined in a *manifestation determination* review that the behavior that led to the student's removal was *not* the result, or manifestation, of the student's disability.

What is a manifestation determination and when is it required? A manifestation determination is "an analysis of the causal relationship between a student's disability and the misconduct for which he or she is being disciplined" (Hartwig & Ruesch, 2000, p. 243). It is required when a student with a disability is removed from his or her current educational setting for disciplinary reasons for more than ten days in a given school year. The student's IEP team, which typically includes the regular classroom teacher, conducts the manifestation determination and must do so no later than ten school days after the disciplinary action is taken. In the review the IEP team must address two questions:

1. Was the misbehavior subject to disciplinary action a result of the school's failure to implement the student's IEP or behavioral intervention plan?
2. Was the misbehavior subject to disciplinary action a result of the student's disability? In answering this question, two guiding questions are typically addressed: (a) Did the disability impair the student's ability to understand the impact and consequences of the behavior? and (b) Did the disability impair the ability of the student to control the misbehavior?

If the answer to question 1 is yes then the answer to question 2 is irrelevant. That is, the misbehavior subject to disciplinary action must be considered a manifestation of the student's disability, and the school must take immediate action to correct its failure to implement the interventions in the IEP or behavioral intervention plan. If the answer to question 2 is yes then the misbehavior is considered a manifestation of the student's disability and thus removal is limited to ten days in a school year (with the exceptions presented previously). If the answer to question 2 is no then the misbehavior is not considered a manifestation of the student's disability and thus the student can be treated the same as other students without disabilities, as long as a FAPE is provided. For example, if the misbehavior is not a manifestation of a disability, the student can be suspended or moved to an alternative education program for any number of days (as long as the same practice applies to students without disabilities).

Are a functional behavioral assessment (FBA) and behavioral interventions required when a student with a disability is placed in an interim alternative educational setting or suspended for more than ten days?   Yes. Recall earlier in this chapter, as well as in Chapters 11 and 12, that it was *recommended* that a functional behavioral assessment be conducted when developing interventions to address misbehavior. An FBA and behavioral intervention plan are *required* when a change in placement (i.e., a removal for more than ten school days), occurs for disciplinary reasons. Both the FBA and behavioral interventions are to address the behavior that led to the student's removal. If a behavioral intervention plan already exists for the student, the team should review the plan and its implementation and make modifications, as needed. The plan should include positive behavioral intervention strategies, program or curricular modifications, and supplementary aids and supports (e.g., counseling, social skills training, anger management training) to address the student's behavior. If the student is, or will be, participating in the regular education classroom, the regular education teacher is to be a member of the IEP team that is responsible for designing the behavioral intervention plan.

Section 504 of the Vocational Rehabilitation Act

In addition to IDEA, all teachers should be aware of another federal law pertaining to students with disabilities: Section 504 of the Vocational Rehabilitation Act (P.L. 93-112). Section 504 applies to any persons, including children, with an identified physical or mental disability that "substantially limits a major life activity." Learning is considered a major life activity. Viewed as a civil rights law, as opposed to an educational law, Section 504 guarantees students with disabilities the civil right to receive a free appropriate education in the least restricted environment. As is true under IDEA, under Section 504 students with disabilities are guaranteed special education and related services, as well as related legal protections (e.g., parental permission for an evaluation and placement, IEP requirements, etc.). Unlike under IDEA, however, the procedures and requirements under Section 504 are much broader, more flexible, and less extensive and specific. For example, Section 504 does not specify categories of disabilities or provide regulations and guidelines as to how to identify a disability that "substantially limits a major life activity."

Because qualification criteria are less specific and rigorous under Section 504, many children and adolescents who do not qualify for special education services under IDEA qualify for special education or related services under Section 504. This is true even if the school determines that they *do not need* special education services and, thus, are not students with disabilities under IDEA. Under Section 504, it may well be determined that although these students do not qualify for special education services, they need certain *educational ac-*

commodations in the classroom because of a disability that substantially limits learning or any other major life activity. For example, students with ADHD or LD may need more time taking tests or preferential seating. These and other common educational accommodations for students with ADHD and LD were presented in Chapter 10 (see p. 210). In most cases, educational accommodations provided under Section 504 are less extensive and less costly than the special education services provided under IDEA (note that whereas the federal government reimburses schools for some of the costs of special education and related services under IDEA, it provides no funding under Section 504).

With respect to school discipline, most of the disciplinary provisions under IDEA apply to students who are eligible for services under Section 504, but there are several important exceptions. Perhaps the most important one is that the school does not have to continue to provide educational or related services under Section 504 when a student with a disability is suspended or expelled for more than ten days. Another exception is in the case of drug or alcohol use. The legal protections of Section 504 do not apply to students with disabilities engaged in the abuse of drugs or alcohol.

Remediation and the Regular Classroom Teacher

As noted earlier, the strategies and techniques presented throughout this book *are effective* for students *with and without* disabilities, as well as students with or without chronic or serious behavior problems. For example, as with all other students, students with disabilities and students with chronic and serious behavior problems respond favorably to effective classroom management practices. These would include warm and supportive teacher–student and student–student relations, high expectations, clear and fair rules, instruction and materials that are motivating and developmentally appropriate, close supervision and monitoring, and ongoing home–school collaboration. Likewise, they respond favorably to strategies and techniques designed to develop self-discipline, including those that focus on social and moral problem solving and emotions. These would include the use of modeling, the teaching of social problem-solving skills, the development of moral reasoning, building positive emotions, teaching anger management, and so forth. Finally, most students with serious and chronic behavior problems certainly respond favorably to the wide range of replacement and reductive techniques. There is substantial evidence supporting the use of these techniques for students with behavioral and emotional disorders (Walker, Colvin, & Ramsey, 1995). Indeed, if one were to examine popular textbooks on working with students with chronic and serious behavior problems, very few additional strategies and techniques would be found.

The major difference in classroom strategies and techniques for addressing the social, emotional, and behavioral needs of students with and without chronic and serious behavior problems lies not in the strategies and techniques per se but in the intensity and frequency of their implementation. For example, most students with chronic and serious behavior problems require more frequent and systematic reinforcement of desired behaviors, more frequent use of reductive techniques, more intensive supervision and monitoring, more direct teaching and practice of social and emotional skills, more adaptations and modifications of curricula and instruction, and greater home–school collaboration. Depending on the individual needs of the student, however, certain strategies and techniques would receive greater emphasis than others. For example, students with serious and chronic misbehavior are more likely than other students to require moderately and severely restricted reductive techniques presented in Chapter 12.

Often the need for greater intensity, frequency, and restrictiveness in intervention techniques requires that a student be placed in a more restricted setting—a setting other than the regular education classroom that is staffed by teachers and mental health specialists with appropriate training and experience. For some students with disabilities IDEA allows for such placement. That is, IDEA requires that schools provide a continuum of educational settings varying in degree of restrictiveness. Typically, the least restrictive setting would be a regular classroom in which consultative services, an aide, and/or a teacher trained in special education (who coteaches with the regular education teacher) is provided. Although a bit more restrictive, one of the most common special education settings is the *resource room.* Students with disabilities go to the resource room that is staffed by a special education teacher for part of the school day to receive educational services, such as remedial reading or the direct teaching of replacement behaviors. For students with disabilities who exhibit the most serious behavior problems, more restrictive special education settings are appropriate, including placement in a "self-contained" classroom housed in the student's school, which is attended by a small number of students with similar disabilities, a self-contained classroom located in a separate school, an alternative school (for students with and without disabilities), a residential school, or a mental health facility or hospital. A similar range of placements, although not funded by special education, is appropriate for students who are not eligible for special education services but, nevertheless, exhibit serious or chronic behavior problems. Among such non–special education settings, the most common are alternative classrooms and alternative schools (which would include interim alternative educational settings discussed earlier). As is true with special education settings, the primary purpose of alternative settings for students with serious and chronic misbehavior should be to provide remedial services, with the aim of increasing the likelihood that the behavior(s) that led to classroom removal will not recur upon the student's return to the former setting (Bear et al., 2001).

Characteristics of Effective Programs

Consistent with the limitations of punishment, as discussed earlier, research indicates that special education and alternative education programs that emphasize punishment and control may be effective in the short term (while the student is there) but tend to be associated with poor student attitudes, negative school climate, and no lasting reduction in behavior problems (Gottfredson, 1997; Sugai & Horner, 1999). This finding strongly indicates that an important feature of effective remedial programs is an emphasis on the use of replacement techniques rather than reductive techniques. Other research, based primarily on observations of successful alternative schools, has identified the following additional important features (Bear et al., 2001). Note that although these features are found to characterize effective alternative schools, they also are likely to characterize effective alternative classrooms that are not housed in a separate school.

1. *Teachers, administrators, and support staff have training and experience to work with students with social, emotional, and behavioral problems.*

2. *Teachers, administrators, and support staff are given flexibility in program management, decision making, and role functions.*

3. *Teachers, administrators, and support staff are sensitive to individual and cultural differences.*

4. *There are clear goals—both for each individual student and for the program overall.* Central among the goals is to prevent misbehavior from recurring, especially after the student leaves the alternative setting and returns to his or her previous setting.

5. *On-site counseling and consultative services are provided.*

6. *Sufficient funding and resources are provided.* The school is able to employ and maintain qualified teachers and support staff and offer a full range of services that address the educational and mental health needs of their students with serious and chronic misbehavior.

7. *A case management approach to student services is employed.* An individual staff member is assigned primary responsibility for each student, helping to assure that the social, emotional, and educational needs of each individual student are met.

8. *A wide range of strategies and techniques supported by research are used that target a combination of individual factors, classroom and school factors, and peer/home/community factors that are linked to behavior problems.*

9. *Networks of additional supports and services are provided* (e.g., social services, parent management training, family counseling, medical and psychiatric services, transitional services).

10. *Strategies, techniques, services, and supports are individualized.*

11. *The program is evaluated as to its effectiveness.*

The foregoing features of effective alternative schools are consistent with research on the effectiveness of programs and interventions for students whose misbehavior is so serious and chronic that they are diagnosed as having a conduct disorder (Brestan & Eyberg, 1998; McMahon & Wells, 1998; Miller, Brehm, & Whitehouse, 1998). That is, these remedial programs are:

- *comprehensive* (addressing multiple factors related to the presence, and absence, of behavior problems)
- *broad-based* (adopting a "systems" perspective in which it is understood that schools, families, and community agencies must work together)
- *guided by research and theory*
- *intensive and sustained over time*
- *delivered early* (i.e., delivered at an early age but also when problems first warrant intervention, irrespective of the age of the student)
- *sensitive to developmental and cultural differences in behavior and the determinants of behavior* (Bear, Webster-Stratton, Furlong, & Rhee, 2000)

Research also indicates that perhaps *the* most critical component of effective programs is parent management training or family therapy (Brestan & Eyberg, 1998). A family- and parent-focused component (which would include ongoing communication and collaboration between the home and school) is particularly effective when combined with student-focused and teacher-focused components. A student-focused component would include the direct teaching of social problem solving and emotional skills and remedial instruction in academics, whereas a teacher-focused component would provide teachers with training and consultative support in preventing and correcting misbehavior in the classroom (Conduct Problems Prevention Research Group, 1999; Webster-Stratton, 1998). This finding has direct implications for the regular classroom teacher. Not only should these components be delivered while a student is in an alternative setting, but also they must be continued upon the student's return to the regular classroom if improvement in behavior is lasting.

STOP AND REFLECT

With respect to the effectiveness of programs for a student with serious and chronic behavior problems, one of the most consistent research findings is that in order to have a lasting impact on the student, the program needs to include an intensive family or parent component. What are the implications of this finding for school-based remedial programs? What are the obstacles to providing this component?

Schoolwide Security and Safety

As discussed in Chapter 2, increased school shootings in the 1990s and the public's (mis)perception of a general increase in school violence sparked many schools to develop and implement school safety plans. Unfortunately, many schools have simply adopted a zero tolerance approach to school violence in which they suspend and expel more students and employ greater security measures, such as the use of metal detectors, surveillance cameras, and law enforcement personnel, and ban book bags and long coats. However, others have adopted a more balanced approach to comprehensive school discipline in which they combine reasonable zero tolerance policies and security measures, as needed, with a variety of strategies and techniques that target prevention and the development of self-discipline. These schools understand that establishing school safety does not necessarily help develop self-discipline or create a school climate that is conducive to learning and experiencing a sense of community.

To be sure, safety should be a foremost concern among all schools, especially those in which acts of violence are common. However, not all schools require the same degree of security measures or the same safety plans. Even in the most disruptive schools, less time, resources, and expense need to be devoted to security and safety when there is a focus on developing self-discipline, preventing misbehavior with effective classroom management, and correcting misbehavior with replacement techniques. Still, safety should be one part of a comprehensive school discipline plan. Common recommendations (e.g., Duke, 2002; Dwyer & Osher, 2000; Dwyer, Osher, & Wagner, 1998) for enhancing safety follow:

Recommendations for School Safety

1. *Ensure that physical facilities are well designed and monitored.*

   - Make sure that the school campus has appropriate lighting, alarm systems, fences, and locks.
   - Monitor and control campus access, screening all visitors and requiring that they wear identification cards.
   - *When necessary,* use surveillance cameras, metal detectors, locker inspections, and identification tags for staff (and high school students).
   - Install a two-way communication system (e.g., telephones, intercom, walkie-talkies, instant message e-mail) between classrooms and the office. Likewise, establish two-way communications for personnel who patrol or monitor the campus.
   - Conduct a building safety audit in consultation with law enforcement experts or using guidelines set by your state department of education.
   - Provide routine supervision and monitoring of students, especially during critical periods (while entering and leaving school) and in areas conducive to close physical proximity (hallways, stairways, playground).
   - Direct traffic flow patterns such that they limit the potential for conflicts, altercations, and accidents.
   - Arrange schedules, recess periods, and lunch periods to minimize potential conflicts between different age groups.

2. *Develop or review school policies and procedures pertaining to safety.*

   - In the student handbook include clear policies pertaining to use of lockers, dress code, possession of weapons and illegal substances (give clear descriptions and examples of each), and searches of lockers, automobiles, and personal property.
   - Carefully screen new employees.

3. *Be well prepared in advance for responding to any potential crisis or violent act.*

   - Develop a plan for responding to a crisis. The plan should include four major components (Dwyer, Osher, & Wagner, 1998):
     - What to look for—key characteristics of responsive and safe schools
     - What to look for—early warning signs of violence
     - What to do—intervention: getting help for troubled students
     - What to do—crisis response
   - Establish a standing *crisis team* or safety team for implementing the plan (and, if needed, for developing the plan). Members of the team should include the building administrator; regular, special, and alternative education teachers; support staff (e.g., school psychologist, counselor, social worker, school resource officer); parents; and representatives of the community (e.g., law enforcement personnel, business leaders, clergy). The team should meet regularly to identify potentially troubled or violent students and situations that may be dangerous.
   - Train all teachers and staff in how to look for warning signs of potential violence and how to prevent and respond to physical violence and crisis situations.

- Teach students about issues of school safety. This would include techniques for developing social and moral problem-solving skills (especially skills of conflict resolution) and emotional competencies (e.g., expressing their feelings, regulating emotion, and coping with stress). This also should include the direct teaching of the dangers of firearms, how to deal with strangers, and when to seek help.
- Practice how teachers and staff should respond to a crisis. Conduct periodic mock crises to evaluate the staff's level of preparedness.

4. *Allocate additional time and resources to those students identified to be at greatest risk for serious and chronic misbehavior, particularly acts of violence.* This would include the implementation of programs for students deemed at risk based on early signs of social, emotional, academic, and behavioral problems (e.g., peer rejection, anger, academic failure, bullying). This might include individual or group social skills training, academic tutoring, mentoring, conflict resolution training, and parent management training.

5. *Work closely with families, community groups, and outside agencies (e.g., law enforcement, social services, juvenile corrections, and faith-based agencies).* Solicit their input, support, and assistance; involve them on planning committees; and keep them informed.

6. *Teach and encourage students to recognize warning signs of potential violence and to share any concerns they might have about potential school violence.* Recognize that students are more likely to share their concerns in schools characterized by warm and supportive teacher–student relations and a sense of community.

S U M M A R Y   A N D   K E Y   P O I N T S

- There are more limitations than advantages to the use of suspension and expulsion. The advantages, however, are that it highlights the seriousness of a misbehavior, deters others, helps establish an environment that is safe, orderly, and conducive to learning, and that removal might help a student receive the level of remedial services that is needed but best provided in an alternative setting.
- The limitations to suspension and expulsion are (1) their effects tend to be short term and nonlasting; (2) punishment is modeled; (3) misbehavior may actually be reinforced; (4) undesirable side effects often follow; (5) they foster a negative climate in the school and classroom; and (6) they decrease time spent in academic learning, while possibly increasing time spent learning undesirable behavior.
- Suspension and expulsion should be used only as "last resorts," in response to serious or chronic acts of misbehavior, and always in combination with more positive strategies and techniques.

- IDEA mandates that all children with disabilities be provided with a "free appropriate public education" (FAPE) in the "least restricted environment" (LRE). It is a violation of the law to use long-term suspension and expulsion with students with disabilities unless they continue to receive special education services.
- The most common disabilities for which regular classroom teachers are likely to be required by law to assist in the development and implementation of the student's individualized educational plan are students with learning disabilities, ADHD, emotional disturbance, and mental retardation.
- IDEA allows schools to remove a student with a disability from the classroom or school. However, special provisions apply when such removal (a) constitutes a change of placement and (b) the parent objects to the change of placement.
- In addition to IDEA, the rights of students with disabilities—including those with disabilities not

included under IDEA—are protected under Section 504 of the Vocational Rehabilitation Act (P.L. 93-112). A student with a disability who does not qualify for special education under IDEA may qualify for educational accommodations under Section 504.

■ Although the strategies and techniques presented throughout this book are effective for students with chronic and serious behavior problems, including those with and without disabilities, students with chronic and serious behavior problems often require that the strategies and techniques be implemented in a more sustained, intense, and frequent manner. In many cases this requires placement in a more restricted setting outside of the regular classroom.

■ Among the characteristics of effective remedial programs for students with serious and chronic behavior problems are that they are comprehensive, broad-based, guided by research and theory, intensive and sustained over time, delivered early, and sensitive to developmental and cultural differences in behavior and the determinants of behavior.

■ For the purposes of prevention and remediation, every school should have a school safety plan that is tailored to its individual needs. Not all schools require the same degree of security measures or the same safety plans. Such a plan should include multiple components, as listed in this chapter.

KEY TERMS AND CONCEPTS

Alternative classrooms and schools
Attention deficit hyperactivity disorder
Behavioral intervention plans
Crisis response team
Emotional disturbance
Expulsion
504 accommodations

Free appropriate public education (FAPE)
Individualized education plan (IEP)
Individuals with Disabilities Education Act (IDEA)
Interim alternative education settings (IAES)

Least restricted environment (LRE)
Manifestation determination
Mental retardation
Related services
Remediation
Specific learning disabilities
Special education
Suspension

RECOMMENDED READINGS AND RESOURCES

Books on Working with Children and Adolescents with Serious and Chronic Behavior Problems

Algozzine, R., Serna, L., & Patton, J. R. (2000). *Childhood behavior disorders: Applied research and educational practice* (2nd ed.). Austin, TX: Pro-Ed.

Bader, B. D., Hoffman, C. C., Warger, C. L., Osher, D., Quinn, M. M., & Hanley, T. V. (2000). *Teaching and working with children who have emotional and behavioral challenges.* Longmont, CO: Sopris West.

Bos, C. S., & Vaughn, S. (2002). *Strategies for teaching students with learning and behavior problems* (5th ed.). Boston: Allyn and Bacon.

Kauffman, J. (2001). *Characteristics of emotional and behavioral disorders of children and youth* (7th ed.). New York: Prentice Hall.

Minke, K. M., & Bear, G. G. (2000). *Preventing school problems—Promoting school success: Strategies and programs that work.* Bethesda, MD: National Association of School Psychologists.

Walker, H. M., Colvin, G., & Ramsey, E. (1995). *Antisocial behavior in school: Strategies and best practices.* Pacific Grove, CA: Brooks/Cole.

Whelan, R. J. (1998). *Emotional and behavioral disorders: A 25-year focus.* Denver, CO: Love Publishing.

Wood, M. M., & Long, N. J. (1991). *Life space intervention: Talking with children and youth in crisis.* Austin, TX: Pro-Ed.

Books on School Safety and Responding to Crises

Duke, D. L. (2002). *Creating safe schools for all children.* Boston: Allyn and Bacon.

Dwyer, K., & Osher, D. (2000). Safeguarding our children: An action guide. Washington, DC: United States Departments of Education and Justice, American Institutes for Research. Available www.ed.gov, www.ideapractices.org, and http://cecp.air.org.

Dwyer, K., Osher, D., & Warger, C. (1998). *Early warning, timely response: A guide to safe schools.* Washington, DC: United States Department of Education. Available www.ed.gov, www.ideapractices.org, and http://cecp.air.org.

Osher, D., Dwyer, K., & Jackson, S. (2003). *Safe, supportive, and successful schools step by step.* Longmont, CO: Sopris West.

Polack, S., & McCormick, J. (1999). *Coping with crisis: Lessons learned.* Longmont, CO: Sopris West.

Poland, S., & McCormick, J. (2000). *Coping with crisis: A quick reference guide.* Longmont, CO: Sopris West.

Websites for Information on Teaching, School Discipline, and Students with Disabilities

www.chadd.org

Website for the largest organization for parents and educators concerned about ADHD—children and adults with attention deficit hyperactivity disorder. Contains a wealth of general information, including appropriate educational accommodations, for children with ADHD.

www.dld.cec.org

Website for the Division for Learning Disabilities of the Council for Exceptional Children. Offers general information on LD and specific information and resources for teaching children with LD.

www.ld.org

Website for the National Center for Learning Disabilities. Includes general information for parents and educators, including general information, recent legislation, fact sheets about LD, and educational resources.

www.ldonline.org

A valuable resource for general information for parents and educators on learning disabilities, as well as ADHD. Includes activities and links for social skills training for students with behavior problems.

www.aamr.org

Website for the American Association on Mental Retardation. Offers general information, including fact sheets and links, on mental retardation.

Websites for General Information on IDEA, Children with Disabilities, and Special Education

www.ideapractices.org

An excellent place to begin when looking for anything pertaining to special education, including legislation, regulations, court cases, research, and teaching techniques.

www.cec.sped.org

Website for the largest professional organization dedicated to helping children with disabilities (and the gifted). In addition to general information and links to other sites, the site has an excellent list of books and resources that are published by CEC.

www.ed.gov/offices/OSERS/IDEA

The federal government's Offices of Special Education and Related Services site for information on IDEA.

www.ed.gov/offices/OSDFS

Website of the Office of Safe and Drug-Free Schools provides resources, research, and statistics related to school safety and violence.

www.nichcy.org

Website of the national information center providing information to parents and professional educators on children with disabilities. Contains excellent free publications and fact sheets, answers to common questions about disabilities, and links to other sites.

www.nsba.org

Website for National School Boards Association. Provides updates and links to court cases and legislation regarding school discipline.

Websites on School Safety and Crisis Response

http://cecp.air.org

The Center for Effective Collaboration and Practice offers resources and materials for promoting the "development and the adjustment of children with or at risk of developing serious emotional disturbance."

www.naspcenter.org

Website for the National Mental Health and Education Center for Children and Families hosted by the National Association of School Psychologists and dedicated to fostering best practices in mental health and education for children, schools, and families. Among resources provided are those on school safety, school violence, and crisis intervention.

www.nssc1.org

Website of the National School Safety Center. Offers resources and products on school safety. Good site for national statistics on school violence.

http://smhp.psych.ucla.edu

Website for the UCLA School Mental Health Project/Center for Mental Health in Schools. Provides resources on mental health in the schools, including information and resources on responding to crises and links to annotated lists of evidence-based interventions for school-aged children and adolescents.

REFERENCES

Advancement Project/Civil Rights Project. (2000). Opportunities suspended: The devastating consequences of zero tolerance and school discipline policies. Retrieved from Harvard Law School Website: http://www.civilrightsproject.harvard.edu/research/discipline/opport_suspended.php.

American Psychiatric Association (1994). *Diagnostic and statistical manual of mental disorders* (4th ed.). Washington, DC: Author.

American Psychological Association (1999). *Warning signs.* Washington, DC: Author.

Barkley, R. A. (1997). *ADHD and the nature of self-control.* New York: Guilford.

Bear, G. G. (2000). School suspension and expulsion. In *Encyclopedia of Psychology.* Washington, DC: American Psychological Association.

Bear, G. G., Quinn, M. M., & Burkholder, S. (2001). *Interim alternative education settings for children with disabilities.* Bethesda, MD: National Association of School Psychologists.

Bear, G. G., Webster-Stratton, C., Furlong, M., & Rhee, S. (2000). Preventing aggression and violence. In K. M. Minke & G. G. Bear (Eds.), *Preventing school problems—Promoting school success: Strategies and programs that work* (pp. 1–69). Bethesda, MD: National Association of School Psychologists.

Brestan, E. V., & Eyberg, S. M. (1998). Effective psychosocial treatments of conduct-disordered children and adolescents: 29 years, 82 studies, and 5,272 kids. *Journal of Clinical Child Psychology, 27,* 180–189.

Brooks, K., Schiraldi, V., & Ziedenberg, J. (1999). *School house hype: Two years later.* San Francisco: Center on Juvenile and Criminal Justice. [On-line]. Available at *www.cjcj.org.*

Conduct Problems Prevention Research Group (1999). Initial impact of the Fast Track prevention trial for conduct problems: I. The high-risk sample. *Journal of Consulting and Clinical Psychology, 67,* 631–647.

Costenbader, V. K., & Markson, S. (1998). School suspension: A study with secondary school students. *Journal of School Psychology, 36,* 59–82.

Costenbader, V. K., & Markson, S. (1994). School suspension: A study of current policies and practices. *NASSP Bulletin, 78,* 103–107.

Duke, D. L. (2002). *Creating safe schools for all children.* Boston: Allyn and Bacon.

Dwyer, K., & Osher, D. (2000). Safeguarding our children: An action guide. Washington, DC: United States Departments of Education and Justice, American Institutes for Research. Available *www.ed.gov* (enter "Safeguarding our children").

Dwyer, K., Osher, D., & Warger, C. (1998). *Early warning, timely response: A guide to safe schools.* Washington, DC: United States Department of Education. Available www.ed.gov (enter "Early warning" under search).

Finn, J. D. (1989). *Withdrawing from school. Review of Educational Research, 59,* 117–142.

Gorn, S. (1999). *The answer book on discipline.* Horsham, PA: LRP Publications.

Gottfredson, G. D., & Gottsfredson, D. C. (2001). What schools do to prevent problem behavior and promote safe environments. *Journal of Educational and Psychological Consultation, 12,* 313–344.

Gresham, F. M., & Reschly, D. J. (1986). Social skill deficits and low peer acceptance of mainstreamed learning disabled children. *Learning Disability Quarterly, 9,* 23–32.

Gun-Free Schools Act of 1994. Public Law 103-382. 108 Statute 3907. Title 14.

Hartwig, E. P., & Ruesch, G. M. (2000). *Disciplining students with disabilities: A synthesis of critical and emerging issues.* Alexandria, VA: National Association of State Directors of Special Education.

Individuals with Disabilities Education Act (IDEA), 20 U.S.C. §§ 1401 *et seq;* Individuals with Disabilities Education Act Amendments of 1997, Public Law 105-17, 105th Cong., 1st Sess.; Individuals with Disabilities Education Act Regulations, 34 C.F.R. 3000.1 *et seq.*

Kauffman, J. M. (2001). *Characteristics of emotional and behavioral disorders of children and youth* (7th ed.). Upper Saddle River, NJ: Merrill Prentice Hall.

McMahon, R. J., & Wells, K. C. (1998). Conduct problems. In E. J. Mash & R. A. Barkley (Eds.), *Treatment of childhood disorders* (2nd ed., pp. 111–207). New York: Guilford.

Mendez, L. M., Knoff, H. M., & Ferron, J. M. (2002). School demographic variables and out-of-school suspension rates: A quantitative and qualitative analysis of a large, ethnically diverse school district. *Psychology in the Schools, 39,* 259–277.

Miller, G. E., Brehm, K., & Whitehouse, S. (1998). Reconceptualizing school-based prevention for antisocial behavior within a resiliency framework. *School Psychology Review, 27,* 364–379.

Morrison, G. M., & D'Incau, B. (1997). The web of zero tolerance: Characteristics of students who are recommended for expulsion from school. *Education and Treatment of Children, 20,* 316–335.

National School Boards Association (2003). NSBA recommendations for the reauthorization of the Individuals with Disabilities Education Act. Retrieved July 6, 2003 from www.nsba.org.

Rapport, M. D., Denney, C., DuPaul, G. J., & Gardner, M. J. (1994). Attention deficit disorder and methylphenidate: Normalization rates, clinical effectiveness, and response prediction in 76 children. *Journal of the American Academy of Child and Adolescent Psychiatry, 33,* 882–893.

Rossi, R. J. (1994). *Schools and students at risk: Context and framework for positive change.* New York: Teachers College Press.

Skiba, R. (2002). Special education and school discipline: A precarious balance. *Behavioral Disorders, 27,* 81–97.

Skiba, R. J. (2000). *An analysis of school disciplinary practice* (Policy Research Rep. No. SRS2). Bloomington, IN: Indiana Education Policy Center.

Skiba, R., & Grizzle, K. (1991). The social maladjustment exclusion: Issues of definition and assessment. *School Psychology Review, 20,* 580–598.

Skiba, R., & Grizzle, K. (1992). Qualifications v. logic and data: Excluding conduct disorders from the SED definition. *School Psychology Review, 21,* 23–28.

Slenkovich, J. E. (1992). Can the language "social maladjustment" in the SED definition be ignored? *School Psychology Review, 21,* 21–22.

Sugai, G., & Horner, R. H. (1999). Discipline and behavioral support: Preferred processes and practices. *Effective School Practices, 17*(4), 10–22.

Swanson, H. L., & Malone, S. (1992). Social skills and learning disabilities: A meta-analysis of the literature. *School Psychology Review, 21,* 427–443.

Tilly, W. D., Knoster, T. P., & Ikeda, M. J. (2000). Functional behavioral assessment: Strategies for positive behavior support. In C. F. Telzrow & M. Tankersley (Eds.), *IDEA Amendments of 1997: Practice guidelines for school-based teams* (pp. 151–197). Bethesda, MD: National Association of School Psychologists.

U.S. Department of Education. (2002). *To assure the free appropriate public education of all children with disabilities: Twenty-fourth annual report to Congress on the implementation of the Individuals with Disabilities Act.* Washington, DC: Author. Available at www.ed.gov/offices/OSERS/OSEP.

U.S. Department of Education Office of Special Education and Rehabilitative Services (1999). *Discipline for children with disabilities: Q & A Document from OSEP.* Washington, DC: Author. Available at www.ed.gov/offices/OSERS/OSEP.

U.S. General Accounting Office (2001). *Student discipline: Individuals with Disabilities Education Act. Report to the Committees on Appropriations, U.S. Senate and House of Representatives.* Washington, DC: Author. Available at www.gao.gov.

U.S. Government Accounting Office (2003). *Special education: Clearer guidance would enhance implementation of federal disciplinary provisions.* Report to the Committee on Health, Education, Labor and Pensions, U.S. Senate. Washington, DC: Author. Available at www.gao.gov/cgi-bin/getrpt.

U.S. Surgeon General (1999). *Mental health: A report of the surgeon general.* Washington, DC: Author. Available at www.surgeongeneral.gov/library/mentalhealth/home.html

Vaughn, S. R., & Haager, D. (1994). Social competence as a multifaceted construct: How do students with learning disabilities fare? *Learning Disability Quarterly, 17,* 253–266.

Vossekuil, B., Reddy, M., & Fein, R. (2000). *An interim report on the prevention of targeted violence in schools.* Washington, DC. United States Secret Service National Threat Assessment Center. Available at www.treas.gov/usss/ntac.

Walker, H. M., Colvin, G., & Ramsey, E. (1995). *Antisocial behavior in school: Strategies and best practices.* Pacific Grove, CA: Brooks/Cole.

Walker, H. M., Horner, R. H., Sugai, G., Bullis, M., Sprague, J. R., Bricker, D., & Kaufman, M. J. (1996). Integrated approaches to preventing antisocial behavior patterns among school-age children and youth. *Journal of Emotional and Behavioral Disorders, 4,* 193–256.

Webster-Stratton, C. (1998). Preventing conduct problems in Head Start children: Strengthening parent competencies. *Journal of Consulting and Clinical Psychology, 66,* 715–730.

Recommended Procedures for Conducting Class Meetings Dealing with Social and Moral Problems

The following steps are recommended for conducting a class meeting in which both peers and the teacher challenge the faulty thinking and reasoning of students. The author has found this format best for grades 5–12 and for discussing problems or dilemmas that tend to generate disagreement, such as moral dilemmas. Teachers should use their own creativity in modifying the format to meet their own preferences and grade level and to suit a particular class meeting.

A. Establish Ground Rules

During the first meeting, establish the ground rules. Two types of rules need to be established: rules of conduct and rules for promoting discussion and reasoning. First, establish the standard rules of conduct that apply to class discussions. They should include:

1. Only one person speaks at a time.
2. Listen to and always respect the other person's point of view.
3. No put-downs.

If these rules already have been established, briefly review them. If they have not already been established, either develop the rules jointly with the class or simply develop them yourself and review them. A good compromise between these two methods is to ask students what rules they think should apply. After they brainstorm the rules, present the list of rules you have developed, making any modifications you believe to be appropriate. (In using this method, the author has almost always found that students recommend the same rules that the author desired or stricter ones.) If it becomes clear after the first or second meeting that students do not follow the rules, consider implementing the Good Behavior Game, as described in Chapter 11, as a technique for systematically reinforcing following rules and participating actively in discussion.

In addition to reviewing ground rules, explain that other "rules" will apply for the purpose of encouraging active discussion, reasoning, and debate:

1. Students are to question, challenge, and debate the opinions and reasoning of others (including that of their teacher).
2. Nothing is wrong with changing one's opinion, recommended solution, or reasoning. Indeed, often it would be appropriate to do so!

309

3. In most situations there is more than one "right" answer. Students should not worry about giving a "wrong" answer. However, they should remember that answers will be evaluated by peers and, thus, they should always be able to justify their answers.
4. The teacher will use Socratic questioning and play "devil's advocate," when appropriate. (Explain these terms, emphasizing that if others fail to do so you will argue with them, voicing differing perspectives, right or wrong. Explain that you will do so not because you necessarily disagree with their answers but for the purpose of stimulating critical reasoning and forcing them to consider and analyze the perspectives of others, whether such perspectives are "right" or "wrong").

B. Present, Identify, and Explain the Problem or Dilemma

1. Present the problem or dilemma and clarify any related facts.
2. Ask the students to identify the circumstances, including conflicting values or perspectives, which make the situation a true problem or dilemma.
3. Highlight the meaningfulness of the problem and any conflicting issues or values involved. If the case is a hypothetical one, note how it could be a real-life situation and ask students if they know of similar cases. For example, in discussing promises and peer pressure with students in upper grades, present the moral dilemma of Jackie having promised that she will go to the movies with a friend, but other friends approach her and pressure her to go to the mall. Clarify any facts and answer questions about the case (e.g., Jackie would like to do both but can't decide), ask students to identify conflicting issues or values (e.g., keeping a promise, one's reputation, disappointing others, having fun), and highlight that students often face similar dilemmas (e.g., ask "Does this sound familiar? Might this happen to you?").

C. Divide the Class into Smaller Groups of Four to Six to Allow for Greater Discussion

1. Although certainly not the only way to divide students into smaller groups, one way the author has found to be effective is to survey the initial positions taken by the students, or their recommended solutions, and divide the students into groups based on the results of the survey. For example, ask students "Which of you think that Jackie should break her promise?" Another option would be to ask students "What are some alternative solutions to this problem?" If you choose the latter option (which often is best when the problem is not viewed as a true dilemma), be sure to brainstorm recommended solutions before surveying positions.
2. Remind students that their positions are only tentative ones. ("You may change your position later if you want to.")
3. Divide the class for small-group discussion in one of two ways:
   a. Put students who agree with an action into the same groups as students who disagree.
   b. Break the class into two groups based on the action each group supports.
4. Ask each group to discuss not only their decisional choice but also their *reasons* behind their choice. Challenge them to try to reach consensus on their decision and

on their best supporting reasoning. Have one member of each group record the group's decision and supporting reasons. Challenge them to evaluate the goals and consequences of their chosen action, especially with respect to how the decisional choice might affect the feelings, thoughts, and behavior of everyone involved in the situation.

5. Have students think of questions to ask the other groups for the purpose of challenging their points of view.

6. Proceed around the class, helping the students with their tasks, fostering Socratic dialogue, and playing the role of moral advocate.

D. Begin Debate across Groups

1. Have each group present its decisional choice and supporting reasons. List responses on the board.

2. Have each group challenge the decision and reasoning used by the other group(s) and point out contradictions or inadequacies in their reasoning. Especially encourage students to challenge self-centered, hedonistic, and pragmatic reasons.

3. When others do not challenge irresponsible decisions and faulty reasoning, assume the role of moral advocate and challenge it yourself. Seek agreement on reasons that reflect a concern about the feelings, welfare, and rights of others.

4. When discussion dies out, have the students move back into one large group.

E. Discuss Problems and Steps for Doing What One Intends to Do

1. Seek class consensus on what one *ought* to do and *why*. Summarize on the board the decisional choices and the supporting reasons. Try to find the decision and one or two supporting reasons that most students believe would be best from the perspective of everyone involved in the problem situation.

2. Challenge students to reflect on whether what they decided they *ought* to do is consistent with what they would actually do.

3. Discuss the steps necessary to implement their decisional choice(s). Have students role-play the skills required, as appropriate.

4. Discuss obstacles that might keep them from following through on the decided course of action and how they might address anticipated obstacles.

F. Close Discussion

1. Have students summarize and reflect on their choice of action and the supporting reasons.

2. Highlight any main points that the students overlooked in their summary.

3. Challenge students to apply what they discussed to any real-life problems they have recently faced.

INDEX